EARLY GEORGIAN FURNITURE
1715-1740

Frontispiece. Overmantel mirror (1730-50). Oil on canvas, gilded deal and glass. The painting is unsigned, but in the Continental manner of an artist such as Pieter Casteels. Courtesy of Sotheby's

EARLY GEORGIAN FURNITURE

1715-1740

Adam Bowett

ANTIQUE COLLECTORS' CLUB

For Natalie

©2009 Adam Bowett
World copyright reserved

ISBN 978-1-85149-584-9

The right of Adam Bowett to be identified as author of this work has been asserted by him in accordance with the Copyright, Designs and Patents Act 1988

All rights reserved. No part of this publication may be reproduced, stored in a retrieval system, or transmitted in any form or by any means electronic, mechanical, photocopying, recording or otherwise, without the prior permission of the publishers.

British Library Cataloguing-in-Publication Data
A catalogue record for this book is available from the British Library

Printed in China
for the Antique Collectors' Club Ltd., Woodbridge, Suffolk

THE ANTIQUE COLLECTORS' CLUB

Formed in 1966, the Antique Collectors' Club is now a world-renowned publisher of top quality books for the collector. It also publishes the only independently-run monthly antiques magazine, *Antique Collecting*, which rose quickly from humble beginnings to a network of worldwide subscribers.

The magazine, whose motto is *For Collectors-By Collectors-About Collecting*, is aimed at collectors interested in widening their knowledge of antiques both by increasing their awareness of quality and by discussion of the factors influencing prices.

Subscription to Antique Collecting is open to anyone interested in antiques and subscribers receive ten issues a year. Well-illustrated articles deal with practical aspects of collecting and provide numerous tips on prices, features of value, investment potential, fakes and forgeries. Offers of related books at special reduced prices are also available only to subscribers.

In response to the enormous demand for information on 'what to pay', ACC introduced in 1968 the famous price guide series. The first title, *The Price Guide to Antique Furniture* (since renamed *British Antique Furniture: Price Guide and Reasons for Values*), is still in constant demand. Since those pioneering days, ACC has gone from strength to strength, publishing many of today's standard works of reference on all things antique and collectable, from *Tiaras* to *20th Century Ceramic Designers in Britain*.

Not only has ACC continued to cater strongly for its original audience, it has also branched out to produce excellent titles on many subjects including art reference, architecture, garden design, gardens, and textiles. All ACC's publications are available through bookshops worldwide and a catalogue is available free of charge from the addresses below.

For further information please contact:

www.antiquecollectorsclub.com

Antique Collectors' Club
Sandy Lane, Old Martlesham
Woodbridge, Suffolk IP12 4SD, UK
Tel: 01394 389950 Fax: 01394 389999
Email: info@antique-acc.com

——— or ———

ACC Distribution
6 West 18th Street, 4th Floor
New York, NY 10011, USA
Tel: 212 645 1111
Email: sales@antiquecc.com

CONTENTS

Acknowledgements 4
Abbreviations 4
Preface 5

CHAPTER ONE:
The London Furniture Trade
    The organisation of the trade   10
    Raw materials   32
    The export trade   36
    The influence of the Orient   42

CHAPTER TWO:
Case Furniture Construction
    'Second-phase' cabinet work   54
    Details of style – cornices and mouldings   58
    'Transitional' second-phase cabinet work   65
    Drawer-edge mouldings   72
    Architectural pediments   80
    'Third-phase' cabinet work   81
    Wainscot and mahogany case furniture construction   84
    Standardisation, conformity and innovation   90

CHAPTER THREE:
Other Case Furniture
    Clothes chests   94
    Chests of drawers   96
    Chests with folding tops   105
    Commodes   111
    Chests on stands   112
    Double chests of drawers   118
    Bureaux-tables   120
    Writing bureaux   125
    Corner cupboards   126
    Clothes presses   130
    Bookcases   131
    Cabinets   137

CHAPTER FOUR:
Seat Furniture
    Late pillar-leg chairs   144
    'Indian' feet   148
    The cabriole leg   150
    The 'India' back   156

CHAPTER FOUR continued:

Banister backs and compass backs	160
Compass seats	171
The Houghton Hall suites	173
Chair design in the 1730s	177
Sofas and settees	187
Dressing chairs	188
'Kentian' seat furniture	189
The origins of the fan back chair	196

CHAPTER FIVE:
Tables and Stands

The end of the 'triad'	200
Tables with gilt tops	210
Sideboard tables	216
Neo-Palladian tables	223
Eagle, sphinx and dolphin tables	228
Term stands	232
Dressing and other small tables	234
Tea tables	241
'Dutch' tables	245
Pillar and claw tables	246
Dining tables	251
Folding card and tea tables	260

CHAPTER SIX:
Mirrors

Looking glass production	266
Dressing glasses and 'union suites'	267
Chimney glasses	272
Sconces	277
Hanging glasses	284
Pier glasses	287
The 'tabernacle' frame	294

APPENDIX I:
Cabinet Metalware — 300

APPENDIX II:
Glossary of Woods mentioned in the text — 308

Bibliography — 316
Index — 322

ACKNOWLEDGEMENTS

It is impossible to write a book of this kind without the assistance of many people and organisations. Of the latter I am particularly indebted to Blair Castle Trust, Blenheim Palace, Chatsworth Estates, Cholmondeley Estates, City of London Record Office, Country Life Photo Library, The Ditchley Foundation, English Heritage, The Geffrye Museum, Historic Royal Palaces, Leeds City Art Galleries, London Guildhall Library, the National Archives, The National Trust, The Royal Collection, the Victoria and Albert Museum, and Wilton House. Several firms of auctioneers have responded patiently to my enquires and have helped with photographs. Particular thanks must go to Bonhams (formerly Phillips), Christie's, Sotheby's and Tennants. Other businesses and individuals who have helped in many and diverse ways include Chris Allhusen, Jane Anderson, Harry and Guy Apter, Arlington Conservation, Arthur Brett & Sons, Bruce Bailey, Simon Banks, Geoffrey Beard, David Beaufort, Rufus Bird, Robert Bradley, Peter Brown, Mrs. B.H. Burrough, Roderick Butler, Adrian Butterworth, Carlton Hobbs Ltd, Roger Carr-Whitworth, Charlotte Grant, Major J.B.G. Chester, Christopher Claxton Stevens, Richard Coles, Peter Collyer, Robert Copley, the late John Cornforth, Robert Curtis, David Dewing, Patrick Dingwall, Sebastian Edwards, Ian Fraser, Chris Galloway, Jeremy Garfield-Davies, Tim Garland, John Hardy, Jonathan Harris, Kate Hay, Peter Holmes, Hotspur Ltd, Simon Howard, Jeremy Ltd, Simon Jervis, Eleanor John, David Jones, Tim Knox, Michael and Polly Legg, Melvyn Lipitch, James Lomax, Fergus Lyons, Mallet Ltd, Sarah Medlam, Lady Diane Nutting, John and Susan Parry, Partridge Fine Art, Pelham Galleries, Tim Phelps, Ronald Phillips Ltd, the Earl of Radnor, Mrs. R. Rosier, Treve Rosoman, Anne Rossi-Lefevre, Christopher Rowell, Margaret Stone, Sally Stratton, Susan Stuart, Tennants Auctioneers, Frederick Uhde, Karin Walton, Anthony Wells-Cole, Charles Wemyss, and Lucy Wood. I would especially like to mention Laurie Lindey, whose generosity with hard-won information has been remarkable and whose own research into the London furniture trade will, when published, transform the subject.

I am most grateful to Diana Steel and the Antique Collectors' Club for agreeing to publish this book in these unprofitable times, when antiques in general and furniture in particular seem to be out of fashion. Primrose Elliott has edited the book with her customary diligence and patience – thank you Prim.

ABBREVIATIONS USED IN CITATIONS

CLRO	City of London Record Office
DEF	*Dictionary of English Furniture* (see Bibliography)
DEFM	*Dictionary of English Furniture Makers* (see Bibliography)
GL	Guildhall Library, London
BL	British Library
PRO	Public Record Office (now known as the National Archives)

PREFACE

This book is an attempt to provide an up-to-date and straightforward account of the stylistic and technical development of fashionable English furniture in the first few decades of the Hanoverian age. The short time span has been chosen for several reasons. The wealth of new material that has come to light in recent years meant that even this short period would result in a substantial study. It was a period of rapid technical progress in cabinet-making and major stylistic change in all areas, and to do justice to both meant going into considerable detail. Thus there was more than enough subject matter to consider without going beyond 1740. That date is generally agreed to mark the beginning of the mid-Georgian or rococo period, and to cover that adequately would require a much larger book. Moreover, mid- and late eighteenth century furniture has been reasonably well served by furniture scholars in recent decades, whereas the so-called 'Age of Walnut' has not. The standard texts are still those written by R.W. Symonds between 1923 and 1955 and there is, of course, the *Dictionary of English Furniture*, last revised in 1954. Subsequent publications have added to and built on these works, but none has attempted to reconsider the whole period in the light of new discoveries and modern research methods. Finally, there is probably no period so closely circumscribed by the myths of connoisseurship, which confine the appreciation of walnut furniture to a few chosen types and impose a set of anachronistic aesthetic values which do nothing to further a true understanding of the period.

To greater or lesser extent, all twentieth century collectors, dealers and scholars were in thrall to the myth of 'Queen Anne', an essence of *Olde England* embodied in honey-coloured walnut. 'Queen Anne' was never a reality. It was not an historical period but an idea, created in the late nineteenth century in response to the aesthetic ideal created by the Queen Anne revival in architecture and as a reaction against the ponderous bulk of the Gothic Revival. As Warrington Taylor, manager of Morris & Co. from 1865, wrote: 'Is not Queen Anne furniture more suited to our wants?' 'Queen Anne' took the lightness and elegance of Aesthetic movement furniture, dispensed with its angularity and Oriental rigour, and gave it harmonious lines and gentler tones. It was both historic and modern, in a way that previous revivals – Elizabethan, Carolean and Gothic – had not been; it was also indisputably English.

Somehow 'Queen Anne' became more than just another historicist revival. It captured the imagination of antiquarians, connoisseurs and collectors, and became, for many, the perfect embodiment of old English furniture. The aesthetic appeal was obvious; 'Queen Anne' furniture combined, as the connoisseur/historian John C. Rogers remarked, 'perfect proportion and line…[with] warm golden-brown tones, appearing extremely rich under the original oil varnish and subsequent waxing, and the wonderful grain of the wood'. But there was another, more important aspect to it. 'Queen Anne' emerged at a time when the study of old furniture was developing into a coherent and systematic body of knowledge and this ensured that, unlike previous revivals, it acquired both scholarly credibility and a solid historiography. This was the era of Percy Macquoid and Herbert Cescinsky, the two giants of English furniture studies at the turn of the nineteenth and twentieth centuries, and between them they created a mould for English furniture studies which set hard for most of the twentieth century. Indeed, it was Macquoid who gave popular currency to the phrase 'Age of Walnut'. In his role as adviser and decorator to collectors and aristocrats, Macquoid in particular was able to influence the taste of a generation of rich patrons. His work is still evident in the collections of men like Frank Green (at the Treasurer's House, York) and the 9th Earl of Stamford (at Dunham Massey, Cheshire). Through their books, Macquoid and Cescinsky reached a much wider audience, and while their work was truly ground-breaking it also created many enduring misconceptions about English furniture and furniture-making, of which 'Queen Anne' is the most obvious example.

Macquoid's natural successor was R.W. Symonds, whose books still occupy a central place on any furniture collector's shelf and whose articles are still cited in both popular and scholarly literature. Symonds' work was, by the standards of the time, both rigorous and original, and his interests extended far wider than walnut furniture, but he was deeply imbued with the spirit of 'Queen Anne'. In handling documentary material he was careful and objective, but his reaction to a given piece of furniture was essentially aesthetic rather than empirical. He was concerned not just with authenticity but with 'principles of artistic truth'. These principles were based on apparently objective criteria – design, construction, unity, ornament, workmanship – but ultimately derived from Symonds' own subjective tastes. Such was the eloquent power of Symonds' work that the furniture illustrated in his books, or in collections formed under his guidance, is still highly sought after when it comes on the market. But to the modern historian the ambiguity at the heart of Symonds' work is increasingly problematic. On the one hand his research, particularly that published in his numerous articles for the *Connoisseur*, broke new ground. In its emphasis on contemporary sources and documentary material it brought to furniture studies a level of academic respectability which it had not hitherto enjoyed, and formed the basis for a new wave of furniture scholarship in the 1950s and 1960s. But his books continued to assert the primacy of aesthetic values – of connoisseurship – and consequently to perpetuate the myth of 'Queen Anne'. This was the inevitable consequence of his role as guide and adviser to collectors, and much of the furniture in his books was drawn from collections formed under his tutelage.

Some present-day collectors, dealers and auctioneers maintain there is a way of reconciling the two approaches, of combining academic rigour with aesthetic appreciation. But how much common ground is there? While academic study demands objectivity and temporal sensitivity, the aesthetic criteria on which collections are founded are subjective and, what is worse, anachronistic. There are times when academic and aesthetic values coincide, but often they don't. The historic and academic value of a piece of furniture depends not on whether we think it is beautiful, but on what information it conveys about the past. Many of the best known pieces of 'Queen Anne' furniture, which have passed from collection to collection for successive generations are, from a historian's point of view, irrelevant. They are undocumented, unprovenanced and academically unimportant. This doesn't prevent them realising high prices at auction, for collecting pieces endorsed by Symonds is a form of modern trophy hunting. But, just as stuffed heads teach us very little about wildlife, studying furniture solely from the point of view of form, proportion, colour and patina has limited potential.

This is not to suggest that aesthetic or other potentially subjective judgements have no role to play in furniture studies. They are in any case unavoidable, indivisible from the human intellect, but much depends on the criteria on which those judgements are based. Are they based on sound reasoning? Are they rooted in verifiable fact? Will they stand up to third-party scrutiny? We can distinguish between poor quality and good quality materials or workmanship, and make judgements about them, because these things have objective physical attributes. Pure aesthetics are more difficult, because one man's 'line of beauty' is another's (to misquote Batty Langley) 'monstrous curve'. But it is possible to be aesthetically objective by asking the right question – not, 'Do I like this object?' but, 'Does this object successfully embody the artistic objectives of its maker?' (This, of course, depends on whether we can correctly interpret the objectives of the maker, which is a moot question, and on whether the maker had any artistic objectives to start with.) However, it is important to recognise that this kind of aesthetic judgement is different from that which so often applies in the commercial world. For instance, mellow colour and deep patina are vitally important to dealers and collectors, and hence worth a lot of money, but neither can be said to be original attributes of the object. Both are anachronisms and therefore directly opposed to the notion of historical truth. The key, surely, is as far as possible to be able to judge historic furniture on its own terms, rather than on ours, and this sometimes involves divorcing ourselves from the aesthetic conventions customarily applied to antique furniture. Beauty and historical truth are not necessarily the same.

'Queen Anne' has had a pernicious effect on furniture studies in many ways. Its effect on chronology has already been hinted at. Generally speaking, English 'Queen Anne' furniture has been dated between ten and thirty years too early. The standard 'Queen Anne' chair is typically a chair of the 1720s, not 1710. Unlike previous authors, who saw 'Queen Anne' as a continuation of the 'Anglo-Dutch' style of William and Mary, Symonds considered 'Queen Anne' a precursor to the

Georgian style. In this he was intuitively correct, since most of what is popularly conceived as 'Queen Anne' furniture is in fact early Georgian. He was nevertheless very clear about what constitutes, for instance, a 'Queen Anne' chair – a cabriole leg and a curved back with central splat. But Symonds failed to notice that it was not possible to find a chair of this description that could actually be shown to have been made between the years 1702 and 1714. He too was blinded by 'Queen Anne'. The mismatch between connoisseurial opinion and historical evidence was one which struck the late Benno Forman, when attempting to explain the apparent time lag between the development of the 'Queen Anne' chair in Britain and North America: 'Another equally possible explanation is that the so-called lag did not exist at all, and perhaps our European colleagues have tended to date their examples somewhat too early'. Forman was right, but because he relied on published material (particularly the work of R.W. Symonds) for his discussion of British furniture, rather than primary research, he did not have the evidence to prove his case.

The effect of this backdating on our understanding of the baroque style in English furniture has been profound. By attributing furniture of the 1720s and 1730s to the first decade of the century, the connoisseur/historians created a stylistic vacuum in the early Georgian period which was then filled by the 'Kentian' or neo-Palladian style. The result was that instead of seeing late baroque and neo-Palladian as concurrent styles, with all the complexity and ambiguity that entailed, furniture historians settled for a simplistic but inaccurate model, in which furniture 'periods' followed one another in a clearly demarcated sequence: Queen Anne – Palladian (aka Kentian) – Rococo (aka Chippendale). Not only was this chronologically inaccurate, it failed to acknowledge the close relationship between baroque and neo-Palladian furniture and completely severed the link between the late baroque and rococo styles. In other areas of art history – painting, sculpture, silverware – the continuous transition from the baroque to the rococo is acknowledged, but in English furniture the neo-Palladian style interposed a stylistic and chronological separation between the two. A similar problem has afflicted architectural history, causing the late Giles Worsley to observe: 'This interpretation places a dangerously narrow stylistic strait-jacket on a complicated period of architectural flux'. Although the present book does not seek to analyse the late baroque or neo-Palladianism in any depth, it does aim to show that stylistic plurality was not only perfectly usual but actually underpinned the design of most early Georgian furniture.

Where a given piece of late baroque furniture could not be assigned to 'Queen Anne', because documentary or other evidence placed it firmly in the 1720s or later, two possible explanations were constructed to account for the anomaly. The first was the concept of the 'export market'. High baroque desks-and-bookcases and floridly decorated japanned or gilt chairs are still routinely described as being 'made for the export market'. This supposedly explains both their un-English exuberance and their old-fashioned features. Giles Grendey is probably the most frequently cited Georgian furniture maker whose furniture, or furniture attributed to him, is commonly described as being made 'for export'. In fact we have no idea what proportion of Grendey's output went for export and we do not know whether his exported furniture differed in any respect from that made for the domestic market.

The alternative explanation for anomalous 'Queen Anne' furniture is that it was made by a foreigner. Peter Miller's superlative desks and bookcases are masterpieces of English baroque cabinet-making. As far as I can discover, he was English by birth and training, yet some observers have seen his style as essentially 'un-English'; surely, they reason, his name must originally have been Muller. A better known example of this circular reasoning is the work of John Channon, in which successive scholars have perceived Germanic baroque influences. By a stroke of luck it was found that his father was named Otto and thus art historical prejudice was apparently confirmed by historical fact. But no search of John Channon's antecedents or of what little is known of his career has uncovered any Continental connection. In fact, with later excrescences removed, Channon's bookcase have as impeccable an English neo-Palladian design pedigree as one could wish for.

Stylistic plurality was a key factor in this as in any age, and indeed the extraordinary variety, novelty and originality of English furniture of this period is one of its chief attractions. Despite the efforts of neo-Palladian propagandists such as Lord Burlington, English furniture makers refused to conform to any single aesthetic code or dogma, and neither should modern furniture historians.

Flimsily constructed attributions are just as pernicious as compartmented thinking. The driving force here is both vanity, on the part of historians whose kudos is enhanced by 'discoveries', and profit, on the part of the antiques trade. Where an attribution is soundly based it may indeed contribute appreciably to our understanding of a particular object, maker, patron or period. Where it is not soundly based (and these instances are in the majority) it can mislead, obscure, confuse and generally retard the subject. Historians are as much to blame here as the commercial trade, and it seems we do not learn from our mistakes. Having not long emerged from an era in which any high quality rococo furniture was wrongly attributed to Thomas Chippendale, we persist in applying the same flawed reasoning in attributions to other makers – James Moore, Richard Roberts, John Belchier, John Channon – to name but a few relevant to the period of this book. What do we actually know about these men and their businesses? How can we say that a particular type or style of furniture was exclusive to this or that maker and no other? How can we prove that even a documented piece of furniture was produced in the maker's workshop and not supplied by some unnamed contractor? In fact we can be certain of very little and attributions, on the whole, merely disguise our ignorance.

Here then is the principal difficulty in writing this book about early Georgian furniture. How to overcome the accumulation of received wisdom, preconceived ideas and plain nonsense that is the state of popular knowledge of the subject? How to get rid of 'Queen Anne', long cherished, much loved and widely recognised, and replace it with something closer to the historical reality? How to persuade the connoisseur, the dealer or the auctioneer of the difference between opinion and evidence? How to divorce aesthetic appreciation from academic analysis? The only answer I have is to stick to the evidence. Wherever possible I have used contemporary sources and documented furniture. Where this has not been possible I hope that my conjectures are reasoned and my arguments clear. In most cases I have not cited or illustrated furniture unless I have seen it myself, even if the actual illustration comes from an auctioneer's catalogue or a dealer's archive. In moments of weakness I have offered the occasional opinion on the aesthetic merit of particular objects, for which I hope to be excused. The fact is, from whatever angle one approaches the subject, either as historian, collector or dealer, one usually starts from a visual and emotional response, and without this any art historical subject is essentially lifeless.

My object has been to give as clear as possible an account of the stylistic and technical development of English furniture between 1714 and 1740. As with my previous book, I have not attempted to cover all furniture, but only that made for the upper classes, and typically that made in London. It is actually very difficult to document the furniture even of the 'middling classes', let alone the poor, since so little survives in context. Thus our conception of the early Georgian style in furniture is necessarily limited by the available evidence, and defined by the furnishings of relatively few people – royalty, the nobility, prosperous gentry, landed commoners, urban merchants and professionals. According to Joseph Massie's analysis of English society in 1760, only 75,000 families had an income of more than £100 per annum, while the remainder, some 1,396,000 families, survived on £100 or less. How could they afford even a walnut chest of drawers, at £3 or £4 a time? Thus the fashionable furniture industries of London and the larger provincial towns and cities were sustained by the custom of perhaps five per cent of the population. However, the number of potential customers was less important than their spending power, which was vastly greater than the remaining ninety-five per cent put together. Similarly, the influence of both the furniture makers and their patrons on the furnishing taste of their poorer neighbours was out of all proportion to their numbers. Despite the increased interest in recent years in regional and vernacular furniture, which has demonstrated the tenacity of local traditions in the face of relentless change, it is still true to say that where London led, the rest of the country sooner or later followed.

This book concentrates on mainstream furniture types – chairs, desks, chests of drawers, etc. – and in a way this is a pity, because the variety of Georgian furniture and the ingenuity of its makers is truly amazing. But in writing for the mainstream, rather than the specialised reader, one has to concentrate on the most common forms and answer, in that sense, the most commonly asked questions. Moreover, it is a rare piece of furniture which, however specialised or unique, does not share significant elements of style, materials or construction with its more ordinary peers. It is hoped, therefore, that this book will offer some common themes or criteria by which all furniture of the period can be approached. At the same time, I am aware that one can be too prescriptive. Just because ninety-nine chairs are made in a certain way does not mean that the hundredth will be. By the same token, however, how are we to recognise anomalies when we see them unless by their deviation from an accepted norm? The 'rules', if one calls them that, are there to guide us but not to be slavishly adhered to.

The emphasis on technical details, particularly materials and construction, derives from my belief that furniture-making was a manufacturing process first and an artistic statement second. This is not to deny the consummate artistry of many furniture designers and some makers, nor the powerful aesthetic sense that somehow pervades all aspects of the production process, but ultimately furniture makers were in business to make a living. If the furniture didn't hold together or the pennies didn't add up, no amount of artistic sensibility would clothe the wife and feed the children. Indeed, it is in the development and application of effective construction techniques, efficient production methods and aggressive marketing that we see early Georgian furniture makers distinguishing themselves from their Continental rivals. The French and Italians might have been leaders in style, but in developing a broadly based, modern and efficient furniture industry they were wholly outclassed by the English. This was why England was the world's largest exporter of furniture in the eighteenth century.

In a world where furniture history is increasingly subsumed beneath the broad aegis of studies in 'material culture', a book focusing on design and construction may seem rather narrow in scope. My answer to that is that there is little point in discussing the wider context when we have yet to establish the basic facts. Our chronology is still awry – the legacy of 'Queen Anne' – and nomenclature is still uncertain. We still cannot accurately identify common Georgian items such as a *dressing chair* (although I suggest a potential candidate in this book), and anachronistic terms such as 'lowboy' instead of *dressing table* and 'kneehole desk' instead of *bureau-table* do nothing to enhance understanding. Thus there is still plenty of work to do at the most basic level, and I have no illusions that the present book is any thing more than a step along the way.

A note on dating
The dating of furniture of this period is a thorny point. In many case the dates suggested here for certain pieces of furniture will differ by as much as ten or twenty years from the accepted parameters (by accepted I mean those generally applied in the older literature and the antiques trade). My chief concern is to identify the point at which a particular object, technique or stylistic device was first used, so that it can constitute a firm point of reference. To do so I have tried to find documented furniture or other firm evidence, which establishes the date at which the given object, technique or style first occurs. To argue, as some may do, that the given phenomenon may have occurred earlier, and that it is the evidence that is lacking, is specious. Evidence is the only basis for sound reasoning and therefore I stick with my dating until evidence, not opinion, proves otherwise.

The pace of stylistic change was as rapid in the early eighteenth century as it had been in the late seventeenth. While it is relatively simple to chronicle that change by finding the earliest appearance of particular features, or the earliest occurrence of new terminology, it is less easy to say when a particular style, or motif, or furniture type was no longer fashionable. The persistence of apparently outmoded ideas is a fact of life in furniture design as in any other sphere of human activity, but this book is principally concerned to record change, not inertia. Hence most of the furniture cited is given fairly close date parameters, suggesting when a given piece is likely to have been fashionable, rather than how long it might have continued in production. The point is illustrated by Chippendale's 'sweep back' chairs made for Sir Lawrence Dundas (Chapter 4). That they were made in 1765 is undeniable, but no furniture historian would claim they were still fashionable at that date. Single, unqualified dates (e.g., 1728) are only given to objects whose date of manufacture is known by documentary or other means. Qualified single dates (e.g., c.1720) are given where circumstantial or supporting evidence gives credence to such a date. In most cases a range of dates (e.g., 1715-40) is given. The earlier date should be the year when evidence for a particular object or design or style is first manifested and the later date will be the point at which it might still have been fashionable. Occasionally a date range will be given where a piece of furniture is ascribed to a particular maker whose working dates are known (e.g., 1723-32).

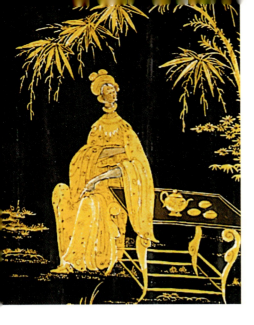

Chapter One
THE LONDON FURNITURE TRADE

Plate 1:44 (Detail). Desk and bookcase (1740-60). See page 51.

The organisation of the trade

In 1715 the population of London was about 550,000, or roughly ten per cent of the population of England and Wales. The populations of the next largest cities, Norwich and Bristol, were about 30,000 and 20,000 respectively.[1] This extraordinary disparity reflects London's dominance in all spheres of human activity – social, political, artistic, religious and economic. The primary engines of national economic growth were manufacturing and overseas trade, in both of which London's pre-eminence was overwhelming. In the West India trade, for instance, of an annual average of £630,000 of sugar imported between 1699 and 1701, 83 per cent went to London.[2] There was a similar imbalance in the furniture export trade. Of a total value of £35,456 of furniture exported in 1700, London accounted for £33,161 (93 per cent).[3] Of course, these figures do not represent the furniture industry as a whole, for the output of furniture made for domestic consumption in provincial centres must have been considerable, but they do accurately portray London's dominance of the fashionable furniture market. Similarly, until the Naval Stores Act of 1721, London received the lion's share of raw materials for high-class furniture-making. Almost 98 per cent of the walnut timber imported into England between 1697 and 1720 went into London. For olive wood and princes wood the figure was 100 per cent.[4]

By modern standards London was not a large city (**1:1**). From Wapping in the east to Charing Cross in the west was under three miles, with Westminster still separated from London by gardens, fields, and a straggle of buildings along the river. From the riverside at Blackfriars' Stairs to northernmost Clerkenwell was less than a mile. Across the river the borough of Southwark extended a few hundred yards in all directions from the end of London Bridge. Within this small area half a million people worked, bred and died.

There were furniture-makers in every part of the city, with most concentrated in a broad swathe from Aldgate and Houndsditch in the east, through Cornhill to St Paul's Churchyard and Ludgate Hill, extending north into Aldermanbury and Holborn, then west to Fleet Ditch, along Fleet Street and the Strand to Covent Garden, Long Acre and Haymarket. Outlying pockets were established in Southwark, St James's and Westminster.[5] Within this overall distribution there were significant concentrations of furniture-makers in particular areas and even individual streets. This

1. Holmes (1993), pp. 403-6.
2. PRO, Cust 3.
3. Joy (1965).
4. PRO, Cust 3; for the 1721 Naval Stores Act see Bowett (1994); for a digest and commentary of the figures for imported walnut between 1698 and 1780, see Bowett (1995).
5. Extrapolated from *DEFM*.

clustering of tradesmen was a characteristic feature of the medieval urban landscape, but its continuance in an age of rapid change and increasing diversity suggests there were still significant benefits from the arrangement. A document in the Corporation of London Record Office lists the names and professions of all householders liable for jury service in and around St Paul's Churchyard in 1721.[6] It shows that certain sections of the Churchyard and its adjoining streets were dominated by particular trades. Along the south side of the Churchyard were listed twenty-six householders, of which fifteen were furniture-makers and a further three were 'leather guilders' who, among other things supplied painted leather screens and seat covers to the trade.[7] The east side of the Churchyard between Watling Street and Cheapside was dominated by the fine classical façade of St Paul's School. Flanking it were eleven businesses, of which six were cane chair-makers and two were cabinet-makers.[8]

Fleet Ditch and Holborn Bridge, just west of the city walls, housed another concentration of furniture-makers, and to the north of them in Holborn and Clerkenwell was the centre of the carving trade. Further west was the cabinet-making hotspot centred on Covent Garden, Long Acre and St Martin's Lane. This area had escaped the fire of 1666, and much of the new building of the mid-to-late seventeenth century had occurred here. This was already a fashionable and expensive area of town, as is shown in the rents paid by furniture-makers on their premises. For instance, between 1700 and 1711 the cabinet-maker John Guilbaud's premises in Long Acre were valued at £30 per annum, whereas John Coxed's workshop in St Paul's Churchyard was valued at only £10.8s. in 1710, declining to less than £6 in the 1720s.[9] Guilbaud's premises may, of course, have

6. CLRO, MISC MSS 83/3.
7. Chair-makers: James Bull, Thomas Bushnell, William Green, Jonathan Puller, John White, William Old, William Gardner, Edward Newman, Daniel Eldin, Samuel Van Ruyvan. Cabinet-makers: ? Jones, John Hodgson, John Belticher (sic). Upholsterers: ? Gibson. Leather gilders: John Rowland, Samuel Williams, Joseph Fletcher. The list includes only those eligible for jury service – non-jurors, papists and females, such as Grace Coxed who owned the White Swan workshop, were not listed.
8. Chair-makers: Joseph Wormell, Henry Buck, Richard Hartland, Robert Gamage, Edward Newman and Richard King. Cabinet-makers: Abraham Avery and Thomas Jones. We know from other sources that the chairmakers also made or supplied other furniture.
9. Westminster Record Office, *Scavenger's Books 1700-11, Poor Rate Books 1702-11*; CLRO, *Castle Baynard Ward Land Tax Books, 1711-37*; GL, *Land Tax Assessment Books St Gregories Parish East*.

Plate 1:1. Anon, A Map of Westminster, the City of London and Southwark, published by Joseph Smith (1724). The Tower of London is clearly visible on the right, with London Bridge to the west of it. St. Paul's Cathedral and the surrounding churchyard is just right of centre, with Fleet Ditch to its west, running north from the River Thames. Further east along the river stretches Fleet Street and the Strand, with the fashionable West End developing rapidly to the north and west of them. St James's Park and Westminster are lower left.
GUILDHALL LIBRARY, CORPORATION OF LONDON

been larger, and the more spacious plots in the West End were undoubtedly an attraction, but the disparity in rents was real. The willingness to pay the higher West End rents reflected the value ambitious furniture-makers placed on a good address close to their wealthy and fashionable patrons.

The close proximity of colleagues and competitors made for a close-knit community, in which most prominent furniture-makers were known to each other. The names of debtors and creditors recorded in furniture-makers' probate inventories reveal an interlaced web of commercial relationships, strengthened by ties of blood and marriage. Together with a skilled and mobile workforce, this resulted in the rapid transmission of ideas and skills from one workshop to another, and this is one reason for the homogenous nature of much London-made furniture. It also ensured fierce competition, which was a major factor in maintaining consistent standards of manufacture and keen pricing.

A career in the furniture trade began with an apprenticeship. Youths were usually apprenticed about the age of fourteen, and the usual term was seven years. The apprentice was 'bound' to his master by an indenture which followed a standard form of words. Below is the indenture of Samuel Butt, who went on to establish a workshop in St Paul's Churchyard in the 1720s:

> 8 July 1707
> Samuel Butt son of Samuel Butt late of Frampton in the County of Gloucester Clerke deceased putts to Samuel Luvarick Citizen and Joiner of London for 7 yeares dat as above.[10]

From these indentures, which survive in large numbers, we learn the apprentice's origins, his father's occupation and the name of his master, all valuable information in building a picture of the largely anonymous and forgotten men who populated the London furniture trade.

Apprenticeships were served under the auspices of the London Livery Companies, which in theory regulated the activities of all the tradesmen operating in the City of London and its immediate environs. Aspiring furniture-makers might join any Company, but most served their time with either the Upholsterers' or the Joiners' Company. Of the two, we know most about the activities of the Joiners' Company because their records are more complete. By 1720 the majority of apprentices (some 60 per cent) in the Joiners' Company came from London itself, but London was also a significant draw for youths from the provinces and, indeed, the furniture trade relied on a constant infusion of labour and talent from the Home Counties and beyond.[11] Most apprentices were the sons of tradesmen; others were sons of merchants, professional men, yeoman farmers and even gentry. The custom of primogeniture often obliged the younger sons of gentlemen to support themselves in a trade.

The quality of a London training was reflected in the high premiums paid for metropolitan apprenticeships compared with those of provincial furniture-makers. The amounts charged reflected both the status of the particular trade and the reputation of the individual furniture-maker. Upholsterers charged the most – between £20 and £50 – with cabinet-makers the next most expensive at between £11 and £22.[12] In addition to paying the premium, the apprentice also had to buy or make his own tools and tool-chest; in the case of a trainee cabinet-maker, whose range of tools was extensive, this amounted to at least 8 or 10 guineas.[13] Thus an apprenticeship was an investment of both time and money, in anticipation of a respectable and potentially lucrative career.

After seven years' training the apprentice could take up the 'freedom' of his Livery Company and begin work as a journeyman. At the same time, he assumed the rights and privileges of a 'citizen' of London. Samuel Butt, whom we saw indentured in 1707, took up his freedom after almost eight years' apprenticeship in 1715:

> 3 May 1715
> Samuel Butt app Samuel Luvarick Citizen & Joiner of London for 7 yeares per Indenture 8th July 1707 was admitted into the freedome by consent.[14]

---

10. CLRO MS 8052/3, f. 124.
11. I am grateful to Laurie Lindey for sharing her research with me. Lindey's unpublished work shows that in the 17th century most apprentices to the Joiners' Company came from outside London, but this trend was reversed from about 1710 onwards. This supports Kirkham's findings for the 18th century that most apprentices were London-born (Kirkham (1988), p. 43 and Appendix I).
12. Kirkham (1988), pp. 43-46; Lindey, personal communication.
13. Anon. (1747), p. 50.
14. CLRO, MS 8051/3, f. 33.
15. Kirkham (1988), pp. 141 et seq.
16. Joy (1955), p. 57.
17. GL., MS 8046/5, *Minutes of the Joiners' Company*, 5 February 1724/25.
18. Anon. (1747), p. 50.
19. Ibid: Campbell (1747), p. 332.
20. Bowett and Lindey (2003).
21. Lindey (February 2006).

However, the proportion of apprentices taking up freedoms declined markedly from about 1725 onwards.[15] The reasons for this are not fully understood, but one significant factor may have been the failure of a legal action by the Joiners' Company in 1726, by which the Company attempted to enforce the by-law obliging all joiners to take up their freedoms.[16] Although the apprenticeship system continued to operate throughout the eighteenth century, it did so much less systematically than before and many, perhaps most, furniture apprenticeships were served by private arrangement rather than under the auspices of the Livery Companies. Because of this, it is impossible accurately to estimate the number of people working in the furniture industry. In February 1724/5 the Joiners' Company presented the Lord Mayor with an estimate of their membership which cited 286 Liverymen, 2,146 'freemen householders' or masters, and 2,925 journeymen. The total of 5,357 was some 60 per cent higher than in 1699.[17] The survey took no account of the many cabinet-makers who were not members of the Company, nor of the upholsterers, turners, carvers, gilders, japanners and other tradesmen. One must assume, therefore, that the figure represented only a fraction of the total number of furniture-makers in London at this date.

The survey reveals that roughly 55 per cent of freemen joiners never became masters of a workshop, but worked all their lives for piecework or a weekly wage. These journeymen (and, in some trades, women) rarely aspired to more than a guinea or perhaps thirty shillings a week, and never amassed the capital required to set up shop.

A rung above the journeyman was the 'working master', one of those who 'keep no shops nor stocks but principally follow making and dispose of their goods as fast as they are finished'.[18] In other words, a working master had a small workshop, perhaps just himself and a couple of apprentices or journeymen, and worked at the bench himself. It was reckoned that to set up on his own and become a working master, a journeyman cabinet-maker required a capital of between £100 and £200 in addition to his tools.[19] This amounted to between one and two years' wages for a skilled journeyman, and there was little prospect of amassing this capital by labour alone. Those who became masters usually had some other source of funds. Many relied on an inheritance, either succeeding to the family business or inheriting sufficient funds from parents or relatives to establish a new one. One relatively common method of acquiring capital, or indeed a ready-made business, was to marry it. In 1708 the journeyman cabinet-maker John Coxed married the widow of his late master, John Mayo, and thereby acquired both a wife and a business.[20] The subsequent success of the White Swan workshop in St Paul's Churchyard must have proved satisfactory to both parties. John Ody, a joiner made free in 1712, became a partner at *The Castle* in St Paul's Churchyard in 1719 by marrying Mary Old, daughter of William Old, a turner and chair-maker.[21] We do not yet know how Samuel Butt managed to establish himself, but he was taking on apprentices by 1718 and by the mid-1720s he was master of the *Greyhound and Hat* at the east end of St Paul's Churchyard, where he 'Makes and Sells all Sorts of the Best *Cabinet* and *Looking-Glass* work, at the Cheapest Rates' (**1:2**).

The working master, while master of his own business, was often dependent on other furniture-

Plate 1:2. Double chest of drawers (1720-30). Walnut on deal and oak. This bears the trade label of Samuel Butt, who had premises at the *Greyhound and Hat* in St Paul's Churchyard in the 1720s. Butt was the son of a clerk from Frampton on Severn, Gloucestershire. He was apprenticed in London in 1707 and made free of the Joiners' Company in 1715. He began taking apprentices in 1718, and established a workshop in St Paul's Churchyard probably after 1721. He twice declined to serve as Steward to the Joiners' Company (1725 and 1730). The date of his death is not recorded, and this is his only known labelled piece. Brassware is replaced.

PHILLIPS OF HITCHIN

The London Furniture Trade

Plate 1:3. Inscription and signature of Peter Miller (1724). This inscription was found behind the prospect mirror on the desk-and-bookcase in Plate 2:31. Miller appears to have been a working master with a small workshop producing work of an unusually high calibre. He was not a member of the Joiners' Company and almost nothing is known of his life. He died in 1729.

Plate 1:4. Inscription and signature of William Palleday, from the double-chest in Plate **3:45**. This is the hand of a literate man. The fact that the inscription is hand-written rather than a printed label suggests the piece might be the work of Palleday himself.

makers or retailers to sell his goods. Many were little better off than journeymen, with no certainty of work and the added burden of maintaining a business. (It was for this reason, among others, that apprenticeships with working masters were less expensive than with more prominent makers.) In 1742 the cabinet-maker John Wierne had so little work that he set his two apprentices to making picture frames. The business finally folded when he had no money to buy wood to continue working.[22]

For a working master to get steady work, good craftsmanship was essential, but that alone did not guarantee riches. The furniture made by Peter Miller, a cabinet-maker working in the Savoy, is of quite exceptional quality (cf. 2:31), but when he died in October 1729 his estate consisted of little more than his tools, his remaining stock in trade and about £40 in cash.[23] His will suggests little in the way of workshop facilities or employees, so he may well have been a working master. Miller's only lasting legacy was his peerless furniture and his name, secretly inscribed behind the mirror on one of his finest pieces (**1:3**).

Much of the working masters' custom probably came from other furniture-makers, who relied on them when the facilities of their own workshops were overstretched, or when specialist skills were called for. Indeed, the use of working masters as sub-contractors probably underpinned the trade as a whole, providing a large pool of manufacturing capacity supporting a relatively few prominent names.

A step above the working master was the 'craftsman-shopkeeper', who still might work at the bench himself, but also employed journeymen and sold the furniture he made from his own premises. It is possible that William Palleday, who worked at *The Crown* in Aldermanbury, was a man of this stamp. He came from well-established stock; his father John was a member of the Joiners' Company, his grandfather William had been Master in 1679-80 and his great-grandfather Richard had been taking on apprentices in the 1640s.[24] After gaining his freedom in November 1706, William succeeded to his father's business in Aldermanbury. He is known to have supplied furniture directly to clients such as Lady Heathcote, for whom he made a looking glass and a table in 1713.[25] On the other hand, he may also have performed work for other masters or retailers, for at least four pieces of case furniture with his name and address on it are known (**1:4** and **3:45**). It is possible that the inscriptions were intended to inform buyers who the maker of the piece was and encourage them to come directly to the source of the goods. The fact that these inscriptions are hand-written strongly suggests he still worked at the bench.

Even the smallest craftsman-shopkeeper ran a multi-faceted business, quite different from the solitary craftsman/artist of popular imagination. The easiest way to get a sense of this is to look at the lists of creditors and debtors recorded in the inventory of an obscure furniture-maker such as Lazarus Stiles, who died in 1724.[26] Stiles was a longstanding member of the Joiners' Company, having taken his first apprentice in 1688.[27] His premises were in the parish of St Mary

---

22. Kirkham (1988), p. 41.
23. PRO, PROB 11/632, sig. 274, f. 309.
24. GL, MS 8046, *Minutes of the Joiners' Company*; MS 8051/2, *Joiners' Company Freedom Admissions*, f. 117.
25. *DEFM*, p. 671. William Palliday (*sic*) was made free of the Joiners' Company in November 1706 and was resident in Aldermanbury by 1716. GL, MS 8051/2, *Joiners' Company Freedom Admissions*, fol. 117; CLRO, 126.21, *Trophy Tax for Cripplegate Within*, 1716-17, f. 24.
26. CLRO, *Orphans' Court Record*, 3197, *Common Sergeant's Book 6*, f. 86.
27. GL, MS 8052/2, *Joiners' Company Apprenticeship Bindings*, f. 158.

Aldermanbury, a few hundred yards north-east of St Paul's Churchyard. When he died he was an old man, living alone, or perhaps with a servant, in a house crammed with furniture parts, tools and materials. His stock-in-trade consisted largely of case furniture and looking glasses, and his workforce consisted of about half a dozen journeymen as well as himself. He owned or held leases on several properties on which he received rent, and acted in a small way as a timber merchant. At the time of his death he owed money to timber merchants and woodmongers, ironmongers, glass-sellers, brass-founders, sconce-makers, frame-makers and gilders, and other cabinet-makers. Thus Stiles' business was interwoven with a host of suppliers, sub-contractors and specialists without whom he could not operate. Was he successful? Perhaps moderately so. After outstanding debts had been accounted for he was worth about £890 in stock-in-trade and personal goods, and he was owed £138 in unpaid debts. In financial terms this places him somewhere in the broad middle range of London furniture-makers. The fact that Stiles' name is virtually unknown to historians and his work has vanished without trace is typical; signed, labelled or documented pieces by known makers are the exception, not the rule.

If a master specialised in a single trade or product he did not require a very large workshop, nor a large workforce, to be able to manufacture on a considerable scale. Thomas Warden, a chair-maker in St Paul's Churchyard who died in 1701, had a workshop with four frame-makers' benches and two carvers' benches, implying that he probably employed six journeymen, or five if he was still working himself.[28] With this small workforce he had over six hundred cane chairs, stools and couches finished or in hand. Such a copious output suggests a well-organised workshop, relying on sub-division of parts and labour to speed production. Warden's chair frames must have come to him ready turned, since there was no lathe in his workshop. His carvers embellished them and his joiners assembled them. For the caned seats and backs he relied on a member of the Basket-makers' Company, Isaac Puller. When Warden died in 1703, Puller was the executor of his estate. Warden's son William was apprenticed to Puller and later married his daughter Sarah. Thus the link between two mutually dependent businesses was secured for the future.[29] This sort of close, inter-familial relationship seems to have been very common, and had obvious social as well as commercial advantages.

Isaac Puller's premises were at *The Golden Plow*, on the south side of St Paul's Churchyard, and his trade card of 1714 states that he made and sold 'Cane-Chairs, Stools and couches of all sorts: and also Easie Chair-Frames, Chair-Stool Frames both round and square, to cover; and sells Rattan-Canes, whole and split'.[30] Thus Puller was a great deal more than a mere basket-maker – perhaps he retailed the chairs Thomas Warden made. When he died in 1720 his son Jonathan inherited the business. At the same time William Warden, son of Thomas and now established as a chair-maker, was living in Black Swan Court, just behind *The Golden Plow*, and it is not difficult to envisage the two men continuing the business relationship begun by their fathers.[31]

Over the period of this study the demand for cane chairs declined markedly, so cane chair-makers had to diversify their output:

> Though this Sort of Household Goods [chairs] is generally sold at the Shops of the *Cabinet-makers* for all the better Kinds, and at the *Turners* for the more common, yet there are particular makers for each.
> The *Cane-chair-makers* not only make this Sort (now almost out of use) but the better Sort of matted, Leather-bottomed and Wooden Chairs, of all of which there is a great Variety in the Goodness, Workmanship, and Price; and some of the makers, who are also Shop-keepers, are very considerable Dealers, employing from 300 to upwards of £500 in Trade, and require with an Apprentice £10. The Work is pretty smart, the Hours from six to nine; and a Journey-man's Wages 12s. a Week
> The white, Wooden, Wicker, and ordinary matted Sort, commonly called Kitchen-chairs, and sold by *Turners* are made by different Hands, but are all inferior Employs.
> Those covered with Stuffs, Silks, &c., are made and sold by the Upholsterers.[32]

28. CLRO, *Orphans' Court Record* 2439, *Common Sergeant's Book* 5, f. 82B.
29. Lindey (2004); PRO, Prob 11/579, *Will of Isaac Puller*, 1 March 1720.
30. DEFM.
31. CLRO, MISC MSS/83/3.
32. Anon. (1747), pp. 57-58.

The London Furniture Trade

Plate 1:5. Trade label of Francis Thompson (1740-50). This informative label records the extraordinarily diverse output of some London turners. Nothing else is known about Thompson's life and work.

FROM HEAL, *LONDON FURNITURE MAKERS*

Plate 1:6. The Bedroom Scene (detail, 1732). This is from *The Harlot's Progress*, by William Hogarth (1697-1764). The turned 'Dutch' chair on the left was made in huge numbers in England, as well as being imported from Holland in considerable quantities. Surviving metropolitan examples have yet to be identified, although the type is well represented in provincial and vernacular traditions in various regions of England.

VICTORIA AND ALBERT MUSEUM

As this passage suggests, chairs made by turners were generally of the cheapest sort. Francis Thompson, who worked at the *Three Chairs* in St John's Lane, advertised 'all Sorts of dy'd Beach Chairs' together with a plethora of household articles and 'many other Things too tedious to Mention' (**1:5**). The ubiquitous 'Dutch' chair, which features in so many engravings of eighteenth century interiors, was one of the turner's most characteristic products (**1:6**). Thompson called himself a turner *and* chair-maker, which suggests that he actually made chairs, but many turners were only retailers:

> The other Part are a Set of Shop-keepers, and many of them in a very large Way, who deal in a vast variety of necessary Household-stuff... In short, they engross, as to the buying and selling Part, almost all the Produce of the *real Turners*, and many Trades besides'.[33]

Plate 1:7. Pillar-and-claw table (1730-1760). Tables such as this were made in vast numbers and, although of a simple form, still required sub-division of labour. The turning of tops and pillars was done by turners, the shaping of the legs and assembly of the table by joiners.   PRIVATE COLLECTION

Turners also played a significant role in supplying ready-made parts to other chair-makers and cabinet-makers. It is striking how few joiners' and cabinet-makers' workshops had lathes; instead, they subcontracted or 'put out' turned work to turners. The probate inventory of Richard Roberts, joiner and chair-maker to George I and George II, reveals a heavy reliance on ready-made turned parts such as pillars for pillar-and-claw tables and fire-screens (**1:7**).[34] Most of the cheaper joiner-made chairs had turned rather than 'O.G.' (cabriole) back legs, and these too would have been put out to a turner. Turners also made circular table-tops, dining table legs, candle-stands, tea-boards and voiders, and a vast range of domestic and kitchen wares.

Richard Roberts' business was at *The Royal Chair* in Marylebone St, Westminster. There were at least seven workmen's benches in his workshops, and the presence of lumber (including 'thirty two feet of rich mahogany'), a sawbench and several saws suggests a limited capacity to convert timber. As well as the 230 chairs, stools and settees in his ware-room and workshops there were dumb waiters, fire-screens, dining tables, pillar-and-claw tables, sconces and other mirrors. This suggests that, although primarily a chairmaker, Roberts was also able to supply other forms of furniture, mostly constructed of solid wood. A similar but probably less prosperous business was that of Edward Newman, who worked at *The Chair and Crown* in St Paul's Churchyard. Although described in several documents as a chair-maker, a wainscot chest of drawers bearing his trade label

33. Ibid., p. 211.
34. PRO PROB 3/32/127; a partial transcript of this inventory can be found in Beard and Cross (1998).

The London Furniture Trade

Plate 1:8. Chest of drawers (1720-40). Oak and deal. This bears the trade label of Edward Newman, one of three furniture-makers of that name. This man's workshop was on the east side of St Paul's Churchyard. Some documents describe Newman as a cane chairmaker, but this chest demonstrates he made or sold other furniture as well. The construction is decidedly old-fashioned, with a frame-and-panel carcase and side-hung drawers. Escutcheons are original, handles are not. PRIVATE COLLECTION

has recently come to light (**1:8**). Newman, like Roberts, may have specialised in chairs but also made other kinds of joined furniture. Other joiners restricted themselves to a sole commodity; the most common of these was the bed-joiner, who made nothing but bed-frames, posts and testers for upholsterers to fit up. One of these was Thomas Bent, who had premises in Fleet Ditch from the 1740s onwards (**1:9**).[35]

The work of cabinet-makers differed from joiners in that they were principally concerned with producing veneered case furniture. They generally produced a wider range of products than chair-makers or joiners, but there were considerable variations in the scale and scope of their businesses. The trade card of Coxed and Woster (fl.1719-1735) records that their workshop made 'Cabinets, Bookcases, Chests of Drawers, Scrutores and Looking-glasses of all sorts' (**1:10**).[36] Neither chairs nor upholstery is mentioned. No doubt the list was not definitive, but it is surprising how often this relatively narrow repertoire is repeated on other makers' trade cards. Samuel Butt, also in

---

35. *DEFM*, p. 66.
36. For more on Coxed and Woster's work, see Bowett and Lindey (2003).

St Paul's Churchyard, John Gatehouse in Fleet Ditch, and Stephen Wood in Southwark all advertised similar goods.[37] The same range of stock is cited in cabinet-makers' bills. John Phillips, a cabinet-maker working in St Paul's Churchyard c.1720-32, supplied a large quantity of furniture to the Duke of Beaufort between 1728 and 1730. It comprised cabinet-work, japanned case furniture, and looking glasses of many different sorts, but no seat furniture. It also included several carved and gilt pier tables, and it is a moot point whether these were produced in-house or contracted out.[38]

According to Campbell, the skills required for cabinet-work were of a relatively high order:

> The Cabinet-Maker is by much the most curious Workman in the Wood Way, except the Carver; and requires a nice mechanic Genius, and a tolerable Degree of Strength, though not so much as the Carpenter; he must have a much lighter Hand and a quicker Eye than the Joiner, as he is employed in Work much more minute and elegant. A Youth who designs to make a Figure in this Branch must learn to Draw; for upon this depends the Invention of new Fashions, and on that the Success of his Business.[39]

The author of *A General Description of All Trades* described the budding cabinet-maker's talents in much the same terms, adding that he must 'be very assiduous during his Apprenticeship, or he may serve seven Years, and turn out but a Bungler'.[40]

Campbell's assertion that cabinet-making was a 'very profitable Trade' is borne out by some wills and inventories. When John Coxed died in December 1718 he left more than £1,480 in cash to relatives; the value of his remaining assets and business, which he left to his wife, was probably considerably greater.[41] Coxed was undoubtedly a successful businessman, but his surviving furniture is not outstanding, either in design or quality. He was typical of a large group of middle-ranking cabinet-makers who formed the core of the London trade, many of whom were based in

37. For more on these makers see *DEFM*.
38. Badminton Archives, *Bill of John Phillips*, 3 December 1733.
39. Campbell (1747), p. 171.
40. Anon. (1747), p. 49.
41. Bowett and Lindey (2003).

Far left:
Plate 1:9. Trade Card of Thomas Bent (c.1760). Bent worked in Fleet Ditch from the 1740s. Few bed-joiners' trade cards have survived, probably because most such businesses operated mainly as subcontractors to upholsterers.
FROM HEAL, *LONDON FURNITURE MAKERS*

Left:
Plate 1:10. Trade label of Coxed and Woster (1719-c.1725). Coxed and Woster's output typifies the good but usually unexceptional furniture made in St Paul's Churchyard. As the label indicates, their repertoire was limited to cabinet-makers' goods, with no upholstery or chair-making branch. The firm operated from 1719 to 1735, and this style of label was used by the firm between 1719 and c.1725.
PRIVATE COLLECTION

The London Furniture Trade

Plate 1:11. Trade label of William Old and John Ody (1717-33). William Old was a turner and chair-maker who formed a partnership with John Ody, a joiner, about 1717. After Old's death in 1728 the partnership continued with Henry Old, William's son, until Ody's death in 1733. The combination of cabinet-maker's and chair-maker's goods advertised here was a common one.

CHRISTIE'S IMAGES LTD 2001

42. *DEFM*.
43. Ibid.
44. Campbell (1747), p. 171.
45. The information in the *DEFM* concerning the Old and Ody partnership is incorrect. John Ody was apprenticed in 1704 and made free in September 1713. He was made Liveryman in 1723. William Old's daughter Mary married Ody in May 1719, and Old is recorded as a chair-maker in St Paul's Churchyard in 1721. Old died in 1728, and John Ody in 1733. However, Old's widow did not sell off the stock in trade until 1738 [Lindey (February 2006)].
46. Charleston (1984), pp. 98 et seq.; Campbell (1747), p. 173.

and around St Paul's Churchyard. His contemporaries and neighbours included such well-known and apparently successful makers as John Belchier, John Brown, Henry Buck, William Old and John Ody, John Phillips and James Rodwell.[42] The otherwise obscure but evidently wealthy Mr Mash is known only by a paragraph in the *General Advertiser* of 4 September 1749:

> Thursday last died at his House at Chelsea Mr. Mash formerly an eminent Cabinet Maker in Wardour Street, Soho, having acquired a handsome fortune, had retir'd from Business.[43]

According to Campbell, one of the secrets of success in cabinet-making was to keep the upholsterer at arm's length; 'A Master Cabinet-Maker is a very profitable Trade; especially, if he works for and serves the Quality himself; but if he must serve them through the Chanel of the Upholder, his Profits are not very considerable'.[44]

Chair-making and cabinet-making were complementary trades, and commonly gave rise to partnerships. William Old, who had premises in St Paul's Churchyard, was a chair-maker and member of the Turners' Company. The marriage of his daughter Mary to the joiner/cabinet-maker John Ody in 1717 probably marked the inauguration of an expanded business at *The Castle*, offering both veneered case furniture and chairs. Their stock included: '… all Sorts of Cane & Dutch Chairs, Chair Frames for Stuffing and Cane-Sashes. And also all Sorts of the best Looking-Glass & Cabinet-Work in Japan Walnut-Tree and Wainscot'(**1:11**). The mention of 'Chair Frames for Stuffing' tells us that Old and Ody did not perform upholstery. This would either have been contracted out or Old and Ody might have been sub-contracted themselves to supply frames to the upholsterer.[45]

Francis Croxford, 'eminent in his profession for his many new and beautiful designs', sold a similar chair-making and cabinet-making business in 1733. The range and quantity of goods he produced was impressive:

> … magnificent large and noble glass sconces, and chimney glasses in rich carved and gilt Frames, made after his own design, and several fine walnut-tree, mahogany, mehone [*sic*] and other desks and bookcases with glass doors, and several fine mahogany clothes chests ornamented with brass, mahogany, walnut-tree and pigeon wood quadrille tables, fine mahogany dining tables of all sizes, and dressing glasses and dressing tables of several sorts, walnut-tree, mahogany and other desks, fine walnut-tree chests upon chests, and about one hundred dozen chairs of several sorts.
>
> *The Daily Post*, 12 July 1733

The association of cabinet-making with the production and sale of mirrors dated back to the 1660s, when the fashionable ensemble of table, candlestands and looking glass had become one of the cabinet-maker's staple products. Although these suites gradually declined in popularity after about 1710, mirrors remained an integral part of the cabinet-maker's stock-in-trade. The rough plates, manufactured in glass-houses situated in various parts of the City, and across the river at Vauxhall, were ground and polished by glass-grinders.[46] This was 'a cold, wet business, and does not want for Labour: They are not indeed very numerous, and the Pay pretty good, a Journey man getting 15 or 20s. a Week, by working from five to eight; and a Master can set up with about £50 or less (for they commonly work for Looking-glass-makers and coach-makers)'.[47] It was usually the glass-grinder who also 'foiled' the plates with tin and mercury.

A few cabinet-makers had the means to grind and foil their own plates. Samuel Jakeman, a cabinet-maker with premises in the parish of St Catherine Coleman, in the east of the City, had a silvering room with slate and stone tables, weights, quicksilver, foil and grinding benches, together with 265 looking glass plates in preparation. The rest of his premises were given over to a cabinet workshop and a ware-room containing all the usual cabinet-maker's stock of furniture and looking glasses.[48]

The carving of mirror frames was commonly put out to carving workshops, 'For there are a Class of Carvers who do nothing else but carve Frames for Looking-Glasses'.[49] The carvers in turn received the basic chassis or frames from frame-makers, who were often 'no more than a cobbling Carpenter or Joiner'.

Elite master-carvers such as John Boson (fl.1720-1743) and Matthias Lock (1710-1765) were not restricted to one type of product, but worked on all kinds of carved furniture:

> Though *Frame-making* is certainly a Part of *Joinery*, yet making those [frames] for Pictures and Looking Glasses, Tables and Slabs, especially the most curious Sorts of them, in which there is usually a good deal of *Carving*, is a particular Trade; the Masters are not many in number, but most of them take Apprentices, and require from 5 to £10, whose work will not be hard, but his Hours must be from six to eight: At this Handicraft a Workman can get from 10 to 20s a Week; and about £50 will supply one as a Master in common.[50]

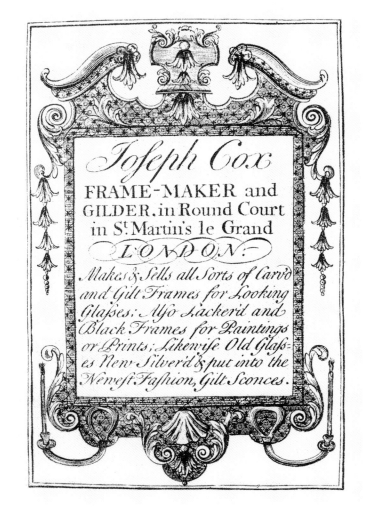

Plate 1:12. Trade card of Joseph Cox (c.1740). It is not clear what sort of apprenticeship qualified a man to be a 'frame-maker and gilder'. Cox may have been a cabinet-maker, joiner or carver.
FROM HEAL, LONDON FURNITURE MAKERS

Carvers usually gilded their own work, to the extent that 'Carver and Gilder' was a commonly cited combination on carvers' trade cards. 'Frame-maker and gilder' was an equally common label (**1:12**).

The mechanics of the relationship between cabinet-makers and master-carvers like Boson is not well understood. Numerous items of furniture have been attributed to Boson on the strength of bills for furniture made for Lady Burlington at Chiswick Villa in 1735 (see Chapter Three). But the bills state that Boson charged for carving only, not cabinet-work. Whether it was usual for a carver to invoice his work independently in this manner, rather than as a sub-contractor to the cabinet-maker, is not known. One suspects that it depended very much on the status of the individual carver. Boson's reputation and talent were probably sufficient to ensure that he was dealt with as a principal rather than as a subcontractor, but this may have been exceptional. One should also remember that top-flight carvers ran busy workshops, so that the carving billed in their name was very probably the work of one or more journeymen. In Matthias Lock's notebooks dating from the 1740s, his sketches of pieces executed for Hinton House, Dorset, are accompanied by the names of the several craftsmen (including himself) who carved them.[51]

To achieve any reputation in this field a man needed not only to be an excellent carver but to have skill in drawing and artistic sensibility or, as Campbell puts it, 'a good Invention to find out new Patterns'.[52] Indeed, the example of men like Matthias Lock (1710-65) and Thomas Johnson (1723-99) suggests that it was draughtsmanship rather than craftsmanship which marked out the men of genius in the carving trade.

47. Anon. (1747), p. 106.
48. Jakeman (1731).
49. Campbell (1747), p. 174.
50. Anon. (1747), pp. 97-8.
51. Victoria and Albert Museum, W.106a.
52. Campbell (1747), p. 175.

The London Furniture Trade

Plate 1:13. Desk-and-bookcase (1715-30). English japanning on a deal and oak carcase veneered with pearwood. Brasses are original; feet are original but reduced in height. This is typical of many japanned pieces in placing more value on the japanning than the cabinet work, which is of poor quality. TENNANTS AUCTIONEERS

In contrast to the master carver, routine carving on chairs and case furniture was likely to be performed in-house by chair-carvers, 'a species of Carvers peculiar to themselves; who are employed in carving Chairs, Posts and Testers, or any other Furniture whereon Carving is used. Their Work is slight, and requires no great Ingenuity to perform it; I mean, he needs no elegant Taste in the general Arts of Carving who performs that used at present upon Furniture'.[53] Chair carvers were further subdivided according to the type of chairs on which they worked. When in January 1734 William Byrom was indicted for theft at the Old Bailey, he described himself as a 'Cane-Chair-Carver by Trade, and my Father [in law] is a Cane-Chair-Maker in Moorfields'.[54]

Many cabinet-makers and chair-makers advertised japanned goods, and some appear to have specialised in them. When Thomas Halfhide left off trade in March 1723/4, his stock included the following:

> Several fine scarlet and gold desks and book-cases, several blue and gold, and black and gold, fine cabinets, chests of drawers, desks, and bowfets of all sorts; large lacquere'd trunks, chests and screens… fine lacquer'd tea-tables, several chimney-glasses, peer-glasses, and sconces in gold frames; and several union suits.
>
> *The Daily Post*, 18 March 1723

Whether all this stock was actually japanned in Halfhide's workshop is debatable; japanning was a specialised, if largely anonymous, craft. Japanners are sometimes mentioned as either debtors or creditors in furniture-makers' probate inventories, but they rarely merit more than 'by a Japanner…£2. 8. 0.'. Thomas Clinch, who worked at 'The Clock Case' in Moorfields, was a japanner who specialised in clock cases. His trade card states that he 'sells all sortes of lackquard work for clock cases' as well as 'all sortes of varnish'.[55] It is not clear if Clinch also made his clock cases, but one suspects not. The need for a clean, dust-free workshop makes it probable that the carcases for japanned work were made elsewhere. Given the scarcity of information regarding japanners, it seems likely that most worked as sub-contractors to joiners and cabinet-makers. One of the few practitioners to achieve prominence was Abraham Massey, whose workshops were in Great Queen Street. On his death in 1746 he was described as 'the most eminent Japanner in England'.[56] Another prominent japanner was Daniel Mills, who worked at 'The Japan Cabinet and Cistern' in Hatton Garden. His trade card reveals that as well as cabinet ware 'for Exportation, Wholesale or Retail', he japanned 'upon all Sorts of Goods made of Copper, Brass, Tin, Lead &c. to ye utmost perfection'. As well as this, he sold materials to other japanners.[57] Philip Arbuthnot (fl.c.1702-27), who had premises off the Strand, is variously described as a cabinet-maker, looking glass seller and japanner. He sold all kinds of cabinet-makers' goods, including case furniture, mirrors and japanned work. He died in 1727 and his will describes him as a 'japanner'; one wonders which of the many facets of his business was his real trade.[58]

The division between construction and decoration in japanned furniture is implied by the stamped initials found on some japanned furniture. The desk-and-bookcase in **1:13** is one of four known pieces stamped RF on the carcase (**1:14**). Since the black wash of the japanning overlies the stamp, it is likely that the stamp is that of the joiner or cabinet-maker who made the carcase. In common with many japanned pieces, the quality of the cabinet-work is poor, which suggests that buyers of this class of goods were concerned more with outward appearance than structural integrity.

Plate 1:14. Detail of **1:13**, showing the stamp RF, overlaid by a black wash. This may well be the stamp of the joiner who made the carcase prior to japanning. Three other pieces bearing the stamp are known, of which two are at Erddig, near Wrexham.

53. Ibid., p. 172.
54. Old Bailey Proceedings Online (www.oldbaileyonline.org), *trial of William Byrom, 16 January 1734* (t17340116-7).
55. *DEFM*.
56. Ibid.
57. Heal (1953), pp. 110 and 118; *DEFM*.
58. *DEFM*.

Opposite:
Plate 1:15. Desk-and-bookcase
(1715-30). Blue and gold japanning on a deal and oak carcase veneered with pearwood. The quality of both the japanning and the cabinet-work on this piece are far above the norm.
PARTRIDGE FINE ART

Below:
Plate 1:16. Detail of 1:15, showing the back of one of the interior drawers. Each drawer is numbered and initialled in the same red pigment used to decorate the inside of the drawers. These are probably the initials of the japanner.

59. Fennimore (1996), pp. 428 et seq.
60. Campbell (1747), p. 177.
61. Perkins (1723).
62. Stiles (1724).
63. Legg (1994).
64. Pattern-maker – 'someone who constructs the mould assembly in metalwork' (Wooler, 2002). For an account of the materials and processes involved in brass-founding, see Fennimore (1996).
65. Campbell (1747), p. 178.
66. Ibid., p. 179.
67. BM, *Banks Coll.*, 85.54

Occasionally, however, one finds pieces which combine japanning and cabinet-work of the highest quality. The desk-and-bookcase in **1:15** suggests the work of two highly skilled workshops, one a cabinet-maker's and the other a japanner's. The cabinet-work is unusually good for japanned furniture, and the japanning is of an equally high standard. The interior drawers are all numbered and marked on the back with the initials BA, drawn with a brush (**1:16**). These are almost certainly the initials of the japanner, who must have taken considerable pride in his work. Through the japanner, the furniture industry supported a host of colour-men and varnish-makers who supplied the raw materials of the trade.

Cabinet metalware became an increasingly important adjunct to cabinet-making as the industry developed. It is clear from the prevalence of standard designs for handles, hinges and catches that the mass-production of cabinet metalware was already well advanced in the early eighteenth century. In the later eighteenth century the production of cabinet metalware developed in Birmingham and its environs, but in the first half of the century London appears to have been the principal manufacturing centre.[59] The metalware was retailed directly by smiths and founders, or through braziers' and ironmongers' shops which, as well as a vast range of household goods, sold 'Chases and Handles for Cabinet-Work, Nails, Wood-Screws, and generally all Sorts of Brass and Iron Work that are useful for Furniture, or any Part of Furniture'.[60] Many furniture-makers' inventories include quantities of metalware, although there was a significant difference between cabinet-makers and chair-makers in this respect. The chair-maker Thomas Perkins had plenty of wood but no metalware, and this was fairly typical.[61] By contrast, in the front shop of cabinet-maker Lazarus Stiles there were escutcheons, handles, 'corner pieces', 'buttons', butt-hinges, side-hinges, 'dolphin' hinges, locks and keys.[62] A comprehensive joinery and furniture-making concern like that run by the Bastard brothers in Blandford, Dorset, needed a vast range of metalware, too extensive and varied to list here.[63]

The separate classes of metalwork were made by specialists in each branch, so that screws were made by the screw-maker, iron hinges and bolts by the blacksmith, and brass handles by the brass founder. The founder 'has Models generally of the Work designed, to which he fits the Mould to cast his Metal in; he seldom designs anything himself, and his chief Skill lies in melting the Brass and running it into the Mould evenly.' The implication here is that the models for the metalware were not devised by the founder, but were made by carvers or engravers. From these, 'patterns' were made by pattern makers to create the moulds for the brass-founder.[64]

The founding trade was further subdivided into specialisations: 'Founders who only cast for the Braziers; Founders who cast for the Coach-Makers; and those who cast Buckles, Studs and Bars for the Sadlers'.[65] The rationale behind these minute specialisations was commercial, because of the economies of scale: 'Thus the Founder, who casts Candlesticks and Brasses for Stoves, &c. is furnished with Moulds and Instruments proper to these Articles, and if he is desired to cast a Buckle in the Coach-Maker's Way, he cannot do it; not that he is ignorant of the Manner, but because he must make a Mould for that Purpose, which is not worth his while unless he had several Customers in the Branch'.[66] For this reason, cabinet brassware is likely to have been produced by specialist founders. One such was John Giles, whose premises were *The Two Candlesticks and Bell*, in Addle Street. Giles' trade card lists an extensive range of products:

> …all Sorts of Brass Handles, Escutcheons, Cloak Pins, Jointed Turnbuckles and Screw Rings, Plain and Wrought Joint & Hollow Drops, Rings & Roses, Buttons, Sash Knobs, Chimney Hooks, Watch Hooks, Fine & Common Curtain Rings, & Oes, Brass Curtain Rods Cas'd or Solid, Plain or with Pulleys & Hooks for the same. Likewise Brass Leather or Wood Casters, Brass Bolts, Butts, Desk Side Tumbler & Rule Joint Hinges, Brass Coach, Chair & Coffin Nails, Lath & Dovetail Door Hinges, Brass and Iron Door Locks & Brass & Iron Cabinet Locks of all Sorts. Brass & Iron Knockers, Implements for Hanging of Bells & Furniture for Coffins, in Brass or Tin, Square, Octagon, Round, Corner & Side Lanthorn Frames, Plain or Ornamented Hanging Glass Bell Lamps, Globe or Bell Lamps for Passages, Glass Arms & Lustres, Plain or Wrought Single Double & Treble Brass Branches, Plain or Wrought Chandeliers for Churches, Halls, or Assembly Rooms.[67]

The London Furniture Trade

The London Furniture Trade

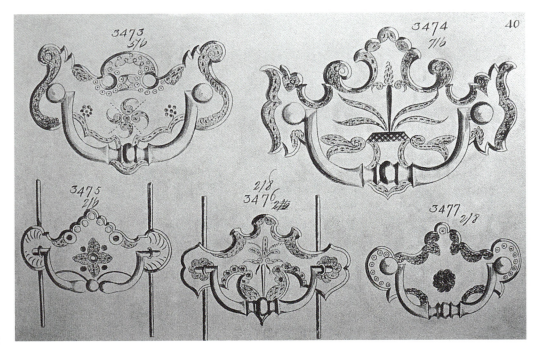

Plate 1:17. Brass backplate (1730-40). This backplate has the initials J*G cast into it. This is one of the most common identifying marks found on backplates of the period, and may identify brasses produced in the foundry of the cabinet brassfounder John Giles.

Plate 1:18. Page from a cabinet-founder's pattern book (c. 1750). The style of these patterns ranges in date from c.1730 (bottom left) to c.1750 (top right). Each pattern is numbered and priced, per dozen. It was from pattern books such as these that cabinet-makers ordered their furniture fittings. The mass–production of standard patterns explains the relative uniformity of much Georgian cabinet brassware.
VICTORIA AND ALBERT MUSEUM

This astonishingly wide range of articles was not all produced in-house. Giles described himself as a 'Cabinet Founder and Ironmonger', the latter term denoting a retailer rather than a maker of goods. Many of the things he advertised, such as locks, nails and glass arms for lustres, and possibly some of the brassware also, would have been supplied by other specialists. Along with other brassfounders and metalworkers, Giles is recorded as a creditor in the probate inventories of several furniture-makers.[68]

It is not uncommon to find initials stamped into the backplates of brass furniture handles. In theory, the marking of wares was a requirement of the London Company of Founders after an Ordinance of 1615, but the degree to which it was enforced is unclear.[69] One of the most common stamps is JG (**1:17**), and it is tempting to speculate that these are the initials of John Giles. Other initials found on furniture brasses up to 1740 include EH, ET, IC, II (or JJ), IP and TT.[70]

By the middle of the eighteenth century, and probably earlier, retailers and cabinet-makers were able to order handles from printed catalogues.[71] A number of these survive, most from the second half of the eighteenth century, but some contain early patterns of handles. The example in **1:18** shows five designs annotated with the price per dozen for each pattern. In this case all the designs are embellished with surface decoration which was usually engraved rather than cast. Another method of marketing brassware was to produce 'pattern cards' of full-size samples.[72]

The 'abundantly ingenious' locksmith was another essential supplier: 'The Keys, Wards, Springs, and Plates he makes himself; and employs the Founder to cast his cases, if in Brass'.[73] Iron cases were made by the blacksmith. As with cabinet brassware, the economies of scale resulted in the prevalence of standard patterns of both iron and brass locks. However, furniture of exceptional quality often had locks of equivalent quality to match. Although there must have been a considerable number of locksmiths supplying the furniture trade, few are known by name. One exception is Henry Walton, a locksmith in St Martin's Lane. His trade label of 1694 survives at Dyrham Park, and states that he made 'all Sorts of Brass Locks for Chamber Doors and all Sorts of Cabinet Locks…'.[74]

With so many different workmen and sub-contractors to supervise, and with clients to cultivate and attend, the master of any sizeable furniture business was unlikely to work at the

---

68. For example, the inventory of Samuel Jakeman records him as owing Giles £41.19.0, sufficient to buy a lot of cabinet brassware. (Jakeman 1731).
69. Fennimore (1996), pp. 42-3.
70. Butler (2002). The author's own researches into founders' marks supports the findings of Butler and Fennimore.
71. Goodison (1975); Fennimore (1996), p. 35 et seq.
72. Fennimore (1996), pp. 34-35
73. Campbell (1747), p. 166.
74. Lenygon (1927), p. 245.

bench himself. The following account, although dating from 1767, is probably applicable to our earlier period:

> The master himself no longer touches a tool. Instead he oversees the work of his forty journeymen, evaluates what they have produced, corrects their mistakes, and shows them ways and methods by which they can better their work or improve their technique. He may invent new tools and will observe what is going on in the development of fashion. He keeps in touch with people of taste and visits artists who might be of assistance to him.[75]

Like the cabinet-makers, upholsterers were also dependent on a host of suppliers and subcontractors. Horsehair, webbing, hessian, nails and tacks, fringes, braid, and cloth of all kinds and qualities were essential to the upholsterers' trade, and all were bought in from other tradesmen or merchants. Sadly, we know almost nothing about this intricate web of commercial relationships, a lack which is all the more surprising when one realises that upholsterers or 'upholders' comprise the largest single group of furniture-makers recorded in the *Dictionary of English Furniture Makers*. Most remained journeymen or working masters all their lives. Such a man 'has a Mind only to be a mere Upholder, and has no Prospect of setting up in the Undertaking Way'.[76] Journeyman upholsterers needed few skills: 'He must handle a Needle so alertly as to sew a plain Seam, and sew on the Lace without Puckers; and he must use his Sheers so dextrously as to cut a Valance or Counterpain with a genteel Sweep, according to a Pattern he has before him.... The stuffing and covering a Chair or Settee-Bed is indeed the nicest Part of this Branch; but it may be acquired without any remarkable Genius. All the Wooden-work they use is done by the Joiner, Cabinet-Maker, and Carver'.[77]

A journeyman upholsterer might earn twelve or fifteen shillings a week, and a woman, 'if good for any thing', a shilling a day. A working master needed a modest level of capital, perhaps £100, to establish himself, but at this level his business was limited in its scope. In 1720 John Meller ordered a new bed for his house at Erddig from the upholsterer John Hutt, who worked at *The Three Pillows* in St Paul's Churchyard. In April he asked his son-in-law to report on progress, and was told that 'ye Bed as to their [Upholsterers'] work hath been finished long since, but ye Gilding & Carving is not ready nor will be till towards ye latter end of next weeke'.[78]

Hutt's reliance on other workshops for carving, gilding and perhaps even basic joinery was probably typical of the smaller upholstery shops who worked only within their own trade. A much wider range of goods and services was provided by the 'undertaking' upholsterer, whose role was described by Campbell in 1747:

> He is the Man upon whose Judgement I rely in the Choice of Goods; and I suppose he has not only Judgement in the Materials, but Taste in the Fashions, and Skill in the Workmanship. This Tradesman's Genius must be universal in every Branch of Furniture; though his proper Craft is to fit up Beds, Window-Curtains, Hangings, and to cover Chairs that have stuffed Bottoms: He was originally a Species of the Taylor; but, by degrees, has crept over his Head, and set up as a Connoisseur in every Article that belongs to a House. He employs Journeymen in his own proper Calling, Cabinet-Makers, Glass-Grinders, Looking-Glass Frame Carvers, Carvers for Chairs, Testers, and Posts of Beds, the Woolen-Draper, the Mercer, the Linen-Draper, and several Species of Smiths, and a vast many Tradesmen of the other mechanic Branches.[79]

In fact it was not only upholsterers who took on this 'undertaking' role. James Moore, the king's cabinet-maker, was employed by the Duchess of Marlborough in place of an architect to oversee the completion and furnishing of Blenheim Palace: '... for he certainly has very good sense, and I think him very honest and understanding many Trades besides his own'.[80]

The multi-faceted business of the undertaking upholsterer required a great deal of capital to set up. It was perhaps for this reason, as well as the need to combine skills in the different branches of furniture-making, that many upholstery businesses were partnerships. The trade card of Nash,

---

75. Moser (1767).
76. Campbell (1747), p. 170.
77. Ibid., p. 170.
78. Flintshire Record Office, D/E/1542/54. For Hutt's career see *DEFM*, p. 468.
79. Campbell (1747), p. 170.
80. Quoted in Murdoch (2003).

The London Furniture Trade

Plate 1:19. Trade card of Nash, Hall and Whitehorne (c.1730). Thomas Nash worked at this address from c.1714; the partnership with Hall and Whitehorne probably lasted from c.1722 to c.1740. Together the partners were able to offer the whole range of domestic furnishings.
FROM HEAL, *LONDON FURNITURE MAKERS*

Plate 1:20. Billhead of Robert Webb (1716). Webb was made free of the Upholsterers' Company in 1712 and operated from Covent Garden from about 1716 onwards. This is one of the first billheads to advertise the combined roles of upholsterer and appraiser.
FROM HEAL, *LONDON FURNITURE MAKERS*

Plate 1:21. Trade card of George Browning (c.1750). Browning was clearly a comprehensive furnisher of both new and second-hand goods, but the most significant omission from the list of his services was the actual making of furniture.

FROM HEAL, *LONDON FURNITURE MAKERS*

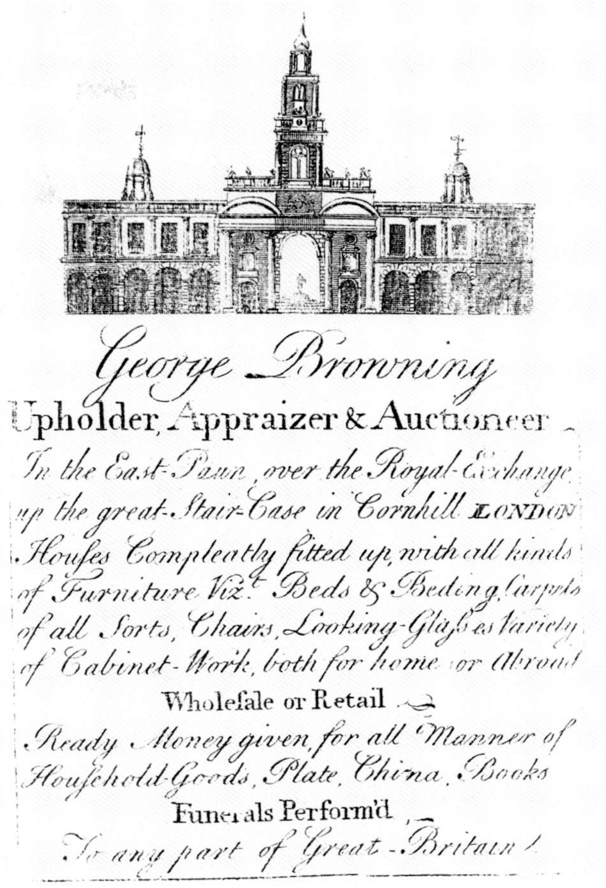

Hall, and Whitehorne claims they 'made and sold' upholstery, cabinet ware, seat furniture and looking glasses at *The Royal Bed* on Holborn Bridge (**1:19**). Thomas Nash was certainly an upholsterer, and it seems probable that at least one of his partners was a cabinet-maker. When Nash died in October 1748 he was described as 'an eminent upholsterer… a person of good Character and esteem'd by all his Aquaintances'.[81] At least one of his customers had a different opinion. Joseph Banks, who bought a bed from Nash's shop in 1716, complained that 'upon examining the bed Mr. Nash of Fleet Ditch has sent me I find it the most scurvy thing that ever was imposed upon any body'.[82]

Nash and his partners at *The Royal Bed* also acted as appraisers. Appraising or valuing was a natural extension of the undertaking upholsterers' work, which commonly involved the repair or remaking of goods, part-exchange of furniture or furnishings, renting or leasing furniture and dealing in second-hand furniture. Campbell comments:

> The Appraising Business is generally joined to that of the Upholder, and as such he makes Estimates of Goods upon all Occasions, when that is necessary: But, for the most part, the Business is carried on by Brokers of Household Goods: They are called Sworn-Appraisers, because they take an Oath to do Justice between Parties who employ them; but they generally value Things very low, not out of Respect to any of the Parties, but because they are obliged to take the Goods if it is insisted on at their own Appraisement.[83]

One of the earliest trade cards mentioning appraisals is that of Robert Webb, 'Upholsterer and Appraiser' of Covent Garden, printed in 1716 and bearing scribbled invoices for 1718 and 1719 (**1:20**). It is likely that appraising had long been part of the upholsterers' business. Certainly it was common in the late seventeenth century for upholsterers to deal in second-hand or part-exchanged goods, and to rent or lease furniture.

John Wills, a cabinet-maker with premises on Fleet Ditch near Holborn Bridge about 1730, was both a furniture-maker and dealer in second-hand furniture. His trade card relates that he makes and sells cabinet-work, japanned goods, seat furniture and joiner's work 'Wholesale and Retale', and also 'Appraiseth, Buyeth, and Selleth all Sorts of Household Goods'.[84] One wonders how much of his stock was actually made in his workshop. George Browning, who had premises in Cornhill, was both an upholsterer and auctioneer. He offered not only to furnish and fit up houses, but sold cabinet-work for home or export, wholesale or retail and bought and sold second-hand goods (**1:21**).[85] Charles Maxwell, at *The Lion & Lamb* in Drury Lane, had a similar business, buying, selling and appraising 'all Sorts of Household Goods, also Useful and Ornamental Old China.

81. *DEFM*.
82. Ibid.
83. Campbell (1747), p. 175.
84. Gilbert (1996), fig. 988.
85. Heal (1955), p. 15; *DEFM*.

Funerals Decently Performed. Sackings for Beds of all Sorts & Sizes, Wholesale & Retail'. Significantly, neither Browning nor Maxwell claimed to make furniture.

Like the furniture industry as a whole, the appraising business grew in scope and scale throughout the eighteenth century, and with it came a burgeoning second-hand market. London newspapers frequently advertised domestic house clearances and sales of stock-in-trade, often by public auction. In at least one case the sale of private domestic goods was combined with the sale of stock-in-trade of a famous cabinet-maker:

> To be Sold by Auction
> About the Middle of this Month, the Dwelling-House of the Hon. General Webb, deceas'd, in Great Marlborough Street, near Golden-Square. At the same time will be sold all the rich Furniture of the said House, consisting of all manner of useful and handsome furniture. To which will be added, The Entire Stock of Mr. James Moor, deceas'd Cabinet-Maker to his late Majesty, consisting of the finest old Japan and India Cabinets, Screens, Chests, Tables, &c. in Walnut-tree, Mahogany, and other fine Wood, Bookcases, Drawers, Buroes, Desks, Tables, Chairs, and all the newest Fashion'd Goods, in the greatest Perfection of Workmanship and Arts, with many other Valuable Effects. *The Daily Post*, 5 June 1728

It seems probable that some furniture-makers used auctions to get rid of surplus stock and raise ready money. This at least is the inference to be drawn from the number of advertisements for furniture 'To be Sold by the Maker' at auction. One such was advertised in *The Daily Courant* of 15 November 1723:

> At the Looking-Glass and Cabinet Ware-house, at the Golden Cup against the Royal Exchange in Cornhill, and at his House in Lincoln-street, alias Little Wild-street, near Lincoln's-Inn-Fields, all Sorts of Looking Glasses and Cabinet Work, both Walnut-Tree and Japann'd; and all Sorts of Tables, as Writing Tables, Wist-Tables, Ombre-Tables, Gilt-Tables, and Mahogeny Dining Tables, Beaufets, curious Wallnut-Tree Cabinet Beds, Desks and Book-Cases with Clocks, both Wallnut-Tree and Gilt, and fine Chairs.

In some cases the instigator of such sales was said to be 'leaving off trade', but in others the maker seems to have used this method of selling as a deliberate selling strategy. James Faucon, a cabinet-maker and glass-grinder with premises in Soho Square, advertised his stock for sale no less than 119 times in the *Daily Post* between February 1731 and September 1732.[86]

With the growth of upholders as general furnishers, the division between those who made furniture and those who sold it became more apparent. The description of John Gumley's new premises in the Strand, which opened in 1714, sounds more like a retail outlet than a manufacturing concern:

> This is to give Notice, That John Gumley hath taken for a Ware-house, and furnished all the upper Part of the New Exchange in the Strand... with the largest and finest Looking Glasses in Frames, and out of Frames... Likewise all sorts of Coach Glasses, Chimney-Glasses, Sconces, Dressing Glasses, Union Suits, Dressing-Boxes, Swinging-Glasses, Glass Schandeleres, Lanthorns, Gilt Brockets, Desks and Book-Cases, India Chests and Cabinets, Screens, Tea Tables, Card-Tables of all kinds, Strong Boxes, and the like.... *The Lover*, 24 April 1714

The raw material for much of this stock was no doubt produced at Gumley's own glasshouse in Lambeth, but whether his workshops had the capacity to produce such a large range of carved, cabinet and japanned work is open to question. He may well have employed a network of working masters and journeymen operating in small workshops throughout the city.

---

86. DEFM.

Many furniture-makers' trade cards advertised the availability of their products 'wholesale or retail'. This is a clear indication that they not only sold from their own premises but were willing to manufacture and sell to other businesses. There is no doubt that this went on. In the Heal Collection in the British Museum is one of John Belchier's billheads recording the receipt of £5.10s. for a mahogany chest of drawers delivered to Samuel Bennet.[87] This is presumably the same Samuel Bennet who traded as a cabinet-maker from premises at *The Cabinet* in Lothbury.[88] The transfer of goods between workshops raises questions about the traditional methodology of furniture connoisseurship, based as it is on attribution by stylistic analogy.

Plate 1:22. Billhead of John Hodson (1733). Hodson avoids the usual formula of 'makes and sells' and emphasises that everything is made 'in his own house'. John Hodson was apprenticed in the Upholsterers' Company in 1709 and became free in 1718. He moved to the Frith Street address in 1723 and operated from there until the 1740s. This particular bill was sent to a Mr Stanwix in December 1733, detailing goods delivered in 1732. Several of these billheads are known, dated from 1731 onwards.

CHETHAMS LIBRARY, MANCHESTER

Some makers resisted the temptation to buy in stock. The billhead of John Hodson, a Soho cabinet-maker, claims that all his goods were made by workmen 'employ'd in his own house' (**1:22**), thereby ensuring a consistent quality of material and workmanship and timely delivery.[89] We have already seen (page 27 above) how the reliance on subcontractors was a source of delay in the case of John Meller's bed.

The division between retail and manufacturing affords a clue to the purpose of trade cards themselves. If a patron bought furniture directly from the maker, then such advertising would be unnecessary, but if the furniture was bought from a general upholder or retailer, a trade card pasted into a drawer was an obvious way of letting the buyer know the original source of the merchandise. Thus it was a way of attracting repeat business and cutting out the middleman or retailer. If this hypothesis is correct, then the increase in the number of makers using trade cards in the early eighteenth century is a good indication of the growth of furniture retailing. It may be significant that in the period covered by this book, makers using trade cards tended to be situated in the less fashionable areas of the city, such as St Paul's Churchyard, Fleet Ditch and Holborn. This may be an indication that they were more reliant on furniture retailers than were the more fashionable makers of St Martin's Lane and Covent Garden.

Retailing as distinct from manufacturing is reflected in the change in meaning of the term 'warehouse'. At the beginning of the eighteenth century the warehouse was the part of a furniture-maker's premises where wares were displayed for inspection and sale. Thus most furniture-makers had a workshop, where goods were manufactured, and a warehouse where the finished goods were displayed. This was usually at the front of the building, facing the street. By the middle of the century warehouse had taken on a slightly different meaning. Mortimer's *Universal Director* of 1763 makes a distinction between cabinet-makers 'such as either work themselves or employ workmen under their direction' and 'one of the those numerous warehouses which sell ready-made furniture bought of the real artist'.[90]

Some furniture-makers used the term 'shop' instead of warehouse. Thus Lazarus Stiles (1724) had a 'Work Shop' at the rear of his premises and a 'Shop' at the front.[91] Samuel Jakeman (1731) had a 'Great Ware Room and Shop' and an 'Auction Room'.[92] The latter may have been devoted to the sale of second-hand goods, for the valuation of £61 seems very low for the quantity of goods it contained.

Although a great deal more research is needed before we have a full picture of the extent of furniture retailing in the early part of the century, it is clear that by the 1740s the phenomenon was well advanced:

> Many of their Shops are so richly set out that they look more like Palaces, and their Stocks are of so exceeding great Value. But this business seems to consist, as do many others, of two Branches, the Maker and the Vender; for the Shop-keeper does not always make every Sort of Goods that he deals in, though he bear away the Title.[93]

87. Heal (1955), p. 6.
88. *DEFM*.
89. For more on Hodson see *DEFM*.
90. Mortimer (1763), p. 11.
91. Stiles (1724).
92. Jakeman (1731).
93. Anon. (1747), p. 49.

The incentive to establish partly or wholly retail establishments was commercial. By offering the widest possible range of goods the retailer, who was often an 'undertaking' upholsterer, could engross the business which otherwise went to a variety of individual tradesmen. He or she could cater to all levels of custom, benefit from economies of scale and control costs by manipulating subcontractors and suppliers. From the point of view of the sub-contracted furniture-maker, selling to the retailer must have entailed some reduction in profit margins, but on the other hand it provided work which he might not otherwise have. Commercial logic dictated that a workshop could not be idle, but must manufacture goods to keep hands employed and create cash flow. When bespoke orders were scarce, the retailer offered an outlet for goods made for stock which might otherwise remain unsold.

The financial rewards for the 'undertaking' furniture-maker and/or retailer could be impressive. John Gumley's premises in the New Exchange, together with his glasshouses and other business interests, allowed him to build a country house on the Thames at Isleworth, designed by Sir John Vanbrugh. One of his four daughters married William Pulteney, later to become the Earl of Bath. His indolent eldest son lived as a gentleman on £150 a year, and his second son John succeeded to his business and stood for Parliament in 1727. The youngest, Samuel, purchased a Colonel's commission in the army. This was a remarkable change in fortune and status for a family whose head, at the start of his career in the 1690s, could barely read or write.[94] In 1747 William Hallet senior (c.1707-1781) bought the Cannons estate of the Duke of Chandos, building himself a great house to which he retired while still in his prime.[95] Giles Grendey (1693-1780) bought a country house in Middlesex in 1743 in addition to his business premises in Clerkenwell, and died a 'gentleman'.[96] These are just three of many London furniture-makers who became successful businessmen in the first half of the eighteenth century. Pat Kirkham has cited others who are otherwise largely unknown, such as William Dale (c.1720), Hibbert (c.1717), and Simms and Metcalf (1729-40) who each made fortunes of fifty thousand pounds upwards. It is perhaps significant that all were described as upholsterers.[97]

In contrast to the retail warehouse in which furniture was sold but not manufactured was what Pat Kirkham has called 'the comprehensive manufacturing firm', in which upholstery, cabinet-work, chair-making, carving and glass-grinding were carried out under one roof.[98] The career of Samuel Norman, who began as an apprentice carver and gilder in the 1740s and ended with a complete carving, furniture-making and upholstery business in the 1760s, demonstrates how such businesses might develop, but there is scant evidence that they existed in the early eighteenth century.[99] The creation of comprehensive manufactories, typified by firms such as Chippendale, Rannie & Haig, or Seddon, appears to have been a phenomenon of the second half of the eighteenth century.

Raw Materials

We have already touched on some of the suppliers of manufactured materials on which London's furniture-makers depended – brass-founders, blacksmiths and locksmiths – but the greatest need was for timber. Most of the timber employed by the London trade was imported. From Norway and the Baltic came *deal* (boards and planks of pine, larch, spruce and fir), and from Holland came *wainscot* (quarter-sawn oak). Walnut board, plank, log and veneer were imported from various parts of Europe and the Mediterranean and increasingly, after the 1721 Naval Stores Act, from North America.[100] Some native walnut timber was also employed (Richard Roberts' walnut timber was predominantly English, according to his inventory),[101] but there are no data by which to estimate the relative quantities of home-grown and imported wood. English oak does occur in some inventories and bills, but wainscot was always preferred for high quality work. Mahogany was imported either directly from the West Indies or via North America. Other exotics such as ebony or padouk were carried from Asia by the East India Company and in smaller quantities from West Africa. The only native wood used in any quantity was beech, which was extensively used by chairmakers and upholsterers. Daniel Defoe tells us that 'a vast quantity' came from Buckinghamshire, whence it was carried by boat down the Thames to London. Defoe adds that the quantity of beech quarters used by chair-makers and turners was

---
94. Gumley's lack of education is apparent in bills submitted by him to clients in the 1690s [Bowett (2002), p. 210].
95. DEFM.
96. Ibid.
97. Kirkham (1988), pp. 90-92.
98. Ibid., pp. 57-71.
99. Kirkham (1969).
100. For these and other woods see Appendix II.
101. Roberts (1733).

'almost incredible'.[102] Richard Roberts had large quantities of beech on hand in 1733, in thicknesses of four-inch down to two (10 to 5cm), as well as clapboards and quarters.[103] Holly, maple and other native woods are mentioned in workshop inventories, usually in veneers, and usually in small parcels. Pearwood is cited quite frequently. It was commonly used for picture frames and as a veneer for case furniture prior to japanning (cf. 1:13 and 1:15).

The heavy reliance on imported timber meant that access to the River Thames was an important consideration. The siting of so many furniture-makers in and around St Paul's Churchyard may have been linked to the proximity of wharves and timber yards on Thames Street, immediately to the south. Of twelve men eligible for jury service in the Castle Baynard section of Thames Street in 1721, seven were timber merchants and four others were 'wharfingers' or wharf-keepers.[104] Lazarus Stiles, whose workshop was in the parish of St Mary Aldermanbury to the north-west of St Paul's Churchyard, owed money to one 'Wm Astell', who was one of the Thames Street timber merchants recorded in the 1721 survey. Access to the Thames via the Fleet River was also probably a factor in explaining the number of furniture-makers in Fleet Ditch and Holborn.

The timber merchant, as Campbell tells us, 'is the Importer of Timber from abroad in his own Bottoms', and this distinguishes him from a mere 'wood-monger' or seller of wood.[105] However, Campbell goes on to point out that 'Every Man who keeps a Timber-Yard is not a Timber-Merchant... most of the Timber-Yards, especially at the Court End of the Town, are kept by Carpenters or Master-Builders. These buy their Timber from the Importer, and retail it to the Trade'.[106] Some furniture-makers were also timber merchants. Samuel Richardson (father of the novelist) imported timber on his own account, as did George Seddon at a later date. Both probably sold on timber to other makers.[107] Samuel Jakeman bought at least some of his timber direct from ships at anchor, and was drowned in 1731 while being rowed out to make a purchase. One assumes, however, that most furniture-makers bought their stock from timber merchants or wharfingers.

Workshop inventories suggests that some furniture-makers kept surprisingly little timber in stock. There are at least three possible explanations for this: the first is that the furniture was actually made elsewhere and the workshop owner did little more than finish and prepare the furniture for sale; the second is that space was often limited, so keeping large stocks was simply not possible; and the third is that it did not make financial sense to tie up capital in wood. Providing the supply was reliable, why not let the importer bear the cost of seasoning, converting and storing the timber?

It was nevertheless necessary for a furniture-maker with a high output and plenty of storage to keep sufficient timber for the work in hand. In 1731 Samuel Jakeman had in stock 65 half-inch, 96 three-quarter inch, and 71 one-inch wainscots; 3,272ft. of one-inch mahogany boards, 'a parcel' of holly, pear and walnut veneers and eleven walnut logs.[108] In 1724 Lazarus Stiles had quantities of wood scattered throughout his house, workshops and yard, and he seems to have acted as dealer in a small way. The largest stock was in his yard and workshop, including; 338ft. of four-inch mahogany plank, 1,240ft. of one-inch mahogany board, 390ft. of irregular mahogany slabs; 747ft. of sweet chestnut in two, one and half-inch boards; 434ft. of two and one-inch Virginia walnut; 58ft. of two-inch cedar; 72 pieces of maple; 3,118 wainscot boards in two and a half, one and a half, one and a quarter, one-inch, three-quarter and half-inch boards; 509 deals; 271 three-quarter and half-inch beech boards; 130 pieces of walnut quarter stuff;[109] some yew veneers and much sundry lumber. The whole stock was valued at £247.13. 6d.[110]

Another well-stocked workshop was that of Richard Roberts, chair-maker to the crown. The timber in his yard and workshops in Westminster included walnut, beech, wainscot and deal in many different scantlings and a sizeable quantity of mahogany in plank and board. The total was valued at £79.16.0. There were in addition some walnut veneers in the workshops.[111]

When sold wholesale, deals and wainscots were generally sold by the 'long' hundred of 120 boards, or fractions thereof. Deals typically cost £6-£14 per hundred, depending on size and quality. When retailed, deals were sold in scores, dozens and individually, and priced per deal, for example, '17 Ten ft whole deals at 1s.6d. each'. Wainscots were sometimes retailed by the piece

---

102. Defoe (1724-5), II, p. 72.
103. *Clapboards* – thin boards of tapering section, originally riven (from medieval German *claffen* to cleave); *quarters* – battens 4 x 2in. (10 x 5cm) in section.
104. CLRO, MISC MSS/83/3.
105. Campbell, (1747), p.167.
106. Ibid., p. 168.
107. *DEFM*.
108. Jakeman (1724).
109. *Quarter stuff* – a scantling 4in. (10cm) broad and 2in. (5cm) thick.
110. Stiles (1724).
111. Roberts (1733).

but more usually by the superficial foot (12in. x 12in. x 1in.), for example, '1 inch wainscot at 5d p[er] ft'. Large deals (2in. and over) and oak planks were priced per linear foot, e.g., '2in. fir plank at 5d ft, 4in. oak at 1s 4d'. Timber in balk or log was usually sold by the cubic foot. Fine timber, such as walnut and mahogany in board, plank and log was sold by the superficial foot.[112]

Mahogany was frequently sold at auction by speculative importers and timber merchants:

To be Sold together, or in Parcels

> About fifty or sixty Mahogany Timber Tress, about 12 Inches square, and 12 Foot long, being very sound, and fine colour'd, fit for Cabinet-Makers or Turners, for Tables or Stands, at Mr Naylor's Toy-Shop in King-Street, Covent Garden. Where is likewise to be had, the Ladies Spinning Wheels, and all sorts of rich Gold and Silver Toys.
>
> *The Daily Journal, 10th August 1724.*

The usual procedure was to advertise a time and a place and sell 'by the candle', i.e., to sell to the highest bid offered during the time taken to burn a given length of candle. The sales were usually conducted by professional brokers who charged 5 per cent commission. As the advertisement suggests, mahogany was often imported in the log, which was squared to save space and cost in shipping. It was also imported as plank (i.e., sawn timber over 2in. (5cm) thick) and as boards. The latter were risky, since they were more liable to damage in transit. Richard Roberts had mahogany in various thicknesses from six-and-half inches (16.5cm) down to one inch (2.54cm) in stock in 1733 and some of this might well have been sawn after importation.[113] In the 1720s the relative cost per foot of the commonly used woods was roughly as follows; deal 1½d.-2d., wainscot 3d.-5d., mahogany 3d.-5d., walnut 6d.-9d. (walnut veneers cost much more).

Interposed between the timber merchant and the furniture-maker was the sawyer. The sawyers jealously guarded their monopoly of the work:

> ... the Sawyer's Business is quite a separate Trade, and only preparative to the other [Carpentry]; nay, they are so strict, that a *Timber-merchant* or *Carpenter*, cannot employ indifferent Servants to *saw* their large Timber &c., but must have regular-bred Sawyers to do that Work, most of which is pretty laborious, therefore requires stout healthy Lads.[114]

The sawyers' insistence on their monopoly gave rise to frequent disputes, like that between the sawyers on one side and the Joiners and Carpenters on the other, which began in 1702 and was still unresolved in 1708.[115] As with most of these inter-trade disputes, the nub of the question was money, for the woodworking trades disliked paying the rates which the sawyers demanded. It is difficult to see how in the long run the sawyers' monopoly could be policed, and the incentive among both the suppliers and the users of timber to employ non-freemen at a cheaper rate must have been strong. Whether freemen or not, quite a number of furniture-makers' inventories include sawyers among their creditors. Thomas Perkins, a joiner and cane-chair maker in St Giles Cripplegate (on the northern fringe of the City) who died in 1723, owed more than £16 to one Shaw, a sawyer. It was perhaps he who was responsible for sawing the planks of walnut (French and Virginia) and beech stored in Perkins' yard.

A key reservation in the description quoted above was that sawyers were concerned only with 'large Timber'. There were two reasons for this. The first was that much of the wood imported for furniture-making was converted in the country of origin. Deals were generally imported in thicknesses between one and three inches. One or one-and-a-quarter-inch deals were ideal for primary carcase work and needed no further reduction by sawing. For framing and carved work, two and three-inch deals were often suitable. Similarly, wainscots were imported ready-sawn in scantlings from two inches downwards, reducing by increments of a quarter of an inch. The signatures of the mechanised and multi-bladed frame saws used to produce deals and wainscots are

112. Examples and prices taken from the Records of the Commissioners for Fifty New Churches in Lambeth Palace Library, London. These contain prices quoted for masonry, paving, timber, joinery and many other aspects of early 18th century building work.
113. Roberts (1733).
114. Anon. (1747), p. 185.
115. CLRO, *Court of Aldermen, Reps.* 97-98; GL, MS 8046/3 and 4, *Minutes of the Joiners' Company.*

Plate 1:23. Wainscot oak. This is from the base of an early 18th century drawer, showing the distinctive signature of a Dutch wind or water powered frame saw in fine, regular and closely-spaced kerfs. The closely-spaced growth rings, straight grain, pale colour and fine medullary rays are all typical of imported wainscot.

Plate 1:24. Red deal (*Pinus sylvestris*). This is an 18th century deal board from the underside of a piece of case furniture. It was imported from Norway or the Baltic. The rough, unfinished surface is typical, as are the broad, regular kerf marks of the water-powered frame saw used to convert it from the log.

Plate 1:25. 'Slit' deal. This is the back of a walnut veneered chest of c.1730. The top and bottom boards show the rough, raised grain of the outer surface of the deal, and the middle board shows the kerf marks of a deal 'slit' by manual sawing. The horizontal alignment of the boards is unusual.

characteristic features of English case furniture in the eighteenth century. The fine-bladed saws of the Dutch 'wagenschot molen' (wainscot mills) were very different from the much coarser blades of the Norwegian deal mills (**1:23** and **1:24**). The second reason for restricting the sawyers to dealing with large timber was that sawing was an indivisible part of furniture-making; it was only sawing in bulk or for sale that required a professional sawyer. It is likely that some large workshops had the means to saw timber themselves, and were even mechanised to a degree. The Bastard workshop in Blandford had an 'Engin and wheel for sawing' probably powered by manual labour.[116] Of course, Blandford was a long way from London. The Bastards' reliance on home-grown timber was probably greater than their London contemporaries, and there was no body of professional sawyers to impose their monopoly.

If wainscots and deals needed to be reduced into thinner boards for drawer linings, dustboards and backboards, to say nothing of veneers, then a sawyer was needed. These jobs could be done in house, but it required skilled men, for if labour was cheap timber was not, and skimping the job was a false economy. If a furniture-maker needed a constant supply of thin deals or wainscots, it was probably more cost-effective to sub-contract the work to a sawyer. A good sawyer and his mate were able routinely to 'slit' a standard 1in. deal, 10-14ft. (3-4.3m) in length, exactly down the middle to produce two thinner boards (**1:25**). Walnut and mahogany were commonly imported as logs or planks, and in both cases sawyers were required to convert the timber into scantling suitable for the furniture-maker's requirements.

There is some evidence that sawyers did not necessarily have their own yards, but operated in a peripatetic manner, moving from yard to yard or workshop to workshop as the need arose. How else could Samuel Jakeman convert his '11 Wallnuttree Loggs' except by calling in a sawyer? It is also probable that much sawing was done in the timber yards, prior to delivery to furniture workshops. This is the implication of the statement (above) that timber merchants could not employ non-sawyers to saw their large timber.

116. Legg (1994).

The London Furniture Trade

Plate 1:26. Chair (1730-40). Japanned beechwood. This is part of a large commission exported by Giles Grendey to the Duke of Infantado in Spain. Although such large suites of japanned furniture were not typical of English houses, the basic design of the chair has not been modified for the export market. The seemingly archaic retention of stretchers is made necessary by the narrow rails of the caned seats. TEMPLE NEWSAM HOUSE, LEEDS CITY ART GALLERIES

The export trade

England exported furniture to every part of the world with which it traded and, with the exception of the East India trade which will be discussed separately, the balance of trade in furniture weighed heavily in England's favour. The quantity and range of London's exports is a reflection of the popularity of the English style in furniture not only in English overseas possessions but throughout Europe and beyond.[117] The great majority was exported from London, and the principal categories of goods were looking glasses, cabinet-work, clock-cases and chairs. Japanned goods and upholstery were also exported in sizeable quantities.[118]

The West Indian and North American colonies were naturally important markets for furniture as for other British manufactures, and the trade to North America is particularly well documented. The best customers were the middle and southern states – Virginia, Maryland and the Carolinas – whose tobacco exports generated the cash to pay for furnishings from London. Indeed, because of the shortage of skilled labour it was often as cheap or cheaper to ship furniture from England than to acquire it locally. Further north in New York and New England the local economies were more self-sufficient and the domestic furniture-makers were better able to compete against English imports.[119] For some commodities, however, such as lacquerware and canes for chair-making, they remained wholly dependent on East India goods imported from London until the colonies became independent in 1783.

In northern Europe, Holland and Germany were the most consistent customers, although Scandinavia, the 'Eastland' or Baltic states and Russia also imported furniture. The influence of English furniture in Holland was particularly strong, with Dutch furniture-makers emulating English models for cabinets and scriptors, desks-and-bookcases, chairs and clock cases.[120] The phrase 'Engels Cantoor Cabinet' (English writing cabinet) often occurs in Dutch sales notices, and could refer either to an English import or a Dutch piece in the English style. From 1711 aspiring furniture-makers in the Hague were permitted to submit English-style writing cabinets as their 'masterpiece'.

In Germany the taste for English furniture extended well beyond the Hanoverian possessions, and the popularity of the English style induced a number of German furniture-makers to create

---
117. For a detailed analysis of the imports and exports of furniture in the 18th century, see Joy (1955).
118. PRO, Cust 3.
119. Joy (1955).
120. Baarsen (1993), pp. 66-7, 38-9, 86-7, 90-1.

their own versions of it. The court archives of Prussia in the 1720s contain references to 'English writing cabinets' and other English-style pieces produced by Prussian furniture-makers. Caned chairs, although made in Prussia, were known as 'Englische Stuhl'. In Saxony, also in the 1720s, cabinet-makers such as Peter Hoese were supplying 'English tables' to their patrons, while in Mainz, as in the Hague, writing cabinets of English design were accepted by the guilds as 'masterpieces'. The vogue for English furniture extended north into Sweden, where the makers of cane chairs were known as 'English chair-makers', and south into Italy, where the *scrivania all'inglese* received royal approval, being made for the Queen's apartments in Turin.[121] Small quantities of furniture went east as far as Turkey, and south to the 'Straits' (this was a general term for Gibraltar and the coast of North Africa). Even France imported more English furniture than was exported to England, although the trade was never significant in scale, partly due to the frequent wars between the two nations.

The single largest export market was the Iberian peninsula, where Spain and Portugal together accounted for about a quarter of total furniture exports. In 1730 furniture worth more than £3,197 was exported to Spain and £3,451 to Portugal. This trade has received more attention than most, largely because of the famous suite of red japanned furniture supplied by Giles Grendey to the Duke of Infantado (**1:26**). We should be wary, however, of the common assumption that because furniture by this or that maker was sent abroad, he or she necessarily specialised in the export trade. That Grendey had a sizeable export business is not in doubt, for when his premises were destroyed by fire in August 1731 he lost (among others things) furniture to the value of £1,000, 'pack'd for Exportation against the next morning'.[122] But it does not necessarily follow, as is often assumed, that Grendey's business was principally an export one.[123] The Infantado suite is wholly English in design, and what has been called its 'retarded character' is more a reflection of historians' preconceptions than stylistic reality.[124] The retention of stretchers, often identified as a *retardataire* feature, is due to the narrow seat rails of the caned seats, so that the legs require additional support. On the other hand, it is fair to say that such a large suite of matching japanned furniture, amounting to at least seventy-two pieces, is unknown in any English collection. It may also be true, as R.W. Symonds observed, that the caned seats were peculiarly suitable to the warmer climates of southern Europe even while they declined in favour in England.[125] The poor quality of much japanned furniture may also be relevant. The standard of carcase work and drawer construction of most japanned desks-and-bookcases, for instance, is well below the norm for English veneered walnut furniture, but compares with contemporary Italian, Spanish or Portuguese pieces.

One of London's most valuable but unquantifiable exports was training. A London training was regarded as the best in Great Britain, and furniture-makers setting up in provincial towns after training in London were sure to advertise the fact in local newspapers. In May 1728 the *Ipswich Journal* carried an advertisement for a furniture business in Framlingham, Suffolk, where could be bought '... Cabinets, Desks and Book-Cases, Desks, Chests of Drawers of all Sorts, Card-Tables, Gammen-Tables, Chairs of all Sorts, Dressing-Tables, Close-Stools, Ovel-Tables at Reasonable Rates, by John Marshall, Maker from London'.[126] Similarly, furniture-makers emigrating to the North American colonies used the fact of their London training to suggest acquaintance with the latest fashions and techniques. In the *South Carolina Gazette* of 27 January 1732 James McClellan advertised that he was '... from London, living next door to Mr. Joseph Massey, in Church Street, Makes and sells all sorts of Cabinet Ware...'.[127]

The migration of trained men to provincial centres was one of the primary mechanisms by which the London style of furniture-making was transmitted beyond the city, and provincial makers claimed to supply fashionable, London-style furniture almost as soon as it emerged in London. About 1730 Francis Lomax, a furniture-maker of Mardol, Shrewsbury, advertised 'all maner of Cabinet Work and fine Compass Seat Chairs with Upholster'd Seats both in Mohogany and fine Walnut after the newest and best fashion, all sorts of *India* Back Chairs either with Upholster'd Seats or fine Dutch or Matted Bottoms, Cane Chairs and Dutch Chairs both Course and fine...'.[128]

---

121. Hayward and Medlam in Gilbert and Murdoch, eds. (1993), pp. 29-31
122. For more on Grendey see *DEFM*.
123. Gilbert (1971).
124. Ibid.
125. Symonds (December 1935).
126. *DEFM*.
127. Ibid.
128. Ibid.

Plate 1:27. Chair (1735-50). Walnut and ash. This chair bears the stamp of Samuel Sharp, a chair-maker working in Norwich between 1737 and 1761. With the exception of its ash seat rails, it is indistinguishable from London work in either style or construction. One of a pair. RONALD PHILLIPS LTD

---

129. For Sharp see *DEFM* and Stabler (2005 and 2006).
130. Hayward and Medlam in Gilbert and Murdoch, eds. (1993), p. 30.
131. Ibid., pp. 24-26.

This poses interesting problems for anyone attempting to classify a given piece of furniture as either 'London' or 'provincial'. The chair in **1:27** bears the stamp of Samuel Sharp, a chairmaker recorded in Norwich between 1737 and 1761.¹²⁹ In terms of construction, there is nothing to distinguish this chair from a London-made example. In terms of quality (both of materials and workmanship) it does not match the best London chairs, but not all London furniture was of the best quality.

Perhaps the most significant endorsement of London's reputation was the number of foreigners who came to work and in many cases learn their trade in London. This was not a case of necessity, as it had been with the Huguenot immigrants of the late seventeenth century, but choice. As Hayward and Medlam have commented: '… the use of the title 'English cabinet-maker' was a general term of self-advancement in Holland, Germany and Denmark' by the middle of the eighteenth century.¹³⁰ As a consequence, even experienced foreign furniture-makers found a period of work in England gave them a commercial advantage at home. Little is known of these men, and no reliable data are available to assess their numbers. The best known was Abraham Roentgen, who arrived in London around 1733. Roentgen was already a skilled workman by this time, but it may have been in London that he learned to inlay in brass, a technique which became one of his trademarks after his return to Germany in 1738. The form of Roentgen's furniture was clearly influenced by contemporary English designs, and he maintained links with the English trade throughout his life, even sending one of his journeymen to work with his old London master.¹³¹

A contemporary of Roentgen and a member of the same Moravian brotherhood was Frederick Hintz. Hintz probably established his business in London in the early 1730s, where he appears to have specialised in cabinet-work inlaid with brass and mother-of-pearl (**1:28**). In June 1738 he returned to Germany, and the sale of his stock-in-trade was advertised in *The Daily Post* of 22 May that year:

> To be Sold, at the Porcupine in Newport Street, near Leicester Fields
>
> A Choice Parcel of Desks and Book-Cases of Mahogany, Tea-Tables, Tea-Chests and Tea-Boards, &c. all curiously made and inlaid with fine Figures of Brass and Mother of Pearl. They will be sold at a very reasonable Rate, the Maker, **Frederick Hintz**, designing soon to go abroad.

Plate 1:28. Desk-and-bookcase (1740-50). Mahogany, oak and deal, with inlay of brass and mother-of-pearl. Furniture with this style of inlaid decoration is now routinely attributed to the German emigré J.F. Hintz on the strength of his newspaper advertisement of June 1738 (see text). It is clear, however, that Hintz was not the only manufacturer to produce such work.
TEMPLE NEWSAM HOUSE, LEEDS CITY ART GALLERIES

Plate 1:29. Desk (1732/3). Walnut on oak and deal. This was made by a German craftsman working for an English master, Robert Hyde of Maiden Lane, Covent Garden. In common with many narrow desks and bureaux it has full-thickness dustboards but is otherwise of conventional London construction. It originally had a dressing mirror on top, and the drawer immediately below the slope is fitted for dressing. Brasses are original. PRIVATE COLLECTION

Hintz returned to England in the 1740s, and ultimately established himself as a musical instrument maker. He died in 1772.[132] It has been suggested that it was the Moravians who introduced brass and mother-of-pearl inlaid cabinet-work to London, forming a close-knit network of specialists in this field, but recent research has found little evidence to support the hypothesis.[133] Furniture inlaid with brass and other materials features in the stock-in trade of a number of English furniture-makers, and brass-inlaid furniture made by or attributed to Antrobus, John Channon, J. Graveley and Thomas Landall survives.[134] Perhaps the most notable supplier of brass-ornamented furniture was Benjamin Goodison, who supplied the Royal Household with two walnut cabinets and a desk-and-bookcase 'adorned with brass' in 1734.[135]

Much less is known of the other German furniture-makers working in London, but several craftsmen recorded in the *Dictionary of English Furniture Makers* have German surnames, including Henry Dieckard (1713-14), Nathaniel Spindler (1703-1717), Heinrich Steinfeldt (1711-59), and Joachim Falck (1727). Numerous others of German, Dutch and Scandinavian origin may have escaped historians' notice by anglicising their names. Two pieces of furniture made by Joachim Falck are known, a double chest of drawers and a chest on stand, both dating from c.1725-30.[136] Both are purely English in style and construction.

The desk in **1:29** was made by a German craftsman working in the Maiden Lane workshop of Robert Hyde. An inscription in German on the base of a drawer translates roughly as follows: *John George Troester, of a foreign country, joiner's assistant to master Heid in Maiden Lane, London, made this desk, March 9th 1732*.[137] Like Falck's work, it is typically English in style and construction, and were it not for the inscription its German maker would have remained unsuspected. Pieces like this go a long way to explaining the strong stylistic and technical affinity between English cabinet-work and some contemporary German work (**1:30**).

A similar stylistic affinity links English and some Russian cabinet-work of this period. During his time studying ship-building in London in 1717, Tsar Peter I had a walnut-veneered desk made to his own design, and returned with it to St Petersburg, where it remains. In June 1717 he ordered that twenty-four young Russians be sent from Amsterdam to London, of whom nine were

132. Ibid., pp. 26-28.
133. Boynton (1993); Gilbert and Murdoch (1993), pp. 24-36 *et passim*; Graf (2004).
134. Gilbert and Murdoch (1993).
135. PRO LC 9/289.
136. These are in private collections. The chest-on-chest was sold at Christie's, New York, 28 March 1981, lot 159, and is illustrated in Gilbert (1996), fig. 328. The chest on stand (with restored apron and legs) was for sale with Roger Grimes Antiques, Polranny, Co. Mayo, in 2005.
137. I am grateful to Robert Copley for drawing this piece of furniture to my attention. For more on Robert Hyde see *DEFM*.

Plate 1:30. Desk-and-bookcase (1730-60). Walnut, padouk, tortoiseshell and brass on oak. This piece is attributed to the Dresden cabinet-maker Peter Hoese (1686-1761). It is inspired by contemporary English examples, but has several idiosyncrasies of style and construction which distinguish it as German work. In many cases English locks, handles and other fittings are also found on Dutch and German furniture.
COURTESY OF SOTHEBY'S

The London Furniture Trade

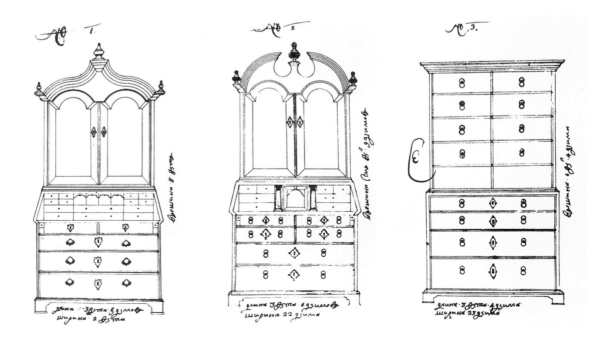

Plate 1:31. Designs for case furniture (1738). These designs were drawn for the Empress Anna Ioannovna by Fedor Martynov, one of the Russian craftsmen sent to train as furniture-makers in London in 1717.
REPRODUCED FROM GUSEVA (1994)

to train as furniture-makers. When they finished their apprenticeships in 1723-4 they returned to St Petersburg to work. Among the returnees was Fedor Martynov, whose drawings of furniture made for the Empress Anna Ioannovna in 1738 are identical in every respect to London made cabinet-work of the 1720s (**1:31**).[138] The Empress Anna also had a throne made in London in 1731, copies of which survive in Moscow and St Petersburg.

The influence of the Orient

The published histories of the English East India Company make little mention of furniture imports in the eighteenth century. This is because, relative to other commodities such as silk, porcelain, tea, drugs and spices, the quantity of furniture carried was insignificant and its value negligible. The value of a typical return cargo on a 350-ton East Indiaman in 1730 was around £35,000, so a dozen chairs worth a few shillings each or a desk worth a pound or two were of very little financial consequence. But in terms of design the importance of the East India trade is difficult to overstate, for several popular Georgian furniture types owe their origins to Oriental models.

The range of furniture imported by the East India Company before 1720 was relatively limited – lacquered cabinets, screens, trays, tops for stands and tables, boxes and trunks of various sorts.[139] It is no accident that many of these items were essentially two-dimensional, so that they could be packed flat and carried at minimal cost, or in the case of trunks and boxes, filled with other goods. The low value of furniture relative to other commodities like porcelain, silk and tea ensured that it was often carried to make up freight when other goods were lacking, and this is one reason for the rather sporadic nature of furniture imports recorded in the customs returns.[140] Another is the fact that some furniture, perhaps most, came in by private trade. Unofficial private trade had always featured in the East India Company's activities, and in 1674 it was regularised to allow Company officers to trade in all but a few commodities over which the Company retained a monopoly. Ship owners and ship's officers were allotted a percentage of their vessel's tonnage to carry their own goods, and most took advantage of this if they could afford to.[141] Thus the volume of imported furniture recorded in the Customs returns considerably understates the true quantity. In 1735, a year in which the Customs returns recorded the importation of only four cabinets and eleven lacquered chests, seven East India Company officers imported a total of thirty-three pieces of furniture, comprising cabinets, scriptors, screens, chairs, card tables, chests of drawers, bookcases and trays.[142]

138. Guseva (1994).
139. Bowett (2002, p. 149 *et passim*).
140. Clunas (1987).
141. Farrington (2002), p. 77.
142. PRO Cust. 3; Clunas (1987).

Plate 1:32. Cabinet and stand (1725-50). Chinese lacquer cabinet on an English stand. Although the volume of importations declined after 1700, Chinese and Japanese lacquer cabinets retained their luxury status in English houses.

MONTACUTE, THE NATIONAL TRUST

During the War of Spanish Succession (1702-13) there was a marked drop in the East India trade as a whole, and a corresponding decline in the amount of furniture and general 'lacquered ware' imported.[143] Even after the end of the war the paucity of lacquered goods is noticeable when compared with the record importations of the late 1690s. For instance, 157 cabinets were imported in 1699 and 146 in 1700, whereas the most imported in any subsequent year to 1740 was thirteen.[144] Although it is impossible to verify in statistical terms, it is conceivable that the market for Oriental lacquerware was undercut by the thriving English japanning industry, which produced a vast range of goods in imitation of Oriental lacquer. Nevertheless, importations of lacquered furniture continued, albeit on a reduced scale, throughout the 1720s and 1730s, and lacquered articles feature prominently in the domestic inventories of the wealthy houses.

The most conspicuous and expensive of these imports were lacquer cabinets, which maintained the luxury status they had acquired in the seventeenth century. Whereas English cabinets were largely superseded by newer types of furniture such as the desk-and-bookcase, cabinets of Chinese and Japanese lacquer continued to be highly valued. The only change was in the style of their English-made stands, which generally kept pace with contemporary fashions (**1:32**). These cabinets were among the most expensive items of furniture in any English house; at Cannons there were 'India' cabinets valued at £50 and £40, whereas japanned examples rated a mere £18.[145]

143. PRO, Cust 3.
144. The Joiners' Company petition of 1701 recorded the following lacquered goods imported in the previous four years: 244 cabinets, 6,582 tea tables, 428 chests, 70 trunks, 52 screens, 589 looking glass frames, 655 tops for stands, 818 lacquered boards, 597 sconces, 4,120 dressing, comb and powder boxes. (B.L., 'THE CASE OF THE JOYNER'S COMPANY AGAINST the Importation of Manufactured CABINET-WORK from the EAST INDIES'.)
145. Cannons (1725).

The London Furniture Trade

Plate 1:33. Chest and stand (1730-60). Chinese lacquer chest on an English japanned beechwood stand. This was probably the most common form of Chinese case furniture imported in the 18th century. Numerous English japanned examples also survive, as well as those in walnut and mahogany.
HAM HOUSE, THE NATIONAL TRUST

Opposite page:
Plate 1:34. A Tea Party, by Joseph Van Aken (c.1725). In this intimate scene set in a back parlour or closet, the family take tea around a lacquered tray on a frame. This is the genesis of the Georgian tray-top tea-table, as seen in 1:35. Note the kettle stand, which is probably 'French plated', that is, covered with silver leaf on a brass core.
MANCHESTER ART GALLERY

Left:
Plate 1:35. Tea table (1700-15). Lacquer or japanned tray top on a japanned beechwood frame. This closely resembles the tea table shown in 1:34. It is a rare survival, and the precursor of many thousands of Georgian tray-top tea tables. Photographed at Bramshill Park, Surrey; its present location is unknown.
COUNTRY LIFE

The role and status of lacquered screens was similarly unchanged. The Customs returns show that screens were imported in twelve out of the twenty-one years between 1720 and 1740. The largest number imported in one year was thirty-two (in 1729), but this does not take into account the private trade. As in the late seventeenth century, these were either used as their makers intended or adapted for room panelling and furniture. A number of eighteenth century rooms panelled with Oriental lacquer survive in English houses (there is a particularly good example at Burton Agnes, Yorkshire), and many more have been lost.

Lacquered trunks and chests featured prominently in both the import statistics and domestic inventories. They were usually adapted by placing on low frames, and were used for storing clothes, bed-linen and hangings (**1:33**).

'Tea tables' or trays were conspicuous in number if not in value; indeed, they were the single most numerous class of imported lacquerware throughout the period. In the boom years of 1697-1702 importations of tea tables averaged well over a thousand per annum. These quantities were never again reached, but precise figures are difficult to estimate because in some years large amounts of goods were simply recorded in the customs returns as 'lacquered ware'; again, the scale of the private trade is also unknown. However, some indication of their popularity can be gained from their ubiquitous presence in domestic inventories.

For early eighteenth century English artists the tea table became a favourite centrepiece for family portraits and conversation pieces. Many of these are painted in sufficient detail to identify Oriental lacquer trays in use. In **1:34**, a painting by Joseph Van Aken, a group of people takes tea in a closet or back parlour. The table has a rectangular tray top which is either lacquered or japanned, raised on a japanned frame with scrolled legs joined by flat stretchers. The table-top is slightly off-centre on its stand, suggesting that it is probably a removable tray. A table of this design was formerly at Bramshill Park, Surrey, but its whereabouts are now unknown (**1:35**).

The London Furniture Trade

From the 1720s onwards the most common form of tea table had a rectangular tray top on a conforming frame with cabriole legs. This type of table appears repeatedly in conversation pieces of the 1730s, usually with the tea equipage upon it (5:77). Many of these were made with imported lacquer tops; others were japanned, or executed in solid walnut and mahogany, but retaining the tray-top form. Another table design of the 1720s was almost certainly inspired by Chinese prototypes. It had a convex-moulded frame and straight square legs. This form of table had no obvious English precedent, but similar tables had long been made in China (**1:36**). The earliest known English example was a table with a lacquer top and gilt frame, made by James Moore for the Prince of Wales' apartments in Hampton Court Palace in 1715 (5:4).[146] If Moore first introduced the form to an English clientele, he is unlikely to have remained the sole maker for long. In 1730 George Nix made a similar straight-legged frame for a lacquer panel made from the top of a Japanese cabinet at Ham (**1:37**). His bill describes the process:

Opposite page:
Above:
Plate 1:36. Chinese table (1550-1650). Huali wood. High tables such as these were probably the prototypes for English straight-leg tables like that in 1:37.
VICTORIA AND ALBERT MUSEUM

Below:
Plate 1:37. Table (1730). Created by George Nix from the top of a Japanese cabinet at Ham House. The cabinet, with Nix's replacement top, also survives.
HAM HOUSE, THE NATIONAL TRUST

Right:
Plate 1:38. Chair (1720-40). Walnut, with later seat. The curved 'India back', inspired by Chinese originals, revolutionised the design and construction of English chairs.
FREDERICK PARKER COLLECTION

for Sawing the Top of an Indian Cabinet & putting on a Deal Top, & Japanning the Top & new pollishing the Cabinet…	£3.10.0.
for altering the Cabinet frame and new Gilding it…	£4.10.0.
for making a Table of the Top of the Cabinet, and a Neat Japann'd frame for the Table…	£2.15.0.
for a Leather Cover for the Table lined wth flannell…	£0. 6.0.[147]

It seems likely that the Chinese straight leg was the origin of the plain 'Marlborough' leg which became almost universal from the mid-eighteenth century onwards.

The most significant of all borrowings from the Chinese was the 'India' or bended back, which was adopted by English chair-makers from about 1715 onwards (**1:38**). This development is discussed more fully in Chapter Four; it is sufficient to state here that the India back revolutionised English chair design and, by export or imitation, also transformed chair-making throughout Europe and North America.

From the 1720s onwards, a new element entered the East India trade with the importation of solid rosewood furniture made to English patterns. The precise identity of the 'rosewood' employed in such furniture has been the subject of much connoisseurial and botanical debate (see Appendix II), but the majority appears to have been made from what is now called padouk (*Pterocarpus* spp.).

146. Royal Archives, GEO/81174-5, 'for a Table and Stands with Indian Tops and the fframes finely carved and gilt… £50.0.0'.

147. Ham House, Bills, George Nix, 12 September 1730.

The London Furniture Trade

Plate 1:39. Hall chair (1725-40). Huali wood inlaid with mother-of-pearl, later mahogany seats. This is one of a set of eight made for Sir Gregory Page. They bear the arms of Page impaled with those of Martha, third daughter of Robert Kenward, who married Sir Gregory in 1721. The design is a combination of X-frame, *sgabello*, and India-back models. Note the arched fore-and-aft stretcher, typical of English *sgabelli* of this date.
SIR JOHN SOANE'S MUSEUM

Plate 1:40. Chair (1730-40). Huali wood, with modern seats. This is one of a set of six, together with twelve plainer ones, made for Sir Matthew Decker, a Director of the East India Company from 1713 to 1743. The cartouche in the back represents the Chinese symbol for *shue*, or good luck. WILTON HOUSE

Plate 1:41. Locking joint. Detail of 1:42, showing the locking joint with square pin used by Chinese craftsmen to join the two halves of the back post and leg on chairs made for the English market. English chairmakers made the leg and post in one piece.

The first official record of imported rosewood furniture dates from 1726, when twenty-four 'Chairs of rosewood inlaid with Mother of Pearl' were imported, valued at £12.[148] Chairs inlaid in this fashion were never common and are now even less so. A set of eight, bearing the impaled arms of Sir Gregory Page and his wife Martha, survives at Sir John Soane's Museum, London (**1:39**). In 1730 forty-eight chairs, three desks, two card tables and six boxes of rosewood were imported, and more followed in subsequent years.[149] In some cases chair frames appear to have been imported as 'pieces' (perhaps disassembled?), and others are recorded as having caned seats. Although very little is known about the production of Chinese export furniture at this early date, it was probably made at Canton, since from 1729 onwards Canton was the only Chinese port open to European traders.[150]

Considerable numbers of Chinese export chairs survive in English collections. The most common model is the 'India-back' style, which itself was an English borrowing of a traditional Chinese form. The example in **1:40** is from a set of six (together with a set of twelve plainer ones) which was almost certainly made for Sir Matthew Decker, a Director of the East India Company from 1713-1743.[151] The exaggerated curvature of the back is typical, but in some cases the Chinese versions are difficult to separate from their English contemporaries, save for their characteristic method of assembling the back leg (**1:41**).

148. PRO, Cust 3.
149. Ibid.
150. Amin Jaffer has raised the possibility that furniture made by Chinese craftsmen might have been produced elsewhere in Asia, since they are known to have settled in the Philippines, India and elsewhere (Jaffer (2001), pp. 92-95). However, since Canton is known to have been a centre of production for the English trade, it is reasonable to assume that most, if not all, these chairs were made there
151. The chairs are stamped on the inner seat rails with a crowned F for the Viscount Fitzwilliam of the Kingdom of Ireland, and S H for Sidney Herbert, 11th Earl of Pembroke. Fitzwilliam's mother Catherine was Decker's daughter; on Fitzwilliam's death the chairs were left to his cousin Sidney Herbert and since then they have remained at Wilton House.

The London Furniture Trade

Plate 1:42. Chair (1730-40). Tropical hardwood frame decorated with Chinese lacquer. The lacquer has been much degraded and is now overlaid with later japanning. Modern leather seat. Probably made in Canton, whence almost identical examples were exported to Denmark in 1735 (see text).
BENINGBOROUGH HALL,
THE NATIONAL TRUST

Plate 1:43. Detail of 1:42, showing brackets secured by square pegs. On English chairs these brackets were glued in place.

152. For example, a piece illustrated in Clunas (1987), fig 9.
153. Clemmensen (1985); Clunas (1987), V&A FE.116-1978.
154. Clunas (1987).
155. Jaffer (2001), p. 91.
156. B.L., 'THE CASE OF THE JOYNER'S COMPANY AGAINST the Importation of Manufactured CABINET-WORK from the EAST INDIES' [1701]; Dampier (1729), II, p. 62.
157. Jaffer (2001), p. 95.

Many export chairs are decorated with carving in shallow relief. This style of decoration is often assumed to be Chinese, and indeed it frequently has an exotic appearance, but the repertoire of motifs is wholly European, deriving from Baroque engravings of the sort popularised by Jean Berain and his successors. The same style of work occurs, less commonly, on Canton-made cabinets and desks.[152] Occasional examples do exhibit indigenous influences, where the Chinese carver has strayed from the relatively formulaic Berainesque baroque into a more fluid, Oriental style incorporating specifically Chinese motifs. The fact that such work is relatively uncommon on English chairs suggests that it might have been done more cheaply in China than in England.

Lacquered chairs were also imported from the 1730s onwards. A set of chairs with their original leather seats survives at Fredensborg Castle, Denmark. These were imported in 1735 and sold to King Christian VI. Chairs of identical form, varying only in the decorative detail, survive in English collections (**1:42**).[153] The restrained form of the chairs is so close to contemporary English models that it might easily be taken for an English chair. However, some details of construction, such as the pegged scroll brackets, are decidedly un-English (**1:43**).

The question of how the Chinese workmen obtained their designs is still a matter of conjecture. Craig Clunas has suggested that the limited scope of the trade in furniture meant that it was not worthwhile to ship out full-size furniture as models,[154] but against this is the fact that many East India ships went out in ballast or part-freighted, so that there was no shortage of shipping space even for large pieces of furniture. In the 1680s the East India Company sent out chests, chairs, couches, looking glass frames and tables to Tonkin, along with a cabinet-maker to supervise their production.[155] The Joiners' Company Petition of 1701 describes how 'Patterns and Models' of all sorts of furniture were sent East by merchants concerned in the trade,[156] and there is no reason to suppose that the practice was any different in later years. Nor must one forget that when the English established their trading posts and 'factories' they probably brought furniture with them, and these too could have served as models for the local workmen.[157] Case furniture made for the English market replicates details of style and construction whose exact configuration would have been difficult to determine except at full size. For instance, the different styles of rail mouldings, drawer cockbeads and ovolo-lip moulds can all be found faithfully reproduced on Chinese-made pieces, as can the transition from thin to thick-railed carcases (see Chapter 2). These features result from English working practices being faithfully followed by the Chinese craftsmen without necessarily understanding their purpose.

Other opportunities to study English furniture at first hand occurred when English-made carcases were sent out to be lacquered. The desk-and-bookcase in **1:44** has a conventional English-made carcase of deal and oak decorated with Chinese lacquer. The interior drawers are marked with Chinese characters to allow the artist to replace them in the correct position. This class of furniture is rare; the expense and delay of the double voyage may have been inhibiting factors.

The London Furniture Trade

Plate 1:44. Desk-and-bookcase (1740-60). Oak and deal, with Chinese lacquer decoration. This is a rare survival of a piece of furniture whose carcase was made in England and sent out to Canton to be lacquered. GODSON & COLES

The London Furniture Trade

Plate 1:45. Elbow chair (1700-1720). Ebony, ivory and cane. This is one of a set of chairs produced in Vizagapatam, India, either for an East India Company official or for export to England. It is closely modelled on contemporary English chairs. CHARLECOTE, THE NATIONAL TRUST

With the attention of most historians and collectors focused on China, it is easy to forget that India played a lesser but none the less important role in the Oriental furniture trade. In 1722 the Customs returns recorded thirteen chairs 'inlaid with ivory' and two couches imported from the East Indies.[158] The most probable source of these was the town of Vizagapatam, at the northern end of the Coromandel Coast of India. Many items of Vizagapatam furniture survive in English collections, including a set of banister-back chairs probably made for Edward Harrison, Governor of Fort St George (1711-17), and brought back by him from thence about 1717.[159] An almost identical set of nine chairs and a couch survives at Charlecote Park, Oxfordshire (**1:45**). In the late eighteenth and nineteenth centuries chairs of this type were thought to be English, dating from the sixteenth century. The Charlecote chairs were acquired in 1837 on the strength of a rumour that they had been presented to the Earl of Leicester by Elizabeth I in 1575.

Such chairs, however, are not common, and the most frequently imported articles were boxes of either ebony or rosewood inlaid with ivory. Large case furniture was also made, and the best documented examples are those commissioned in India by British officials and brought back on their return to England. One such is the desk-and-bookcase made for Sir Matthew Decker and now in the Peabody Essex Museum (**1:46**).[160] It is modelled on contemporary English examples, even to the extent of having similar moulding profiles for cornice, surbase and base mouldings. It is assumed that such pieces were made by Indian craftsmen, but it is also known Chinese artisans were present in a number of Indian centres.[161]

158. PRO, Cust 3.
159. Jaffer (2001), p. 177., fig. 75
160. Ibid., pp. 182-5.
161. Ibid., pp. 94-5.

Plate 1:46. Desk-and-bookcase (1720-40). Padouk, teak, ebony and ivory. Made in Vizagapatam for Sir Matthew Decker. The design closely follows English prototypes and employs English-style mouldings derived from classical architectural profiles. It also has the narrow-railed carcase typical of English case furniture before 1740.
PEABODY ESSEX MUSEUM

Chapter Two

CASE FURNITURE CONSTRUCTION: THE DESK-AND-BOOKCASE

Second-phase cabinet-work

In the late seventeenth century the most technically advanced pieces of cabinet-work routinely produced by English furniture-makers were cabinets and their close variants, scriptors. The evidence of bills and trade cards suggests that scriptors continued to be made until about 1730, and these late examples can usually be identified by 'second-phase' carcase and drawer construction (**2:1**).[1] From about 1700, however, the desk-and-bookcase represented an increasingly popular alternative, and by about 1710 the design was well established and familiar to most London furniture-makers (**2:2**).[2] Visually imposing and highly functional, it fulfilled the role of both cabinet and scriptor. In addition, the mirrored doors on the upper case added an entirely new dimension to case furniture, allowing it to stand in for a pier glass or sconce while retaining its function as a bookcase or cabinet. A bill for furniture supplied by Gumley and Moore in 1716 describes positioning a cabinet with mirrored doors on the 'jaumb' or pier between windows where a pier glass would normally be placed: 'For a fine Walnuttree Cabinett with two large Glasses in Glass frames for the middle Jaumb in his Royal Majesties New Dressing Room…£140.0.0'.[3] The correlation in shape between the mirrors on desk-and-bookcase doors and pier or other mirrors is therefore not accidental, for their roles to some extent overlapped.

Inventories record that desks-and-bookcases were usually placed in bedchambers or dressing rooms rather than saloons, parlours or libraries. At Erddig in 1726 there were three desks-and-bookcases, all in bedrooms or dressing rooms, and at Cannons there were japanned desks-and-bookcases in several dressing rooms, varying in value between £7 and £25.[4] However, none was in the state apartments. Desks-and-bookcases contained books, writing materials, correspondence and, in the lower part, clothes. Some doubled as dressing tables and many probably stored ready cash, which explains the good quality locks and hidden compartments which are characteristic of the more expensive examples.

Because of their high technical specification, and because many labelled or otherwise documented desks-and-bookcases survive, they are our best guide to the technical development of cabinet-work over this period. The account which follows is based wherever possible on firmly dated or documented pieces which might be said to represent 'best practice' in London cabinet-

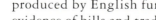

Plate 2:24 (Detail). Cabinet door (1719). See page 65.

---

1. Scriptors continued to be supplied even to the royal palaces into the 1720s, e.g., 'For a large walnuttree Scrutoire for his Majesties Great Closet… £27.0.0' (1721) (PRO, LC 9/286. There is, however, some overlap in terminology at this period, so that some compilers of inventories referred to desks-and-bookcases as 'scriptors', when it is plain from the details of the description that a desk-and-bookcase is meant, e.g., 'A Japan'd Scruptore wth glass doors' (Cannons 1725).
2. For a discussion of the early development of desks-and-bookcases, see Bowett (2002), pp. 218-223.
3. PRO, LC 9/286.
4. Erddig (1726); Cannons (1725).

Case Furniture Construction: The Desk and Bookcase

Below:
Plate 2:1. Scriptor (1700-20). Walnut, oak and deal. This early 18th century scriptor is outwardly indistinguishable from its 17th century forebears, but drawer and carcase construction are standard 'second-phase' work. The handles are not original, but are typical of the 'drops' and 'roses' that continued to be advertised by brass–founders into the 1730s.
TENNANTS AUCTIONEERS

Right:
Plate 2:2. Desk-and-bookcase (1700-1720). Walnut, oak and deal. This is typical of early desks-and-bookcases in being conceived as three distinct sections – a chest of drawers, a desk and a bookcase. Some of these early pieces have first-phase carcases and drawers, but many have second-phase construction throughout.
APTER-FREDERICKS

Case Furniture Construction: The Desk and Bookcase

Plate 2:3. Second-phase carcase construction (1700-1735). Standard second-phase carcases are externally indistinguishable from first-phase ones, but internally they are characterised by their 'stepped' dustboards.

Plate 2:4. Stepped dustboards (1700-1735). This was the most common method of stepped dustboard construction, whereby the groove ploughed for the dustboards was widened at the front to accept the front rail. The rail was usually dovetailed into the carcase.

Plate 2:5. Stepped dustboards (1700-1735). A less common technique was to plough the whole groove to the thickness of the front rail, then wedge the dustboards from below. This construction did not allow the front rail to be dovetailed to the carcase, and was inherently weak. From the desk-and-bookcase by John Gatehouse (d.1721) shown in 2:12.

work between about 1714 and 1740. As always, however, individual pieces of furniture must be assessed on their merits, and while a significant majority will conform to the patterns described below, exceptions can always be found.

The earliest desks-and-bookcases, made around 1700-1710, have first-phase carcase and drawer construction, but these are not common (a first-phase carcase is defined by having dustboards of a uniform thickness without a separate front rail). Some examples have first-phase carcases and second-phase drawers, a transitional arrangement found, for instance, on the Pardoe desk and bookcase of 1717 (2:13), but by about 1715 it was usual to employ a second-phase lower carcase (**2:3**). Second-phase carcases had 'stepped' dustboards, comprising a half-inch (12.5mm) front rail with thinner dustboards behind. The front rail was either of deal or oak, and varied in depth from one to four inches (2.5 to 10cm), according to the individual maker's preference. Occasionally one finds full-thickness dustboards used even after 1730, but this is not common.

There were two standard methods of housing the rails and dustboards in the carcase. The most common was to plough a narrow groove into the carcase wall; this was then widened at the front to accept the front rail (**2:4**). Alternatively, the groove was ploughed to the same thickness as the rail, and the thinner dustboards were then wedged from below to keep them in place (**2:5**). In both cases the rails and dustboards were glued in position, but the first method was superior, since it allowed the rails to be dovetailed into the carcase rather than simply housed in their groove. Thus the strength of the carcase was actually enhanced despite the thinner dustboards.

Thinner dustboards were viable because second-phase drawers had runners to transfer their weight to the sides of the carcase. The bottom boards of the drawer, generally with the grain running from front to back, were nailed up the drawer front, back and sides, and a runner glued at each side (**2:6**). The runners not only ensured that the weight of the drawer bore on the strongest part of the dustboard, but also raised the base of the drawer well clear of the boards to prevent friction or binding.

The drawer sides were joined to the drawer front with either 'through' or 'lapped' dovetails (**2:7** and **2:8**); the rationale behind these alternatives will be discussed later in the chapter. The drawer sides were usually slightly lower than the drawer front, and the top edges of the sides were rounded off. Rounding the top edges made them less vulnerable to the sort of minor damage suffered in everyday use, as well as giving the drawers a better 'feel'. Lowering the drawer sides meant that the fit between these and the drawer aperture was no longer important, and therefore less accuracy was required in the drawer's making. In the same vein, drawers were usually tapered from front to back, so that the fit was initially slack, but tightened as the drawer was pushed home. The taper is not usually evident to the naked eye, but it can be measured.

Second-phase drawers allowed furniture-makers to resolve a further problem, which was the correct alignment of the drawers in the carcase. On first-phase carcases the drawers were aligned by stops glued to the backboards of the carcase or to the backs of the drawers, and these stops are also

Case Furniture Construction: The Desk and Bookcase

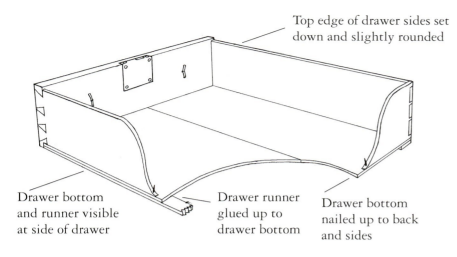

Top edge of drawer sides set down and slightly rounded

Drawer bottom and runner visible at side of drawer

Drawer runner glued up to drawer bottom

Drawer bottom nailed up to back and sides

Plate 2:7. Through-dovetailed second-phase drawer (c.1715). From a secretaire-cabinet by John Coxed (fl.1711-18). Through dovetails remained in common use until about 1730. Note that both the drawer bottom and drawer runner are visible.

Plate 2:6. Second-phase drawer construction (1700-1730). This type of drawer was in common use in London by c.1710. The bottom was nailed up to the front, back and sides, and runners were then glued to each side. The weight of the drawer was transferred to the edges of the dustboards and the runners were easily replaced when worn.

found on early second-phase carcases (**2:9**). The disadvantage of this was that if the stops dropped off the drawer became misaligned. Additionally, if the drawers were pushed in too vigorously the backboards suffered. Attempts to improve on this construction can be seen as early as 1713. W. Price, the maker of the desk-and-bookcase in 2:15, took advantage of the fact that the drawer sides were lower than the drawer front and fitted a batten under the leading edge of the dustboards which acted as a stop along the whole width of the drawer.[5] A similar but more laborious solution was adopted by the maker of 1:15. In this case, stops were created above and below the front rails by ploughing a rebate on both sides of the leading edges. The fronts of the drawers were rebated top and bottom to butt against the stops along the whole length of the rail. However, the simplest and ultimately the most common solution was to nail small stops on to the front rail (**2:10**). When the drawer was closed, the inside bottom edge of the drawer front butted against the stop, preventing it from going any farther into the carcase. With first-phase drawers this had not been possible, because the bottom of the drawer ran directly on the dustboard, but with second-phase construction the drawer bottom was raised clear of the boards, allowing a stop to be fitted. This type of stop was generally adopted by 1720.

Plate 2:8. Lap-dovetailed second-phase drawer (1700-20). From the desk-and-bookcase by John Gatehouse (d.1721) shown in 2:12. The smaller, shallow-angle dovetails are typical of lapped construction. Note the groove ploughed for the drawer bottom, rather than a simple rebate shown in 2:7. Both methods were common.

Plate 2:9. Drawer stop (1700-10). This is an early second-phase carcase. Small blocks of wood are glued to the carcase to prevent the drawers being pushed in too far. An alternative was to glue stops to the backs of the drawers

Plate 2:10. Drawer stop (1715-30). The raised bottoms used on second-phase drawers meant that drawer stops could be fitted to the front rails. The main advantage of this method was that it allowed easy alignment of the drawer. Note the scribe mark parallel to the edge of the front rail marking the position of the stop.

5. I am grateful to Peter Lang of Sotheby's New York for information on the construction of this desk-and-bookcase.

Case Furniture Construction: The Desk and Bookcase

Plate 2:11. Rebated drawer bottom with slips on four sides (1720-30). This is a sophisticated and time-consuming method of drawer construction which, where found, is usually indicative of high quality manufacture. It may represent the persistence of earlier cabinet-making traditions, as distinct from the ordinary second-phase drawer which owes as much to contemporary joinery as to cabinet-work. From the desk-and-bookcase in 2:40.

The combination of second-phase carcase with second-phase drawers with either lapped or through dovetails was the most commonly used configuration employed on London-made cabinet-work between about 1710 and 1730. The same system of construction was also used in provincial England and in North America, where it persisted much longer. The driving factors behind the transition from first to second-phase cabinet-work seem to have been economy and speed of production. Drawers with nailed-up bottoms and glued runners undoubtedly required less time and labour than drawers with rebated flush bottoms. Stepped dustboards might have taken longer to make than full-thickness ones, but they used less material and produced a lighter but stronger carcase. Rail-mounted drawer stops were quick, robust and effective. All these were decided improvements for any furniture-maker working in the competitive and cost-conscious environment of early eighteenth century London.

Some makers were clearly more concerned with quality than cost. One example of this is the use of raised rebated drawer bottoms with runner slips on all four sides (**2:11**). This feature, which first appeared on English case furniture in the 1690s, recurs throughout the period, and is invariably associated with high quality materials and workmanship.[6] There are several possible interpretations of this construction. Some makers might have regarded it as a better, albeit more expensive, method. Alternatively, it might be the manifestation of an alternative system of training. Raised rebated drawers derived logically from the first-phase, flush-bottomed rebated drawers found in late seventeenth century cabinet-work, whereas second-phase drawers related more closely to contemporary joiner's work. Raised rebated bottoms might therefore represent the persistence of a seventeenth century cabinet-making tradition in the face of simpler, more cost-effective second-phase construction adopted by the majority of London's furniture-makers trained under the auspices of the Joiners' Company.

Details of style – cornices and mouldings

The design of case furniture was heavily influenced by the conventions of classical architecture, albeit with a considerable degree of licence, as Batty Langley took pains to point out. The upper case was conceived as the main body of a building, surmounted by a frieze and cornice, and the lower as the base or plinth. The junctions between the different sections were defined by mouldings whose profile was taken from the classical Orders of Architecture.

The largest and most significant moulding was the cornice. In this respect the chief difference between desks-and-bookcases and scriptors was that the greater height of desks-and-bookcases meant that the pulvinated or 'cushion' frieze drawer was no longer practical. The omission of the frieze gives most early desks-and-bookcases a rather compressed appearance, and the cornice moulding itself is often rather mean (**2:12**). This was soon remedied by the adoption of the coved frieze. The earliest firmly dated example of this occurs on the desk-and-bookcase supplied by John Pardoe to John Meller in 1717 (**2:13**), but it also occurs on secretaire-cabinets made by John Coxed (fl.1711-18).[7] Whether coved or plain, the friezes and cornices of veneered furniture were constructed of cross-grained sections (usually walnut) backed on to a deal core (**2:14**) and glued directly on to the carcase.

---

6. For the introduction of this construction in the 1690s see Bowett (2002), pp. 202-3.
7. For Pardoe see *DEFM* and Gilbert (1996); for John Coxed see Bowett (2002), pls. 7:59 and 7:60, and Bowett and Lindey (2003), figs. 6 and 7.

Case Furniture Construction: The Desk and Bookcase

Left:
Plate 2:12. Desk-and-bookcase (1715-20). Walnut on deal and oak. This bears the trade label of John Gatehouse (d.1721). It has a second-phase carcase and drawers and, unusually at this early date, lacks both a waist moulding and a well. The flat cornice gives a rather compressed look to the upper case. Brasses are not original.
TEMPLE NEWSAM HOUSE, LEEDS CITY ART GALLERIES

Above:
Plate 2:13. Desk-and-bookcase (1717). Walnut on deal and oak. This was supplied by John Pardoe to John Meller of Erddig in March 1717 at a cost of £10.5s. It has a hybrid construction, with a first-phase carcase and second-phase through-dovetailed drawers. The coved frieze, seen here for the first time, was probably the most common style of the 1720s and 1730s. ERDDIG, THE NATIONAL TRUST

Below:
Plate 2:14. Cornice profiles, early eighteenth century
a. Flat cornice from the desk-and-bookcase by John Gatehouse (2:12). This was placed directly above the doors, lacking either a frieze or architrave to complete a true entablature. Cheaper versions had fewer sections.
b. Coved cornice, from the desk-and-bookcase by John Pardoe (2:13). Coved cornices became common from c.1715 onwards.

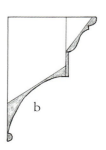

Case Furniture Construction: The Desk and Bookcase

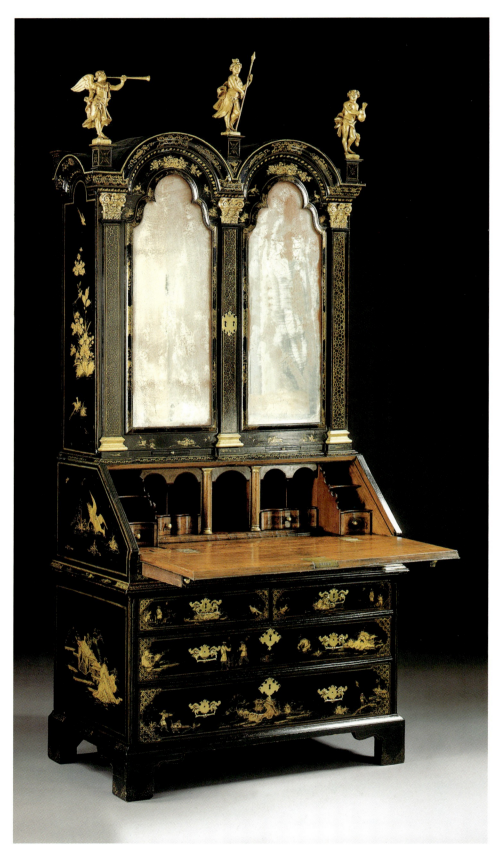

Left:
Plate 2:15. Desk-and-bookcase (1713). Black japanning on oak and deal. This is signed on one of the dustboards 'W. Price Maker 1713'. It has a first-phase lower carcase. The drawers have sunk bottoms rebated all round, typical of many high quality pieces at this date. The bracket feet might be original fitments; brasses are not original.   COURTESY OF SOTHEBY'S

Opposite:
Plate 2:16. Desk-and-bookcase (c.1720). Red japanning on an oak and deal carcase. This piece is standard second-phase work throughout, with a two-part carcase. It is in wonderful condition, with original locks, brassware and feet. Stamped RF on the top of the lower case.   ERDDIG, THE NATIONAL TRUST

The most common alternative to the flat cornice was the double-arched cornice. Because of the labour and materials involved in its creation, it represented a more expensive option, and this perhaps explains its popularity on japanned pieces, which did not require cross-grained veneered mouldings. The first firmly dated double-arched cornice occurs on the Price desk-and-bookcase of 1713 (**2:15**), and most extant examples have standard second-phase construction of the period 1710-30.[8] Some 'transitional' pieces dating from the 1720s also survive (see below), but examples with post-1730 features, such as cockbeaded drawers, are uncommon.

The red japanned desk-and-bookcase at Erddig was recorded in the Blew Mohair Room in the inventory of 1726 (**2:16**).[9] This spectacular object probably dates from about 1720, and has been tentatively attributed to John Belchier, whose label has been recorded on at least three other japanned pieces, and who is known to have supplied other furniture to the house.[10] The top of the lower carcase is stamped RF which, it has been suggested in the previous chapter (page 23), are probably the initials of the joiner or cabinet-maker marked prior to japanning. Three other pieces with this stamp are known (cf. 1:13 and 1:14).[11] The flashy exterior combined with relatively crude construction is typical of most japanned furniture of this date.

---

8. There are three William Prices recorded in the Joiners' Company apprentice bindings, but the only one whose dates fit this desk and bookcase is William Price from Cobham, Surrey, who was apprenticed in November 1682 (GL MS 8052/2, fol. 100).
9. Erddig (1726).
10. Drury (1978), pp. 52-3; *DEFM*.
11. One, a black japanned desk and bookcase, is also at Erddig. An almost identical piece was sold at Tennants Auctioneers, Leyburn, 23 July 2004, lot 1333 (1:13), and a black japanned cabinet-on-chest was sold at Christie's New York, 18 October 2001, lot 332 (3:82).

Case Furniture Construction: The Desk and Bookcase

61

Case Furniture Construction: The Desk and Bookcase

Opposite:
Plate 2:17. Desk-and-bookcase (1715-30). Green japanning on a deal and oak carcase. This is a second-phase piece with the addition of a shaped plinth, perhaps the forerunner of the plain bracket foot. Locks, brassware and feet are original.　　　　GODSON & COLES

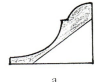
a

b

c

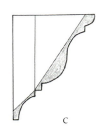
a　　　　b　　　　c

Plate 2:18. Double-arched cornice profiles.
a. W. Price, 1713 (2:15). b. Erddig, c.1720 (2:16). c. c.1725-30 (2:17).

Plate 2:19. Surbase moulding profiles.
a. was the most common, with b. and c. popular alternatives.

A variant of the double-arched cornice was the truncated double-ogee. The example in **2:17** is also a second-phase piece in remarkably original condition. Aside from the cornice design it is interesting chiefly because of its shaped plinth, into which the ball feet are fixed. It was perhaps from plinths of this kind that the bracket foot was developed; this feature will be discussed in more detail later in the chapter.

The cornices on these three pieces are all ostensibly similar, but actually vary considerably in the complexity of their profiles. The simplest is the Erddig piece (**2:18b**); the other two are more complex but differ slightly in detail (**2:18a** and **c**). The choice of profile must relate primarily to cost (simple profiles requiring less work and fewer tools), and there is usually a good correlation between the complexity of the cornice and the overall quality of materials and workmanship. To some extent the choice of profiles also reflects the preferences of individual makers, and this could be a significant factor in identifying workshop groups.

The smaller carcase mouldings tended to be much less varied. Surbase mouldings served to locate the bookcase on the lower case, and there were several common variants, of which **2:19a** was the most popular. Properly speaking, the moulding was the base mould of the upper case, but it was almost invariably glued to the top of the lower case. Some makers dispensed with a proper surbase mould, instead carrying the half-round or double-bead moulding from the desk slope over the top of the desk (**2:20**). In such cases there was usually no moulding at all in front of the bookcase, which finished directly above the top edge of the fall. The most probable reason for this was that the desk was made to a standard design to which the bookcase could be added if desired. To allow sufficient front-to-back depth for the bookcase, the surbase moulding was omitted.

Up to about 1730 most desks-and-bookcases had waist mouldings defining the division between the desk proper and the drawers beneath. In most cases its function was purely aesthetic, since the desk and its drawers were made as one unit, but some

Plate 2:20. Double-bead surbase moulding (1717). The lack of any moulding in front of the bookcase suggests that the desk was a standard model adapted to take a bookcase. Detail of 2:13.

Case Furniture Construction: The Desk and Bookcase

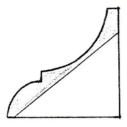
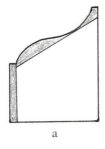
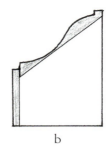
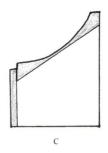

a   b   c   d

Plate 2:21. Waist moulding profile. This was the most common moulding profile used on second-phase desks-and-bookcases.

Plate 2:22. Base moulding profiles. a. *cyma reversa*. b. *cyma recta*. c. cove. d. ovolo.

were made in separate carcases. Although this entailed greater expense in labour and materials, it allowed the two parts to be constructed independently, perhaps allowing the craftsmen to work more efficiently. With some exceptions, the profile was as shown in **2:21**. Although the waist moulding remained more or less standard up to c.1730, some makers omitted it at an early date, perhaps simply to reduce cost. The desk-and-bookcase by John Gatehouse not only lacks a moulding but also has no well; instead, two drawers occupy the same space (2:12). Since Gatehouse died in 1721, his piece must predate this.[12] This is apparently a precocious example, however; the arrangement became more common later in the 1720s.

The most popular base mould throughout the period was either the *cyma reversa* (ogee) or the *cyma recta* (reverse ogee), above a shallow fascia (**2:22a** and **b**). In the 1720s a small coved moulding was introduced; it was used, for instance, on the Berry desk-and-bookcase of 1725 (2:32) and is commonly found on furniture from 1730 onwards. A slightly later version was the quarter-round or ovolo, which is characteristic of the 1730s (**2:22d**). Both these were probably quicker and cheaper to produce than the *cyma*.

In almost all cases these mouldings were produced by gluing cross-grained sections of walnut on to a backing of deal or oak, then planing or scraping them to section. Mouldings for japanned furniture were run out of solid wood (usually deal or, for small mouldings, pearwood), as were the mouldings on most wainscot and mahogany furniture.

Two further points about mouldings on second-phase furniture are worth noting. The gap between the desk slope and the carcase was usually covered by a half-round or double-bead moulding, usually (but not always) glued to the edge of the slope rather than the carcase (**2:23**). This meant that the face of the slope closed level with the carcase sides. The mirrors on the bookcase doors were set proud of the face of the doors and retained by a bold moulding, usually of ovolo section (**2:24**). As we shall see, both these details changed in the course of the 1720s.

Summary of second-phase construction

Carcase:	boards of deal or, less commonly, of oak, usually ⅞in. to 1⅛in. thick (22-29mm).
Dustboards:	'stepped', with ½in. (12.5mm) front rail and thinner dustboards behind.
Carcase mouldings:	half-round or double-bead.
Drawers:	through-dovetailed or lapped, with nailed-up bottoms and added runners. Drawer sides usually stepped down from drawer front, with slightly rounded top edges.
Feet:	ball
Other features:	desk slope level with carcase sides, finished with half-round or double-bead moulding; mirrors in bookcase doors set proud of the surface of the doors and retained by a bold moulding, usually of ovolo section.

12. PRO PROB 11/581. A wainscot desk-and-bookcase without waist mouldings, dated 29 January 1719, was sold by Sworder's Auctioneers in February 2005, lot 730.

Plate 2:23. Desk slope closure (1710-25). The moulding is glued to the edge of slope and covers the gap with the carcase. The surface of the slope is level with the carcase sides. An alternative was to glue the moulding to the carcase around the slope.

'Transitional' second-phase cabinet-work, 1720-35

The 1720s saw the introduction of a number of modifications to second-phase cabinet-work. The degree to which some or all of these changes were implemented by individual cabinet makers varied considerably, so that it is perhaps best to regard this as a 'transitional' period rather than a fully developed third phase.

From about 1720 lapped dovetail drawers became increasingly common. Prior to this lapped dovetails were routinely used on solid wainscot furniture, where through dovetails would show on the drawer fronts, and on japanned furniture, where movement or shrinkage of the joint might cause the japanning to crack. But with veneered furniture, providing the construction was sound and the veneers sufficiently robust, through dovetails performed their task adequately. The most commonly cited drawback of through dovetails, that the joint would in time 'telegraph' through the veneer, does not seem to have worried most makers, and some of the very best, like Peter Miller, continued to use through dovetails into the 1720s (2:31). Nevertheless, there is no denying the increasing occurrence of lapped dovetails on furniture of no great technical distinction. The most probable explanation for this is that lapped dovetails could save both time and labour. Since lapped dovetails were visible only from the side, all the hidden faces of the joint could be undercut to give a slack fit, thereby ensuring that the joint would fit first time without adjustment. Proof that this was the case can be seen if a lapped dovetail joint is dismantled (**2:25**).

Another advantage of lapped dovetail drawers was in fitting the drawer to the carcase, for no matter how careful the measurement and making of the drawer, it was likely to need some adjustment for the drawer front to align absolutely flush with the face of the carcase. The use of lapped dovetails made this relatively simple, because the face of the drawer could be planed flush without cutting into the dovetails. Thus the cabinet-maker could try his drawer, mark it where the face stood proud, and plane it to that mark. For the cabinet-maker in a hurry, the advantage of this system was obvious. One often finds drawers whose fronts are thicker at one end than the other, indicating that the drawer has been 'faced off' in this way (**2:26**). Finally, we should note the obvious point that the general introduction of drawer cockbeads and ovolo lip-mouldings between c.1725 and c.1735 dictated that (with some odd exceptions) all drawers had to be made with lapped dovetails thereafter. These developments will be discussed in more detail in due course.

Plate 2:24. Cabinet door (1719). This door is all that remains of a fine japanned cabinet or desk-and-bookcase. The embroidery is dated 1719 and is initialled ES, for Elizabeth Sidney (1713-81), niece of the 6th Earl of Leicester. She was six years old at the time this was completed. The bold ovolo moulding was the usual method of retaining panels or mirrors until c.1725.
PENSHURST PLACE

Plate 2:25. Drawer front with lapped dovetails. This photograph shows pockets of dried glue lying in the dovetail sockets where they have been undercut for an easy fit.

Plate 2:26. Planed drawer front. This image shows a drawer front from a japanned desk-and-bookcase of about 1720. One end of the drawer front is fully 1/4in. (5mm) thicker than the other, indicating that the drawer front was not square to the carcase and had to be planed flush. This could not safely be done with through-dovetailed drawers.

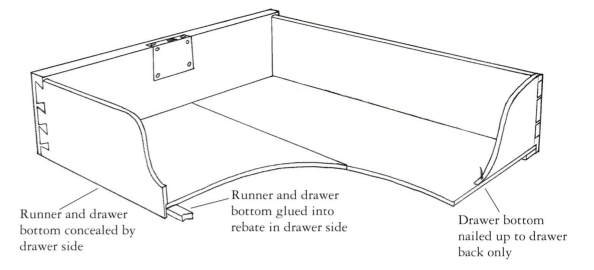

Plate 2:27. Drawer with rebated bottom and runner. In this type of construction both the drawer bottom and its runners are housed in a rebate ploughed in the drawer sides. The joint is glued, not nailed, and the result is both neat and strong.

Runner and drawer bottom concealed by drawer side

Runner and drawer bottom glued into rebate in drawer side

Drawer bottom nailed up to drawer back only

One of the most important technical advances made in the 1720s was the introduction of rebated bottoms and runners for drawers (**2:27**). The standard second-phase drawer had two main drawbacks. The first was that it looked crude, with both the drawer bottom and the runner being visible from the side. The second was that it was not particularly strong; the junction between the drawer bottom and the drawer sides was not a true joint, and relied for its strength on both nails and glue. The rebated drawer bottom successfully solved both these problems and, indeed, remained the standard method of making a drawer for the rest of the eighteenth century. A deep rebate was cut into the lower edge of the drawer sides, sufficient to admit both the drawer bottom and the runner (**2:28**). The three elements combined were held by glue alone, but the joint was strong; perhaps the additional time taken in construction was even paid for by the saving in nails. The back of the drawer was still nailed in the usual way (**2:29**).

The first firmly dated desk-and-bookcase having the new style drawer construction was made by Peter Miller in June 1724 (**2:30-1**). A desk-and-bookcase by William Berry, dated 7 February

Plate 2:28. Drawer with rebated bottom and runners. This rear view shows the drawer bottom and runner neatly rebated into the drawer side. Note the wear on the outside bottom edge of the drawer side. In extreme cases this wore through completely, exposing the runner and destroying the joint.

Plate 2:29. Drawer with rebated bottom and runners. The drawer bottom is nailed up to the back of the drawer in the same way as on standard second-phase drawers.

Plate 2:30. Drawer with rebated bottom and runners (1724). Detail of 2:31. This is a through-dovetailed drawer with rebated bottom and runners. Note that the rebate cut into the base of the drawer front is now much deeper, to accommodate the runner as well as the drawer bottom.

Case Furniture Construction: The Desk and Bookcase

Plate 2:31. Desk-and-bookcase (1724). Walnut veneers on oak. This is a pre-eminent piece of English cabinet-making. It is inscribed 'Peter Miller Cabenet Maker, in the Savoy in London the 13 June Ao 1724' (cf. 1:3). Although of conventional construction, the workmanship and materials are of peerless quality throughout. The carcase is built in three sections using no secondary wood other than the finest wainscot oak. All locks and brasses are original.
JEREMY LTD

Left and opposite:
Plates 2:32 and 2:33. Desk-and-bookcase (1725). Walnut veneers on oak and deal. One of the interior drawers in the upper case is signed W. Berry and dated 7 February 1724/5. William Berry was apprenticed in June 1716 and made free of the Joiners' Company in March 1724. He was serving his statutory two years as a journeyman when he made this bookcase interior. The rest of the piece, including the desk interior, appears to be by a different hand. This is the earliest firmly dated piece of case furniture with bracket feet as original fittings. PETER LIPITCH

1724/5, also has this type of drawer construction (**2:32-3**), as does furniture made by Coxed and Woster from about 1719 onwards.[13] It is probably safe to assume that most good quality London makers had adopted this method by 1730, although standard 'second-phase' drawers remained popular in provincial England and in North America into the second-half of the eighteenth century.

The Berry desk-and-bookcase features several significant innovations of the 1720s. The omission of the interior well in favour of drawers, first seen on the Gatehouse desk-and-bookcase, is here seen again.[14] More significantly, this is the first dated piece to have an ovolo-moulded edge to the desk slope, which causes the slope itself to sit proud of the carcase sides when closed. It is also the first to have its mirrors sunk below the face of the doors and retained by a small ovolo bead. All these features occur on desks and bookcases produced by other London makers in the 1720s and were widely adopted by 1730 (**2:34**).

---

13. Bowett and Lindey (2003).
14. See note 11, above. The well was nevertheless retained into the 1730s by some makers. A walnut-veneered desk with well and waist moulding, dated 1737, is illustrated in Symonds (1946), pl. 48.

Left:
Plate 2:34. Desk-and-bookcase (1725-30). Stained burr maple veneers on oak and deal. This bears the trade label of Grace Coxed and Thomas Woster. It exhibits two newly-introduced features of the 1720s: the raised, ovolo-moulded slope and mirrors sunk below the face of the doors. The brasses and feet are not original. CHRISTIE'S

Case Furniture Construction: The Desk and Bookcase

69

Case Furniture Construction: The Desk and Bookcase

Plate 2:35. Cabinet on stand (1720-50). Japanese lacquered cabinet on an English japanned stand. The valance or plinth fitted to Japanese export cabinets is one possible design source for the bracket foot introduced into English furniture-making in the 1720s.
CANONS ASHBY, THE NATIONAL TRUST

The Berry piece is also the first dated example to have bracket feet as original fittings. The origins of the bracket foot are obscure. It might represent a plinth, perhaps introduced in conformity with contemporary developments in architectural taste. On the other hand, it could derive from Oriental prototypes. Imported Japanese lacquer cabinets were usually fitted with fascias or brackets linked by a shaped valance (**2:35**), and it is possible that English cabinet-makers sought to mimic this feature, regarding its exotic appearance as a desirable selling point. This might explain the appearance of the ball-and-bracket combinations shown on 2:31 and 2:40, as English furniture-makers adapted the Oriental design to a conventional ball foot. If so, it was a short-lived fashion, for no documented examples of ball-and-bracket construction made after 1730 have come to light. By way of contrast, the plain bracket, seen on the Berry desk-and-bookcase for the first time, proved eminently practical, and became the standard form of foot for English case furniture until the end of the eighteenth century.

The bracket was essentially a fascia, supported behind by blocks which, if properly constructed, bore the real weight of the carcase. They were commonly made as shown in **2:36**, but this was a relatively weak construction. A better method was to stack the blocks with the grain running horizontally and in alternate directions (**2:37**). Later in the century this technique was described as 'Blocking the brackets with inch stuff, cross'd', and cost 6d. extra.[15] Where found, stacked blocking usually indicates a better than common standard of manufacture.

A stylish variant of the bracket foot occurs on a labelled desk-and-bookcase by Old and Ody (**2:38**), which was probably made about 1730.[16] The sinuous ogee shape and bold ovolo base moulding have an Oriental look, and might tend to reinforce the impression that the bracket foot was an innovation adopted from Chinese or Japanese originals.

Plate 2:36. Bracket foot construction, showing the rear foot of a walnut desk-and-bookcase. This was the usual way of constructing a bracket foot, using one or more vertically aligned blocks to support the brackets. It was not, however, very robust.

Plate 2:37. Stacked blocking. This method of supporting the brackets, using horizontal blocks laid in alternate directions, was far stronger than the common method shown in 2:36.

15. *The Cabinet-Makers' London Book of Prices* (1793), p.2
16. See Ch 1, fn. 45.

Case Furniture Construction: The Desk and Bookcase

Above:
Plate 2:38. Desk-and-bookcase (c.1730). Walnut, oak and deal. This bears the trade label of William Old and John Ody. The bold ovolo base moulding and ogee feet are very unusual and possibly unique to this workshop. Note the carcase cockbead; this is the first occurrence of this feature on a piece by a known maker. JEREMY LTD

Right:
Plate 2:39. Desk-and-bookcase (1720-30). Walnut veneers on deal and oak. This is a very high quality piece, with its original bracket feet. Brasses and locks are original. New features include the bracket feet and lip-moulded fall, combined with old double-bead carcase mouldings and prominent old-style door mouldings. CHRISTIE'S IMAGES LTD 2001

The impression that the 1720s were a period of transition, both technically and stylistically, is strengthened by the number of pieces which combine old and new features. Peter Miller's desk-and-bookcase of 1724 (2:31) combines old-style mirror and slope mouldings with rebated drawer runners and ball-and-bracket foot construction. The cabinet-work is of superlative quality and yet still employs through-dovetailed drawers. A similar transitional quality is evinced by **2:39**. This has proud mirror plates but a raised, ovolo-moulded slope. There is no waist mould, two short drawers instead of a well, and plain bracket feet. As with many high-quality pieces of this date, the drawers are through-dovetailed with rebated bottoms and slips on all four sides. The locks, handles and other metalware are all of high quality.

Plate **2:40** shows one of a small group of tiny desks-and-bookcases, barely 5ft. (1.5m) tall, which combine high quality materials and construction with transitional features suggestive of the 1720s.[17] The mirror fixing and slope closure are standard second-phase features, as are the half-round carcase mouldings, but the neat ball-and-bracket feet are transitional. As with 2:39, the drawers are through-dovetailed with rebated bottoms and slips all round. There is a fitted dressing drawer below the slope, and a fold-out writing surface below that. The diminutive size suggests this was probably intended for a girl's dressing room or bedroom. In 1716 Gumley and Moore supplied something similar to St James's Palace: 'For a Walnuttree Desk & Bookcase with a Glass Door for the young Princess' Dressing Rooms… £12.0.0.'.[18] Since the princesses Anne and Amelia, the first two daughters of the future George II, were only seven and five years old at the time, the piece must have been quite tiny.

The increasing confidence and sophistication of London's furniture-makers during the 1720s is manifested by their penchant for more complex and imposing cornice designs. To some extent this might reflect the increasing interest in architecturally inspired furniture and fittings which are manifest in the interior schemes of James Gibbs, William Kent and others, but many designs relate only vaguely to architectural precedent. There is no known source for the top of Peter Miller's desk-and-bookcase (2:31), nor for the ogee top employed by the maker of 2:39. Both appear to be a development of the double-arched cornice, resolving its non-architectural 'unresolved duality' by a strong upward central emphasis. The open segmental pediment used on the Berry desk-and-bookcase is more obviously architectural (2:32); examples can be found in numerous design books by the Italian baroque masters, and in their English derivatives. One aspect they all share is their solid construction; that is, the pediment is enclosed, extending backwards to the full depth of the carcase. This was a style of construction developed for the first double-arched tops which was both complex and wasteful, since the space enclosed by the pediment was only notionally usable. From about 1730 it became more usual to make the pediment as a two-dimensional fascia applied to the top of the cornice (cf. Plate 2:57).

It is worth noting how on the pedimented bookcases of the 1720s the mirror plates break through the line of the cornice. This is a typically baroque trait, breaking strict architectural proprieties for the sake of dramatic effect. It illustrates Batty Langley's opinion that, compared with joiners, cabinet-makers lacked basic understanding of the classical orders: ''tis a very great Difficulty to find, one in Fifty of them; that can make a Book-Case, &c., indispensably true, after one of the Five Orders; without being obliged to a Joiner for to set out the work; and make his Templets to work by'.[19] Langley's strictures (of which this is only a brief extract) smack more than a little of pedantry, but they accurately convey the freedom with which cabinet-makers modified their classical models. With the advent of neo-Palladian ideas from the mid-1720s onwards baroque licence was noticeably curtailed and cornices and pediments tended to be more 'correctly' conceived and executed, with square mirror plates finishing below the line of the cornice. There is an obvious correlation here with the introduction in the 1720s of rectangular plates for 'tabernacle' pier glasses, sconces and hanging mirrors.

Drawer-edge mouldings

One of the most significant changes to second-phase case furniture in the 1720s was the introduction of the drawer-edge cockbead. The origins of the drawer cockbead are somewhat obscure, although the principal of protecting a vulnerable edge with a projecting bead was a well-established one. Cockbeads were commonly used, for instance, on the lower edges of card and side tables from about 1700, and the desk-and-bookcase in 2:39 is cockbeaded along the entire length

17. The other examples from this group are: a green japanned example at Clandon Park, formerly in the Gubbay Collection; a red japanned one in the Victoria and Albert Museum; another red japanned one formerly with Mallett and now in a private collection; a white japanned example in a private collection; a black japanned one in a private collection; a yewtree veneered one in a private collection. Additionally, the Rijksmuseum has a piece very similar which has yet to be verified as part of the group.
18. PRO, LC 9/286, f. 14.
19. Langley (1740), p. iii. See also pp. 22-23 of the same work.

Plate 2:40. Desk-and-bookcase (1720-35). Walnut veneers on deal and oak. This exceptional piece is one of a group of diminutive desks-and-bookcases from a common but as yet unidentified source. Apart from this example and one veneered in burr yew, all the others are japanned.
APTER-FREDERICKS

Case Furniture Construction: The Desk and Bookcase

73

Case Furniture Construction: The Desk and Bookcase

Plate 2:41. Desk-and-bookcase (1730). Mahogany and other woods. This extraordinary piece of furniture encapsulates a key moment in English furniture design, since it is the first firmly dated example with cockbeaded drawers. PRIVATE COLLECTION

Plate 2:42. Detail of 2:41, showing the label inscribed 'Antrobus *Fecit* 1730', pasted inside a desk drawer.

Plate 2:43. Detail of 2:41, desk interior. This was built as a distinct unit before fitting into the carcase. The cabinet-work is different from that employed on the main carcase. This suggests that the workman responsible for this interior – 'Antrobus' – was not the man who built the rest of the piece.

of its base moulding. The first firmly dated piece of English furniture having cockbeaded drawers is the desk-and-bookcase shown in **2:41**, which is labelled in a neat hand *Antrobus Fecit* and dated 1730 (**2:42**).

Judged by any criteria this is an exceptional piece of furniture. The design is apparently unique, the workmanship and materials both idiosyncratic and superb, and its condition remarkable. While the use of brass inlay in conjunction with mahogany and other exotic woods is not unique to this piece, it is the only dated example to survive other than the Powderham bookcases of 1740 (cf. 3:80).

The cabinet-work is by at least two different craftsmen. The interior fittings of the desk, although of wonderful quality and execution, are essentially conventional in their construction. (**2:43-4**). The small drawers in the bookcase and the drawers in the main carcase are made differently. There are no top and bottom dovetails, and all four corners are mitred. The dovetailing of the large drawers in the lower case is the same (**2:45**), and the drawer bottoms are deeply rebated to raise them clear of the drawer stops (**2:47**). No runners were fitted originally, so that the weight of the drawers bore on the drawer sides, which are unusually thick. In order to clear the drawer stops the backs of the drawers have cut-outs on their lower edges. The cockbeads are of brass, fixed by brass pins whose heads have been ground flush to render them almost invisible.

The carcase work is equally unconventional. It is entirely in solid mahogany except for rails and dustboards of oak. The front rail is unusually deep, extending 5in. (12.7cm) into the case, and slips or 'kickers' are fitted below the dustboards to prevent the drawers sagging as they are withdrawn. Both the rails and dustboards are dovetailed into the carcase sides. The ogee bracket feet are supported by stacked blocking.

It must be admitted that this apparently unique desk-and-bookcase raises more questions than it answers. It is so unusual in its design and execution that it cannot be regarded as typical of its type and period. One is tempted to look for Continental parallels which are, however, difficult to substantiate. The surname Antrobus is certainly English, deriving from the Cheshire village of the same name, and there were at least two men named Antrobus who were members of the Joiners' Company. John Antrobus was apprenticed in 1675, and served as an officer of the Company at various times, but it is not known when he died.[20] In June 1710 a youth named Richard Antrobus was apprenticed to the otherwise unknown Paschal Tennet or Tennant who, despite his exotic name, was a Londoner who took up a Joiners' Company apprenticeship in 1689.[21] In the 1720s Tennet worked in Gutter Lane off Cheapside, a street occupied almost exclusively by silversmiths and engravers.[22] This raises interesting possibilities about the source of the engraved brass, and speculation is further encouraged by the fact that Richard Antrobus' father Daniel was a member of the Goldsmiths' Company.

Since it is clear that the maker of the desk interior and the maker of the main carcase and drawers were two different men, and since the Antrobus label is pasted to a drawer in the desk interior, it is possible that Richard Antrobus was the maker of the desk fittings, but not the entire piece. At the time of writing no analogous examples of the carcase and main drawer construction have been found, although brass cockbeads do occur on contemporary German furniture. The suspicion that the maker of the main carcase was not English but European cannot be avoided.

If such an idiosyncratic piece of furniture can be said to belong to any group or class, then it fits into a broader context of elite, London-made furniture employing exotic woods and brass inlay, most of which have an advanced technical specification and some peculiarities of construction. There are obvious stylistic similarities between the Antrobus desk-and-bookcase and the one in **2:48**, and indeed the desk interiors are closely comparable, but the cabinet-work in general is different.[23] The carcase is of oak, veneered with padouk. The brass cockbeads are mounted on the carcase, not the drawers, and the drawers have rebated bottoms with runner slips on three sides. The dustboards, which are entirely of oak, are constructed in a curious fashion,

Above left:
Plate 2:44. Detail of 2:41, desk drawer, showing lapped dovetails. Despite being unusually fine and small, the dovetailing looks like conventional English work.

Above right:
Plate 2:45. Detail of 2:41, drawer from lower case, showing the unusual dovetailing and the brass cockbead on the lower case drawers. The bead is fixed by four brass-headed pins whose heads have been ground flush with the bead.

Plate 2:46. Detail of 2:41, drawer front. All the brass is inlaid, including the handle, which is of an advanced style.

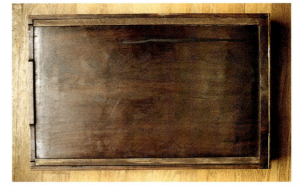

Plate 2:47. Detail of 2:41, showing the deeply rebated drawer bottom and unusually thick sides. The runner strips are later additions. Note the rear cut-outs, allowing the back of the drawer to clear the drawer stops on the rails.

---

20. GL, MS 8052/2.
21. GL, MS 8052/3; 8052/2.
22. CLRO MISC MSS/83/3
23. This piece is briefly discussed in Gilbert & Murdoch (1993), pp. 59-60, where stylistic analogies with the Samuel Bennet desk-and-bookcase in the Victoria and Albert Museum are noted.

Case Furniture Construction: The Desk and Bookcase

Plate 2:48. Desk-and-bookcase (1725-40). Padouk, mahogany and oak. The similarities between this and the previous piece are intriguing, but so are the differences.   CARLTON HOBBS

Plate 2:49. Desk-and-bookcase (c.1730). Walnut veneers on a deal and oak carcase. This piece can be closely dated by its label, which gives John Phillips' address as *The Cabinet* in St Paul's Churchyard. Phillips was established there by 1725 but moved to premises in Cornhill in February 1732. Note the carcase cockbead.   FROM HEAL, *LONDON FURNITURE MAKERS*

being run through to the front of the carcase and thicknessed at the front with a fillet of oak to create the front rail.

The two foregoing examples demonstrate that cockbeads could be either carcase-mounted or drawer-mounted, and for a short period both were equally popular. Carcase-mounted cockbeads occur on the work of several well-known London makers, including William Old and John Ody,

Plate 2:50. Desk-and-bookcase (1730-35). Walnut veneers on a deal and oak carcase. This bears the trade label of Coxed and Woster, and belongs to the final phase of their output before Grace Coxed's death in 1735. The drawers are through-dovetailed with rebated side and bottoms, in a conventional second-phase carcase. The brasses are not original, and the cartouche in the pediment is probably a replacement. HOTSPUR LTD

Plate 2:51. Desk-and-bookcase (1725-35). Red japanning on a deal and oak carcase, one of a pair. Bears the trade label of John Belchier. This has a second-phase carcase with wedged dustboards and the drawers are standard second-phase types with lapped dovetails. More advanced features include sunk mirrors in the doors and a lip-moulded slope. The construction is palpably inferior to Belchier's veneered walnut furniture but typical of most japanned carcases. The brasses are not original. GODSON & COLES

John Phillips, Coxed and Woster and John Belchier (2:38, **2:49-51**).[24] Several of these pieces have 'transitional' or 'old-fashioned' features, such as standard second-phase drawers rather than the more advanced rebated bottoms and runners. Both the Coxed and Woster and Belchier desks-and-bookcases (2:50 and 2:51) have through-dovetailed drawers; indeed, it may have been this which determined the use of carcase cockbeads, since fitting drawer cockbeads would have entailed

24. For more on these makers, see *DEFM*.

Case Furniture Construction: The Desk and Bookcase

Plate 2:52. Desk-and-bookcase (1730-40). Walnut veneers on deal and oak. Inscribed by William Palleday. This is a fine example of a late second-phase desk-and-bookcase, incorporating all the 'textbook' features; thin-railed carcase with stepped dustboards, cockbeaded drawers with rebated bottoms and runners, bracket feet, lip-moulded fall, sunk bookcase mirrors.

PELHAM GALLERIES, PARIS & LONDON

Plate 2:53. Drawer cockbead (1725-50). Many early cockbeads were rather slim. Note that the top of the drawer is bevelled and the cockbead sits slightly proud of it. Both these features helped to create a snug fit when the drawer was shut.

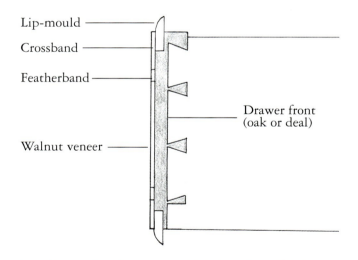

Plate 2:54. Cross section of an ovolo-moulded drawer front (1730-50). The cross-grained moulding allows the grain of the crossband and moulding to be matched into the main veneer.

ploughing through the dovetails. Most furniture with drawer cockbeads, by contrast, is fully realised third-phase work. The desk-and-bookcase in **2:52** is such a piece. It is signed by William Palleday, who worked in Aldermanbury between about 1715 and 1735.[25] It has sunk mirror doors, a lip-moulded fall, no well, cockbeaded drawers and bracket feet, all features to be expected on good quality London work after 1730. The brassware is of a style introduced in the 1720s and popular until about 1740.

In the long term, drawer-mounted cockbeads proved superior to carcase-mounted ones,

---

25. For Palleday see *DEFM* and Chapter One of this book, note 25.
26. It was a different story in Colonial America, where carcase cockbeads continued to be used well into the second half of the 18th century.
27. Gilbert (1996), figs. 63, 65, 70, 72.

Plate 2:55. Desk-and-bookcase (1730-40). Walnut veneers on deal and oak. This bears the label of John Belchier. It is a typical late second-phase piece with ovolo-moulded drawers. Brasses and feet are replaced.
CHRISTIE'S IMAGES LTD 1998

probably because they possessed several practical advantages.[26] The first was that they were more robust, being usually made in the long grain rather than in short grain sections, and being set into a rebate which offered two glued surfaces rather than one. The second was that, if damaged, it was easier to replace a single strip of bead rather than a section of moulding comprising two beads separated by a flat fascia. The third was that drawer cockbeads allowed the fit of the drawer in the carcase to be minutely adjusted. Usually the drawer front was made slightly slack in its aperture to achieve a trouble-free fit, and any play could then be taken up by fitting the cockbead slightly proud. There was also usually a slight bevel on the upper bead to ensure a snug fit as the drawer was closed (**2:53**). Underlying all this was a simple visual trick, which was that the strong shadow created by the cockbead distracted the eye from any slight gap between the drawer and carcase.

An alternative and, for a time, equally popular drawer-edge finish to the cockbead was the ovolo or lip-mould (**2:54**). We have seen that ovolo mouldings were already in use for desk slopes in the 1720s, but their application to drawers was a slightly later innovation. This, at least, is the inference to be drawn from the fact that many desks and bookcases have ovolo-moulded falls combined with conventional half-round or double bead carcase mouldings. Nevertheless, the use of ovolo-moulds on drawers is a logical extension of the principle. Their advantage over any other type of drawer-edge finish was that they concealed the gap between drawer and carcase, thus excluding dust and, perhaps more importantly, disguising slack-fitting drawers. Their disadvantage was that they were vulnerable; if the drawer was shut too forcefully the mouldings were easily forced off, and if this happened a section of veneer or banding usually came with them.

Unlike cockbeads, which almost always run in the long grain, ovolo mouldings on veneered furniture were usually made in short-grain sections. Although time consuming, this looked better, since the grain and figure of the crossband was continued into the moulding. Another advantage of this method of construction was that any damage was usually limited to the short section of moulding immediately affected.

No dated or documented examples of furniture having ovolo-moulded drawers survive from before 1730. John Belchier seems to have favoured this type of drawer finish on his furniture of the 1730s, and at least four of his labelled pieces are known in this style (**2:55**).[27] Another

Case Furniture Construction: The Desk and Bookcase

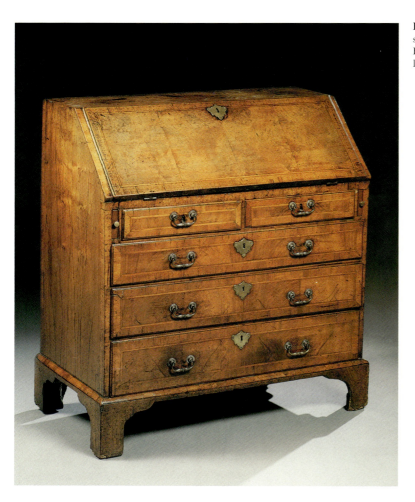

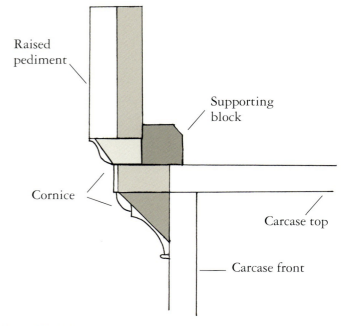

Plate 2:56. Desk (1732-40). Walnut veneers on deal and oak. This is a standard second-phase desk with lip-moulded drawers. It bears the label of Benjamin Crook, who was first recorded working in 1732. Note the full-depth lopers. Brasses are replaced. COURTESY OF SOTHEBY'S

Plate 2:57. Pediment construction.

maker who employed lip-moulded drawers was Benjamin Crook, who worked at 'The George & White Lyon' in St Paul's Churchyard between 1732 and 1748 (**2:56**).[28] However, many, perhaps most, makers produced furniture with both cockbeaded and ovolo-moulded drawers. Labelled examples of both types are known from John Belchier, Henry Bell, Benjamin Crook, Giles Grendey, and Daniel Wild.[29] The criteria governing the choice of cockbead or ovolo-moulded drawers are unclear, but in the long term the cockbead proved more durable. It is unusual to find ovolo-moulded drawers on London-made furniture after about 1750.

One further introduction of the 1730s was the deep loper to support the fall, rather than the narrow version which preceded it. The Antrobus desk-and-bookcase is the first firmly dated piece to have this feature and, while many London makers persisted with narrow lopers for some years, by 1740 the deep loper was virtually universal.

Architectural pediments

There appears to be a correlation between the adoption of triangular and scrolled pediments for desks-and-bookcases from about 1730 and the same features occurring on 'tabernacle' mirrors of the same date. Both were a manifestation of neo-Palladian taste, and their widespread popularity coincided with the publication of numerous design books, from Gibbs' *Book of Architecture* (1728) onwards, to which furniture-makers were able to refer for fashionable designs. It is also noticeable that the pediments tend to be associated with rectangular rather than shaped mirror plates, which do not intrude into the entablature. This again hints at a more correct interpretation of classical architectural conventions.

28. For more on this maker, see *DEFM*.
29. For illustrations, see Gilbert (1996).

Different makers had different ways of constructing architectural pediments, but in general the lower cornice mouldings were glued to the carcase in the usual way. The upper section of moulding, which was raised up in the centre to form the pediment, was glued on top of the cornice and also secured to the top of the carcase by glue blocks (**2:57**). The practice of constructing the cornice and pediment as a separate unit resting on top of the carcase was not introduced until the middle of the eighteenth century.

Summary of 'transitional' second-phase features, 1720-35

Carcase:	as second-phase.
Dustboards:	as second-phase.
Either:	carcase mouldings – half-round, double-bead or carcase cockbead.
Or:	drawer mouldings – cockbead (after c.1725) or ovolo (after c.1730).
Drawers:	lapped or through dovetails, rebated bottoms and runners.
Feet:	ball, bracket-and-ball, or bracket.
Other features:	raised desk slope with ovolo-moulded edge; sunk mirrored doors; interior well to the desk sometimes omitted in favour of two short drawers; waist moulding sometimes omitted.

Third-phase cabinet work

Transitional second-phase construction was the last phase of a style of case construction which originated in the 1660s. With the exception of their stepped dustboards, the carcases of second-phase furniture were unchanged in their basic construction from their seventeenth century progenitors. The addition of bracket feet, cockbeaded drawers and different patterns of moulding did nothing to alter the specification of the carcase proper, which was still constructed of approximately ⅞in (22mm) deal or oak boards braced by ½in. (12.5mm) horizontal dustboards and rails. This 'thin-railed' construction characterises almost all English cabinet-work made between c.1670 and c.1735. One of the key weaknesses of the design was that the rails on which the carcase's rigidity partly depended were often simply tenoned into the carcase sides, relying wholly on glue for their bond. If the glue failed or the carcase warped, there was nothing to prevent the carcase spreading and eventually failing altogether. Even if the rails were dovetailed into the sides, as was usually the case with second-phase carcases, the thin rail meant the dovetail was relatively weak (**2:58**). Between c.1735 and c.1740 a new form of carcase came into use which addressed this fundamental problem. The solution was to use thicker rails to provide a more substantial dovetail into the carcase sides.

Third-phase case furniture is therefore distinguished from second-phase chiefly by its thicker rails. In most cases the rails are equal to or only slightly thinner than the carcase sides, typically about ¾in. (21mm) thick. The rails are fitted from the front, and the dovetail is hidden either by a cross-grained veneer or, in the case of solid wainscot and mahogany furniture, by a long-grained facing. In many cases subsequent shrinkage of carcase has caused the dovetails to stand proud, thereby revealing their presence and frequently causing the veneer or facing to part company with the carcase (**2:59**) The damage, however, is superficial and does not compromise the integrity of the carcase.

Far left:
Plate 2:58. Carcase damage. This photograph illustrates the key weakness of thin-railed case construction, which was that the rails had very little purchase in the carcase sides, and hence could not always prevent them from spreading. As a consequence, the dustboard has dropped out of its housing.

Left:
Plate 2:59. Carcase damage. Thicker rails increase the strength of the joint between carcase and rail. Shrinkage of the carcase has caused the dovetails to stand proud, forcing off the veneer. This common problem is easily remedied by removing the veneer and planing down the protruding rail.

Case Furniture Construction: The Desk and Bookcase

Plate 2:60. Desk (1736-40). Walnut veneers on deal and oak. This bears the trade label of Henry Bell, who succeeded Coxed and Woster at the White Swan in St Paul's Churchyard in 1736, and died in 1740. This is a second-phase carcase with cockbeaded drawers.
CHRISTIE'S

Below left:
Plate 2:61. Desk (1736-40). Unidentified veneers on deal and oak. This desk bearing Bell's label has the new thick-railed carcase, although the ovolo-moulded drawers partially disguise the thickness of the rails.
STAIR & CO

Below:
Plate 2:62. Desk (1740-55). Walnut veneers on deal and oak. This is a standard third-phase desk bearing the trade label of Elizabeth Bell, Henry's widow. The handles suggest a date in the 1740s or 1750s.
PHILLIPS OF HITCHIN (ANTIQUES)

Below:
Plate 2:63. 'Kicker', glued below the dustboard of a thick-railed carcase. This slip of wood kept the drawer running true as it was pulled out, preventing it from dropping.

Right:
Plate 2:64. Desk-and-bookcase (1730-40). Walnut, oak and deal. This plain but fine quality piece bears the label of James Fordham, who worked near Moorgate between 1727 and 1744. The combination of thin-railed carcase and cockbeaded drawers suggests a date between 1730 and 1740.
APTER-FREDERICKS

The first recorded maker to use thick-railed carcase construction was Henry Bell, who succeeded Coxed and Woster at the White Swan in St Paul's Churchyard in 1736.[30] Only two pieces bearing Henry Bell's label have so far been discovered; one, a walnut desk, has a thin-railed third-phase carcase with cockbeaded drawers (**2:60**). The other, a desk veneered in elm or ash, has a thick-railed carcase with ovolo-moulded drawers (**2:61**). Since Bell died in 1740, this suggests an approximate date for the introduction of the third-phase carcase between 1736 and 1740. His widow, Elizabeth, who continued the business from 1740 until about 1758, seems to have produced third-phase carcases exclusively (**2:62**).

The thicker front rail made the step on the underside between rail and dustboards more pronounced, and meant that the clearance between the drawer and the dustboard above was increased, allowing the drawer front to drop as it is drawn out. It is therefore more common to see 'kickers' fitted beneath the dustboards on thick-railed carcases than on earlier types (**2:63**).

The success of the third-phase carcase can be gauged by the fact that it continued in use, essentially unmodified, until the end of the eighteenth century. This presents the historian with a peculiar difficulty, since there is nothing in terms of construction or materials to distinguish a walnut desk of c.1740 from one of c.1760. If the brassware is original then this is the best indicator of date, but brasses can easily be changed, thereby adding twenty or thirty years to the piece's apparent age. The desk and bookcase by James Fordham in **2:64** is clearly a second-phase piece

30. For more on Henry Bell see *DEFM*; Gilbert (1996), p. 17; Bowett and Lindey (2003), pp. 72 and 80. Furniture by Elizabeth Bell is illustrated in Gilbert (1996), figs. 76-81.

Case Furniture Construction: The Desk and Bookcase

Plate 2:65. Desk-and-bookcase (1745-60). Walnut veneers on oak and deal. The rococo-style handles are original, suggesting a date after c.1740. The thick-railed carcase is consistent with this dating.
CARLTON HOBBS

31. PRO, PROB C107, 126; PROB 3 21/271.

with a thin-railed carcase, suggesting a date before c.1740, whereas the anonymous example in **2:65** is equally clearly a third-phase piece with a thick-railed carcase which even the overlapping ovolo-moulded drawers cannot disguise. The rococo handles, which are original, are unlikely to predate 1740, and thus are consistent with the thick-railed construction. However, it is impossible to determine on technical grounds alone whether this is a piece of 1740 or 1760.

With provincial work, archaic features may persist for years or even decades. The desk in **2:66** was made by Peter Fish, of Hopton, Suffolk, in 1744. The brassware is of a fashionable pattern found on London pieces of this date, but the desk retains an old-fashioned interior well, narrow lopers and an old-fashioned ogee base moulding. With a different style of handle this could easily pass for 1730, but the thick-railed construction cannot be so easily disguised.

Summary of third-phase construction (after c.1735)

Carcase: 'thick-railed' – rails approximately similar in thickness to carcase sides.
Dustboards: stepped, with abrupt change in thickness between front rail and dustboard. 'Kickers' sometimes added to the underside.
Drawers: lapped dovetails, rebated bottoms and runners, with cockbeads or ovolo-mouldings.
Feet: Bracket.
Additional features: sunk mirrored doors, ovolo-moulded slope, interior well rarely found. Deep lopers.

Wainscot and mahogany case furniture construction

There is a common assumption in the world of antiques that oak furniture is by definition provincial or 'country', but the bills and trade labels of scores of Georgian furniture-makers found on oak furniture prove this to be untrue. 'Wainscot' furniture was a staple of the London trade, distinguished from most provincial furniture by its workmanship and the use of fine textured, straight-grained, quarter-cut wainscot oak imported from Holland. It was, naturally, a cheaper option than veneered walnut, but none the less respectable and suitable for secondary bedrooms and offices in high-status houses and for public rooms in more modest homes. At Sherborne House, Dorset, in 1726, there was wainscot furniture in the entrance hall, library and servants' hall, but not in the drawing room, parlour or best bedchambers. Similarly, at Catherine Morgan's house in Teddington in 1722 there was wainscot furniture in garrets, closets and the servants' hall.[31] Further up the social and financial scale we find much the same pattern, with wainscot furniture occurring in the lower and upper storeys, but not on the main or 'parade' floor. By way of contrast, in professional or middle-class urban houses wainscot furniture was to be found in some parlours and best bedchambers. Until mahogany became widely available, wainscot dining tables were found even in the best houses.

In form and proportion London-made wainscot case furniture generally conformed to contemporary veneered furniture, using moulding profiles in common (**2:67-8**). Backboards and

Case Furniture Construction: The Desk and Bookcase

Above:
Plate 2:66. Desk (1744). Walnut veneers on deal and oak. A pencilled inscription on the underside of a drawer reads 'Maker Peter Fish for Mrs. Verlander Hopton Suffolk – Debr 15th 1744'. The brassware is typical of the 1740s, but the interior well and narrow lopers are by London standards obsolete.
ROBERT WILLIAMS

Below:
Plate 2:67. Desk (1730-35). Oak and deal. This bears a Coxed and Woster label, and belongs to the last phase of their work before Grace Coxed's death in 1735. It is typical of the modest wainscot furniture produced in large quantities by London makers. It has a second-phase carcase and drawers in solid oak, with deal rails and dustboards. Brasses are replaced.
VICTORIA AND ALBERT MUSEUM

Plate 2:68. Desk-and-bookcase (1725-40). Oak and deal. This conforms to contemporary veneered walnut in all respects save that it is made of solid wainscot. Note the balanced proportions, crisply detailed mouldings and fine, straight-grained wainscot oak. This could be provincial, but is more likely to be London made. Brasses are replaced.
SHORT, GRAHAM & CO.

85

Case Furniture Construction: The Desk and Bookcase

Plate 2:69. Desk (1730-45). Mahogany, oak and deal. The plain workmanlike character of this desk is typical of much early mahogany furniture. Carcase and drawer fronts are solid mahogany, drawer linings and rails of oak and dustboards of deal. Second-phase construction throughout. Brasses are original. PRIVATE COLLECTION

Opposite:
Plate 2:70. Desk-and-bookcase (1725-40). Mahogany, oak and deal. A fine example of a desk-and-bookcase in solid mahogany. Note the mahogany backboards and interior fittings. Expenditure of mahogany on this scale was possible because of the low price of the wood. Second-phase construction throughout. Brasses are original. JAMES BRETT

32. Gilbert (1985).

dustboards tended to be of deal, and drawer linings were either of deal or wainscot. One clear difference between wainscot and veneered walnut furniture was in the thickness of the boards used for carcase sides, which were often worked down to ¾in. (19mm) or less, rather than the ⅞in.-1⅛in. (22-29mm) deal used for veneered carcases. Thus the difference in thickness between the carcase sides and the rails, which is so obvious with veneered walnut, is often not so apparent. Another difference was in the construction of mouldings. Wainscot mouldings were almost invariably run along the grain, rather than in cross-grained sections. Small mouldings were also frequently solid, instead of being glued to a deal core. When half-round and double-bead carcase mouldings were replaced by cockbeads and ovolos, the carcase sides and rails were faced with long-grain strips to conceal the joints between them. All these factors, together with the important fact that wainscot furniture was not veneered, meant that the difference in price between wainscot and walnut case furniture was in the order of 100 per cent or more. A list of prices agreed in May 1764 by furniture-makers in York stated that a plain walnut desk cost £1.10s., whereas one of wainscot cost 15s. This price was for labour only, and did not take into account the cost of materials which, in the case of walnut veneers, was considerable.[32]

References to mahogany case furniture in the 1720s are scarce. Probably the earliest is the bill for a 'Mohogany Clothes Chest' supplied by Gumley and Moore to the Royal Household in 1724 at a cost of £16. A few years later, mahogany case furniture was offered for sale by auction from a deceased estate:

> The Entire Library of the Learned Dr. Wellwood (Fellow of the College of Physicians deceased:) likewise all his Household Furniture: consisting of … Walnut-tree and Mahogany Book-cases, Burows, Tables &c.'   *The Daily Post*, 6 June 1727

The notion that mahogany case furniture was relatively scarce in the 1720s but increasingly more common thereafter is consistent with the technical and structural attributes of surviving examples. Second-phase drawers are relatively uncommon, whereas drawers with rebated bottoms and runners, as might be expected from about 1725 onwards, are the norm. As with wainscot, it is sometimes difficult to categorise mahogany carcases as thin or thick-railed because they tended to be made of thinner boards than walnut-veneered pieces. Carcases with half-round or double-bead mouldings certainly survive, but these features probably persisted with some London makers after 1730, and in provincial centres longer still. As a general rule of thumb it is probably safe to assume that most mahogany case furniture dates from 1730 or after, with some precocious exceptions.

In both construction and style mahogany furniture was much closer to wainscot than walnut (**2:69-70**), primarily because both woods costs around the same price (3-5d per superficial foot) and tended to be used in the solid. This accounts for the plain, workmanlike character of much early mahogany case furniture. Solid colour, straight grain, wide boards and stability in use were the chief attractions of mahogany for most furniture-makers in the 1730s. Nevertheless, mahogany furniture was generally more expensive than wainscot because of the greater degree of labour involved. The 1764 York list of prices reveals that the cost of making a dining table in wainscot

Case Furniture Construction: The Desk and Bookcase

Plate 2:71. West Indian mahogany (*Swietenia mahagoni* Jacq.). Note the white mineral deposits in the pores which tended to blunt even the best tools. These deposits are only visible on untouched surfaces, vanishing when wax or oil is applied.

Plate 2:72. Mahogany board. The underside of a tea table, showing the marks left by the toothing plane used to work the surface. This is often mistaken for evidence that the surface was intended to be veneered.

was 1s.5d., compared with 1s.7d. in mahogany.[33] The extra labour arose because mahogany was on the whole more difficult to work than wainscot and contained mineral deposits which blunted tools (**2:71**). When the mahogany room at Seaton Delaval was being installed in 1726, the Clerk of Works wrote to the architect, Sir John Vanbrugh: 'Thomas Harles and two of his men are sett on to wainscott the North East Roome with the mahogonny wood, which is so well dryed & seasoned that it works extremely fine... there is two more of Harles' men sawing the mahogany continually and the crust of that wood is very hard'.[34] Mahogany tends to have an interlocked grain (meaning that the grain changes direction in alternating strips) which makes it difficult to plane and finish cleanly. To avoid tearing out the grain on interlocked sections, furniture-makers often worked across the grain with a toothing plane whose marks can still be seen on undersides and hidden surfaces (**2:72**). This is often mistaken for evidence that the surface was intended to be veneered. Show surfaces needed to be finished with steel scrapers followed by abrasives of increasing fineness, ending with brick dust or fine *tripoli*.[35]

So far as we can tell, mahogany at this date was routinely polished with oil. Sheraton's remarks on this, published in 1803, were probably equally applicable to the earlier period:

> The general mode of polishing plain cabinet work is however with oil and brick dust... If the wood be hard, the oil should be left standing upon it for a week; but if soft, it may be polished in two days. The brick-dust and oil should then be rubbed together, which in a little time will become a putty under the rubbing cloth, in which state it should be kept under the cloth as much as possible; for this kind of putty will infallibly secure a fine polish by continued rubbing; and the polisher should by all means avoid the application of fresh brick-dust, by which the unskilful hand will frequently ruin his work instead of improving it: and to prevent the necessity of supplying himself with fresh brick-dust he ought to lay on great quantity at first, carefully sifted through a gauze stocking; and he should notice if the oil be too dry on the surface of the work before he begin, for in this case it should be re-oiled, that it may compose a sufficient quantity of the polishing substance, which should never be altered after the polishing is commenced, and which ought to continue till the wood by repeated friction become too warm, at which time it will finish in a bright polish, and is finally to be cleared off with the bran of wheaten flour.[36]

---

33. Gilbert (1985).
34. James Mewburn to Sir John Vanbrugh, 21 January 1726/7. Document at Seaton Delaval Hall.
35. *Tripoli* – a very fine powdered earth originally imported from North Africa.
36. Sheraton (1803), II, pp. 289-90.

Plate 2:73. Drawer (1740-50). Mahogany and oak. This type of drawer–edge finish, where the ovolo moulding does not overlap the rails, is often found on plain mahogany furniture. It presumably saved a few pence in labour and materials, as well as being less prone to damage than the overlapping version. Note the square-edged top to the drawer side, rather than the rounded top of earlier pieces.

The putty of brick-dust and oil acted initially as an abrasive, driving a mixture of oil, brick and wood particles into the grain of the wood, filling up pores and creating an almost case-hardened surface on which a thin film of oil gradually polymerised to produce a thin but very tough finish. Under microscopic analysis the original oil finish is often visible under subsequent layers of waxing and re-finishing. If the mahogany was pale or uneven in colour, a red pigment such as alkanet root was added to the oil.[37] Uneven or carved surfaces, on chairs and tables for instance, were 'generally polished with a hardish composition of wax rubbed upon a polishing brush, with which the grain of the wood is impregnated with the composition, and afterwards well rubbed off'.[38] According to the *Cabinet-Makers' London Book of Prices*, a finish superior to the standard oil polishing could be obtained with turpentine and wax, or with 'hard wax', but these cost half as much again and twice as much respectively.[39]

Working and finishing apart, wainscot and mahogany case furniture was constructed in similar ways, with solid carcases and solid, long-grain mouldings. The differences between them become more apparent in their internal construction. Mahogany furniture generally employed wainscot for drawer linings and carcase rails, and this is a clear indication of the relative status of the two woods. Smaller drawers for desk or bookcase interiors are often entirely of mahogany, and the backboards of bookcases are also often of mahogany. A common trick used on plain mahogany furniture was to run ovolo drawer edge mouldings out of the solid drawer front without an overlap. The rationale for this is obscure; the saving in timber and labour was very slight. The most probable reason was that it was difficult to repair a damaged ovolo mould in solid wood, since the patch could not be disguised by a crossband. By avoiding an overlap damage to the moulding could be minimised (**2:73**).

A small proportion of mahogany case furniture was more ambitious in both its design and use of materials, and it is clear that some makers recognised the decorative potential of mahogany at an early date. Mahogany veneers were employed by John Phillips for the reredos of St George's,

37. Ibid, I, pp. 6-7; II, p. 289.
38. Ibid. II, p. 290.
39. *The Cabinet Makers' London Book of Prices* (1793), p. viii.

Bloomsbury, in 1727-28.[40] More commonly it was used in the solid, but quarter-cut to emphasise its striped figure. Quarter-cutting also meant that the wood remained dimensionally stable. A more imaginative use of the wood is evident in **2:74**, the work of an unknown but sophisticated London workshop.[41] The desk slope and drawer fronts are veneered with curl or crotch mahogany, a figure more commonly found in the second half of the eighteenth century. The baroque style and solid pediment suggest a relatively early date, but on the other hand the thick-railed carcase points to a date probably after c.1735. It has been suggested that this piece corresponds closely to a desk-and-bookcase advertised for a raffle in 1737:

> John Renshaw, Cabinet-Maker, in Brook-Street, Holbourn, over against Gravel Street, having now finish'd a very curious Desk and Book-Case, which is allow'd by the Best and Most Impartial Judges to far excel any Thing of the Kind that has ever been made, for its Beauty, Figure and Structure, which are very extraordinary. It chiefly consists of fine mahogany, embellished with Tortoiseshell, fine Brass Mouldings and Ornaments, with Palasters curiously wrought after the Corinthian Order. The Inside is compos'd in the most beautiful and convenient Manner; and it being Propos'd by Several Persons of Distinction to have it raffled for; Mr. Renshaw intends to dispose of it accordingly, at so easy a Rate as 2s 6d, each Chance, which doth purchase one 1699th Part of the said Desk and Book-Case, which is agreed to be raffled for by Mr. Foubert's Patent Mathematical Machine, it being impossible to use any Fraud or Deceit with it   *London Evening Post*, February 1737

The hyperbole is typical of many such advertisements, disguising the fact that raffles were often used to get rid of unsaleable or unprofitable goods. If Renshaw managed to sell all his tickets he would have made over £200, or many times what the piece was worth.

The steep rise in prices caused by the beginning of the war against Spain in 1739 put an end to the era of cheap mahogany, at least until the advent of Honduras wood in the 1760s.[42] From 1740 onwards, English furniture-makers had to be much more discriminating in their use of mahogany.

Standardisation, conformity and innovation

The analysis presented in this chapter argues that the technical and stylistic development of case furniture in London was both logical and systematic. Changes which were purely technical, such as the introduction of lapped dovetails or rebated runners, seem to have been driven by considerations of performance, economy or manufacturing efficiency. Stylistic changes, such as the vogue for rectangular rather than arched doors, were prompted by contemporary developments in architectural design and interior planning. Few changes, however, were solely technical or purely stylistic; the introduction of drawer cockbeads seems to have been performance related, but nevertheless had a significant impact on the appearance of case furniture for the rest of the eighteenth century. Equally, the sunk mirror plates adopted in conformity with the fashion for 'tabernacle' pier glasses affected not only the appearance but also the making of bookcase doors.

One of the most striking aspects of case furniture development in this period is that it evinces a high degree of conformity in what is traditionally regarded as an individualistic and unregulated craft. While one cannot deny the importance of individual initiative and talent, particularly among elite craftsmen, and while 'non-standard' furniture can be met with every day, the overwhelming evidence of the furniture itself points to an industry in which standardisation of both materials and methods was fundamental. There clearly was a consensus about how a desk-and-bookcase should look and how it should be made. Changes to that consensus as a result of practical experience or fashionable impulse were tempered by rational considerations such as cost, speed of production and economy of materials. The level of consistency between the work of different workshops, and the remarkable degree to which changes were adopted at the same time across the trade, argues for a high degree of conformity in the industry as whole.

The mechanisms by which this conformity arose are not easy to pin down. One possibility is that it was enforced by regulation, perhaps through the authority of the Joiners' Company. There

---

40. Bowett (1999). It is possible, however, that Phillips' decision to employ veneers was dictated by the curved form of the reredos, rather than any decorative intention.
41. This is discussed in Gilbert & Murdoch (1993), pp. 18-19, 60-62, figs 47-49.
42. Bowett, *Mahogany Trade* (1997).

Case Furniture Construction: The Desk and Bookcase

Plate 2:74. Desk-and-bookcase (1735-45). Mahogany and other woods, oak, deal, tortoiseshell and brass. This is a sophisticated piece in the late baroque style. It has a rather archaic solid pediment combined with advanced thick-railed carcase and high quality brassware. The upper case is solid mahogany with applied pilasters and tortoiseshell-veneered cornice. The lower case is of deal, veneered with mahogany, and kickers are fitted to prevent the drawers dropping. Drawers are of oak, veneered with mahogany and cockbeaded with brass. VICTORIA AND ALBERT MUSEUM

is evidence to show that the Company's 'searches' to root out substandard goods and workmanship were still effective into the 1730s, but as the uptake of both apprenticeships and freedoms declined after c.1725, so the Company's ability to enforce its ordinances must have diminished.[43] A more subtle conformity may have come about through training. Until the 1720s an apprenticeship regulated by the Joiners' Company was still the most common route to becoming a cabinet-maker, and this must go a long way towards explaining the common conventions of materials, style and construction which are so evident in London cabinet-work. Even as Joiners' Company apprenticeships declined in the 1730s and 1740s, private apprenticeships continued to operate throughout the eighteenth century. Both within and without the Company, most apprentices were taught by men whose expertise had developed within a common ethos borne out of a combination of inherited tradition and acquired experience. Workshop practices were thus transmitted from one generation of workmen to the next, ensuring a continuity at both a practical and an ethical level.

A significant factor in encouraging conformity was the London trade's dependence on imported timber, which tended to encourage standardisation of both the types and sizes of wood used in metropolitan furniture construction, and this gives urban furniture generally, and London furniture in particular, a characteristic look and feel. The deal boards used for carcases, for instance, tended to be either ⅞in. (22mm) or (less commonly) 1⅛in. (29mm) in thickness, which were probably the sizes reached when standard 1in. and 1¼in. (25 and 31mm) deals were planed down.

Standardisation was not incompatible with innovation and change, when it did come, could be rapid. This was partly the consequence of a free labour market. Even apprentices enjoyed considerable freedom outside working hours, and when they gathered in the tavern after work professional secrets were no doubt divulged. Once qualified, a journeyman was free to take his skills to whoever would pay him. As he moved from workshop to workshop, he passed on techniques devised in one place to another. Thus innovations rarely remained novel for long. A second force for change was commercial competition, and this, paradoxically, also encouraged standardisation. Competition naturally drives prices down, which in turn encouraged workshops to find the most cost-effective answers to manufacturing tasks.[44] Ultimately, this resulted in most workshops arriving at similar solutions to common problems. Hence mobility of labour and economic pressures tended towards the same end, which was uniformity of trade practices. The same process can be observed operating in modern economies, where technologies developed and perhaps patented by one company are soon copied by others, driving prices down and making what were once exclusive commodities generally available.

The impact of patrons and clients on design and innovation was double-edged: on the one hand the desire for fashion and novelty was a driver of innovation and change; on the other, social status and reputation required conformity with one's peers and neighbours. Taste in furniture, like everything else, followed fashion and fashion followed the crowd. In other words, furniture-makers' customers mostly wanted the same type of furniture as everybody else. The trick for the furniture-maker was to combine conformity with invention, so that all patrons could be satisfied that their furniture was *à la mode*, but no two patrons had furniture exactly alike. Conformity was thus not incompatible with choice. Within broad conventions of style and technique London's furniture-makers produced an almost limitless variety of furniture. A desk-and bookcase could be made in two parts or three, with or without a well, with any combination of drawers and pigeon-holes, and the bookcase fitted with arrangements ranging from simple shelves to combinations of drawers, holes, cupboards and folio slots of quite unnecessary complexity. This was the secret of success, combining the economies of scale necessary to keep prices low with the variety and individuality which customers demanded. One often finds furniture which has been altered at the time of making or soon after, suggesting a change of mind on the part of the maker or client. The desk-and-bookcase made for John Meller in 1717 was altered by John Pardoe before it left the workshop, presumably on Meller's instructions (2:13).[45] The desk-and-bookcase in 2:32 was originally intended to have a plain shelved interior to the bookcase, but was re-fitted with a more elaborate unit by William Berry. One can easily imagine a client buying the desk-and-bookcase from stock, but asking for the interior to be improved to create something more showy.

---

43. The minutes of the Joiners' Company record regular searches and seizures of 'insufficient goods' well into the 1730s (GL, MS 8046/3-7).
44. This is probably the root of the price books agreed between journeymen and masters in the later 18th century, since after fixed and material costs had been reduced to their minimum, labour costs were the only remaining negotiable factor.
45. Drury (1987).

One of the most striking things about London furniture is how little bad furniture there is, either in terms of workmanship or materials. Some of it is very good indeed, but most falls within a broad middle ground of sound design, good materials and workmanship and unexceptionable style. This may, of course, be merely the accident of survival, the bad furniture having long since disintegrated or been discarded. But somehow this does not ring true. There seem to have been powerful forces at work maintaining a minimum level of quality below which most London furniture-makers did not fall. The standardisation of materials and working practices must have been a major factor in this, and perhaps the Joiners' Company played its part in enforcing standards, but equally important was the role of patrons and consumers. Research into the networks of patronage of makers like James Moore, to give one example, shows that there were family and/or personal connections which linked several of his major patrons, and this argues for the power of word of mouth.[46] This could operate equally powerfully in a negative way, and the correspondence of some furniture-makers shows them to be painfully aware of the fact. Even when quite legitimately chasing unpaid bills from relatively minor clients, Gerrit Jensen was obliged to choose his words carefully:

> I am very Sorry y^t I must give ye Trouble of a L[ette]r but 'tis to desire you to let me know what it is you Design to doe for I have not had the Honour to See you never Since you Spoke to me wch is above a Twelvemnth agoe I have often been at your House but you was never at Home... And therefore S^r I desire you Send me Word or else I must goe to ye Severity of the Law wch if I doe you Cannot blame me for its is your own Fault... So S^r hoping you will not put me to that Trouble I Rest your humble Servant – and I leave y^r Bill your own Moderation that things may be done in Friendship.[47]

No matter how exalted his status among fellow craftsmen, a furniture-maker remained a tradesman, dependent on the goodwill of his patrons. The freedom of clients to withdraw their custom and that of their friends must therefore have tended to encourage not only social deference but high standards of materials and workmanship. In some case it must be admitted that fashion or superficial appearance seems to have taken precedence over quality; only this could explain the poor quality of much japanned furniture, but this is perhaps a special case. In general, poor workmanship must soon have become apparent with furniture in everyday use, with predictable consequences for the maker's business.

If we were to seek one factor which explained the generally high quality of London furniture, its consistency of style and method, as well as its unlimited choice, it was probably the open, self-regulated nature of the trade and its markets. The success of the furniture trade is a strong argument for the efficacy of the eighteenth century free market in labour and goods within the protective ring of a mercantilist foreign policy.

The conformity of style, technique and materials has important implications for present day furniture scholarship. Both scholars and connoisseurs have traditionally focused on furniture by known makers to which unattributed furniture can be assigned on the basis of stylistic or technical analogy. The analysis presented in this chapter suggests that this approach is flawed, because of the essentially uniform nature of most London furniture production. Were it not for trade labels or other forms of documentation, the output of most London cabinet-makers would be indistinguishable one from another. Occasionally it is possible to assemble a sufficient number of pieces from a given workshop to identify small idiosyncrasies or preferences which identify the output of that maker.[48] And occasionally one encounters a maker such as Peter Miller whose work is so distinctive as to stand out clearly from that of his contemporaries. On the whole, however, one London-made desk-and-bookcase is much like another, and rarely distinctive enough to warrant an attribution without supporting evidence. The use of subcontracted labour, discussed in Chapter One, compounds the problem further, for who knows whether one is looking at a genuine workshop product or the work of an anonymous subcontractor who might also work for other employers? All these factors threaten to make attribution by stylistic and/or technical analogy an inexact science, and one which takes little account of the complex structure of the furniture trade. But so long as attributions make it easier to sell antique furniture, then attributions based on the merest stylistic similarity will continue to be made.

---

46. For Moore's patronage see *DEFM* and Murdoch (2004).
47. Kendal Record Office, Levens Archive, Box C.I, *Gerrit Jensen to Colonel James Grahme*, 23 April 1708.
48. E.g., Bowett and Lindey (2003).

Chapter Three
OTHER CASE FURNITURE

Plate 3:82 (Detail). Cabinet on chest (1715-30). See page 138

Clothes chests

The quantity of bedding, curtains, and other fabrics associated with beds and their furniture was often greater than could be accommodated within bed chambers, so many large establishments had a store or 'wardrobe', usually in the attic storey, where it was stored, particularly when the house was not occupied. Cannons had its own Wardrobe, which housed a large wainscot chest 14 feet long and three feet wide which contained a vast quantity of bed hangings, curtains, quilts and counterpanes.[1] At Drayton in 1724 one closet was entirely given over to '5 chests to put up the furniture' of a bedchamber and its associated suite of rooms.[2] Storage chests were also often located in passages, closets and antechambers. The Duke of Montagu's bedding at Montagu House was kept in the closet next to his bedchamber, in a walnut chest lined with blue silk,[3] and at Dalkeith Palace in 1739 the housekeeper noted that in the Blue Dressing Room 'the backs and cushions for the 6 chairs are put in the Indian Chest'.[4] At Erddig there was an 'Indian chest' in the dressing room next to the Second Best Bedchamber, a 'Walnuttree large chest' in the Breakfast Room, a 'Wenscote Chest' in a closet next to the Yellow China bedroom, and a 'Black Japan Chest' in the Worked Bedroom.[5]

Storage for clothes and bed linen within bedchambers was also provided by presses and chests, rather than chests of drawers. The Ditchley inventory of 1743 suggests that one contemporary term for these articles was 'chamber chests'. Several are cited in walnut, mahogany and japan, including two 'old fashioned' examples with carved fronts. Some of them had drawers, but they were not chests of drawers, which were noted separately.[6] These chests for clothes and linen had changed little in design since the late seventeenth century (**3:1**), and early eighteenth century versions differed significantly only in the adoption of bracket or cabriole feet and more up to date metalware. Inventories suggest walnut chests were the most numerous, but lacquered or japanned examples were almost as common. In 1722 Gumley and Moore supplied a japanned chest for George I: 'For a Japan'd Trunk for his Maties Cloths & Linnens… £12. 0. 0.'.[7] The term 'trunk' rather than 'chest' probably implies a domed lid. After about 1730 mahogany chests also occur (**3:2**).

The most extravagant clothes chests were entirely gilt (**3:3**). It is commonly thought chests of this kind were inspired by Italian cassoni, or marriage chests, and it may well be that only a dynastic matrimonial alliance would warrant such exceptional expenditure. Nevertheless, most

---

1. Cannons (1747).
2. Drayton (1724).
3. Montagu House (1709).
4. Dalkeith (1739).
5. Erddig (1726).
6. Ditchley (1743).
7. PRO, LC 9/287, f. 24.

Other Case Furniture

Plate 3:1. Chest (1680-1710). Walnut on deal and oak. With either a flat or arched lid, the chest remained a common form of storage for clothes, linen and bedding for many years after the general introduction of the chest of drawers. Brasses on the drawer are replaced, others are original. The interior is lined with red silk.

DUNHAM MASSEY, THE NATIONAL TRUST

Plate 3:2. Chest (1730-60). Mahogany and oak. This is probably the 'large Mahogany Chest, Drawers ith [sic] Bottom' recorded in the Stamford Gallery at Dunham Massey in the inventory of 1758. The carcase is solid mahogany, with a veneered lid and oak-lined drawers. Mahogany chests of this sort were once common, but have been out of favour in the antiques trade for a long while and are often considered 'provincial'. The evidence of inventories suggests this was not the case. Brassware is original.   DUNHAM MASSEY, THE NATIONAL TRUST

English chests are closer in form to contemporary French coffers than Italian cassoni, and some can be closely related to designs by Jean Berain and others.[8] The example shown here was probably made for the marriage of Sir William Bateman with Lady Anne Spencer, a granddaughter of the Duchess of Marlborough, in 1718. The stiff shallow relief decoration on the front is similar to that executed in marquetry of brass and tortoiseshell on contemporary French furniture, but the decoration of the top is more freely drawn, similar to that found on the tops of contemporary English gilt-gesso tables. One wonders whether the front elevation was taken from an engraved French source, and the top improvised to suit.

8. Wilk (1996), p. 86.

Plate 3:3. Gilt chest (c. 1720). Carved and gilt wood and gesso. This chest was probably made to celebrate the marriage of Sir William Bateman to Lady Anne Spencer in 1720. It represents the apotheosis of the common clothes or chamber chest. The design is inspired by the large chests or commodes designed by André-Charles Boulle, Jean Berain and others about 1700. It is attributed to James Moore on the strength of his connection with the Duchess of Marlborough, Lady Anne's grandmother and sometime guardian.

VICTORIA AND ALBERT MUSEUM

Other Case Furniture

Plate 3:4. Chest on stand (1725-40). Walnut on oak. The cockbeaded drawers suggest a date after c.1730, but the form of the stand, with its angular legs and pendent apron, is relatively early. All metalware is original.
DUNHAM MASSEY, THE NATIONAL TRUST

Plate 3:5. Chest with drawers (1735-55). Walnut and ebony on oak and deal. This superb chest was made for the 2nd Earl of Warrington (d.1758), with a pair of close stools en suite. The cockbeads are of ebony, and all metalware is original with the exception of the two uppermost handles. The thick-railed carcase and style of brass handles suggest a mid-18th century date.
DUNHAM MASSEY, THE NATIONAL TRUST

Chest of drawers

The relative scarcity of chests of drawers in noble and upper-class houses before 1700 has been noted elsewhere.[9] Even after 1700 some large houses had very few. At Dyrham Park in 1710, for instance, there were only three chests of drawers in a house of more than eighty rooms, and at Montagu House in 1709 there were three among seventy-six rooms.[10] In the latter case, none was in principal rooms; there was a wainscot chest of drawers in the nursery, another in the footmen's room and one next to the Duchess Dowager's apartment. A similar picture emerges from the Duke of Montagu's country seat at Boughton, where chests of drawers, although relatively numerous, did not appear in the State

9. Bowett (2002), p. 50.
10. Walton (1986); Montagu House (1709).

Plate 3:6. Chest with drawers (detail). This shows the interior of 3:5, lined with its original sky-blue quilted silk.   DUNHAM MASSEY, THE NATIONAL TRUST

Apartments or other public rooms.¹¹ At Drayton House in 1710 chests of drawers were again placed in secondary rooms – dressing rooms, closets, nurseries, workrooms and secondary bedrooms.¹² At Erddig in 1726 there were only two chests of drawers in the house, of which one was in a secondary bedroom furnished with a field bed and the other was in a dressing room to another secondary bedroom. The 1747 sale catalogue of the Duke Chandos' palatial home at Cannons in Middlesex records just three chests of drawers – one mahogany, one walnut and one described as 'India'.¹³

The inconvenience of having a large amount of clothes or bed linen stacked in a chest made the addition of drawers a sensible modification. A group of six chests of various configurations made for the 2nd Earl of Warrington survives at Dunham Massey, in Cheshire. Two are shown in Plates **3:4-3:6.** Chests of this type are now relatively uncommon, but this may reflect their lack of adaptability for modern living rather than the historical status quo. On the whole surviving examples tend to be rather early (before c.1750), except in a provincial or vernacular context, where they continued to be made until the nineteenth century. The antiques trade calls these hybrid chests 'mule chests', but this was not a contemporary term.

The evidence of urban inventories suggests a higher incidence of chests of drawers in middle-class and professional homes. When the eminent French upholsterer Francis Lapiere died in 1715 he had three walnut chests of drawers in his London house.¹⁴ All were in secondary bedrooms or closets. A similar picture emerges from the inventory of Catherine Morgan of Teddington, near London, taken in 1722. Here chests of drawers, some 'on frames', were placed in closets off the principal bedchambers, or in secondary bedchambers.¹⁵ We should remember that by modern standards the amount of storage required for personal effects was relatively small. Lapiere's will reveals that he had only two suits (one 'sad' colour, one blue), one great coat, eleven shirts and two hats, and this relatively modest wardrobe was typical of all but the richest men and women. Additional storage was provided by presses, and in the base of scriptors, cabinets and desks-and-bookcases, which were by now routinely made with drawers in the base. In Lapiere's case he had both a 'Wainscott Cloths Press' and a 'Scrutore' in his principal bedroom.

At the beginning of the eighteenth century chests of drawers were identical to their late seventeenth century antecedents, at least in external appearance. Analogies with contemporary clock cases suggest that floral marquetry continued popular until at least 1710, and arabesque

11. Boughton (1709).
12. Drayton (1710).
13. Cannons (1747).
14. Westman (1994).
15. Elmfield House (1722). I am grateful to Mary Green for her transcription of this inventory.

Other Case Furniture

Plate 3:7. Chest of drawers (1700-15). Walnut and marquetry on deal and oak. This chest has a 'second-phase' carcase and drawers typical of post-1700 construction. The crowded floral marquetry extending across the whole drawer front is typically 'late' in style and matches that found on contemporary longcase clocks.   WILLIAM COOK

Plate 3:8. Chest of drawers (1700-20). Olivewood and holly veneers on deal and oak. Stylistically unchanged, this chest is distinguished from its 17th century forebears only by its second-phase carcase and drawer construction. Metalware replaced.   PRIVATE COLLECTION

Other Case Furniture

Above:
Plate 3:9. Second-phase carcase construction, showing the stepped construction generally used for dustboards after about 1710. However, single thickness dustboards were occasionally used into the 1730s.

Right:
Plate 3:10. Chest of drawers (1728). Oak. This chest is inscribed 'May the 21st 1728 Made for Mrs Mary Reynolds by Thos Reynolds in Bell Lane Spittle Fields'. It is the earliest firmly dated English chest of drawers with bracket feet as original fitments. Note the *cyma* top moulding, proving that this profile does not always indicate that the chest once stood on a stand.
PRIVATE COLLECTION

marquetry until the 1720s.[16] Although the style of marquetry may often indicate a 'late' example (**3:7**), plain oyster-veneered olivewood or walnut examples were stylistically unchanged (**3:8**) However, the interior construction should indicate whether a piece is likely to be of late seventeenth or early eighteenth century manufacture. Chests made before 1700-1710 should have a first-phase carcase and drawers, with full thickness dustboards and flush-bottomed drawers; later examples (after c.1710) should have second-phase carcases with stepped dustboards and drawers with nailed-up bottoms and runners (**3:9**). Transitional examples with first-phase carcases and second-phase drawers are often found, probably dating from between 1700 and 1720.

Double bead and half-round carcase mouldings around the drawer apertures continued to be used until at least 1730. A small chest made by the Spitalfields joiner Thomas Reynolds for his wife Mary in 1728 retains half-round mouldings while sporting newly introduced bracket feet (**3:10-11**). This combination of old and new features also occurs on walnut veneered desks-and-bookcases of the 1720s (cf. 2:39). Within a very few years the appearance of chests of drawers was dramatically altered

16. Dawson *et al.* (1982); Robinson (1981).

Plate 3:11. Detail of 3:10. The shaped valance and bracket feet are formed by extending the carcase sides below the base of the chest and cutting them to shape. The conforming base moulding or fascia is simply glued in place. Some full-size case furniture was made in the same way.

Other Case Furniture

Plate 3:12. Chest with folding top (1730-40). Walnut on deal and oak. The introduction of drawer or carcase cockbeads about 1730 provides a useful rule-of-thumb for dating. The carcase cockbead shown here was a short-lived variant, rarely found on London furniture after 1740. PHILLIPS

Plate 3:13. Top mouldings for chests of drawers. a. ovolo mould, commonly used from c.1670 to c.1730; b. inverted *cyma recta*, commonly used for chests on low stands and chests of drawers from c.1690 to c.1730; c. *cyma recta*, introduced about 1715 for chests of drawers, side tables, bureaux-tables, etc.; d. ovolo-bead, first introduced for case furniture in the 1720s and commonly found on chests of drawers of the 1730s and 1740s.

a · b · c · d

by the adoption of cockbeaded or ovolo-moulded drawers. No datable examples are known from before 1730, which date therefore offers a useful rule-of thumb starting point for chests with these features. The example in **3:12** has carcase cockbeads, an alternative to drawer cockbeads which enjoyed a short period of popularity between about 1730 and 1740.

Top and base moulding profiles can offer useful clues to dating. The large ovolo top moulding continued in use into the 1720s (3:7, 3:8 and **3:13a**), as did the inverted *cyma recta* or reverse ogee (3:10 and **3:13b**). This latter profile can be an indication that the chest originally stood on a stand, but the example of Thomas Reynolds' chest proves that this was not always the case. From about 1715 onwards the *cyma recta* was introduced on some chests of drawers and bureaux tables (**3:13c**; 3:51), and this profile remained a popular one throughout the eighteenth century. However, the most characteristic profile for the period 1725-40 was the small ovolo (**3:13d**), which gives early Georgian chests their neat, uncluttered lines. For base mouldings *cyma* profiles continued to be commonly used. Coved base mouldings are unlikely to date from before 1720, and ovolo base mouldings seem to be characteristic of chests after 1730.

A high proportion of early Georgian chests have slides beneath the top. Later in the century Sheraton described chests of this kind as a: 'Lobby chest… is a kind of half chest of drawers, adapted for the use of a small study, lobby or small lodging room. They usually consist of four drawers in height, rising to 3 feet in height, and their length about the same. The top drawer is usually divided into two: and sometimes there is a writing slider which draws out under the top'.[17] The example in **3:14** has carcase cockbeads, an ovolo-moulded top and ovolo base moulding, all indicative of a date of c.1730-40. The arrangement of three drawers in the top row is unusual, but the right-hand drawer is sham, allowing a fitted pen drawer to be inserted in the side (**3:15**). This is clear evidence that the slide, which modern day collectors often call a 'brushing-slide', was intended for writing. However, it would be unwise to be too prescriptive, since there is no reason why the slide could not also function as a dressing table.

Above left:
Plate 3:14. Chest of drawers (1730-40). Walnut on oak and deal. The high quality of this chest is evident from the fine burr veneers and neat cabinet work. The back is also veneered, which is highly unusual. The cockbeaded carcase suggests a date not much earlier than 1730, but the thin-railed construction indicates that it is unlikely to have been made after 1740. Note the ovolo base moulding and re-entrant corners to the top.
PRIVATE COLLECTION

Above right:
Plate 3:15. Detail of 3:14, showing pen drawer fitted to one side. The carrying handle is a common 1730s pattern. PRIVATE COLLECTION

17. Sheraton (1803), II, p. 26.

Other Case Furniture

Plate 3:16. Chest of drawers (1730-50). Walnut on deal and oak. The thin-railed construction of this carcase is made less obvious by the reduced thickness of the sides. The original handles and escutcheons are of a pattern popular from c.1715 onwards, but the bracket feet and cockbeads suggest a rather later date. The top is ovolo-beaded but does not have re-entrant corners. Perhaps a provincial piece.

CHRISTIE'S IMAGES LTD 1997

Plate 3:17. Chest of drawers (1730-50). Walnut on oak and deal. This chest has a flush or 'caddy' top, much sought after by collectors. The ovolo bead on the top is repeated on the front vertical corners, which is a nice refinement. It also reduces the apparent thickness of the carcase sides, making the thin-railed construction less obvious. Brassware is original. CHRISTIE'S IMAGES LTD 1997

Plate 3:18. Methods of flush top construction: a. shows the corner of the carcase planed at an angle, on to which a thick cross-grained veneer is laid. The veneer is then rounded off to create the ovolo, and the top and sides veneered up to it. This works for veneered carcases only. b. shows the rebate ploughed into the top of the carcase into which a solid bead is laid. This works for both veneered and solid construction.

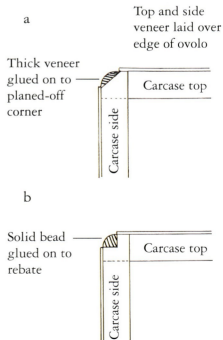

The thin-railed carcase of **3:14** is clearly visible in the photograph, but in other cases the difference in thickness between the carcase sides and the rails is less clear, usually because the carcase sides are almost as thin as the rails (**3:16**). In such cases other features such as moulding profiles, drawer construction and brassware might help with dating. The ovolo base moulding of **3:16** suggests a date after 1730 and the handles are of a type unlikely to have been fashionable after 1740.

Plate **3:17** has what the antiques trade calls a 'caddy top', after the ovolo-beaded flush top which is also found on contemporary tea caddies. Collectors regard this as a desirable feature, but it may well have represented a cheaper option to the conventional overhung top, since less labour was required in making it. Plate **3:18** shows the two methods most commonly used to create this moulding. The same methods were also used to make the ovolo mouldings on conventional, over-hung tops.

Other Case Furniture

Plate 3:19. Chest of drawers (1740-60). This bears the trade label of Giles Grendey. The cabinet-work is in every respect typical of third-phase London work. The handles are original, but the escutcheons are not. MALLETT

Plate 3:20. Trade label of Giles Grendey, from the chest in 3:19.

Plate 3:21. Base of 3:19, showing the hardwood rollers behind the bracket feet. Note the crude battens to which the base moulding is applied. This is typical.

Although caddy-top chests are generally considered 'early', there is no doubt that they were made well into the middle of the eighteenth century. The chest in **3:19** bears the trade label of Giles Grendey (**3:20**). It has a thick-railed carcase, suggesting a date after c.1740, and this is consistent with the style of handle which is a common design found on labelled pieces of the 1740s.[18] The bracket feet conceal hardwood rollers (**3:21**). Other caddy-top chests and bureaux by Giles Grendey are known, all dating from roughly the same period.[19]

18. For more on Grendey, see *DEFM*, pp. 371-2.
19. Gilbert (1996), figs. 439 and 440.

Other Case Furniture

Plate 3:22. Chest of drawers (1740-60). Walnut on deal and oak. This chest has a horizontal rail above the slide, a feature associated with third-phase construction and generally adopted after about 1740.
CHRISTIE'S IMAGES LTD 1997

A feature which is associated with the change from second to third-phase (thick-railed) carcase work is the insertion of a rail between the uppermost drawer and the top of the chest. Hitherto, the top was usually fixed directly above the drawer, with no intervening rail, but from about 1740 many furniture makers began to insert a rail between the two (**3:22**). This provided a structural tie at the top of the carcase, allowing it to be fully assembled before the top was fitted. There was also an aesthetic benefit, for thick-railed carcases which lack a top rail often have a rather compressed look, with the wide spacing between the drawers contrasting oddly with the lack of space above the top drawer.

Chest with folding tops

Chests with folding tops are usually termed 'bachelor's' chests, although this was not a contemporary term. They are generally smaller than ordinary chests, and when open the top is supported on two bearers or lopers which draw out from the carcase. The purpose of the folding top has been variously interpreted by modern writers. Some view it as a surface for laying out or preparing clothes, others as a writing surface. The fact that many chests have drawers fitted for inkwells and pounce-pots suggests that some were certainly intended for writing, but this does not exclude the possibility of also using them as dressing tables.

It is not clear how bachelor's chests were described in the early eighteenth century. It may be that they were not deemed significantly different from ordinary chests of drawers, or it may be that they were conceived in a fundamentally different way. The inventory of Sherborne House, Dorset, taken in 1726, refers to '2 folding walnut dressing tables drawers to the bottom' in a bedchamber,

Other Case Furniture

Above:
Plate 3:23. Dressing table/chest with folding top (1700-1730). Japanned deal and oak. Is this the progenitor of the 'bachelor's chest'? Escutcheons and knob handles are replaced, and the japanning has been restored. Feet are probably replaced.
CHRISTIE'S IMAGES LTD 2003

Opposite:
Plate 3:24. Chest with folding top (1715-30). Walnut on oak and deal. Brasses and feet original. Early bachelor's chests with ball feet and half-round carcase mouldings are rare.
APTER FREDERICKS

20. Sherborne (1726). I am indebted to Michael Legg for pointing out this intriguing and possibly unique reference.
21. It is possible that chests with slides were also conceived as dressing tables by their makers. In 1730 Benjamin Goodison supplied 'three Wallnuttree Dressing Tables upon Castors with Large Drawers to the Bottoms and a Sliding Tables to each of them… £15.0.0.'. These were made for the apartments of the Princesses Royal, Amelia and Caroline at St James's Palace, and the description sounds very much like a chest of drawers with a slide.
22. Cannons (1725).

while in a closet stood another 'Walnut dressing Table to fold up with drawers to bottom'.[20] These sound very like bachelor's chests, raising the intriguing possibility that such chests might have developed from folding tables with drawers underneath, rather than from conventional chests of drawers.[21] Thus the dressing table/chest in **3:23** may well be the sort of thing described in the Sherborne inventory, and the progenitor of the now familiar 'bachelor's chest'. The hinged gates which support the folding top placed obvious constraints on the configuration of the lower case, but once these were replaced by sliding lopers, the lower case could be fitted with drawers across its whole width (**3:24**). Another contemporary term which might describe a bachelor's chest was 'Twylet [toilet] chest'. There were several of these in the dressing rooms at Cannons in 1725, in walnut, wainscot and mahogany.[22]

Other Case Furniture

Other Case Furniture

Plate 3:25. Chest with folding top (c.1730). Walnut on oak and deal. This bears the trade label of William Old and John Ody. A typical London-made piece with second-phase carcase and cockbeaded drawers. CHRISTIE'S

Plate 3:26. Chest with folding top (1730-40). Walnut on oak and deal. A handsomely-figured chest with second-phase construction throughout. No firmly dated furniture with lip-moulded drawers is known before 1730. Brasses are original.
BENINGBOROUGH, THE NATIONAL TRUST

The scarcity of folding-top chests with ball feet and half-round or double-bead carcase mouldings suggests that they were not produced in great numbers before about 1720, and most examples have cockbeaded or lip-moulded drawers which suggest a date after 1730. The example in **3:25** bears the trade label of William Old and John Ody, dating it before 1733. The carcase is second-phase work, and the cockbeaded drawers are among the earliest recorded occurrences of this feature. The chest in **3:26**, with ovolo-moulded drawers, is probably of about the same date. Both chests have coved base mouldings. Plate **3:27** has a thick-railed third-phase carcase and handles of a type introduced around 1740. The two top drawers are sham, and fitted writing drawers pull out to each side. This neat arrangement prevents the writing drawers being masked when the top is open.

Folding tops necessitated some modifications to carcase construction. It was possible to make the carcase in the usual way, apply mouldings around the edges of the top and simply fix a hinged leaf to these. But this was not very secure, since the hinges were screwed to the side mouldings, and these were only held by glue to the main carcase. A more robust construction was to make the top separately and fix it to the carcase by means of a tapered dovetail (**3:28**). The advantage of this was that the side mouldings, instead of being simply glued to the carcase, could be properly jointed to the top boards, thus making a firm fixing for the hinges. This method of construction can also be found on conventional chests of drawers.

Other Case Furniture

Plate 3:27. Chest with folding top (1740-60). Walnut on oak and deal. This is thick-railed, third-phase construction. Both top drawers are sham, allowing drawers to be housed in each side, one of which is fitted for writing. Brasses are original. FAIRFAX HOUSE, YORK

Plate 3:28. Sliding dovetail construction. This is the top of 3:32, constructed in solid mahogany. Veneered sliding dovetail tops were generally composed of two butt-jointed boards cleated at the ends.

109

Other Case Furniture

Plate 3:29. Chest with folding top (1730-50). Mahogany, oak and deal. A neat chest with cockbeaded drawers. Because of the relatively thin sides of solid mahogany, it is difficult to categorise this as either second or third-phase construction. However, the lack of a rail above the top drawer suggests a relatively early date, probably before 1750. Brasses are replaced.
Christie's Images Ltd 1997

Plate 3:30. Chest with folding top (1735-50). Mahogany, oak and deal. This is a third-phase carcase with lip-moulded drawers. In this case the rails are actually thicker than the carcase sides. Brasses are original.
Christie's Images Ltd 1997

Other Case Furniture

Mahogany chests of drawers began to be made in significant numbers from about 1730 (**3:29-31**). As with solid wainscot furniture, many mahogany chests do not fall easily into thin or thick-railed categories because the carcase sides, being usually of solid mahogany, tend to be made thinner than a veneered carcase. With the plainer mahogany chests there was a decided preference for ovolo-moulded drawers (**3:30**). It has already been remarked that the ovolo-mould was often worked in the solid within the perimeter of the drawer front, and the consequences of this are evident in the photograph of the chest of drawers by John Pardoe,[23] where a gap between the top of the drawer and the rail above has been exposed by wear of the drawer runners (**3:31**).

Plate **3:32** shows a chest with high quality brasses and unusual sledge feet. These are necessary to prevent the chest falling forward when the heavy solid mahogany top is opened.

Commodes

The contrast between the private and utilitarian nature of English chests of drawers and the French *commode*, which in the early eighteenth century developed into a high-status object for public rooms, is very marked.[24] There are, however, some English chests of drawers whose size, style and quality place them above the common run, and which might well have been intended for public rather than private rooms. Our difficulty in understanding how these relate to the French *commode*, and when commodes first emerged in England, is initially one of nomenclature. Among later eighteenth century furniture-makers 'commode' was usually a synonym for a bowed or serpentine-shaped front, but whether this was its meaning at an earlier date is open to question. In 1712 Thomas Roberts supplied the Royal Household with 'a wallnuttree Commode Chest of Drawers' at a cost of £5.10s.[25] We can only speculate on what form this took, but the cost suggests something rather modest. The 'walnut tree commode chest of drawers' in the 1722 inventory of Catherine Morgan of Teddington is also a mysterious object, but manifestly a piece of bedroom furniture.[26] The paucity of early references to commodes may partly be explained by the interchangeable roles of commodes and bureaux. The 'very fine large Wallnuttree Burrow Table and Drawers' supplied in 1716 at the enormous cost of £70 for the Princesses' Library at Hampton Court Palace may well have been a commode by another name.[27] Equally, the three 'very large Mohogany Chest[s] of Drawers' supplied by Benjamin Goodison to the Royal Palaces in 1737 could also have been what

Above left:
Plate 3:31. Chest of drawers (1740-48). This bears the trade label of John Pardoe, active between c.1717 and 1748. The thick-railed construction is obvious. Note the gaps between each drawer and the rail above caused by wear. This is revealed because the ovolo-moulded drawer edges do not overlap the rails.
COURTESY OF SOTHEBY'S

Above right:
Plate 3:32. Chest of drawers (1735-60). Mahogany, oak and deal. The brasses on this chest are of unusually high quality. The sledge feet are intended to stop the chest overbalancing when the heavy, solid mahogany top is opened.
PRIVATE COLLECTION

23. For John Pardoe see *DEFM* and Gilbert (1996), figs. 708-13.
24. For a discussion of the evolution of commodes in France and England see Wood (1994), pp. 1-38.
25. PRO LC 9/ 284.
26. Elmfield House (1722).
27. PRO, LC 9/286, f. 15.

Other Case Furniture

Plate 3:33. Chest of drawers or commode (1735-50). Mahogany, oak and deal. Chests of sufficient quality and presence to play a role in state or parade apartments were rare before 1740. This example is conceived in a typically massive neo-Palladian manner, replete with classical iconography. The brassware, however, is derived from baroque rather than Palladian design sources.
BENINGBOROUGH, THE NATIONAL TRUST

we now call commodes.[28] The pair of commode-tables made for Lady Burlington in 1735, which are discussed in more detail below (pages 124-125), were described in the 1770 inventory of Chiswick Villa as 'commodes', but both Lady Burlington and John Boson referred to them in 1735 as 'tables'.[29] One of the earliest references to a 'commode' in its formal, French sense occurs in the 1747 inventory of Cannons, where the State Bedchamber contained 'A most exquisite fine *Commode* of the very rare old raised *Japan*'. This was the only piece of case furniture in the room, and was valued for sale second-hand at the enormous sum of £25, more than twice the price of any other piece of case furniture in the house.[30]

The relative scarcity of surviving commodes, and the paucity of references to them in contemporary documents, suggests that the form had still to take hold among furniture makers and their patrons at large. There are, none the less, a number of impressive mahogany chests of drawers in the neo-Palladian style, probably dating from 1730 onwards, which can be regarded as commodes in the true sense, precursors of the fine English rococo commodes of the mid-eighteenth century (**3:33**).[31]

Chests on stands

In the late seventeenth century chests of drawers were often placed on a low stand or 'frame', usually with a drawer in it (**3:34**). The top of the chest, being low enough to be visible, was veneered. Chests of this sort continued to be made in the early eighteenth century. In 1714 Gerrit Jensen supplied a 'walnut chest of drawers on a frame' for Hatfield House, Hertfordshire, which was perhaps of this type.[32] The trade card of John Kendall, a Colchester furniture-maker, shows a later version, with a deep two-drawer base and squat scroll or cabriole feet (**3:35**). To modern eyes

28. PRO LC 5/48, f. 16.
29. Jackson-Stops (1985), p. 221; Rosoman (1986).
30. Cannons (1747).
31. A pair of these, with kneehole bureaux-tables en suite, was supplied to Rokeby Park, Yorkshire, in the 1730s and is now in the Royal Collection. Goodison's putative authorship of these commodes is discussed in *DEFM*.
32. Hatfield House, 3/179, Bills 475.

Other Case Furniture

Plate 3:34. Chest on frame (1700-1720). Walnut, deal and oak. This is probably a provincial piece, employing rather bland solid walnut for the sides and re-used linenfold panels for the drawer bottoms. It has second-phase drawers with through dovetails, suggesting an early 18th century date. Escutcheons are not original. Most of the handles are replacements, modelled on the surviving originals.
CANONS ASHBY, THE NATIONAL TRUST

Plate 3:35. Trade card of John Kendall (1726). Little is known of Kendall's career in Colchester, but he clearly aspired to fashionable furniture-making. The engraver has attempted to show that the chest is veneered and the sconce above it has a double-arched top fashionable in the 1720s. It is interesting that, although his card depicts a chest on stand, he calls it a 'chest of drawers'. This may explain the paucity of contemporary references to chests on stands.
COLCHESTER MUSEUMS

Other Case Furniture

Above left:
Plate 3:36. Chest on stand (1710-30). Walnut, deal and oak. Chests with low stands often look as though the legs have been cut short, but this example appears always to have had ball feet like this. PRIVATE COLLECTION

Above right:
Plate 3:37. Chest on stand (1710-30). Walnut on deal and oak. Details of construction are unrecorded, but it clearly has a first or second-phase carcase. Legs are apparently original. The full-skirted stance is typical of early chests on stands.
HY DUKE AND SON

the chest seems awkwardly proportioned, but numbers of chests on low stands of this type survive (**3:36**); these are often assumed to have been reduced in height, but Kendall's card suggests this might not be the case.

Chests on high stands of the kind shown in **3:37-39** are popularly associated with the 'William and Mary' style, but no securely dated pieces are known prior to 1700. Most surviving examples are characterised by second-phase carcase and drawer construction, half-round or double-bead carcase mouldings, and turned pillar legs. Pillar legs were still produced by London makers even in the 1720s; in 1725 John Gumley and James Moore supplied George I with '6 walnuttree pillars & Balls for the frame of a Chest', and in 1729 Elizabeth Gumley billed 'a neat Wallnuttree writing Desk on pillars'.[33] In North America high chests with pillar leg stands were made well into the 1730s, and the same was probably true of provincial England. However, pillar-leg chests with third-phase features such as cockbeaded or ovolo-moulded drawers are uncommon, which suggests that among fashionable furniture makers the pillar-leg stand was in decline by 1725-30. Mahogany examples also survive, although these are not common (**3:39**).

The change from low to high chests implied more than a concern for improved storage capacity, for it raised not only the height but the status of the chest, giving it a visible presence equal to other large case furniture. Plate **3:40** shows a rare contemporary sketch of a chest on cabriole-leg stand in the best bedchamber of William Stukeley's house at Grantham in 1729. The sketch demonstrates, if proof were needed, that this was a piece of bedroom furniture.

33. PRO LC 9/287.

Other Case Furniture

Above left:
Plate 3:38. Chest on stand (1710-40). Oak, ash and deal. This is a provincial joiner-made piece in wonderful condition. The face of the carcase and drawer fronts is solid oak with ash banding and mouldings. It has a framed and panelled back. Original brasses, locks and feet.
CANONS ASHBY, THE NATIONAL TRUST

Above right:
Plate 3:39. Chest on stand (1730-50). Mahogany, oak and deal. Mahogany chests on stands are not common. The cockbeaded carcase suggests a date of c.1730 or later, as does the brassware, which is original. ARTHUR BRETT & SONS

Left:
Plate 3:40. The four sides of the best bedchamber, Grantham (1729). Watercolour, by William Stukeley. This sketch shows a chest on stand with coved cornice *in situ* in Stukeley's bedchamber. The stand has no drawer, and many similar pieces have now probably been converted to ordinary chests of drawers. BODLEIAN LIBRARY

Other Case Furniture

Plate 3:41. Chest on stand (1715-40). This chest has a double-bead carcase moulding, suggesting an early date, but the flush surbase moulding probably puts it after 1730. The brasses are of a type popular 1720-40.

BENINGBOROUGH, THE NATIONAL TRUST

Plate 3:42. Chest on stand (1730-45). Walnut on deal and oak. This chest has ovolo-moulded drawers, probably dating it to after 1730, but retains the old-style projecting surbase moulding, giving the piece a full-skirted appearance. Well figured veneers and a nicely detailed cornice are indications of quality. APTER-FREDERICKS

Analogies with seat furniture suggest that cabriole-leg stands for chests might have been introduced about 1715, and many chests with cabriole-leg bases have conventional second-phase construction with either half-round or double-bead carcase mouldings (**3:41**). Most are relatively unsophisticated in design and construction, suggesting provincial work, and it is possible that the form was unpopular with London furniture makers. Documented or labelled examples by London makers are scarce, nor are chests on stands mentioned on London trade cards or furniture-makers' bills.[34] This may be a question of terminology; John Kendall's trade card seems to imply that a chest on stand might routinely be described as just a chest of drawers. Support for this notion comes from the *Prices of Cabinet and Chair Work* published in Philadelphia in 1772. Here chests on stands or 'high chests of drawers' were still commonly made and even those with one or more drawers in the lower frame were simply described as 'chests of drawers'.[35] Similarly, Chippendale's *Gentleman and*

---

34. The author has seen a third-phase chest on stand with its legs missing bearing the trade label of Joachim Falck, a cabinet-maker in Southwark. For more on Falck see *DEFM* (1986) and Gilbert (1996), fig. 328.
35. Kirtley (2005), p. 5.

Other Case Furniture

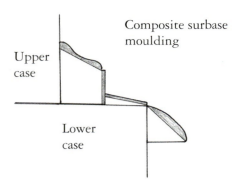

Plate 3:43. Surbase moulding (1700-1730). This style of projecting surbase moulding is common to most two-part case furniture made before 1725-30. Although the upper section of the moulding was nominally the base moulding for the upper case, in practice it was usually attached to the lower carcase. The projecting moulding was superseded by the less vulnerable flush moulding from c.1725 onwards.

Plate 3:44. Chest on stand (1745-65). Walnut on oak and deal. Thick-railed carcase and rococo-style handles clearly point to a date after c.1740 and perhaps as late as the 1760s. APTER-FREDERICKS

Cabinet-Maker's Director (1754) included engravings of a chest on drawers, a chest on chest and a chest on stand, each described simply as a 'Chest of Drawers'. A chest on chest or 'double chest of drawers' might also be called just 'a chest of drawers'; in a newspaper advertisement of 1736, the Norwich cabinet-maker William Gillman offered to raffle a 'Beautiful and Genteel Chest of Walnut-Tree Draws of Eight Guineas Value, commonly called a Chest upon Chest'.[36]

The projecting waist moulding shown in **3:41-43** is an early feature which gradually went out of use in the late 1720s and early 1730s. As with other case furniture, the transition from thin to thick-railed carcase construction is also usually a good indicator of a late date. In the case of **3:44** this is corroborated by the handles, which are unlikely to date from before 1750.

36. Stabler (2006).

Other Case Furniture

Plate 3:45. Double chest of drawers (1715-30). Walnut on deal and oak. Inscribed in a drawer by William Palleday, who worked at the *Crown* in Aldermanbury between c.1713 and c.1740. This is a rare early double chest in wonderful condition. Brasses and locks are original, the feet are replaced but modelled on the original pattern. The three-drawer configuration at the top relates to the same arrangement on chests on stands.
PRIVATE COLLECTION

Plate 3:46. Double chest of drawers (1730-45). Walnut on oak and deal. A good example of a second-phase double chest with ovolo-moulded drawers and angled corners. The coved bottom drawer is probably intended to reduce damage to the base moulding when the writing drawer is being used. Brasses are original.
REINDEER ANTIQUES

Double chests of drawers

The chest on chest or 'double chest of drawers' was a Georgian innovation. The earliest known description of such an article occurs in a bill submitted by Gumley and Turing for furniture supplied to Kensington Palace in 1727: 'for a very neat double Chest of Drawers wth Wallnuttree Doors… £15.0.0'.[37] The high price suggests something out of the ordinary, and as it was enclosed by doors it cannot have looked much like the chest on chest with which we are now familiar. Nevertheless, the double chest had certainly entered the repertoire of London furniture makers by the 1720s. In July 1729 the stock-in-trade of Elijah Chupain was sold off, including '… Mahogany and Walnut-tree double Chests, with a Desk in them or without; quadrille Tables, fine Writing-Tables, Spring Tables, dining, Right, Corner, Square and other Tables…'.[38] A few years later the stock in trade of Francis Croxford, sold in July 1733, included 'fine walnut-tree chests upon chests…'.[39]

The double chest superseded the chest on stand by virtue of its more robust design and better use of space, but the transition was probably a gradual one. Early examples, with second-phase construction and ball feet, are rare. The one shown in **3:45** is inscribed by William Palleday, scion of a long established London furniture-making family.[40] The chest has second-phase construction throughout, suggesting a date of c.1710-30. A virtually identical double chest bearing the trade label of Samuel Butt is shown in 1:2.

37. PRO LC 9/ 287, f. 151.
38. *DEFM*.
39. *DEFM*.
40. For more on Palleday see *DEFM* and page 14 above.

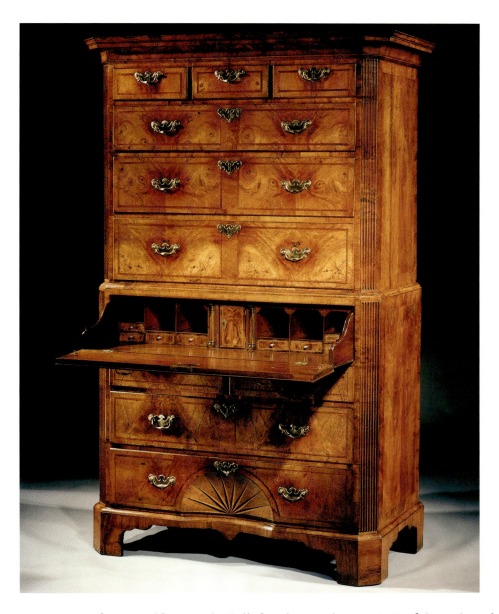

Plate 3:47. Double chest of drawers (1740-50). Walnut on oak and deal. This is a third-phase example with a thick-railed carcase and original brasses. APTER-FREDERICKS

The projecting surbase moulding on the Palleday chest is characteristic of the earliest double chests. From about 1730 it was gradually superseded by a flush moulding which was less vulnerable to damage, and there may be a correlation between this development and the abandonment of waist mouldings on desks and bookcases. In general, the abandonment of the waist moulding is associated with the adoption of cockbeaded and ovolo-moulded drawers from c.1730 onwards. A refinement introduced about the same time was to angle the corners of the upper case to reduce its visual bulk, at the same time endowing it with quasi-architectural reeded pilasters (**3:46**). The coved 'sunburst' decoration to the bottom drawer is usually an indication that the piece is fitted with a secretaire. The cove was presumably an attempt to minimise damage to the base moulding from a person seated or standing at the secretaire. The 'sunburst' style of inlay was not merely decorative; it disguised any flaws in the jointing between the sections of radially-orientated veneers on the coved section.

The basic form of double chest established in the 1730s continued essentially unaltered thereafter. There were many degrees of quality and complexity, ranging from the fitted secretaire chest with sunburst and angled pilasters on both upper and lower cases (**3:47**) to the

Other Case Furniture

Plate 3:48. Double chest of drawers (1740-60). Walnut on oak and deal. This chest labelled by Giles Grendey is typical of the plain but sound furniture made for stock by many London furniture makers. Its plainness is relieved only by a small quirk on the corners of the upper case. The veneers are well chosen and the construction exemplary. The thick-railed carcase suggests a date after c.1740. The handles are replaced.
PRIVATE COLLECTION

Plate 3:49. Double chest of drawers (1740-1748). Mahogany, oak and deal. This bears the trade label of John Pardoe. Like the previous piece it is plain but functional. Handles are replaced.
PHILLIPS

straightforward double chest without any elaboration shown in **3:48** and **3:49**, labelled by Giles Grendey and John Pardoe respectively.

Bureaux-tables

English references to 'buroes' or 'burows' first occur in the late seventeenth century and become increasingly common after 1700. They were an adaptation of the French *bureau*, a table with two banks of drawers flanking a central recess, and were used either as dressing/writing tables in bedchambers, dressing rooms and closets, or as writing tables. The trade card of Nash, Hall and Whitehorne, who traded from the *Royal Bed* in Holborn from about 1722 to 1749, depicts a bureau-table against a bed-chamber wall, with a mirror above (1:19). In this context, the bureau was certainly used as a dressing table, and some examples have their top drawers fitted with

Plate 3:50. Bureau-table (1700-1720). Black japanning on oak and deal. This bureau has a first-phase carcase and drawers, suggesting an early date. Note also the half-round carcase mouldings and ovolo-moulded top. CHRISTIE'S IMAGES LTD

Plate 3:51. Bureau-table (1719-c.1725). Walnut, oak and deal. This bears the trade label of Coxed and Woster. It is a typical 'transitional' piece, having a second-phase carcase with drawers with rebated bottoms and runners. Note the reverse-ogee top moulding, and the inset featherband on the drawers, which occurs here for the first time on a documented piece of furniture. The brasses are replaced, and ball feet were originally fitted.
COLONIAL WILLIAMSBURG FOUNDATION

compartments for the purpose. Others, however, were intended for writing. A very grand example made for the Princesses' Library at Hampton Court Palace in 1716, has already been cited above (page 111). Others made for the Royal Palaces cost as little as £4, which is only a fraction more than a common chest of drawers.[41] The multi-functional role of bureaux is also evident from domestic inventories. At Cannons the Duchess' dressing room contained 'A Dressing Buroe wth Drawers'.[42] In the Chintz Bed Chamber was both 'a wainscot dressing table' and 'a walnut-tree dressing buroe table', which tells us that the bureau was not the same as an ordinary dressing table.[43] It appears, therefore, that the term bureau described a particular form of furniture, with a kneehole flanked by drawers or cupboards, but not necessarily its function. In general they were placed in bedchambers and dressing rooms but not in saloons or parlours.[44]

Bureaux were sometimes made with pairs of stands en suite. In 1716 Gumley and Moore supplied 'a walnuttree Burrow Table and Stands' for Madame Kilmansegge's lodgings at Kensington at a cost of £8, and another set was supplied for Kensington in 1727.[45] Thus the bureau could also act as an updated version of the conventional 'triad' of table, stands and looking glass.

Plate **3:50** shows an early bureau-table, japanned black, with its original ball feet and brass furniture. The construction is first-phase work throughout, and the date perhaps 1700-1720. The essential difference between this and earlier bureaux is that the earlier type had a let-down writing surface and a top which folded half-way back to allow access to the interior. This rather unwieldy arrangement was replaced by a conventional drawer.

A slightly later version is shown in **3:51**. This bears the trade label of Coxed and Woster, and dates from between 1719 and c.1725.[46] It has a second-phase carcase and through-dovetailed drawers with rebated bottoms and runners. The conventional ovolo top moulding has been replaced by an ogee, and the inset featherband on the drawer fronts is another feature associated with the 1720s and later.

41. PRO LC9/284.
42. Cannons (1725).
43. Cannons Catalogue.
44. By the third quarter of the 18th century kneehole bureaux were no longer fashionable and the term bureau came to be applied to a slope-front desk, which meaning it retains today.
45. PRO, LC 9/286., ff. 15, 151.
46. Bowett and Lindey (2003).

Other Case Furniture

Plate 3:53. Detail of **3:52**, showing the construction of the ball-and-bracket foot.

Plate 3:52. Bureau-table (1720-30). Walnut on oak and deal. This is another transitional piece, having some old-fashioned features such as the ovolo-moulded top and half-round carcase mouldings, but with rebated drawer bottoms and ball-and-bracket feet. Brasses are not original.
PRIVATE COLLECTION

A rather atypical bureau is shown in **3:52**. Its drawers have lapped dovetails and rebated bottoms and runners, but it retains the old-style ovolo top moulding and half-round carcase mouldings. The ball-and-bracket feet are constructed by extending the carcase sides downwards to form the bracket (**3:53**). The ball feet are simply dowelled into supporting blocks, and the base moulding is omitted in favour of a rather perfunctory half-round bead.

By about 1730 the bureau-table had arrived at more or less its mature form. Plate **3:54** shows a bureau bearing the trade label of John Belchier which is typical of bureaux made in the 1730s. Similar pieces bearing the trade labels of Thomas Cleare, Giles Grendey and John Pardoe are known, and were it not for the labels it would be impossible to distinguish the output of one workshop from another.[47] Their good but unremarkable quality suggests that these were standard furnishing items, to be found in many Georgian households of the 'middling sort'. Plate **3:55** shows a neat example of a similar date but with cockbeaded drawers. Note that all the examples shown have the first drawer placed directly beneath the top, with no intervening rail.

The bureau-table by Elizabeth Bell, widow of Henry Bell and proprietor of the White Swan workshop between 1740 and c.1758, is virtually identical to the Belchier example, save for the later type thick-railed carcase (**3:56**).[48] It cannot be earlier than 1740 and the style of handle suggests a date in the late 1740s or early 1750s. Unlike the previous examples, this bureau has bracket feet on the outer corners only. The choice of two or four front brackets was presumably primarily determined by cost, but it may also have been the case that the inner brackets were increasingly omitted as being vulnerable to damage.

47. Gilbert (1996), figs. 71, 72, 213, 439 and 712.
48. *DEFM*.

Other Case Furniture

Right:
Plate 3:54. Bureau-table (1730-40), labelled by John Belchier. Walnut on oak and deal. This is a typical bureau of the 1730s, with lip-moulded drawers and thin-railed construction. The handles are original. CHRISTIE'S IMAGES LTD 1999

Below left:
Plate 3:55. Bureau-table (1730-40). Walnut on deal and oak. A nicely made example with original brasses. Note the thin-railed construction, suggesting a date before 1740. The difference in thickness between rails and carcase is not always so obvious. Feet are replaced.
BENINGBOROUGH HALL, THE NATIONAL TRUST

Below right:
Plate 3:56. Bureau-table (1740-58). Walnut on oak and deal. This bears the trade label of Elizabeth Bell and Sons. Elizabeth succeeded her husband Henry in 1740 and her son Philip succeeded her in or before 1758. APTER-FREDERICKS

123

Plate 3:57. Bureau-table (1730-40). Mahogany, oak and deal. A plain mahogany bureau with an obviously narrow-railed carcase. Brasses are original.

PRIVATE COLLECTION

Plate 3:58. Bureau-table (1730-50). Mahogany, oak and deal. Another plain example, this time with ovolo-moulded drawers worked in the solid. Brasses are original.

PRIVATE COLLECTION

As with other case furniture, mahogany bureaux-tables follow the same stylistic trends as walnut examples, with variations due to their construction from solid timber. On **3:57** the thin-railed construction is obvious, suggesting an early date, and the handles are of a pattern introduced about 1730. Plate **3:58** is probably slightly later, with a thick-railed carcase. The drawers are edged with ovolos worked out of the solid and not overlapping the rails.

Some bureaux-tables rise above the mundane. The pair made for Lady Burlington's Summer Parlour at Chiswick Villa in 1735 are probably the most stylistically ambitious to survive from this period (**3:59**). Indeed, when they were recorded in the 1770 inventory at Chiswick, they were described not as bureaux but 'Two Mahogany party gilt commodes', which raises them to a different level of importance.[49] This problem of nomenclature has already been alluded to. Lady Burlington herself described them merely as 'tables' in a letter of 1735,[50] and in form they resemble bureaux more than anything else. In mid-eighteenth century design sources, such as Chippendale's *Director* (1754) and Ince and Mayhew's *Universal System* (1759-62), bureaux-tables, bureaux dressing tables, commode tables and commode dressing tables are all very similar. This reinforces the impression that the distinction between them was essentially one of function.

The Burlington tables have been attributed to the carver John Boson, on the strength of a surviving bill 'for carving done for ye Honble lady Burlington' which includes 'two Rich Glas frames with folidge and other ornaments' at £15, and 'two Mahogany Tables with Tearms folidge and other Ornements' at £20.[51] However, although Boson's responsibility for the carving is clear, he was not a cabinet-maker; the furniture on which he worked was made by others. This is made explicit by the wording of the bill ('for carving done') and by another entry in the same bill, where two term stands were charged at £5 each, of which £1.16s. was to be paid to Mr Davis, the joiner who made them. The sum of £20 charged for the tables, which included carving 'modles for ye Brass work', is too small to account for their total cost. All the carved elements are independent of the main carcase, being carved separately and applied to it. While the maker of the tables remains

49. Rosoman (1986).
50. Jackson-Stops (1985), p. 221.
51. Jackson-Stops, (1985), p. 221; Rosoman (1985, 1986)
52. An attribution to Goodison was suggested by Geoffrey Beard, who later retracted this after the Boson's bill came to light. However, if my reasoning is correct, then Beard's initial attribution seems perfectly plausible (Beard (1977) and (1986), p. 1283). In an analogous case, Beard cites a bill for seat furniture made for the Earl of Tankerville's London house in 1731, for which the carver James Richards charged only £10.2.6. Beard comments on the 'modest cost', but it is probable that, like Boson, Richards was only charging for the carving (Beard 1986).
53. Illustrated in *DEF*, III, p. 244, figs 9 and 11.

Other Case Furniture

Plate 3:59. Bureau-table (1735). Mahogany, oak and walnut. This is one of a pair, almost certainly designed by William Kent and carved by John Boson. The cabinet-maker is unknown, but Benjamin Goodison is a possibility. These tables are exceptional in almost every respect. The carcases are of oak and mahogany, with walnut drawer linings. ©DEVONSHIRE COLLECTION, CHATSWORTH
REPRODUCED BY PERMISSION OF CHATSWORTH SETTLEMENT TRUSTEES

unknown, Benjamin Goodison must surely be a strong candidate. Two tables of similar form attributed to Goodison and made for Rokeby, Yorkshire, survive in the Royal Collection, and Goodison is known to have worked in association with William Kent on other occasions.[52] The brasses whose patterns or 'modles' were carved by Boson may also have been designed by Kent; they reflect the design of the painted cartouches in the ceiling of the Summer Parlour (**3:60**).

Writing bureaux

Bureaux were also associated with libraries or studies, although less commonly than with bed and dressing chambers. In the Yellow Damask Room next to the great Library at Cannons was 'A large Grenoble walnut-tree buroe-desk on castors, with brass mouldings and handles, double folding doors and 12 drawers'. This is clearly what would later be called a writing or library table. At Houghton Hall there is a mahogany bureau made for Sir Robert Walpole which is modelled closely on the French bureau Mazarin, and in the Pepys' Library at Magdalene College, Cambridge, is an earlier wainscot example of more typically English form.[53] Another bureau reputedly made for Sir Robert Walpole in veneered walnut is now at Sir John Soane's Museum.

Plate **3:61** shows a large bureau almost certainly intended for writing. It has unusual bracket feet and it is fitted with castors made with a hand-forged iron plate and armature and a wooden

Plate 3:60. Detail of 3:61. Gilt brass escutcheon, from a model carved by John Boson. Bespoke brassware such as this was very much more expensive than 'off the shelf' brass-founders' ware. It required the personal attention of a designer (Kent?), a carver (Boson), a pattern maker, a brass founder and a gilder. There are significant similarities between the brassware on the Burlington tables and that on the Rokeby commodes.

Plate 3:61. Bureau or writing table (1730-40). Walnut, oak and deal. The greater width of this bureau suggests it was intended for use in a library or study/closet. The feet are highly unusual, but other examples are known. PRIVATE COLLECTION

125

Other Case Furniture

Plate 3:63. Bureau or writing table (1735-50). Mahogany, oak and deal. A number of large, architecturally conceived bureaux like this are known. In this case its size and the leather-lined top clearly suggest library or office use. Carved half-round carcase mouldings between the drawers are archaic, but emphasise the architectural quality of the piece and tie it in with the internal architecture of the library for which it was made. One of a pair, probably made for Gosfield Hall, Essex. CHRISTIE'S IMAGES LTD 2002

Plate 3:62. Castor (1730-40). Detail of 3:61. Large bureaux and commodes were often fitted with castors, and at this early date they were often hand-made of wrought iron, rather than cast brass. The roller is wooden.

roller (**3:62**). Plate **3:63** shows a mahogany example of emphatically architectural form, one of a pair probably made for the library at Gosfield Hall, Essex.[54] The pattern of the brassware suggests a date in the 1730s, which coincides with the remodelling of the hall from 1736 onwards. By this time the half-round carcase mouldings were in theory rather old-fashioned, but in this case they were used to strengthen the architectural quality of the desk and tie it in with the architectural woodwork of the library itself. Other mahogany desks of a similar architectural form are known, including one at Temple Newsam House, thought to have been made for the 6th Viscount Irwin.[55]

It is a moot point when such articles cease to be bureaux and become writing or library tables. At Montagu House in 1746 there was 'a Mahogany writing Table with Drawers in it and Covered with black Leather & Castors to D°'.[56] Having drawers and castors, this was probably of bureau form (we might now call it a pedestal desk), but was not considered a bureau. Similarly, the large pedestal desks in Chippendale's *Director* (1754) were called 'writing tables', whereas smaller dressing tables of a similar form were called 'buroes'. The distinction seem to be one of both size and function; it is also possible that there was a semantic shift about the middle of the eighteenth century, when what were originally bureaux became writing tables.

Corner cupboards

Corner cupboards are among the most common items of domestic furniture surviving from the eighteenth century, and were found in households at all levels of society. Their origins are obscured by an uncertain nomenclature which hints at the emergence of a hitherto unknown furniture type. In 1691 Gerrit Jensen submitted a bill to the Lord Chamberlain 'For making up two corner shelves of Jappan with doors to them… £4.0.0.', for Kensington Palace.[57] This sounds very like a pair of corner cupboards in all but name. In 1700 Jensen submitted another bill 'for polishing a corner cupboard in the late Queen's Apartment at Kensington'.[58] This is probably the earliest known use of the term. It is tempting to speculate that the cupboard was used by Queen Mary

---

54. Bonhams, London, 13 March 2007, lot 33.
55. Gilbert (1998), No. 829.
56. Montagu House (1746).
57. PRO, LC 9/280, f. 44
58. PRO LC 9/281.

Other Case Furniture

Plate 3:64. Corner cupboard (1710-40). Japanning on deal and oak. This small corner cupboard retains most of its original japanning, and the brassware is also original. However, it originally had two shelves on top, not one. The half-round door moulding suggests an early date. Note the left-hand figure holding a wine glass by the foot, in the Georgian manner. Definitely not a Chinaman. PRIVATE COLLECTION

(d.1694) to store or display some of her famous collection of porcelain. An inventory of Kensington Palace drawn up the same year records 'two india Jappan corner cubborts with blacke carved feet' in the Queen's Bedchamber.[59] These were almost certainly the 'corner shelves' supplied by Jensen in 1691 and, having feet, were free-standing rather than hanging. Another early reference occurs in the 1703 inventory of Dyrham, where in Madam Blathwayt's Room there was 'a Corner Looking glass Cubbord', presumably with a mirrored door.[60]

From 1715 onwards corner cupboards are mentioned in the Lord Chamberlain's accounts with greater frequency. In 1716 Gumley and Moore made 'a fine walnuttree Corner Cupboard for her Royall Highnesse the princess of Wales Bedchamber at St James'.[61] In 1721 they made 'a Wallnutree Corner Cupboard with a Glass Door' costing £4.10s. and 'a Japan'd Corner Cupboard' at £2.[62] The first reference to a bowfronted cupboard occurs in 1729, when Benjamin Goodison supplied 'a large wallnuttree Corner Cupboard with Compass Doors' for £2.2s.[63]

The stock-in-trade of furniture-makers at large reflects a similar progression from scarcity to abundance in the first thirty years of the eighteenth century. The earliest public reference to come to light occurs in *The Post-man* of 8-10 March 1711/2, when Isaac van den Helme advertised corner cupboards for sale. In December 1720 *The Daily Courant* advertised '... a Parcel of fine Goods... the stock of Richard Jones; at the Sign of the Japan Cabinet near King Edward's Stairs in Wapping, he leaving off his Trade: The Goods consisting of very fine Japan Cabinets, Desks, and Book-Cases, Chests of Drawers, Japan and Wallnut, likewise plain Wainscot, and fine Japan Trunks, Beaufets, Corner Cupboards, Looking-Glasses and Sconces &c.'. In October 1724 Anne Alden disposed of stock including 'very large and fine Corner Cupboards, or ordinary ones...'.[64]

Many surviving early cupboards are japanned, and this may be no accident. One of the most common functions of corner cupboards was to house the cups, saucers, bowls and pots associated with tea drinking, so that the beverage, its equipage and the cupboard were connected by a common Oriental theme. In the Eating Parlour at Erddig in 1726 there was a 'conner cubberd' containing china placed over or near a 'Tea Table' with six china teacups on it.

Black, red, blue and green were the most common colours for japanned cupboards.[65] Some early cupboards have graduated shelves on top, mimicking the tiered shelving on corner chimney pieces used to display porcelain or other blue and white ware (**3:64**). Corner cupboards might also be found in dressing rooms, as at Erddig, where in one was a 'blew Japan connered cubard,' and in another a 'walnutree connered cubbard' was placed over a 'walnutree connered table'.[66] At Chandos

59. *DEF* (1954), II, p. 175.
60. Dyrham (1703).
61. PRO, LC 5/45.
62. PRO.LC 9/287, f. 117.
63. PRO LC 9/288, f. 35.
64. *DEFM*.
65. Many blue cupboards now appear green because of the yellowing of the varnish. The same is true of other blue japanned articles, such as clock cases.
66. Erddig (1726).

Other Case Furniture

Plate 3:65. Corner cupboard (1710-40). Japanning on deal and oak. Another early example. The mirrored door would have made it considerably more expensive than the previous example. The arched top relates to those on contemporary cabinets and desks-and-bookcases.
AVON ANTIQUES

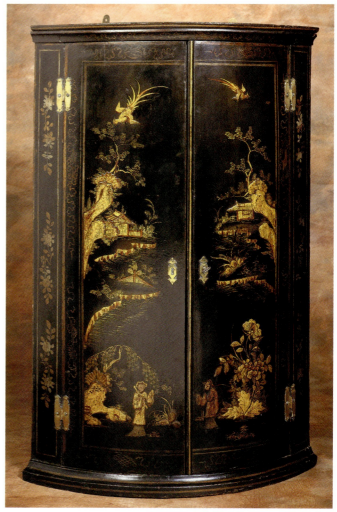

Plate 3:66. Corner cupboard (1720-40). Japanning on deal and oak. This bears the trade label of John Belchier, who worked in St Paul's Churchyard from 1717. The plain bow-fronted form is one of the commonest to survive.
LENNOX CATO

House in London in 1725 there was in her Grace's closet 'a Corner Cupboard wth Looking:glass doors' valued at £1.10s., perhaps similar to the one shown in **3:65**.[67]

Although the tiered shelves on top of the cupboard tended to go out of use later in the century, their form otherwise changed very little. Those with half-round or double bead mouldings around the door are probably early (perhaps before 1740). The example in **3:66** bears the trade label of John Belchier, and probably dates from the 1730s.

Standing corner cupboards seem to have been less common at this period than they became later in the eighteenth century, and were sometimes described as 'buffets'. These were free-standing versions of the built-in buffet found in the parlours and dining rooms of many Georgian houses. The buffet was a receptacle for eating and drinking equipage and a station from which food and drink could be served. Some were fitted with hinged tables which could be brought into use when the doors were open.[68] Just as built-in buffets were conceived as part of the architectural fabric of the room, so standing corner cupboards were frequently architectural in character, with correctly modelled cornice, architrave and base, and often with pilasters to each side. The walnut example in

---

67. Chandos (1725).
68. Buffets of this form are shown in the Gillows Estimate Sketch books, and a number of Gillows' examples are known to survive complete with their folding tables. See also Gow (1994).

Other Case Furniture

Left:
Plate 3:67. Corner cupboard or buffet (1730-50). Walnut, deal and oak. This richly decorated corner cupboard is veneered in a similar manner to the pulpits and altarpieces in the 'Queen Anne' churches, and may be the work of a joiner rather than a cabinet-maker. The glass is modern and the piece may originally have had a panelled rather than a glazed door.   CHRISTIE'S IMAGES LTD 2001

Below:
Plate 3:68. Standing corner cupboard (1746). Mahogany, oak and deal. This high quality piece combines an architectural form with rich carved detail similar to that found on other fine mahogany case furniture. It is stamped ' I. RICHARDS 1746'.   PRIVATE COLLECTION

3:67 has numerous affinities with the sort of joiner's work seen in the 'Queen Anne' churches of 1715-30, where the pulpits and altar-pieces are veneered with similar parquetry with 'sunburst' decoration to the heads of the niches. The mahogany cupboard in **3:68** is rather more sophisticated, with all mouldings beautifully and correctly detailed. It is stamped by an otherwise unknown furniture maker – I RICHARDS – and dated 1746.

Other Case Furniture

Plate 3:69. Press (1710-30). Walnut, oak and deal. This is an early example of what became a standard configuration for a clothes press. Ball, feet, prominent surbase moulding and half-round carcase mouldings all suggest a date before 1730. The upper case has sliding shelves, rather than trays. Drawer handles and feet not original. BONHAMS

Plate 3:70. Press (1730-40). Walnut, oak and deal. A very high quality press with carcase cockbeads, suggesting a date of c.1730. As with the previous example, the interior has shelves rather than trays, which is characteristic of early presses. Brasses are original.

PRIVATE COLLECTION

Clothes presses

A press was by definition a piece of storage furniture enclosed by doors, which might be fitted or free-standing. Depending on their location in the house, presses might contain china, glass, cooking ware or soft furnishings. Clothes presses are recorded in some early eighteenth century inventories but were apparently not common for, as we have seen (pages 94-96), clothes and linen were usually stored in chests. At Montagu House in 1709 there were clothes presses in several bedrooms in the attic storey but not in principal bedchambers or dressing rooms.[69] In the Duke of Montagu's much larger country house at Boughton there were only two presses tucked away in obscure chambers and at Dyrham Park in 1710 there were none.[70] Other houses had presses that were built in and therefore not recorded as part of the movable furniture. In Catherine Morgan's house in Teddington in 1724

---

69. Montagu House (1709).
70. Boughton (1709); Walton (1986).

Plate 3:71. Clothes press (1730-40). Walnut, oak and deal. Another fine quality press, with a nicely detailed cornice and projecting waist moulding. The glass in the doors is modern, and it is conceivable that the doors were originally panelled rather than mirrored. Brasses are original but the feet have been cut short.
MONTACUTE, THE NATIONAL TRUST

there was 'a walpres for clothes' on the top floor, which sounds very like a built-in feature, but none of the bedrooms below had presses. The press made by Richard Roberts for St James's Palace in 1723 might have been something similar: 'a large wainscot press for Cloths… £9.00'.[71] The general impression is that free-standing presses were not as common at this time than later in the century, and this explains the relative scarcity of surviving examples.

Unlike earlier joined 'hanging' presses, in which clothes were hung from pegs, cabinet-makers' presses contained trays or shelves on which clothes could be stored folded. The press in **3:69** is an early example, fitted with shelves in the upper case and a chest of drawers below. The projecting surbase moulding and double-bead carcase mouldings suggest a date before 1730. An early reference to this two-part design occurs in one of Gumley and Moore's bills for 1725: 'for a Wallnuttree Press wth folding Doors & Shelves above and Drawers below… £35.0.0'. The bill records that the press was for 'his Maty's Body Linnen at Windsor'.[72] The example in **3:70** is of the same configuration. A more ambitious example of about the same date is shown in **3:71**. Both are of exemplary quality. A common characteristic of all these early presses is that they had shelves rather than sliding trays. It appears that trays were a later introduction, probably devised to improve ease of access.

Bookcases

The history of English domestic bookcases traditionally begins in 1666, with a discussion between Samuel Pepys and Simpson the Joyner; 'And then comes Simpson the Joyner, and he and I with great pains contriving presses to put my books up in; they now growing numerous, and lying one upon another on my chairs…'.[73] The glazed oak presses, eventually twelve in number, survive at Magdalene College, Cambridge. Pepys used the word 'press' rather than 'bookcase' to describe his furniture, and this was the usual term until the beginning of the eighteenth century. A pair of very similar bookcases, originally made for Pepys' friend Thomas Povey and sold to William Blathwayt of Dyrham Park, were recorded in Dyrham's Library in the 1703 and 1710 inventories as 'Two Glass Presses wth Books'.[74] By this time, however, the word 'bookcase' was certainly current, as in the phrase 'desk-and-bookcase', and it might also have been applied to bookcases on their own. In *The Daily Courant* of 14 January 1716/17, Philip Arbuthnot advertised 'all Sorts of Looking Glasses, Glass Pannels and sconces, Cabinets both English and Japan, Scrutores, Tables, Stands, Writing Desks, Book Cases, Card Tables, Dressing Suits and Chests of Drawers both of Japan and Wallnut-tree; likewise carved and Gilded Sconces, and all sorts of China, Tea Tables, Screens and Fire-Screens, Oyl Pictures, Strong Boxes…'.[75] In 1717 Gumley and Moore supplied 'a fine Book Case on a Walnuttree frame with a Glass Door' for the Princesses' Library at Hampton Court Palace.[76] From the 1720s the term 'press' was used increasingly rarely in relation to glazed bookcases.

71. PRO, LC 9/286, f. 63.
72. LC 9/286, f. 82.
73. Pepys, *Diary*, 23 July 1666.
74. Gloucestershire Record Office, D1799/E254; Walton (1986).
75. *DEFM*.
76. PRO LC 9/286, f. 15.

Other Case Furniture

Plate 3:72. Bookcase (1710-30). Walnut, deal and oak. This is a rare piece, although documentary evidence suggests that bookcases on frames or stands were not uncommon. The half-round glazing bars are typical of this early period.
PRIVATE COLLECTION

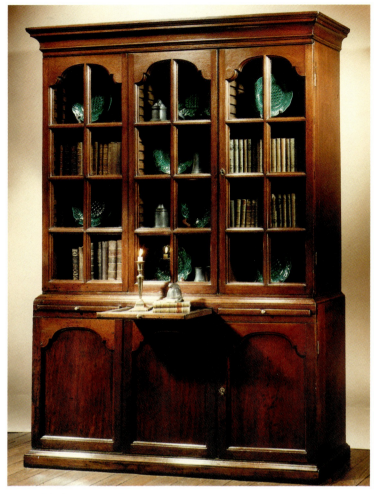

Plate 3:74. Bookcase (1710-40). Oak. A well-made wainscot bookcase whose proportions and stylistic details, such as the arched doors and thick glazing bars, suggest a relatively early date. The slides are practical features. ADAMS ANTIQUES

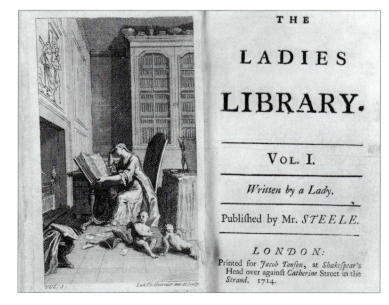

Plate 3:73. *The Ladies' Library* (1714), frontispiece. Aside from the bookcase with its fashionable arched doors, this engraving is full of period detail. Note the china on top of the bookcase, the pillar-and-claw reading stand, and the swing glass standing on a dressing table covered by a cloth or 'toilette'. Behind the reading stand there appears to be a desk with its fall open. JEROME PHILLIPS

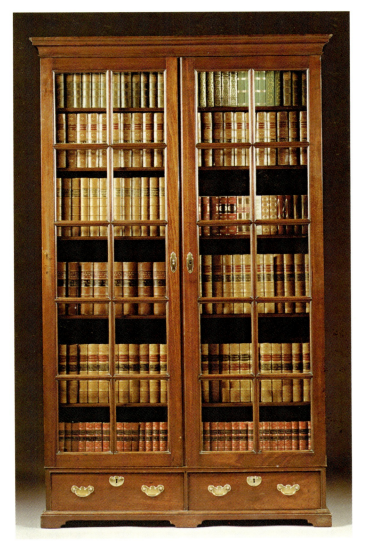
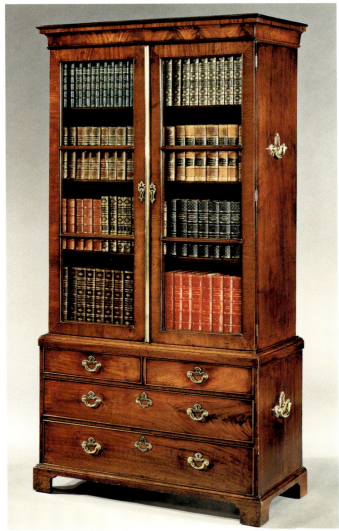

Gumley and Moore's bookcase on a frame may have looked something like the one in **3:72**. More commonly, bookcases have enclosed bases with cupboards or drawers in them. One such is shown in the frontispiece of *The Ladies' Library*, published in 1714, with the fashionable addition of arched glazing to the doors (**3:73**). An oak bookcase made on very similar lines is shown in **3:74**. It is interesting to note from the engraving that the shelves are not aligned with the glazing bars, and the strip of cloth or leather tacked to the leading edge of the shelves to exclude dust is clearly visible. Some bookcases reveal evidence of having had cloth pinned to the inside of the doors, perhaps to exclude dust or sunlight, but it is not clear whether this was fitted by the maker or subsequently by the owner.

Mahogany bookcases appear to have been more common than walnut ones. This is possibly because bookcases were often considered to be a piece of joinery rather than cabinet-work, so that the choice was usually not between mahogany and walnut but between mahogany and wainscot. The example shown in **3:75** is probably early, with carcase cockbeads and handles of a pattern introduced about 1730. The relatively thick glazing bars are typical of this early type. A little later in date is the example in **3:76**. The handles are a pattern probably dating from after 1740, and the drawer fronts, door framing and cornice are all veneered. The effect is decorative, but it also suggests some economy in the use of wood.

Above left:
Plate 3:75. Bookcase (1730-40). Mahogany, oak and deal. The carcase cockbeads and thick glazing bars suggest an early date. Handles are of a pattern introduced about 1730.
COURTESY OF SOTHEBY'S

Above right:
Plate 3:76. Bookcase (1740-60). Mahogany, oak and deal. Bookcases of this simple form were probably made in large numbers and over a very long period. The brassware suggests a date after 1740.
RONALD PHILLIPS LTD, LONDON

Other Case Furniture

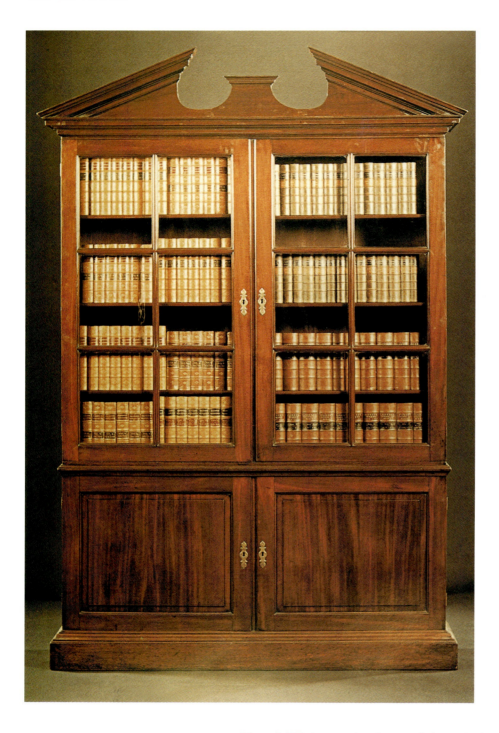

Left:
Plate 3:77. Bookcase (1730-50). Mahogany, oak and deal. This bears the trade label of John Belchier. It is a plain workmanlike piece given presence and status by the architectural pediment. COURTESY OF SOTHEBY'S

Below:
Plate 3:78. Ionick Book Case (1739). Engraving from Batty Langley, *The City and Country Builder's and Workman's Treasury of Designs,* published in 1740. Langley's designs for bookcases were strongly architectural, reflecting both his joiner's training and his penchant for neo-Palladian forms. Because of their large size and because they were often fitted into the internal architecture of the house, bookcases lent themselves to robust architectural interpretations.

Plate **3:77** shows a bookcase of about 1730-50 bearing the trade label of John Belchier. Its strongly architectural form emphasises the link between bookcases and interior joinery. This link was strengthened by the advent of neo-Palladianism. Batty Langley's *City and Country Builder's and Workman's Treasury of Designs* (1740) include bookcases in the Tuscan, 'Dorick' and 'Ionick' styles, all with a powerfully architectural character (**3:78**). This is perhaps another reason for the predominance of mahogany rather than walnut, for solid mahogany was capable of expressing mass and substance in a way that veneered walnut could not. The double-pedimented example in **3:79** is taken almost directly from plate CLXII of Langley's *Treasury*.

Other Case Furniture

Plate 3:79. Bookcase (1740-60). Mahogany, oak and deal. The design for this bookcase appears to have been taken from plate CLXII of Langley's *Treasury*. It was originally fitted as part of a run of bookcases in a library. CHRISTIE'S IMAGES LTD 2005

Other Case Furniture

Plate 3:80. Bookcase (1740). Indian rosewood, brass, oak and deal. This is one of a pair supplied to Powderham Castle in Devon bearing a brass plaque engraved '17 J. CHANNON 40'. Scholarly attention was for many years side-tracked by a raised plinth with dolphin-carved feet which was discovered in 1993 to be a later addition. This photograph shows the bookcase in its original form. Although initially identified as being veneered with padouk (*Pterocarpus* spp.), subsequent work on veneer samples at Temple Newsam House has revealed it to be Indian rosewood (*Dalbergia latifolia*).
VICTORIA AND ALBERT MUSEUM

The best known of these architectural bookcases is the pair made in 1740 by John Channon for Powderham Castle, Devon (**3:80**).⁷⁷ These have attracted a good deal of attention from furniture historians because of their overbearing architectural form and profuse Berainesque brass inlay, a combination which was perceived as somehow un-English and more typical of contemporary German baroque.⁷⁸ However, recent scholarship has unearthed a considerable body of high status, brass inlaid English furniture within which Channon's bookcases sit quite comfortably.⁷⁹ The design source for the bookcase was probably plate 27 of Isaac Ware's *Designs of Inigo Jones and others* (1733), combined with the frontispiece of Palladio's *Second Book of Architecture* as reprinted by Ware in 1738.⁸⁰

Of course, in many houses the bookcases were not free standing, but were considered fitments and sometimes not recorded in inventories. Their presence can only be inferred from the other furnishings of the rooms (library steps, for instance) and from the presence of the books themselves. One exception is the Kiveton inventory, which recorded a 'Large Wallnut Book Case wᵗʰ Glass Doors fixd' in the North East Closet. On the other hand it is not clear whether the '2 Wainscot Book Cases, glaz'd Dʳˢ Brass hinges & Locks' in the Library were 'fixed' i.e., built in, or not.⁸¹ At Cannons the Great Library contained eighteen walnut-tree bookcases of various configurations, some with mirrored doors, others with brass wire doors. Some were 'low', some raised on a frame, and some with three drawers in the bottom. Were these built in or free standing? There was, in addition, a small library furnished with seven bookcases all with mirrored doors. A fine run of fitted bookcases in wainscot and elm, probably installed in 1747, survives at Burton Constable in Yorkshire.

Cabinets

Cabinets are cited on furniture-makers' trade labels well into the eighteenth century, and are also depicted on trade cards of the period, but their status as masterpieces of the furniture-maker's art was substantially eroded by the desk-and-bookcase, which combined the showiness of the cabinet with the practicality of the scriptor, threatening both with redundancy. Desks-and-bookcases tended to be placed in bedchambers, dressing rooms and closets, exactly the places occupied by cabinets in the late seventeenth century. The similarity in status and function is highlighted by the Erddig inventory of 1726, in which the two japanned desks-and-bookcases still at Erddig were described as 'cabinates'.⁸² The relative decline in importance of cabinets over the century is illustrated by the casual way they are described in Sheraton's *Cabinet Dictionary*:

> [Cabinet] is applied to those curious and neat pieces of furniture, used by ladies, in which to preserve their trinkets, and other curious matters.
>
> The cabinets of gentlemen, consist in ancient medals, manuscripts, and drawings &c. with places fitted up for some natural curiosities.⁸³

While their function as repositories of precious objects and curiosities remained, their predominant status in furniture-making had lapsed. There were exceptions, however. Oriental lacquer cabinets retained their luxury cachet throughout the eighteenth century, and continued to be placed on stands in the seventeenth century manner (**3:81**). In this respect it may be significant that most of the cabinets depicted on trade cards are either lacquered or japanned, on carved stands.⁸⁴ There was also a continuing role for imported European cabinets. There were agents in London who dealt in Continental pictures and furnishings, such as William Hubert, an emigré Frenchman whose stock was sold off in 1735. It included a '... Great Variety of most Beautiful Florence and French Cabinets, inlaid with Oriental Agates, Mocos, Jaspers, Bloodstones and Lapis

Plate 3:81. Cabinet on stand (1725-45). This is one of a pair, probably the property of Samuel Shepheard, M.P. (d.1748), a very wealthy London merchant. The cabinet is Japanese, c.1660-80, and the stand is English; both parts are of superb quality. The Renaissance masks at the top of the legs are in the guise of 'green men' of the forest while in the centre is the mask of Diana the huntress.

TEMPLE NEWSAM HOUSE,
LEEDS CITY ART GALLERIES

77. John Channon (1711-79) was the son of an Exeter joiner. He was established in St Martin's Lane from 1737 to 1779. For more on this maker see *DEFM* and Gilbert and Murdoch (1993).
78. Hayward (1965); Gilbert & Murdoch (1993), pp. 5-12 *et passim*; Wilk (1996), pp. 90-91.
79. Gilbert and Murdoch (1993).
80. Bowett (November 2002).
81. Kiveton (1727).
82. Erddig (1726).
83. Sheraton (1803), I, p. 115,
84. See, for instance, the trade cards of John Hodson, John Knowles, John Pardoe, John Price, John Townsend, Stephen Wood. For these see Heal (1955) and Gilbert (1996).

Other Case Furniture

Left:
Plate 3:82. Cabinet on chest (1715-30). Black and gold japanning on deal and oak. Second-phase carcase and main drawers with original brassware. This carcase bears the stamp RF, which also occurs on the japanned desk-and-bookcases at Erddig (2:16). If those are from the workshop of John Belchier, then this may be too. CHRISTIE'S IMAGES LTD 2001

Opposite:
Plate 3:83. Cabinet on chest, open. The interior layout of the upper case differs markedly from the 17th century format, most obviously in the absence of a central cupboard. The secretaire drawer is also an 18th century innovation. CHRISTIE'S IMAGES LTD 2001

Lazuli etc...'.[85] Some of these were probably second-hand, and many English country house collections include seventeenth century Italian, French or Antwerp cabinets on eighteenth century English stands. Englishmen also bought cabinets abroad. The most spectacular example of these was the astonishing Badminton Cabinet, commissioned in Florence by the 3rd Duke of Beaufort in 1726 and delivered four years later in August 1732.[86]

Just as some pieces of furniture, such as chests of drawers, are typical of middle-class urban households, so cabinets do not usually appear in any but high status inventories. In some houses these might be survivors of the seventeenth century furnishings, but in newly built houses we might assume the cabinets were also new. At Sherborne House in 1726 there were four cabinets in various upstairs rooms, three of them described as 'Indian', of which one stood on a gold frame.[87] At Blenheim in 1740 there were eight cabinets (four walnut and four lacquered) of which seven were in rooms on the principal floor. The Duke and Duchess of Marlborough had a cabinet each in their bedchambers. The Duke's was described as a 'large Walnut tree Cabinet with Drawers & Looking Glass Doors', a description which could conceivably apply to a grand desk-and-bookcase. The Duchess had 'An Indian Japan Cabinet with a Gilt Frame very fine and much larger than the Common Size'. The State Bedchamber and the room next to it both had large lacquered cabinets on gilt frames.[88] At Cannons there were four cabinets, relatively few for such a large and rich house, but there were also a number of fine desks-and-bookcases which performed a similar function.[89]

By way of contrast, cabinets occur in a minority of metropolitan inventories. This was partly a question of money, since cabinets were expensive, but perhaps also of class and attitude. The Orphans' Court Records contain the inventories of numerous members of London's trade and business community, some of them men of real wealth and substance. Some did own cabinets, such as the 'India Cabinett & fframe' in the parlour of Richard Cooke, a merchant tailor who died in 1714.[90] More commonly, cabinets are listed without description or qualification, but the valuations given are low, suggesting something rather functional. However, large numbers of London's wealthier citizens did not own cabinets, despite having houses otherwise richly furnished. Instead, scriptors feature prominently, and it may be that the preference for this impressive but functional piece of furniture reflects the pragmatic, business-like attitude of London's merchant classes.

The most common form of early eighteenth century cabinet had an upper case with two doors, sometimes mirrored, enclosing an arrangement of drawers, on a lower case of drawers. Some were also fitted with secretaire drawers in the lower case. The example in **3:82** and **3:83** has second-phase construction throughout and brassware in the style of about 1715-30. This is almost certainly the sort of 'cabinet on a chest of drawers' described in the inventory of William Lucas, a

---
85. Quoted in Gilbert and Murdoch (1993), p. 18.
86. The cabinet was sold from Badminton at Christie's, London, on 5 July 1990.
87. Sherborne (1726)
88. Blenheim (1740).
89. Cannons (1747).
90. CLRO, Orphans' Court Inventory Roll 3013.

Other Case Furniture

139

Other Case Furniture

Plate 3:84. Cabinet on chest (1725-30). Walnut on deal and oak. This bears the trade label of William Old and John Ody, whose working partnership endured from c.1719 to 1733. The brasses are not original and the brackets are replacements for the original ball feet.
CHRISTIE'S IMAGES LTD 2001

Plate 3:85. Hand bill (c.1735). This is signed Potter, possibly the Mr Potter recorded as a cabinet-maker in High Holborn in 1737. A varied array of metamorphic furniture surrounds an impressive baroque cabinet fitted with a multitude of small drawers. Compare with 3:86-7.
VICTORIA AND ALBERT MUSEUM

clothworker who died in 1722.[91] A number of labelled cabinets of this type are known, of which **3:84**, by William Old and John Ody (1719-23) is one.[92] Benjamin Goodison supplied something similar to the Royal Household in 1730, when he billed 'a Walnuttree Cabinet with a large Glass in the Door and a Writing part to pull out and Drawers below it.... £22.0.0'.[93] Subsequent bills show that 'cabinets on drawers' were relatively common in the Royal Palaces in the 1730s.

The interior arrangement of these cabinets immediately distinguishes them from seventeenth century models. The central cupboard is omitted in favour of a more practical array of large and small drawers, and this format remained standard for cabinets of this type and period. In style and construction, all seem to date from the period 1715-40.

The trade card of Thomas Potter, perhaps the cabinet-maker Thomas Potter who had premises

---

91. CLRO, Orphans' Court Roll 3145.
92. The John Coxed piece is illustrated in Bowett and Lindey (2003) and Bowett (2002), p. 226, Pls. 7:59 and 7:60.
93. PRO LC 9/287, f. 82.

Other Case Furniture

Plate 3:86. Cabinet on stand (1720-40). Burr yew, brass, oak and deal. This bears a striking resemblance to the cabinet on Potter's trade card. It is a piece conceived in the 17th century tradition, designed to be the focal point of whatever room it occupied. The flamboyant baroque design is untainted by any hint of neo-Palladian dogma. The use of burr yew veneers is highly unusual at this date.
BRISTOL MUSEUMS AND ART GALLERY

Plate 3:87. Cabinet on stand, open. The arrays of small, shallow drawers, each lined with velvet, was almost certainly intended to contain coins, medals or a similar collection.
BRISTOL MUSEUMS AND ART GALLERY

in High Holborn in 1737,[94] shows a cabinet of a much more ambitious form (**3:85**). It has a prominent baroque pediment adorned with recumbent figures, pilastered and mirrored doors enclosing a multitude of small drawers, on a stand adorned with plumed masks and paw feet. There are at least two cabinets known which relate stylistically to this engraving. One in the Victoria and Albert Museum has been so extensively altered that it is probably unwise to speculate further,[95] but the other, belonging to Bristol Museums and Art Gallery, is in very much better condition (**3:86** and **3:87**). It is veneered inside and out with burr yew and ebony banding, and extensively embellished with inlaid brass and cast and chased mounts.[96] The shallow proportions of the walnut-lined drawers suggest they were intended to contain coins, medals, miniatures or some similar collection, but there is no evidence of any cloth lining or compartments to secure them.

94. *DEFM*.
95. Discussed in Gilbert & Murdoch (1993), pp. 99-102, figs. 113-117.
96. The inner faces of the doors are veneered with thuya wood, and are almost certainly replaced or re-veneered.

141

Other Case Furniture

Certainly some cabinets were purpose-made for this role. Plate CLIV of Batty Langley's *Treasury* shows a 'medal case' of small drawers, and Horace Walpole's wall cabinet for 'enamels and miniatures' made in 1743 survives at the Victoria and Albert Museum.[97] The fashion for collecting these small objects strikes us as curious and quaint, but there is no doubt that eighteenth century connoisseurs took such collections very seriously. When William Hubert's widow sold up in 1751 to return to France there was among her late husband's possessions 'his curious cabinet of casts, pastes and impressions, containing upwards of 3,000 taken (by particular desire) from the most celebrated and valuable antique gems in the King of France's collection'.[98]

In contrast to the deliberately showy Bristol cabinet is the piece in **3:88**, attributed to Peter Miller (d.1729). This is an intensely reserved, private piece of furniture, whose maker has given great thought to the problem of security. As well as high-quality locks and bolts throughout, the cabinet has iron brackets on the inside of the doors which engage with iron mortises in the sides of the carcase, making it impossible to force the doors from their hinges by inserting a lever between the door and carcase. As with all of Miller's work, the cabinet-making is exemplary and the attention to detail almost obsessive. This cabinet must have been made for a wealthy client whose primary concerns were privacy, security and above all quality. The need for security was not mere paranoia. The Old Bailey records reveal that house-breakers regularly targeted cabinets in their search for money and valuables.[99]

The authors of the *Dictionary of English Furniture* observed that 'Cabinets designed under the influence of William Kent and other members of the Palladian school are again scarcely distinguishable from contemporary bookcases…'.[100] This is a difficulty when seeking to classify architecturally derived pieces of the 1730s, compounded by the fashion for glazed rather than solid doors. Whereas it had long been customary to use glazed doors for bookcases, their introduction into cabinets was something new. One wonders, therefore, whether some or most cabinets with glazed doors were originally bookcases or perhaps china cabinets. However, there is no doubting the tendency by c.1750 to use cabinets for open display rather than enclosure. Chippendale's *Director* (1754-62) illustrates both conventional enclosed cabinets and cabinets with either glazed or open shelves.

97. Langley (1740); Wilk (1996), pp. 96-7.
98. Quoted in Gilbert and Murdoch (1993), p. 18.
99. Old Bailey.com.
100. *DEF*, I, p. 178.

Opposite:
Plate 3:88. Desk and cabinet (1720-30). Walnut and oak. This exceptional cabinet is attributed on stylistic and technical grounds to Peter Miller (d.1729). Unlike most cabinets, this piece was not made for show, but to provide a secure repository for documents and/or valuables. The interior of the upper case is fitted entirely with small drawers. CHRISTIE'S IMAGES LTD 1997

Other Case Furniture

Chapter Four
SEAT FURNITURE

Plate 4:4 (Detail). Coronation chair (1714). See page 147.

1. Cescinsky (1912), I, p. 20, fig 16; Graham (1994), pp. 62 and 64.
2. For more on these features see Bowett (2002), pp. 254 et seq.

Late pillar leg chairs

The chair in 4:1 was made for the Master of the Company of Parish Clerks in 1716.[1] Most elements of its design can be traced back several years, some even into the seventeenth century. The pillar leg first became fashionable in the 1690s, as did the outscrolled arm terminals. Other features are more up to date, however. The foreshortened form of the pillar, ribbed like a furled umbrella, is typically 'late', and the scroll feet are introductions of about 1705-10.[2] The raked back leg is very modern, only recently adopted and representing a decisive break with earlier chair-making practice. Also very modish is the flared top to the back. This resembles the back of George I's coronation throne, and it is possible that the throne introduced this style to England (4:4). Thus the maker of this chair was well aware of recent design trends, but chose nevertheless to use the pillar leg. Indeed, stylised pillar-leg designs for both tables and seat furniture continued to be made into the 1720s, reaching their apotheosis in the tables installed in the King's new apartments at Kensington in 1724 (see Chapter Five). Square, octagonal, baluster, ribbed and other variations of the pillar leg abound. One of the keys to identifying these 'late' models is the asymmetric placing of the medial stretcher, about one-third back from the front leg, rather than half-way between front and back as was customary in the seventeenth century (4:2). Plate 4:3 shows a plausibly early version of the asymmetric stretcher, perhaps dating from about 1710, but the first

Opposite page:
Right, above:
Plate 4:1. Chair (1716). Walnut and cane. This was made for the Master of the Company of Parish Clerks in 1716. It combines long established features such as pillar legs and a moulded back with fashionably flared shoulders and scroll feet. Note that the medial stretcher is still centrally placed between front and back legs. There was clearly a period of transition before asymmetric medial stretchers became universal. VICTORIA AND ALBERT MUSEUM

Far right, above:
Plate 4:2. Chair (1710-20). Walnut with modern upholstery. Late pillar-leg chairs typically have strongly raked back legs, which were introduced about 1705-10, but the asymmetric medial stretcher shown here is later still. The earliest known manifestation of the asymmetric stretcher occurs on the coronation chair of 1714 (cf. 4:4). NORMAN ADAMS

Far right, below:
Plate 4:3. Easy chair frame (1710-20). Beechwood. With the exception of a tacking rail added to the back (not visible), this frame is entirely original. It demonstrates how these sumptuous baroque easy chairs were built on very crude foundations. The medial stretcher is positioned asymmetrically, which suggests the chair may be later than initially appears. TENNANTS AUCTIONEERS

Seat Furniture

Seat Furniture

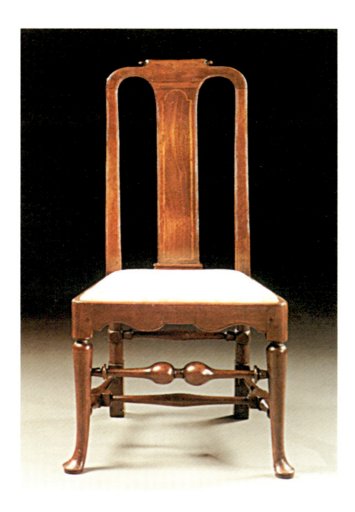

Opposite page:
Plate 4:4. Coronation chair (1714). Carved and gilt wood, with modern upholstery. Made by Richard Roberts for the Coronation of George I in Westminster Abbey. The design of this chair draws heavily on Italian baroque forms. The cartouche back and flared shoulders exerted a powerful influence on English chair-makers at all levels. This chair also documents the first appearance of the reverse-curved or ogee back leg and the asymmetrically placed medial stretcher. The original upholstery was a brocade of gold, silver, scarlet and blue. The gilding is modern and there is no record of the figures having been silvered originally.
PRIVATE COLLECTION

Left:
Plate 4:5. Chair (1720-40). Walnut, with modern drop-in seat. This common model of early Georgian chair turned leg may represent the final development of the pillar leg and not merely a cheap version of the cabriole.
COURTESY OF SOTHEBY'S

Plate 4:6. Stool (1710-20). Walnut with replaced needlework seat. It is not difficult to envisage how this type of pillar leg might develop into the form shown in 4:5.
CLANDON PARK, THE NATIONAL TRUST

firmly dated example occurs on the coronation throne of 1714 (**4:4**). However, as the Parish Clerks' chair shows, the older configuration persisted in many cases.

The fact that the pillar leg had a longer span of fashionable life than is generally recognised may explain the origin of the common Georgian leg design shown in **4:5**. This is usually viewed as a simplified and cheaper variant of the cabriole leg, but it could plausibly be the final version of the pillar leg, brought up to date with the addition of a pad foot. It is also conceivable that the pad foot itself was a highly stylised or vestigial version remnant of the scroll foot. One can see how the design of **4:5** might develop from **4:6**. Alternatively, the pad foot could be a simplified rendering of the French hoof or 'pied de biche', which was highly fashionable in Paris at this time for both chairs and tables. This style of foot will be discussed in more detail later in this chapter.

Seat Furniture

Plate 4:7. Pair of stools (1710-30). Japanned beechwood with later upholstery. These were part of a suite of four stools and a couch, probably made for Kiveton Hall, Yorkshire. The inspiration for the leg design may come from Chinese tables and chairs (cf. 1:36). CHRISTIE'S IMAGES LTD 1998

3. Gilbert (1967). Early 18th century English chair-makers referred to chair legs, from the seat down, as 'feet', not legs.
4. Christie's sale catalogue, London, 9 July 1998, lots 16-18.
5. Kiveton (1727).

'Indian' feet

The influence of Chinese furniture on English chair design was discussed briefly in Chapter One and it seems clear that the period immediately after the end of the War of Spanish Succession (1702-13) brought a number of radical new designs to England, perhaps due to the surge in trade with the Far East. One of these was the so-called 'Indian' foot, which occurs in a small number of furniture-makers' bills before 1720. For instance, among the seat furniture supplied to Lord Irwin by the London upholsterer Remey George in 1718 were several sets of chairs with 'Indian feet',[3] and at this time 'Indian' was a synonym for anything Oriental, usually meaning 'Chinese'. But what was an 'Indian' foot? Some authorities believe that the cabriole leg was a Chinese design, so it is possible that this was an 'Indian' foot but, for reasons which will be explained in due course, a Chinese origin for the cabriole is unlikely. Moreover, the relative scarcity of references to Indian feet suggest something less common than the ubiquitous cabriole. One possible candidate for the Indian foot is the straight, square-section leg shown in **4:7**. This pair of stools is part of a set of four stools and a 'banquette' or couch from Hornby Castle, Yorkshire, but originally made for Kiveton, also in Yorkshire, the seat of the Dukes of Leeds.[4] They can plausibly be identified with the '1 Large Couch, 4 Large Sq^r Stools frames Japand, & black Gold Covered wth ... Indian Satin' recorded in the Best Closet at Kiveton in 1727.[5] The closet in which the stools were placed was hung with 'Indian' satin panels in japanned frames. Kiveton was completed in 1704 and presumably furnished in the ensuing decade or so. The inventory of 1727 suggests its furnishings

were largely unchanged at that date, and depicts a house furnished in the late years of Queen Anne. The stools bear close comparison in their stretcher design with pillar-leg chairs and stools of c.1710-20, and the shaped seat rails suggest a similar date. The japanned decoration implies an Oriental theme, and it is likely that the straight, square-section leg is intended to convey the same message. There is no European precedent for this form of leg on fashionable furniture, but it is commonly found on classical Chinese chairs and tables (1:36).

An equivocally Chinese theme is expressed in **4:8** and **4:9**. The former is of uncertain date, although the gap between the seat and back, and the shaped top to the back are both early features and unlikely to appear much after 1725-30. The straight forelegs, with their peripheral stretchers and small cusped brackets, appear to be direct borrowings from Chinese furniture. 4:9 is one of a set made for Sir Francis Child the younger, a director of the East India Company 1718-19. The back and seat are lacquered and the design of the rails and legs is startling in its simple clarity. It is likely that these 'Indian' feet (if that is what they are) are the progenitors of the ubiquitous 'Marlboro leg' of the mid-eighteenth century. The same leg occurs on tables at much the same date (1:37, 5:4), suggesting the design was perhaps more general at this early date than is commonly assumed. In any case, the style was certainly common currency by 1735, when a set of thirteen chairs with straight square legs was supplied to the Dean and Chapter of Rochester Cathedral, where they remain.[6]

Plate 4:8. Chair (1715-30). Walnut and beechwood frame with original gilded and painted leather cover. One of a set of seven, originally from Parham House, West Sussex.
LADY LEVER ART GALLERY, PORT SUNLIGHT

Plate 4:9. Chair (1715-30). Lacquered seat and back with wooden frame. One of a set made for Sir Francis Child, a director of the East India Company 1718-19. The simplicity of this chair is in stark contrast to most contemporary English chairs. The date is uncertain but 1718-19 is plausible.
OSTERLEY PARK, THE NATIONAL TRUST

6. I am grateful to Christopher Claxton Stevens for drawing these chairs to my attention. The chairs were supplied by 'R. Say', probably Richard Say of Raquet Court, Fleet Street (fl.1712-1752).

Seat Furniture

Plate 4:10. K'ang table (1550-1650). Huali wood. Some authors have suggested this common Chinese leg design as a source for the European cabriole. However, there are other equally or more plausible alternatives. VICTORIA AND ALBERT MUSEUM

The cabriole leg

The innovation which more than any other characterised early Georgian chair design was the reverse-curved or 'cabriole' leg. The term cabriole is an anachronism, for in the eighteenth century a *cabriole* was a type of easy chair, often described as 'French', which sometimes had this type of leg.[7] It was not until the second half of the nineteenth century that cabriole came to be applied to the leg itself. Speculations on the derivation of the term – usually cited as from the Italian *capriola* 'a goat's leap' – are therefore pointless. However, because cabriole is now so universally recognised, it seems sensible to continue using the term for the sake of clarity.

The most common contemporary terms for the cabriole leg were 'French' and 'claw'. The meaning of the latter is made explicit in John Boson's bill for the altar table at St George's, Bloomsbury (1728), which describes it as having 'claw feet'. A drawing of this table shows it to have cabriole legs with leaf-carved pad feet.[8] In a more general sense, the term occurs most frequently in the phrase 'pillar and claw' or 'claw table', which was the eighteenth century name for a table on a central pillar with scrolled or cabriole legs. 'French' feet are cited in numerous furniture-makers' bills. In 1728 Thomas Roberts supplied Sir Robert Walpole with: 'Two large wallnuttree Elbow Chairs with French Feet and carved wallnuttree Elbows stuffd back and Seat and stuffd Elbows cover'd with black Leather and nailed with fine double varnish'd brass nails' at £4.10s a piece.[9] A year later, Henry Heasman, a prominent London upholsterer with premises in Covent Garden, used the term in a bill for chairs supplied to the Earl of Dysart in 1729: 'For 12 pollisht Wallnutree large Chair frames wth ffrench feet... £15.0.0..., For a pollisht Wallnutree large Easy chair frame wth scrole cheeks role off Elbows & ffrench feet... £2.2.0'.[10]

That 'French' and 'claw' feet were the same is made clear by the following advertisement in the *Stamford Mercury* of 23 August 1722:

These are to give Notice to all Persons that have Occasion for fine Chairs of the Newest Fashion; crooked Back with French or Claw feet, or of any stain upon the polished Work, that they may be furnished by Edward Mason, Chair-Maker in St Martin's Stamford Baron, as cheap as in London, and the work as good'.[11]

---

7. Hepplewhite (1794), pl. 10; Sheraton (1803), I, p.120.
8. The drawing is reproduced in Bowett, 'St George's Church, Bloomsbury' (1999), fig 4.
9. Houghton Hall, Mss RB 1 57.
10. Ham House, Bills No. 925, Henry Heasman to the Earl of Dysart, 13 August 1729.
11. *DEFM*, p. 583.

The term 'French' foot was still current in 1788, when George Hepplewhite's *Guide* illustrated several chairs with 'French' feet as an alternative to the neo-classical tapered square leg.[12]

The wide currency of the 'French' foot contradicts the view that the cabriole leg had a Chinese origin. Some scholars have argued that the curved legs found, for instance, on Chinese k'ang tables, are the direct precursors of the European cabriole (**4:10**).[13] While the visual similarity is obvious, there are equally compelling comparisons closer to home. Engravings by Pierre Le Pautre (c.1659-1744) and André-Charles Boulle (1642-1732), show cabriole legs employed for several different types of furniture (**4:11**), and it is probable that some of Boulle's designs were executed in the furnishing of the Ménagerie at Versailles in 1701.[14] A portrait by Hyacinthe Rigaud, dated 1702, shows the Bishop of Meaux standing beside a *bureau plat* raised on angular cabriole legs headed by gilt-metal masks, leaving us in no doubt that the cabriole leg existed in France by this date.[15] It seems more likely, therefore, that the cabriole leg was a development of the baroque scrolled leg or 'horsebone', as it was known by English chairmakers. In the hands of French designers such as Boulle and Le Pautre, this became refined into a more graceful, sinuous form by the turn of the seventeenth and eighteenth centuries, which we now recognise as a 'cabriole' leg.

It is worth noting that eighteenth century chair-makers considered cabriole front and back legs to be different designs. 'Claw' or 'French' foot applied to the front leg only; the reverse curved rear leg first seen on the coronation throne (4:4) was known by English chairmakers as an 'OG (ogee) back foot'. Both the OG and the cabriole were derived from the architectural scrolled bracket or truss, so that its use as a support for chairs and tables was, from a structural point of view, entirely logical.

If the cabriole leg appeared in France about 1700, when was it adopted by English furniture-makers? In the first decade of the eighteenth century 'horsebone' and pillar-leg chairs continued to predominate, and no documented English cabriole leg chairs from this period are known.[16] Some of Thomas Roberts' bills mention chairs and stools with 'French' feet, but it is not clear what form these took. A bill of 1700 describes: '30 back Chairs of Wallnuttree ye foreparts carv'd horse bone French feet and fore-Railes' supplied for the Council Chamber at Kensington Palace.[17] It is difficult to conceive of a chair whose feet were both horsebone and 'French', and were the fore-rails also 'French'? An intriguing bill of 1713 describes how Thomas Roberts altered a set of stools and an elbow chair at St James's Palace, including 'new carving the claws'.[18] Might this be a reference to

12. Some North American chair-makers seem to have used the old English term 'horsebone' for the new style of leg. Between 1729 and 1733 the Boston upholsterer Samuel Grant supplied his clients with numerous items of seat furniture with 'horsebone round feet' (Forman (1988), pp. 286-7). American scholars generally take this to mean cabriole legs with pad feet.
13. Ellsworth (1971), p.18; Grindley (1990).
14. Lunsingh Scheerleur (1985).
15. Paris, Musée du Louvre, no. 7506.
16. A portrait of Queen Anne by Michael Dahl in the collection of the National Maritime Museum (BHC2515) shows the queen standing by a table with cabriole legs of the type shown in 4:7-8 and 4:66. However, the portrait is likely to be posthumous, since it was painted for the dedication of St Alfege parish church, Greenwich, the first of the 'Queen Anne' churches to be completed. The church was dedicated in 1718. I am grateful to Robert Bradley for drawing this painting to my attention.
17. PRO LC9/281, f. 49.
18. PRO, LC 9/285.

Plate 4:11. Designs for tables (c.1700). This is one of a suite of engravings by Pierre Le Pautre (c.1659-1744), depicting pier tables at Versailles. They were made to replace the original silver tables which were melted down in 1689. The left-hand table has two designs for cabriole-type supports. From *Livre de Tables qui sont dans les apartements du Roy*, published in Paris.

Seat Furniture

Right:
Plate 4:12. Chair (1715). Walnut and beech, with original woollen needlework upholstery. Supplied by Thomas Phill to Edward Dryden of Canons Ashby, Northamptonshire. These superb chairs are the earliest documented English cabriole-leg chairs to survive.
CANONS ASHBY, THE NATIONAL TRUST

Far right:
Plate 4:13. Chair (1715-30). Walnut and beech, with modern upholstery. This is a common model which, with variations in leg and stretcher design, survives in considerable numbers. Compare the leg and stretcher design with 4:39.
SUDBURY HALL, THE NATIONAL TRUST

cabriole legs? Perhaps, but the earliest documented examples are on chairs supplied by the London upholsterer Thomas Phill to Edward Dryden, of Canons Ashby, Northamptonshire (**4:12**).[19] The bill for these chairs, dated 12 February 1714/15, runs as follows:[20]

For 6 wallnuttree back chaire frames of ye newest fashion Stufft up in Lynnen & ye seats covered a 2nd time att 25s p. piece [sic]	£7.10. 0
for green serge for ye backs of ye 6 Chairs	0. 5. 6
for making ye needleworke covers and fixing ym on ye chairs & for sewing silke used about ye same	£1.13. 0
for 17¼ yds of gold Colour serge for false caises at 22p[er yard]	£1.11.7½
for sewing silke tapes and making ye 6 false cases at 2s.6d. p[er] piece	0.15. 0

The basic price for the chairs – 25s. each – included the cost of making the frames, stuffing and covering them in plain linen. The needlework covers were fitted at a cost of 5s.6d. each, but there was no charge for the needlework itself, which suggests that it was supplied to the maker by Edward Dryden, and was possibly fashioned by members of his household. The chairs retain their green serge backs, fitted at a cost of 11d. per chair, but the gold serge 'false caises' (loose covers) have long gone. However, they must have survived long enough to perform their protective task for many years, for the needlework is in marvellous condition. The total cost of these chairs, including false covers, was just under £2 each.

There is so much that is new about these chairs that it is difficult to know what precisely Thomas Phill meant by 'ye newest fashion'. The foreleg is very similar to contemporary French examples;

19. For more on Edward Dryden and Thomas Phill, see Jackson-Stops (1975), and the National Trust guide book for Canons Ashby.
20. Northamptonshire Record Office, D (CA) 129.

Plate 4:14. Sofa (1715-30). Walnut and beech, with modern upholstery. This is en suite with the chair in 4:13. Note the 'rowled elbows', a characteristic feature of English sofas from c. 1700 onwards.
SUDBURY HALL, THE NATIONAL TRUST

Plate 4:15. Elbow chair (1716). Walnut and beech with modern upholstery. One of a pair, together with sixteen stools en suite. The frame was supplied by Richard Roberts, and the upholstery was by Thomas Phill and Jeremiah Fletcher. It is not difficult to see how English chair-makers might have adapted the reverse-curved 'horsebone' design popular from the 1680s onwards to the more up to date French-style cabriole leg.
HAMPTON COURT PALACE, ROYAL COLLECTION

slim, angular, and with a slight flat on the leading edge. The stretcher design is in the new style first seen on the coronation chair, with the medial stretcher placed well forward, and the rear legs are strongly raked. This contrasts with contemporary French practice, which favoured diagonal cross-stretchers and more or less vertical rear legs. There is a gap between the chair back and seat, a hangover from seventeenth century practice, but the raised and scrolled-over top was a new introduction. Numerous bills submitted by Phill for chairs supplied to the Royal Palaces suggest that this was known as a 'scrowle back'.[21]

Judging by the number of comparable examples surviving, the Canons Ashby model was a popular one. They frequently vary in style of leg, stretcher design and other details, but the basic form is the same. It probably represented a standard choice for a modestly priced 'back chair' (**4:13**). Settees were made en suite, of which numerous examples also survive (**4:14**).

A year later than the Canons Ashby suite is the elbow chair in **4:15**. It is one of a pair, made together with sixteen stools and a State Bed, for the Prince of Wales' use at Hampton Court Palace, where it was delivered in May 1716.[22] This chair has a fashionably 'scrowled' back, but still with a gap between back and seat. The form of the legs and arm supports is reminiscent of the late 'corner horsebone' style and suggests that the transition from 'horsebone' to 'French' foot was a fairly natural one for English chair-makers. Unlike the Canons Ashby chairs, the medial stretcher is still centrally placed.

21. PRO LC 9/286.
22. Rutherford (1927).

Seat Furniture

Plate 4:16. Hall chair (1714-20). Lacquered back with japanned seat and legs. One of a set made for Sir Gregory Page, who died in 1720. These are the earliest known datable chairs with this style of leg. Could the design have a Chinese origin?
COURTESY OF SOTHEBY'S

Plate 4:18. Chair (1716-22). Gilded wood with modern upholstery. Attributed to James Moore. This is one of a set supplied for one of the State Rooms at Blenheim Palace before the 1st Duke of Marlborough's death in 1722. Note that there is still a gap between the back and seat, in the 17th century manner.
BLENHEIM PALACE, THE DUKE OF MARLBOROUGH

Plate 4:17. Couch (1550-1650). Huali wood. This common form of Chinese foot is one possible source for the 'broken' cabriole found on English chairs and tables of c.1715-30.
REPRODUCED FROM SHIXIANG (1990)

Seat Furniture

Left:
Plate 4:19. Pair of chairs (1717-22). Walnut and beech with later upholstery. This and the companion easy chair (4:20) are part of a suite made for Streatlam Castle, Co. Durham, probably during the refurbishment of 1717-22. The widow's lozenge containing the Bowes arms suggests they were made for Elizabeth Bowes-Blakiston, who died in 1725. Unlike earlier chairs, this has no gap between seat and back.
CHRISTIE'S IMAGES LTD 2001

Below:
Plate 4:20. Easy chair (1717-22). Walnut and beech with later upholstery. Part of the same suite as the chair in 4:19. PHILLIPS OF HITCHIN

23. Murdoch (2003).
24. Wills & Coutts (1998).

The exotic-looking cabriole variant shown in **4:16** is a stylistic puzzle. The chair is one of a set of six made for Sir Gregory Page (1688-1720), a director of the East India Company. The arms on the back of the chair allow it to be dated between the creation of his baronetcy in 1714 and his death in 1720. The leg is formed of three distinct components: a bold, semicircular 'knee', a straight, square-section shaft, and a squared 'hoof' foot. The foot can be read either as a stylised version of the scroll foot or as a moulded plinth, supporting the pillar above. The flying brackets were apparently optional, since they occur on some examples but not others. The design is now usually called a 'broken' cabriole but, unlike the conventional cabriole, there are no analogies for it in contemporary French furniture, and it might therefore derive from a different source. The boldly-curved first section of the leg bears a strong resemblance to a popular Chinese type found on *k'ang* tables and beds of the Ming and early Qing dynasties (**4:17**). Was this perhaps adapted by English chair-makers by being superimposed on a conventional pillar leg and scroll foot? In view of the previous discussion of the 'Indian' foot, this style of leg should be borne in mind as a potential candidate.

The best-known exponent of the 'broken' cabriole leg was James Moore, to whom seat furniture and pier tables at Blenheim Palace are attributed (**4:18**).[23] The Blenheim chairs follow seventeenth century practice in having a gap between back and seat, but within a few years it became usual to upholster the back and seat contiguously. The now dispersed suite made for Elizabeth Bowes-Blakiston of Streatlam Castle, County Durham (**4:19** and **4:20**), about 1720, demonstrates the change.[24]

155

Seat Furniture

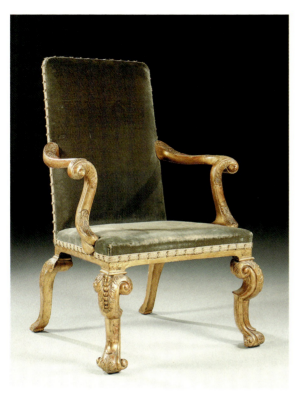

Above:
Plate 4:21. Elbow chair (c.1724), attributed to James Moore. Gilded wood with modern upholstery. This is one of a set of chairs made for the London house of Viscount Harcourt, probably in 1724. The scrolled arm terminals were a recently introduced feature which remained popular for about twenty years. CHRISTIE'S IMAGES LTD 2000

Right:
Plate 4:22. Pair of chairs (1715-30). Japanned wood with modern upholstered seats. These stylish chairs have leg and back designs taken from contemporary Chinese furniture. The back legs and stretchers, however, are characteristically English. The seat upholstery is modern; the original seat would have had a much flatter profile, and was perhaps caned or rushed. BONHAMS

Another suite attributed to Moore has a less angular and more richly decorated version of the leg which gives it a more European feel (**4:21**). These chairs were made for the London house of Viscount Harcourt, for whom Moore supplied furniture between 1724 and 1726.[25] Payments to Moore among the Harcourt Papers amount to several thousand pounds, indicating a very considerable furnishing commission, although little other than the seat furniture survives. The outward-scrolled arm terminals, seen here for the first time, occur quite commonly on elbow chairs of the 1720s, '30s and '40s.

The 'India' back

The introduction of the 'India back', also called a 'bended', 'crook'd' or 'sweep' back, was the most radical and far-reaching design innovation of eighteenth century chair-making. Up to this time the backs of English chairs were usually constructed as a rectangular panel, with two upright posts joined by horizontal cross-rails, leaving a clear gap between the lower cross-rail and the seat. The 'India back' chair had a vertical board, ergonomically curved to accommodate the sitter, which joined the crest-rail to the seat frame, and was tenoned directly into the latter. There is no doubt that this construction, which revolutionised the appearance of English chairs, was derived directly from China, and the contemporary name 'India back' explicitly acknowledged the debt. In the case of the chairs shown in **4:22** and **4:23**, one pair English, the other Chinese, the similarity extends even to the oversailing top rail, which was known in China as 'guan mao shi yi' or 'shaped like an official's hat'.[26] Plate **4:22** combines the 'India back' with putative 'Indian feet'.

25. *DEFM*; Murdoch (2003); Sotheby's London, *Important English Furniture*, 3 July 2003, lot 95.
26. Clunas (1988), p. 17.

Left:
Plate 4:23. Pair of Chinese chairs (1650-1700). Huali wood with rattan seat. The vertical splat and ergonomically curved rear posts formed the model for the English 'India' or 'bended back' chair. The tenoning of the splat directly into the rear seat rail introduced an entirely new form of construction into English chair-making.

VICTORIA AND ALBERT MUSEUM

Below:
Plate 4:24. Chair (before 1717–c.1715?). Walnut, with cane drop-in seat. This is one of four remaining from a set of twelve recorded at Canons Ashby in November 1717. These are the earliest documented examples of English bended or 'India' back chairs.

CANONS ASHBY, THE NATIONAL TRUST

27. Canons Ashby (1717).
28. There is an identical chair which, at the time of writing, is in store at Hampton Court Palace. This originally came from Kensington Palace, which raises the possibility that it was supplied by Richard Roberts. If so, the Canons Ashby chairs could also be from Roberts' workshop.

The earliest documented India back chairs are six survivors from a set of twelve recorded in the Right Hand Parlour at Canons Ashby in November 1717 (**4:24**). These were originally en suite with a settee and a matching marble-topped sideboard table (cf. 5:31).[27] They formed part of the refurnishing scheme initiated by Edward Dryden in 1710, and were probably contemporary with Thomas Phill's upholstered chairs of 1715 (**4:12**).[28] The central splat and ribs are tenoned directly into the seat frame in the Chinese manner and separated by walnut slips and spacers (**4:25**). The spacers were necessary because, rather than cutting mortises for the splat and ribs, the maker has simply ploughed a channel the length of the rail. It soon became usual to socket the splat into a

Plate 4:25. Detail of 4:24, showing the construction of the splat and seat rail. The splat is tenoned directly into the back seat rail. Spacers are inserted between the splats, either for support or to conceal the mortises, and a continuous slip of wood runs behind the splat. The rather *ad hoc* construction suggests that this assembly was still at the experimental stage.

CANONS ASHBY, THE NATIONAL TRUST

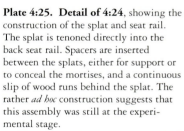

Seat Furniture

Right:
Plate 4:26. Chair (1715-30). Beechwood with red japanned finish. The japanned finish emphasises the Chinese inspiration behind this stylish chair. It also has a Chinese-style 'official's hat' top rail. Note the raised plinth or 'shoe', which became more or less standard on splat back chairs in the 18th century. VICTORIA AND ALBERT MUSEUM

Opposite page:
Plate 4:27. Elbow chair (1715-30). Walnut and cane. This handsome chair is one of a large set with a long history of use at Montacute House, Somerset. It combines an 'India' back with fashionable English features such as the flared shoulders and scrolled top rail. Note that the splat is tenoned into a cross-rail in the conventional manner, rather than directly into the seat rail as on the Canons Ashby chairs. This is a fairly common feature of India back chairs with cane seats.
MONTACUTE HOUSE, THE NATIONAL TRUST

Far right:
Plate 4:29. Chair (c.1725-40). Japanned beechwood. Chairs of this highly decorated type with carved crest rails survive in large numbers. They are often considered Continental, and often described as 'Italian', but the materials and construction of these examples are typically English. TENNANTS AUCTIONEERS

raised pedestal, or 'shoe' in modern parlance, which raised the base of the splat clear of upholstery or cushions (**4:26**). This also made assembly of the chair easier, since the splat and shoe could be fitted after the chair frame had been constructed without impinging on the seat rail. A damaged splat could be replaced simply by removing the shoe without disassembling the chair.

The legs of the Canons Ashby chairs have the characteristic angular section common to many early cabriole-leg chairs; similarly, the scrolled feet are often found at this date, and probably persisted until about 1730. A simplified, squared-off variant is shown in **4:26**. This 'hoof' foot occurs commonly in conjunction with the 'broken' cabriole legs discussed above.

The India back was rapidly assimilated into mainstream chair-making and modified in various ways. The elbow chair in **4:27** is one of a large set with a long association with Montacute House, Somerset. It combines the Chinese bended back and central splat with the flared shoulders of the coronation throne and a shaped and scrolled top rail. The scrolled, out-turned arms are roughly square in section and rest on curved supports which derive from the late 'corner horsebone' models of Queen Anne's time. There are two sets of journeymen's stamps on the rear posts (**4:28**), one probably identifying the joiner and the other the caner.[29]

The retention of a lower cross-rail in the back is a common feature of India back chairs with caned seats (**4:27 and 29**). This was presumably in order to facilitate the caning and avoid weakening the rear seat rail. Richard Roberts' bills in the Lord Chamberlain's accounts reveal that most of the India backed chairs made for the Royal Palaces in 1718-20 were caned. They also show that the caned versions were on the whole cheaper than those described as 'carved and polished'. The latter typically cost £2 each, whereas a set of eighteen caned chairs cost £22.10s., or £1.5s. apiece.[30]

29. Bowett (2002), pp. 89-90.
30. PRO LC 9/286.

Seat Furniture

Plate 4:28. Detail of 4:27, showing journeymen's stamps (MA, IG) on the rear post. Although common on late 17th and early 18th century caned chairs, stamps such as these are found less often after about 1715-20.

159

Seat Furniture

Plate 4:30. Pair of chairs (1719-33). Walnut, with modern upholstery. These chairs bear the trade label of William Old and John Ody. The splats are veneered with burr walnut, but the chairs are otherwise very modest in style. The dipped top rails enhance the chairs' Oriental character, although they do not actually occur on Chinese chairs. CHRISTIE'S IMAGES LTD 2005

'Banister' backs and compass back

The plain rectangular splat continued in vogue throughout the 1720s and probably later. The examples in **4:30** bear the trade label of William Old and John Ody, who worked at *The Castle* in St Paul's Churchyard between c.1717 and c.1733. They have round back posts and Chinese-style inverted top rails, but the splats are straight rather than bended. Plate **4:31** is from a set at Drayton House, Northamptonshire; there are obvious similarities with the Old and Ody chair, but the legs are more powerfully modelled and the 'OG' back leg is usually a sign of a more expensive chair. Chairs with similar backs can be seen in a painting of 1725 by Philip Mercier,[31] and other examples are known at Newhailes, Scotland, Hampton Court Palace and Dunham Massey, Cheshire. The Hampton Court chairs, with matted seats, were presumably supplied by Richard Roberts or his successor, Henry Williams.

---

31. Philip Mercier, *The Schultz Family and Friends* (1725), Tate Gallery, London. This painting is currently on loan to the Victoria and Albert Museum, and is hung in the British Galleries.

Seat Furniture

Far left:
Plate 4:31. Chair (1725-40). Walnut with modern upholstered seat. This is a more expensive version of 4:30, with powerfully modelled legs front and back.   DRAYTON HOUSE

Left:
Plate 4:32. Chair (c. 1720-26). Walnut with modern upholstery. This is a survivor of three similar sets of chairs at Erddig, all with narrow, parallel-post backs and baluster splats with inlaid decoration. The inventory of 1726 records three sets of walnut chairs in the Breakfast Room, Worked Room and Yellow Mohair Room respectively, and this is likely to be a survivor of one of these. If so, it is the first documented example of a baluster or 'banister' back chair, with a vase-shaped rather than rectangular splat.
ERDDIG, THE NATIONAL TRUST

Below:
Plate 4:33. Detail of 4:32. The Berainesque decoration of the splat is sometimes rendered in marquetry, as here, and sometimes in carved relief, as in 4:40.   ERDDIG, THE NATIONAL TRUST

From about 1720 the Chinese-style rectangular splat began to appear in a more Anglicised version, most commonly known as a 'banister' back. Some caution is necessary when interpreting this term, for in the 1690s and early 1700s this term described caned chairs with turned 'banister' or baluster-profiled back posts.[32] This usage was still current at Kiveton in 1727, where there were numerous sets of 'Cane Chairs wth Banester backs'.[33] These were relatively old chairs, probably belonging to the original phase of furnishing at Kiveton shortly after its completion in 1704. However, in the 1720s 'banister back' acquired a new meaning, describing a central splat with a vase or baluster-shaped profile. Furniture-makers' bills also refer to chairs with 'pedestal' backs, which almost certainly describes the same feature.[34] The inventories of Cannons and Chandos House, belonging to James Brydges, 1st Duke of Chandos, reveal that in June 1725 both houses contained several sets of chairs with 'banister backs'. The banister back chairs in the Duchess' dressing room at Chandos House were inlaid with the Duke's cipher and coronet,[35] and may have been similar to the chair in **4:32**. This is from one of three sets of chairs at Erddig recorded in the inventory of 1726, all of which have splats inlaid with cartouches of Berainesque strapwork (**4:33**).[36]

---

32. Bowett (2002), pp. 233-236.
33. Kiveton (1727).
34. The terminology persisted into the 1740s; at Ditchley House in 1743 many rooms were furnished with 'banister back' chairs variously described as having matted, leather, needlework, and silk seats – Ditchley (1743).
35. Chandos House (1725).
36. It is worth noting that the baluster does not actually occur in classical Roman architecture; it was invented, or at least developed as an architectural device, by Italian renaissance architects (Wittkower (1974), pp. 41-48).

Seat Furniture

Left:
Plate 4:34. Chair (1720-30). Walnut and marquetry with modern upholstery. Several examples of this sophisticated linked-splat design are known, differing only slightly in form and detail. The decoration on the foreleg is almost identical to that found on the Cannons chairs (4:51), but executed in marquetry rather than in relief. COURTESY OF SOTHEBY'S

Below:
Plate 4:35. Trade card of Thomas Cleare (c.1730). Thomas Cleare had a house in Holborn in 1724, but it is not certain when he established himself in St Paul's Churchyard. Two pieces of furniture labelled by him are known, dating from c.1725-40.
COURTESY OF SOTHEBY'S

Chairs of this form, tall and narrow in the back and combining parallel rear posts with a baluster splat, survive in huge numbers and in varying degrees of sophistication. Plate **4:34** is one of a group of several similar examples, each differing in detail but sharing a strikingly original basic design.[37] The linked splat is as practical as it is stylish, adding strength to the splat, and the looped shoulders emphasis the yoke-like structure of the top rail. A similar chair is illustrated on the trade card of Thomas Cleare, a furniture-maker who worked at the sign of the *Indian Chair* in St. Paul's Churchyard in the 1720s and '30s (**4:35**).[38] The card also tells us that these chairs, although increasingly unlike the Chinese originals, were still considered 'Indian' or 'India backed'.

One of the most intriguing of these narrow banister back designs is shown in **4:36**. This is one of a set of at least fourteen, now dispersed, some of which were formerly at Arley Castle, Staffordshire.[39] The frame is enriched with low relief Berainesque carving in the manner of contemporary gilt-gesso work, while the legs are superbly modelled with leafy cartouches to the knees and water-leaf feet. The carving is reminiscent of contemporary Chinese chairs made for the English market, and this may be a deliberate imitation, endowing an otherwise conventional chair with exoticism and mystery. The *arc-en-arbalette* shaped seat occurs on other chairs of about 1730, and can also be seen on the 1732 billhead of John Hodson (1:22).

37. One similar example is in the Victoria and Albert Museum (inv. No. W 38-1929); another is illustrated in Francis Lenygon *Furniture in England 1660-1760* (London 1914), p. 247, fig. 379.
38. For more on Thomas Cleare see *DEFM*.
39. I am grateful to Fred Uhde for sharing his research on these chairs with me.

Seat Furniture

Above left:
Plate 4:36. Chair (1720-30). Walnut with modern upholstery. A number of chairs of this design are known, all apparently originating from a set of fourteen or sixteen possibly made for the Lyttleton family. It is an extraordinary mixture of 'Indian' and baroque styles, suggesting the maker was able to draw on a wide range of sources to create his design. The shallow-relief Berainesque carving is more commonly associated with gilt furniture.   PRIVATE COLLECTION

Above right:
Plate 4:37. Chair (1720-40). Walnut with rush seat. It is clear from bills, inventories and contemporary engravings that rushed or 'matted' seats were very much more common than their present scarcity would suggest. The flat profile of the seat emphasises the clean lines of the chair and gives prominence to the shoe, which is often obscured when upholstered seats are fitted at a later date. The seat is kept in place by wooden slips nailed to the tops of the seat rails.   FREDERICK PARKER FOUNDATION

Right:
Plate 4:38. Detail of 4:37. The rush seat is old but not original. It is supported by blocks nailed in the corners of the frame. It can be replaced either by removing these blocks, or by taking off the wooden slips on top of the frame rails.

The rush or 'matted' seat of **4:37** is a rare survival. Inventories and bills suggest these were once very popular, even in the most fashionable houses. In 1720, for instance, Roberts supplied '8 fine Walnuttree matted bottom Chairs with India backs and mouldings' at a cost of £16 for the 'young Princesses' use at St James's Palace. At £2 each these were not cheap, and certainly not just a backstairs option. Matted chairs also appear on the trade cards of fashionable makers such as Nash, Elkington and Whitehorne on Holborn Bridge (1:19) and William Russell in Fetter Lane.[40] As **4:38** shows, the seats were often supported only on nailed blocks or strips, but the better quality examples had rebated seat rails which could support either matted or upholstered seats. Despite their enormous popularity few matted chairs survive, probably due to their unpopularity in the antiques trade, so that matted seats have been routinely replaced by drop-in upholstered ones.

40. Heal (1955), p. 154; *DEFM*.

163

Seat Furniture

Right:
Plate 4:39. Detail from a portrait of Arthur Vansittart (1718). Oil on canvas by Michael Dahl. The chair in this portrait is painted with great attention to detail, suggesting it was taken from life. The legs and stretchers are typical of the period 1715-20 (compare with 4:13). The old-fashioned gap between seat and back is retained, but the waisted shape is new.
LYME PARK, THE NATIONAL TRUST

Far right:
Plate 4:40. Chair (1720-30). Walnut with later upholstery. This is one of a famous set of chairs attributed to Richard Roberts and long associated with a Royal Warrant of November 1717, but the link is tenuous. In stylistic terms it is highly sophisticated, combining the India back with well-considered Berainesque carving. The seats have been re-railed, and may originally have had drop-in frames. Many versions of these chairs survive, including numerous 19th and 20th century copies.
HAMPTON COURT PALACE, ROYAL COLLECTION

 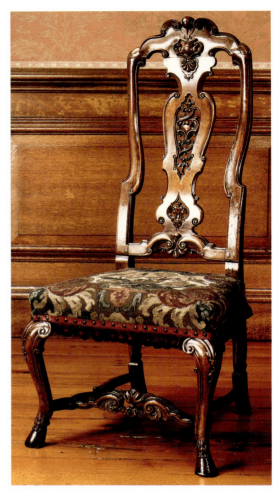

Waisted or 'compass' back posts were a logical corollary of the shaped banister splat and probably introduced about the same time, but it is possible that the compass back first appeared on upholstered chairs. Hitherto upholstered chairbacks had been shaped at the top and bottom, but straight at the sides. A painting by Michael Dahl, dated 1718, shows a chair upholstered in black leather whose back is clearly waisted at the sides (**4:39**). This is probably the earliest known depiction of the 'compass' back form. On wooden chairs the back was conceived as a pair of elongated scrolls, rising sinuously from extensions of the back leg and terminating with an inward curl on to the top of the splat. The idea is elegantly expressed in **4:40**, one of ten chairs surviving from a much larger set at Hampton Court Palace.[41] These are traditionally ascribed to Richard Roberts on the basis of an entry in the Lord Chamberlain's receipts book for 1718: 'Rec'd from H.M.'s Great Wardrobe, eighteen wallnuttree chairs Indea backs and gertwebb bottoms, and Silk upon that, for H.M.'s Eating room at Hampton Court'.[42] In fact there is no way of distinguishing these chairs from the many dozens of India back chairs supplied to the Royal Palaces from 1718 onwards. Indeed, there is no guarantee that the chairs were even made for the Royal Palaces, merely an assumption that because they have been at Hampton Court since the nineteenth century, they have probably always been there.

Nevertheless, the chair represents a well-known design of considerable sophistication and merits closer examination. The lower cross-rail in the back suggests that the seats might originally have been rushed or caned, and this hypothesis is strengthened by the fact that all the Hampton Court chairs have been completely re-railed and upholstered, probably in the first half of the nineteenth century. Many similar chairs survive in private and public collections; some have upholstered seats

41. The chair seats have all been re-railed and re-upholstered, probably in the early 19th century. Each chair is numbered on the rails, the highest number being 27.
42. Rutherford (1927).

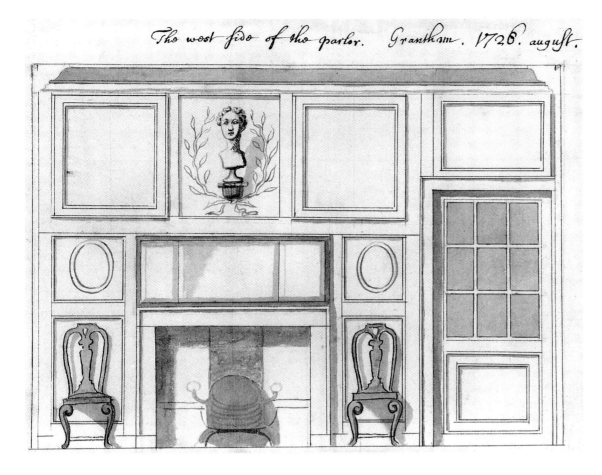

Plate 4:41. The west side of the parlor, Grantham, 1728. Watercolour by William Stukeley, showing chairs with pedestal splats and waisted backs flanking the fireplace. Note the plain tripartite overmantel mirror. Depictions of middle-class interiors of this period are extremely rare.
BODLEIAN LIBRARY, OXFORD

(which may or may not be original) and some have drop-in seats with narrow rails suggesting cane or matted bottoms were originally fitted.

The arched and scrolled medial stretcher has similarities to earlier chairs by Roberts (4:15). The leg design almost certainly derives from Parisian furniture engravings published in the 1720s,[43] and the carved cartouche in the centre of the back mimics both in form and detail the inlaid decoration found on contemporary veneered chairs (c.f. 4:33). The narrow back and delicately scrolled tops to the posts suggest a relatively early date, perhaps 1720-25. One of the most striking aspects of the design is that its decoration is derived entirely from the repertoire of European baroque ornament. There is no hint of the neo-Palladian decoration which became an increasingly prominent feature of English chairs from the late-1720s onwards.

Probably the earliest illustration of compass back chairs in a contemporary setting is shown in **4:41**. This is one of a set of watercolours by Dr. William Stukeley, depicting the furnishing of his new house at Grantham as it appeared between 1727 and 1729. Dr. Stukeley was the son of a prosperous lawyer, whose medical career seems to have taken second place to his interests in antiquity and the arts. In London he was acquainted with a 'whole sett of learned men & Vertuoso's [sic]', among them Sir Isaac Newton, Sir Hans Sloane and Sir Godfrey Kneller.[44] In 1725 he retired to the country and bought a house at Grantham, Lincolnshire. Stukeley's watercolours are significant because he was not a rich man, having an estate of £150 per annum, plus £200-£300 per annum in medical fees. His furnishings are representative of those acquired by the 'middling sort' of comfortable professional and mercantile people in the 1720s.

The compass back was obviously more expensive than the narrow straight back, requiring more work and more wood, and this explains why narrow backs are much more common at this early date. Similarly, upholstered chairs were generally made with straight backs, with compass backs

43. Bowett (2003).
44. Scoones (1999).

Seat Furniture

Left:
Plate 4:42. Chair (c.1720-26). Silvered beechwood frames with original crimson damask upholstery. This is one of six, with a sofa en suite, installed in the Withdrawing Room at Erddig by 1726. The decorated seat rail is only a fascia which is glued to the rails proper. The seat has a drop-in frame, but the back upholstery is fixed. ERDDIG, THE NATIONAL TRUST

Above left:
Plate 4:43. Detail of **4:42**, showing the drop-in seat with its beechwood frame and original webbing.

Above right:
Plate 4:44. The underside of 4:42, showing the seat rails braced by open corner braces. This is normally found only on webbed seats with fixed upholstery. Note the untidy silvered finish; it is not clear whether this is original or the result of later restoration.

being a more expensive option. Several well-documented sets of the early 1720s survive at Erddig, where they formed part of the furnishings of the newly completed suite of state rooms recorded in the inventory of 1726. In the Withdrawing Room, next to the Best Bedchamber, was a suite of eight chairs and a settee with silvered frames and crimson cut velvet covers (**4:42**). The side and front rails have decorated fascias about ½in. (12.5mm) thick glued to the rails proper. The drop-in seats are retained by the raised edge of the fascias (**4:43**) and the seat rails are braced by corner struts dovetailed into the rails from below (**4:44**). This was the standard method of bracing seat frames on upholstered chairs during the eighteenth century. In this case, however, it is unusual, since braces were not normally required for drop-in seats. Together with the added fascias it may suggest that these chairs were originally intended to be webbed and overstuffed, and the removable seats were an afterthought. The late John Cornforth has suggested that John Meller's furnishing at Erddig 'had an element of the Londoner showing off',[45] and this is certainly borne out by these chairs, which lack real quality; the frames are cheaply made and the upholstery crudely applied.

The chairs in the *Salone* were of a similar type, but plainer in style with removable 'Caffoy' top covers.[46] One is shown with its original figured red worsted undercover in **4:45**.[47] The covers are secured by iron sprigs driven into the seat rails which line up with eyes sewn into the edges of the covers (**4:46**). This was a common technique used, for instance, on a set of eighteen chairs, a settee and a pair of large armchairs in the Queen's Bedchamber at Ham House (**4:47**). These are probably slightly later in date than the Erddig examples, and are associated with the refurbishment of Ham which took place after 1730.[48] The suite is very similar to one supplied by William Bradshaw to Belton House, Lincolnshire,[49] and given that the tapestries in the Queen's Bedchamber at Ham are also by Bradshaw, a tentative attribution to this upholsterer has been proposed for the Ham suite.[50]

---

45. Cornforth (2004), p. 281.
46. *Caffoy* – a figured material with a worsted woollen pile and silk or cotton foundation.
47. There is some uncertainty about the exact placement of these chairs at Erddig, since there are the remains of two similar but slightly different sets; one from the Salone and the other probably from the Second Best Bedchamber (Cragg 2001).
48. Thornton and Tomlin (1980), pp. 178-81.
49. The settee from this suite is illustrated in Beard (1997), figs 176-7. For more on Bradshaw see *DEFM* and Beard (1997), pp. 153-4.
50. Thornton and Tomlin (1980), p. 181.

Right:
Plate 4:45. Chair (c.1720-26). Walnut and beech, with original upholstery and fixed worsted undercover. Probably one of the '6 Crimson damask Chairs Walnutree frames' recorded in the Second Best Bed Chamber in 1726.   ERDDIG, THE NATIONAL TRUST

Above:
Plate 4:46. Detail of 4:45, showing one of the sprigs on the underside of the seat rails used to secure the loose top covers. Note the upholstery nails with their faceted heads.

Below:
Plate 4:47. Sofa, (1730-40). Mahogany and beechwood frames with original cut velvet upholstery. This is one of a set of eighteen chairs, two easy chairs and a sofa which relate to the refurbishment of Ham House between 1730 and 1740. Perhaps by William Bradshaw.   HAM HOUSE, THE NATIONAL TRUST

Seat Furniture

Above:
Plate 4:48. Chair (1725-40). Walnut and beechwood with original wool and silk needlework upholstery.
CLANDON PARK, THE NATIONAL TRUST

Right above:
Plate 4:49 Chair (1720-40). Walnut and beechwood with original upholstery. This chair is original throughout, and all the more remarkable because it is clearly a relatively inexpensive model, with Yorkshire broadcloth covers and stained beechwood back legs.
TEMPLE NEWSAM HOUSE, LEEDS CITY ART GALLERIES

Right:
Plate 4:50. Chair (1720-40). Walnut and beechwood with original woollen needlework upholstery. In contrast to the preceding examples, the back of this chair is waisted or 'compassed'.
TREASURER'S HOUSE, YORK. THE NATIONAL TRUST

Plate 4:51. Elbow chair (c.1720). Carved and gilded walnut and beech, with modern cut velvet upholstery. This is one of a pair made for the private chapel at Cannons, seat of James Brydges, 1st Duke of Chandos. A *tour de force* of baroque design, perhaps designed by James Gibbs and made in the workshops of James Moore. The water gilding is original, layers of later gilding having been recently removed.

MALLETT

Further variations on the theme of the square backstool are shown in **4:48** and **49**, which illustrate some of the different styles of top covers then in vogue. By way of contrast, **4:50** has a 'compass' back, representing the more expensive and perhaps more fashionable option.

The compass back chair in **4:51** is a masterpiece of English baroque chair-making. It is one of a pair made for the chapel at Cannons, Middlesex, the palatial house built for James Brydges, 1st Duke of Chandos. The chapel was opened for worship in 1720, which provides a likely date for the making of the chairs.[51] Although no bill has come to light, James Moore has been suggested as a possible maker, and the design has been attributed to Brydges' architect, James Gibbs.[52] A suite of almost identical chairs was made for Cannons house itself, which was completed about 1722-3.[53] Until recent sales four elbow chairs and eight back chairs from this suite were at Houghton Hall, where they were installed in the nineteenth century.[54] The only significant difference between the two suites is that the chapel chairs have an exposed lower back rail, whereas the chairs from the house do not. As we have seen, this reflects a general change in chair-making practice; before c.1720 it was customary to have a gap between back and seat, whereas after that date the back and seat were contiguous.

---

51. Friedman (1984), pp. 52-3.
52. Christie's, London, *Important English Furniture*, 8 June 2006, lot. 50.
53. Collins Baker (1972), pp. 146-50.
54. Christie's, London, *Important English Furniture*, 8 December 1994, lot 135; Cornforth (1987); Beard (1997), figs. 151-4.

Seat Furniture

Like many high quality chairs of the period, the Cannons chairs are upholstered *à chassis*; that is, the upholstery is mounted on a sub-frame which was upholstered independently of the chair frame (**4:52**). This has at least two advantages over conventional fixed upholstery. In the case of chairs with gilded or veneered frames, it meant that the webbing and stuffing could be nailed without damaging the chair, with only the top cover needing to be fixed *in situ*. It also allowed the frame-maker and the upholsterer to work simultaneously rather than sequentially. It is conceivable that this method of manufacture implies the work of an integrated chair and upholstery workshop, rather than one in which the frames are produced in one shop and the upholstery in another.

Drop-in chassis seats are found on a set of stylish chairs from Wimpole Hall, Cambridgeshire (**4:53**). This was the country home of Edward Harley, 2nd Earl of Oxford, and was radically remodelled by James Gibbs in the 1720s. The chairs are probably contemporary with those alterations; as well as deeply waisted backs they have heart-shaped tops, mirroring the inward-curved crest-rails of splat back chairs.

Plate 4:52. Chair seat chassis (1720-40). This type of seat construction with a separate chassis for the webbing and stuffing was introduced in the 1720s. It is usually found on good quality chairs, and might indicate a system of production which allowed the chair frames and the foundation upholstery to be worked on simultaneously. The red wash is not an original finish.
TEMPLE NEWSAM HOUSE,
LEEDS CITY ART GALLERIES

Plate 4:53. Chair (1720-30). Walnut and beech with modern silk upholstery. These were almost certainly made for Wimpole Hall, seat of Edward Harley, 2nd Earl of Oxford. The heart-shaped back is uncommon, but also occurs on wooden chair frames of the period.
CHRISTIE'S IMAGES LTD 2001

Seat Furniture

Compass seats

All the upholstered chairs discussed thus far have straight-sided trapezoidal seats. The introduction of rounded or 'compass' seats is documented by a set of chairs at Erddig which were recorded in the Best Bedchamber in the inventory of 1726: '6 gold stuff chairs with green japan frames... 2 gold stuff stools with green japan frames' (**4:54**).[55] The state bed for this room was made in 1720, so it is reasonable to assume the chairs are roughly contemporary, but it is possible they are a few years later in date. At the time of writing, the earliest documentary reference to compass seats occurs in a bill of February 1726/7, when Thomas Trotter senior billed Lord Irwin for '10 fine Compis seete Chaires covered with Morrocko Leather... £13.0.0.'.[56] The notion that this was a recent stylistic development is supported by evidence from North America, where the Boston upholsterer Samuel Grant supplied a New York customer with a chair with a 'New fashion round seat' in October 1729.[57]

The fully developed 'compass' chair, curved in both back and seat, is documented in a bill for furniture supplied by Thomas Roberts for Sir Robert Walpole's London house in November 1728:[58]

> For 12 fine Wallnuttree Chair Frames with Compass Seates a carved Shell on the Feet a fine Compass India back, vener'd with the finest Grenople Wallnuttree & vener'd Pedestals Girts bottoms Curl'd hair linnen to stuff in and work stuffing and covering them with your own Damask at 50s... £30.0 0.

This bill describes a type of chair which, judging by the number of surviving examples, must have been made in very large numbers by both metropolitan and provincial chair-makers (**4:55**).

The compass seat usually resulted in a more powerful modelling of the top of the leg, allowing

Above left:
Plate 4:54. Chair (c.1720-26). Green and gold japanned beechwood with original upholstery. These are the earliest documented Georgian chairs with 'compass seats'.
ERDDIG, THE NATIONAL TRUST

Above right:
Plate 4:55. Chair, c.1725-40. Walnut with later upholstery. This model of chair, the back compassed in every plane, is typical of good quality London production in the late 1720s and 1730s. Judging by the number of survivors, it was produced in huge numbers. MALLETT

---

55. Erddig (1726).
56. Gilbert (1967).
57. Forman (1988), p. 286.
58. Houghton Hall, Mss RB 1 57.

Seat Furniture

Right:
Plate 4:56. Chair (1725-40) Walnut and cane. The compassed shape and claw feet are all suggestive of the very late 1720s and 1730s. Note how the caned panels in the back make it necessary to retain a lower back rail. The narrow seat rails also make it desirable to retain stretchers. Formerly at Cornbury Park, Oxfordshire.
PRIVATE COLLECTION

Far right:
Plate 4:57. Chair (1730-40). The concave compass seat is shown on trade cards and billheads from about 1730 onwards. The fleshy shell knee is also typical of the 1730s. A good quality chair with exceptionally well-figured veneers on the splat and frame.
BENINGBOROUGH, THE NATIONAL TRUST

Below:
Plate 4:58. Trade card of John Brown (after 1730?). There is some confusion about the date at which John Brown occupied premises at the *Three Cover'd Chairs and Walnut Tree*. Examples of this label have been found with inscribed dates ranging from 1738 to 1755.
FROM HEAL, *LONDON FURNITURE MAKERS* (1955)

stretchers to be dispensed with even on chairs with drop-in seats, and the absence of stretchers was clearly something which some clients saw as desirable. In July 1736 Elizabeth Purefoy wrote to a Mr. King, at the 'King & Queen' in Bicester, Oxfordshire: 'As I understand you make chairs of wallnut tree frames with 4 legs without Barrs for Mr. Vaux of Caversfield… I shall want about 20 chairs'.[59] However, narrow-railed chairs with caned or matted seats were usually still made with stretchers for strength. The chair in **4:56** fits the description given in a bill from the chair-maker Thomas Packer for chairs made for Sarnesfield Court, Herefordshire, in December 1729: '12 Handsome Chairs Compass backs & seat wth fine Cain… £18'.[60]

Plate **4:57** shows an alternative version of the compass seat with a concave front which emerged around 1730. The trade card of John Brown, who occupied the *Three Cover'd Chairs & Walnut Tree* in St Paul's Churchyard from about 1730 onwards, shows a pair of similar chairs (**4:58**).[61] Also clearly depicted is an upholstered chair with compass seat and back.

In terms of iconography or decoration the most significant feature of all the chairs in **4:55-7** is the carved shell on the knee. Thomas Roberts' bill of November 1728, quoted above, is the first recorded description of the 'carved Shell on the Feet'. As such, it marks an important moment in English chair design, heralding the arrival of neo-Palladian ideas into mainstream chair-making.

---
59. DEFM.
60. DEFM.
61. DEFM. Brown took over these premises from William Rodwell, who left off trade in 1727-8. He appears to have been using the same trade card as late as 1755. I am grateful to Laurie Lindey for this information.

The Houghton Hall suites

The seat furniture made for Houghton Hall between c.1728 and c.1732 is probably the most intensively studied group of chairs in England. Analysis has been hampered by the lack of surviving documentation, and the fact that the only chair-maker's bills to survive, those of Thomas Roberts, are mainly concerned with the furnishing of Walpole's London house, not Houghton. Nevertheless, the combined efforts of several scholars have succeeded in making a reasonably coherent account of the original sequence of furnishing, and in placing most of the chairs in their original contexts. One of the most important aspects of the Houghton seat furniture is its systematic use of neo-Palladian iconography – scallop shells, lions' masks, eagles' heads, paw and claw feet. None of these was new in themselves; these motifs had a lineage stretching back through Boulle and Berain to the Italian Renaissance and ultimately to classical Rome. But at Houghton, and at other English great houses of this period, these emblems of the classical past were martialled into a co-ordinated statement of a new stylistic era.

The most problematic of the Houghton suites, in terms of its dating, is the green velvet suite in the Wrought Bedchamber and the Cabinet next to it (**4:59**). It has been assumed that the chairs were made for Walpole's earlier house at Houghton, and predate the building of the new Hall.[62] However, a suite of similar chairs was made for Sir John Chester, whose new house at Chicheley, Buckinghamshire was begun in 1719 and the interiors fitted out from 1722 onwards (**4:60**).[63] The maker of these chairs is unknown, but a furniture-maker named Hodson supplied seat furniture to Chicheley in 1725 at a cost of £34.[64] The Houghton chairs, which are made to virtually the same design and possibly in the same workshop, probably date from the early to mid-1720s, and must have been one of the first suites of furniture to be installed in Walpole's new mansion. Their association with the 'Wrought Bed' lends some credence to this, since it appears that the addition to the bed of the Garter Star, awarded to Walpole in 1726, is an afterthought. Both the bed and the chairs may therefore have been made about 1720-5.

Above left:
Plate 4:59. Chair (1720-25). Parcel-gilt walnut and beechwood with original green velvet upholstery. These simple but very stylish chairs are often dated c.1715 but, for the reasons given in the text, a later date is suggested here. CHRISTIE'S IMAGES LTD 1994

Above right:
Plate 4:60. Chair (1722-6) Parcel-gilt walnut and beechwood with original wool and silk needlework upholstery. This is one of a set originally made for Chicheley Hall, Buckinghamshire, perhaps by John Hodson.
MONTACUTE, THE NATIONAL TRUST

62. Cornforth (1987); Christie's (1994); Moore (1996).
63. Gomme (2000), pp. 348-364.
64. Perhaps Robert or John Hodson of Frith Street, Soho. See *DEFM*.

Seat Furniture

Plate 4:61. Pair of chairs (c.1728). Walnut and beech with original upholstery. This is part of a set of twelve, together with two settees and a couch, made for the Yellow Drawing Room at Houghton. The top covers of yellow and red caffoy, now much faded, were intended to complement the yellow caffoy used to line the walls. CHRISTIE'S IMAGES LTD 1994

Plate 4:62. Pair of chairs (c.1732). Carved and gilt beechwood with original green silk upholstery and gold lace trim. This is part of a large suite which furnished three consecutive State rooms at Houghton. The Houghton seat furniture is the first to employ the full gamut of classical symbolism in a coherent and systematic way. Here the eagles' heads and feet are emblematic of Jupiter.
CHRISTIE'S IMAGES LTD 1994

---

65. Cornforth (1987); Christie's, London, *Important English Furniture*, 8 December 1994, lot 128; Beard (1997), p. 182, fig. 172.
66. Houghton Hall, Mss, RB 1 57.

The 'Yellow Caffey' suite was installed in the Yellow Drawing Room about 1728 (**4:61**). These chairs have been linked to a bill for furniture supplied by Thomas Roberts in November 1728:[65] 'For 12 fine wallnuttree Chair frames stuff'd back & Seat with a Carved Shell on each foot and a small bead round the seat…a wallnuttree Settee frame… a large and strong wallnuttree Couch frame…'.[66] However, the bill refers to furniture made for Walpole's Grosvenor Street house, not Houghton. The Houghton suite comprises twelve chairs, two settees and one couch, and is upholstered with yellow caffoy, not crimson damask. Nor does it have the bead round the seat described in Roberts' bill. While these discrepancies undoubtedly sever the link between the Houghton suite and this bill, they do not necessarily invalidate Roberts' authorship, since the same set of bills confirms that he was involved in supplying upholstery materials to Houghton (including the crimson caffoy for the Saloon), and he had two men working there for sixty-four days in 1728.

The shell-carved knee was a device which soon achieved near universal popularity. As was often

Plate 4:63. Elbow chair (c.1732). Gilded wood with original green velvet upholstery. These are probably the earliest datable 'lion's mask' chairs known. The lions' masks, paw feet and satyrs' masks are all emblematic of Bacchus. CHRISTIE'S IMAGES LTD 1994

the case in furniture design, its introduction appears to have been the result of a gradual evolution rather than decisive change, as chair-makers modified established designs to fit in with new neo-Palladian ideas. Chair-legs of the early 1720s were frequently headed by a leafy scroll or plume, often extending up into the seat rail (similar motifs occur on contemporary Parisian chairs), and it did not require too much modification to render this as a shell. An alternative treatment is shown on the Cannons chairs (4:51) where the knee is carved with an Etruscan mask whose plumes have been carved as a shell-like corona. A similar idea is expressed on the part-gilt mahogany chairs in the Saloon at Houghton (4:101). It was a small step to omit the mask, leaving the scallop shell as the primary motif. This subtle change might stand as a metaphor for the more general transition from the baroque to neo-Palladian style in English furniture.

Another key neo-Palladian motif was the claw foot. There is a popular belief that this had a Chinese origin, deriving from the Chinese motif of the dragon chasing a pearl. However, the context in which it was employed suggests classical iconography as a more likely source. Specifically, the claw is an eagle's talon, symbolic of Jupiter, supreme ruler of gods and mortals. The point is made explicitly on the 'Eagle' suite at Houghton, which combines the claw foot with eagle's head arm terminals (**4:62**). Twelve of these chairs were recorded in the Marble Parlour in the inventory of 1745, together with a settee. (It is curious that their decoration bears no relation to the Bacchic theme which dominates the room, and it has been suggested that the suite was made for another room, and later moved to the Marble Parlour.)[67] A contemporary description of the claw foot occurs in a bill submitted by the Edinburgh furniture-maker Francis Brodie, who about 1740 supplied the Duke of Hamilton with 'Six Mahogany Chairs with Eagles feet' for 25s. each.[68]

Several neo-Palladian themes are combined on another large suite at Houghton which furnished the Velvet Drawing Room, Bedchamber and Dressing Room in sequence (**4:63**). The first of these rooms was described by Lord Hervey in 1731 as still unfurnished: 'The furniture is to be green velvet and tapestry, Kent designs of chimneys, the marble gilded and modern ornaments'.[69] The suite can therefore be dated after 1731. The lions' masks and corresponding paw feet are symbolic of Bacchus, god of wine, while the mask in the centre represents his followers, the satyrs, twinned with the shell of Venus on the side rails. The maker of this extensive suite is not known; William Bradshaw and Benjamin Goodison are the current favourites, although there is no hard evidence for either.[70]

---

67. Cornforth (1987); Christie's, London, *Important English Furniture*, 8 December 1994, lot 130.
68. Pryke (1990). A throne made in London in 1731 for Queen Anne of Russia incorporated eagle's head arm terminals and claw feet with scaly legs. It may not survive, but six copies were made for Czar Paul I in 1797, of which one survives at St Petersburg and two at the Kremlin.
69. Moore (1996), p. 125.
70. Christie's (1994), lot 130; Beard (1997), p. 182.

Seat Furniture

Above left:
Plate 4:64. Chair (1735). Walnut and beechwood; the upholstery is recent, but uses genuine 18th century materials to re-construct the original appearance of the chairs. This is one of eighteen supplied to Lord Irwin by William Hallet in 1735, at a cost of 23s. each. The chair is fitted with a silk 'scarf' to protect the upholstery from wig powder and hair oil. It hangs down the back of the chair when not in use.
TEMPLE NEWSAM HOUSE,
LEEDS CITY ART GALLERIE

Above right:
Plate 4:65. Chair (c.1732). Walnut with original needlework upholstery, dated 1732. The proportions of chairs grew noticeably broader in the 1730s.
CHRISTIE'S

The iconography of these suites is important because the furniture was intended to complement the decorative themes expressed in the rooms themselves. Thus the painted Drawing Room ceiling depicted Venus attended by Jupiter, Juno, Apollo and Cybele, with Apollo's mask repeated on the chimney piece. Opposite the chimney was a pier table designed by William Kent, centred by a mask of Bacchus garlanded with grapes and other fruit (5:49), and on the walls hung paintings of classical subjects. In the Velvet Bedroom next door the dominant theme was Venus, goddess of love, expressed in emphatic fashion by the splendid bed with its scallop shell headboard. Around the walls were Brussels tapestries depicting *The Love of Venus and Adonis*, woven specifically for the room.

Not all houses were as deliberately themed as Houghton, and one must assume that in many, perhaps most, cases furniture was bought from stock or made to standard patterns. By restricting the range of motifs to a handful of key elements, furniture makers were able to ensure that whatever they supplied – beds, tables, pier glasses or chairs – the result would be reasonably coherent and harmonious. The same would be true even if the furniture was bought from more than one maker. A common stylistic vocabulary ensured that all furniture-makers spoke the same language of allegory and symbols. This is one of the chief difficulties in making attributions to particular makers based on stylistic analogy alone. The chair in **4:64** is a case in point. This is from a set of eighteen back chairs and two settees supplied by William Hallet to Lord Irwin in 1735.[71] The style is modest, and the gaitered leg with its claw foot is one of the most common designs of the 1730s. Were it not for the surviving bill, these chairs would be indistinguishable from thousands of similar chairs made in London by scores of different makers.

Plate 4:66. Chair (1730-36). Walnut and parcel gilt with modern upholstery. One of a set made for the 4th Earl of Scarsdale (d.1736). The *verre églomisé* back panel and cast lead knee mounts are highly unusual. The chairs are tentatively attributed to the London upholsterer Thomas How (fl. c.1710-33).

TEMPLE NEWSAM HOUSE, LEEDS CITY ART GALLERIES

Chair design in the 1730s

The typical high quality banister back chair of the 1730s had a compassed back, compassed seat, cabriole forelegs and OG back legs. Plate **4:65** shows an elbow chair bearing the arms of the Suckling family of Suffolk; the needlework seat is dated 1732.[72] The proportions are noticeably broader than chairs of the 1720s and, as well as being bended 'India-fashion' and 'compassed', the back is dished in the horizontal plane. This was an extraordinarily complex shape, and perhaps for this reason it became increasingly common to make the back straight rather than bended, but retaining the horizontal dishing. Plate **4:66** is one of a pair of chairs from Sutton Scarsdale, Yorkshire, a house completed in 1728. It combines a compass back with a linked banister and compass seat.[73] In the centre of the backs is a *verre églomisé* panel bearing the arms of the 4th Earl of Scarsdale, who died in 1736. This highly unusual embellishment is combined with another, in the form of gilt lead mounts on the knees and centre rail.

71. Gilbert (1967).
72. Christie's, London, *English Furniture*, 29 March 1984, lot 33.
73. Gilbert (1998), III, pp. 581-2.

Plate 4:67. Chair (1730-40). Walnut and beech, with modern upholstery. Despite the similarities with Grendey's labelled oeuvre, the large number of surviving examples of this model suggests he is unlikely to have been the only supplier.
TEMPLE NEWSAM HOUSE, LEEDS CITY ART GALLERIES

The chair in **4:67** has been attributed to Giles Grendey on the strength of similarities with labelled examples,[74] but it is shown here simply because it is so typical of its type and period. Even without the bended back, banister back chairs were a product of some complexity, requiring a high degree of workshop organisation as well as individual competence. The fore-legs, back posts and top rail were of solid walnut, and in order to achieve the desired shape without waste of timber, all these elements were thicknessed with additional timber at the necessary points (**4:68**). The splat was either of walnut or a cheaper wood, on to which veneers of figured walnut were glued. The figuring was carefully chosen to continue on to the crest rail and down the forward face of posts above the seat. The curved seat rails were cut from solid timber, usually oak or beech, and then veneered. An ovolo bead was glued to the top of the rails to locate the seat. Because of the complex shaping of the back the frame had to be cut and joined with great precision.

The jointing of the seat rails on compass seats reveals much about the quality of the chair itself. The simplest method was to tenon the rails into the top of the leg, but because of its rounded, triangular shape there was very little room for a conventional tenon, which had a shoulder on each side. A common solution was to use a barefaced tenon with only one shoulder and support the inner, un-shouldered side with a glued block (**4:69**). A much stronger joint could be made by half-lapping the seat rails and then tenoning the top of the leg though them (**4:70**). The joint was then supported by substantial blocking on the underside (**4:71**). Plate **4:72** shows another version of this joint, using the top of the leg cut in a dovetail to lock the joint together.

74. Gilbert (1998), p. 720, note on Cat. No. 56.

Seat Furniture

Plate 4:68. Detail of 4:67, showing how the back posts and splat have been thicknessed to create the shaping of the back.

Plate 4:71. Rear view of 4:70, showing the lapped rails and the substantial blocking beneath. The area has been finished with a rasp after assembly.

Plate 4:69. Detail of 4:67, showing the simplest method of jointing the seat rails to the leg. The side rail has a single scribe line (arrowed) marking one edge of the tenon. The other side of the tenon is formed by the outside face of the rail, which is then supported by the glued triangular block. This is a 'bare-faced' tenon, made necessary by the angle of the rail and the small dimensions of the top of the leg.

Plate 4:70. Alternative seat construction. The front and side rails are half-lapped over each other and secured with a dowel. The top of the leg forms a tenon which passes through both rails and locks them together. This is a very strong joint. Notice how the top of the joint has been faced off with a toothed plane after construction, before the retaining bead for the seat was applied.

Plate 4:72. Alternative seat construction. This method has half-lapped rails locked by the dovetail-shaped top of the leg.

179

Seat Furniture

Above left:
Plate 4:73. Chair (1734). Walnut and beechwood, with later upholstery. One of a set of ten supplied by Daniel Bell and Thomas Moore. The bill for these chairs is the fullest contemporary description known of this classic Georgian type (see text).
LADY LEVER ART GALLERY, NATIONAL MUSEUMS AND GALLERIES ON MERSEYSIDE

Above right:
Plate 4:74. Chair (1730-40). Mahogany and beechwood, with later upholstery. A variant of the design shown in 4:73. The splat and seat rails are veneered, but less expensive versions were usually made entirely in the solid. RONALD PHILLIPS LTD, LONDON

The generally broader proportions of chairs allowed a bolder style of decoration based on neo-Palladian iconography, incorporating the lions' masks, claw and paw feet and other motifs. Plate **4:73** shows one of a set of chairs supplied by Daniel Bell and Thomas Moore to the 'Honourable Counsellor Rider' of Sandon Hall, Stafford, in November 1734. The bill is worth quoting in full since it provides such a complete contemporary description:

To ten hansome Wallnuttree Chairs broad banister backs cutt in a shape with scrole tops finneard with very good wood, loose compass seats, stuft in white Hessings with rich carved fore feet with Lyons faces on Ye Knees and Lyons Paws & O.Ge back feet with scrolls and carved shells to ye fore-rails... £27.10.00.[75]

These chairs were complemented by another set with upholstered seats and backs and matching legs, and a pair of marble slab tables whose frames were carved with lions' masks and paw feet.

The Sandon Hall chairs make an interesting comparison with the mahogany example in **4:74**. The stylistic similarities are obvious, but less so are the differences in construction. Whereas the walnut chairs are veneered on all forward surfaces, the mahogany version is predominantly in solid wood, with a veneered splat and seat rail. The difference between the two is entirely due to the lower cost of mahogany at this date. Cheaper versions were made entirely in the solid, with no attempt to reveal figure in the wood (4:78).

Perhaps the most spectacular versions of the lion-mask model are those reputedly made for Stowe House, Buckinghamshire, and now dispersed among many of the world's great furniture collections (**4:75**).[76] At one time these were attributed to James Moore, but the regal proportions, coupled with the lions' masks and paw feet, suggest a date of about 1735, long after Moore's death in 1726.

75. Strange (1928); for Daniel Bell and Thomas Moore see *DEFM*.
76. For an analysis of the suite's provenance see Christie's, London, *Important English Furniture*, 8 July 1998, lot 100. The most objective discussion of the chairs remains that by William Rieder (1978)

Seat Furniture

Plate 4:75. Chair (1730-40). Gilded wood. One of a set probably made for Richard Temple, 1st Viscount Cobham, for Stowe House, Buckinghamshire. This is perhaps the most regal example of the lion's mask design in existence. COURTESY OF SOTHEBY'S

Seat Furniture

While rich and fashionable patrons demanded the latest in high style seat furniture for their most public apartments, there was a continuing demand for good but modestly styled chairs made to well-established patterns. Plate **4:76** is one of five survivors from a set of twelve made for the Wardens of Rochester Bridge in 1735. The cost of the elbow chairs was 30s. each (with an additional 5s. each for the inlaid motto under the coat of arms) and the seats were originally covered with 'Spanish' leather.

Slightly later in date is the restrained banister back chair in **4:77**, one of six supplied to Stoneleigh Abbey, Warwickshire. One of the set is neatly signed 'Jn York, Warwickshire' and this maker is known to have supplied several items of furniture to Stoneleigh in May 1738.[77] In stylistic terms there is nothing to distinguish this chair from one made at any time in the previous ten or even fifteen years, except that the back is no longer ergonomically curved.

The gradual decline of India backs among fashionable chair-makers is reflected in the relative paucity of bills for such chairs in the Lord Chamberlain's accounts after c.1735 – the last known bill for India back chairs made for the Royal Palaces is dated 1739.[78] The mahogany example in **4:78** is probably of about this date, the only significant difference between this and earlier models being the deep seat rails, which are characteristic of the late 1730s and 1740s. However, the type was still immensely popular in the country at large, for India back chairs are the most common form of seating depicted in portraits and conversation pieces of the 1730s.

---

77. *DEFM*.
78. PRO LC 9/288.

Above left:
Plate 4:76. Elbow chair (1735). Walnut, with later seat. Supplied in October 1735 by Timothy Matthews and Erasmus Delafield, of the *Royal Bed and Rising Sun*, off Fleet Street. The arms and motto in the back are inlaid in holly, and were originally coloured blue, red and black.
ROCHESTER BRIDGE TRUST

Far left:
Plate 4:77. Chair (c.1738). Walnut, with later seat. Made for Stoneleigh Abbey by a local Warwickshire maker, John York. Like the previous example, this is a deceptively late and simple version of the banister back chair. PARTRIDGE FINE ART

Left:
Plate 4:78. Chair (1735-50). Mahogany, with later seat. Unlike the previous chair this still has an ergonomically curved back. The deep seat rails suggest a late date, however.
BENINGBOROUGH, THE NATIONAL TRUST

The unbended but dished banister back design endured longer still. Plate **4:79** shows one of a set of twelve chairs supplied by Thomas Chippendale to Aske Hall, Yorkshire, in May 1765. They were billed as: '12 very large best Red stain'd Chairs wt sweep backs…' and cost 7s. each.[79]

Mythical masks, whether on the legs or the seat rail, were another aspect of neo-Palladian influence. A suite supplied by William Bradshaw for Chevening, in Kent, in 1736 is one of the few documented examples of this style (**4:80**). It comprised '8 Rich carv'd and gilt Chair frames' at £3.15s. apiece, and '2 Settees Do' at £11.11s. The upholstery is the original green Genoa velvet costing 29s. a yard, and this, together with loose covers, almost doubled the cost of the suite.[80] The similarities between these chairs and the satyr-mask chairs at Houghton have given rise to suggestions of a common authorship, but the similarities may be more generic than specific.

The female or Venus mask shown in **4:81** was a common alternative to the satyr mask. The source of these chairs with masks on the rail has been the subject of speculation over the years, but attempts to identify and isolate the products of particular workshops (except the Chevening chairs) has so far not borne fruit.[81] In common with many chairs of this period, **4:81** has a wide ovolo moulding around the base of the seat. When this feature was first introduced in the 1720s the moulding tended to be quite narrow (described in Thomas Roberts' bills as a 'bead'), but in the broader version is characteristic of the 1730s.

79. Gilbert (1978), pp. 158-9.
80. Kent County Record Office, MS., U 1590, A20a
81. Symonds (December 1954).

Top:
Plate 4:79. Chair (1765). Elm with later seat. This is one of a set of twelve supplied by Thomas Chippendale to Aske Hall in 1765. These are probably the latest documented examples of the compassed banister back style originally developed in the 1720s.
ASKE HALL, THE MARQUESS OF ZETLAND

Above:
Plate 4:80. Two chairs and a settee (1736). Gilded wood frames with most of the original blue velvet upholstery. This is part of a suite supplied by William Bradshaw to the Earl of Stanhope in 1736. It is the only documented 'satyr's mask' suite known.
CHEVENING, COUNTRY LIFE

Right:
Plate 4:81. Chair (1730-40). Walnut and beechwood frame with later upholstery in a contemporary style.
APTER-FREDERICKS

Seat Furniture

Plate 4:82. Elbow Chair (1735). Carved and gilt wood with later upholstery. Supplied by Stephen Langley for Lady Burlington's Garden Room at Chiswick Villa. There were originally ten chairs in the set; four survive at Chatsworth and five, formerly at Holker Hall, Cumbria, are now back at Chiswick Villa.
CHATSWORTH,
THE DUKE OF DEVONSHIRE

Stephen Langley's chairs made for the Countess of Burlington's Garden Room at Chiswick Villa stand out because of their idiosyncratic detailing, incorporating oak leaves and acorns, and a key pattern and flowerhead repeat on legs and elbows which would more commonly appear on architectural friezes (**4:82**). His bill describes them in detail, and lengthy descriptions are usually a good indication that something out of the ordinary has been attempted:[82]

For tenn Large Elbow chair frames made wt fine Carved feet, Elbows and Stumps in the Wood, whiting wt Keywork flowers, Oak leaves, Acorns and other Ornaments very richly gilt in Burnish'd gold after the most curious and completed manner at £8 5s each... £82.10.0.[83]

82. Very little else is known of Langley's work. For the few facts available, see *DEFM*.
83. Chatsworth, MS., 247.0.

Seat Furniture

Plate 4:83. Stool (c.1740). Mahogany and beechwood, parcel-gilt with original green damask upholstery. Attributed to Benjamin Goodison. These are perhaps the ultimate expression of the conventional shell knee design which first emerged in the 1720s.
LONGFORD CASTLE, COUNTRY LIFE

Plate 4:84. Elbow chair (c.1740). Mahogany and beechwood parcel gilt frame with original cut velvet upholstery. Attributed to Benjamin Goodison.
LONGFORD CASTLE, COUNTRY LIFE

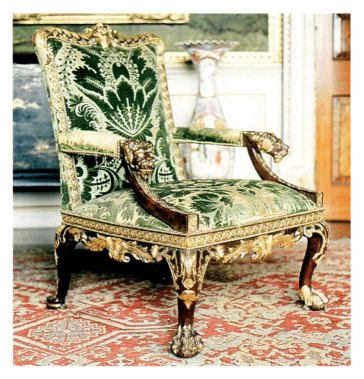

The bill also details bottoming, stuffing, and covering the chairs with green silk, and finishing them with '5,200 Charriot Bullion nailes double gilt wt gold' at 18s. per hundred. The total cost of the suite, which also included two sofas, amounted to just under £200.[84]

The shell knee and claw or paw foot continued fashionable until well after 1740. At Longford Castle, Wiltshire, is a suite of stools almost certainly supplied by Benjamin Goodison (**4:83**). The attribution rests on payments amounting to £1,585.19s.6d. made by the 1st Viscount Folkstone to Goodison between 1737 and 1745. They were made for the Long Gallery, and the green silk damask for the covers and the walls was invoiced in 1740 at 12s. a yard.[85] Although the motifs are conventional, the detail is unusually rich and carved with great precision. Another generously-proportioned suite at Longford combines paw feet with lion's head arm terminals (**4:84**). These were made for the Green Drawing Room; the green 'flowered' velvet cost £1.4s. a yard and was supplied in 1743. Both suites are characterised by the use of pierced and carved ornament overlaying the upholstery around the base of the seats, a technique employed by Goodison on seat furniture supplied to Hampton Court Palace a few years earlier.

84. A drawing by William Kent in the Chatsworth Collection shows Lady Burlington sitting in one of the chairs in her Garden Room at Chiswick House Illustrated in Harris (1994), p. 189.
85. Longford Castle Archives.

Seat Furniture

Acanthus carving appears quite commonly on pier and sideboard tables from the 1720s onwards, but on seat furniture it seems not to have been widely used before the mid-1730s. A large set of acanthus-carved elbow chairs and sofas at Chatsworth exemplifies the generously proportioned style of the late 1730s, with pronounced brackets to the legs enriched with gilt acanthus leaves and scrolls (**4:85**). A set of similarly substantial chairs, this time with lions' masks and paw feet, was supplied for the new Treasury Offices in 1739 (**4:86**).

One of the few fully documented suites with this style of leg is at Bowringsleigh, Devon. It was supplied in 1739 by Elizabeth Hutt & Son of St Paul's Churchyard, and comprised two settees and six chairs.[86] The two 'Seattys' costing £7.10s. the pair are of conventional form with leaf carved knees, claw feet and eagle's head elbows, but the chairs (at 25s. each) have a novel style of back presumably derived from contemporary ladder back 'Dutch' chairs (**4:87**). The ladder back remained a perennial favourite of English chairmakers and their patrons, and is a rare example of a vernacular style being adapted for fashionable furniture.

---

86. Jervis (1993). The Bowringsleigh chairs make an interesting comparison with a set of six walnut chairs of a similar pattern from Newport church, Essex, bearing the trade label of Giles Grendey; Jervis (1974).

Above:
Plate 4:85. Chair (1735-45). Mahogany and beechwood frame with carved gilt enrichments and later upholstery. This is one of a large set at Chatsworth which, although undocumented, epitomises the heavier style of the late 1730s and 1740s. CHATSWORTH, THE DUKE OF DEVONSHIRE

Below:
Plate 4:86. Suite of chairs (1739). Mahogany and beechwood with later upholstery. This suite made for the Treasury in Whitehall by an unknown maker is one of the most powerful expressions of the 'lion's mask' form. COUNTRY LIFE

Plate 4:87. Chair (1739). Mahogany and beechwood with modern upholstery. One of six supplied by Elizabeth Hutt to Bowringsleigh, Devon, costing £7.10s. the set plus 15s. for loose covers. These are the earliest documented examples of fashionable ladder back chairs, a type which remained popular throughout the eighteenth century. PRIVATE COLLECTION

Left:
Plate 4:88. Couch (1730-45). Walnut and beechwood, upholstery possibly original. In 18th century parlance a 'couch' was essentially a day-bed, quite distinct from a sofa or settee.
BENINGBOROUGH, THE NATIONAL TRUST

Below:
Plate 4:89. Settee (1730-45). Walnut and beechwood. The 'settee' derives etymologically from the same Latin root (*sedilia*) as 'settle' and both imply wooden seating, albeit sometimes with an upholstered or cushioned seat. A 'sofa' was usually a piece of fully upholstered furniture. CARLTON HOBBS

Sofas and settees

The terms 'sofa', 'settee' and 'couch' are now almost synonymous, but in the eighteenth century their meaning tended to be more specific. A 'couch' was not a seat but a bed with a raised back at one end – many would now call this a 'daybed'. A bill for furniture supplied by Thomas Roberts to Sir Robert Walpole's Arlington Street house in 1728-9 describes 'a large and strong wallnutree Couch frame with a Scrole head…'. The long cushion on it was described as a 'bed' (i.e., mattress).[87] Plate **4:88** shows a couch which conforms to this description.

A sofa usually had a fully upholstered back and sides, but a settee often differed from a sofa in having exposed wooden arms. Thus the settees cited in Thomas Roberts' bill of 1728 were described as having 'stuffed back and seate and Scrole Elbow'. It is also possible that settees could be entirely of wood. At Montagu House in 1746 the mahogany hall benches (now at Boughton) were described as 'settees', although in George Nix's bill of 1728 they were described as 'couches' (cf. 4:95).[88] A bill of James Moore the Younger for mahogany benches supplied to Sherborne House refers to '2 Mohoggony Settees'.[89] The potential distinction between fully upholstered sofas and wooden or partly wooden settees reflects the respective derivations of the terms. Settee probably derives from the medieval Latin *sedilia*, a seat or bench, usually of wood or stone. The term translated more directly into vernacular usage as 'settle'. Sofa came from the Arabic *suffa*, a bench covered with carpets and/or cushions. When introduced into England in the 1690s, a sofa was by definition upholstered. However, it is a moot point whether these distinctions were universally applied and how long they retained their separate meanings. It is probable that in general usage 'settee' and 'sofa' were to some extent interchangeable – the 'Seattees' supplied by William Hallet to Lord Irwin in 1735 apparently had upholstered arms.[90]

In parts of North America the distinction between sofas and settees was clearer. In the 1772 Philadelphia book of *Prices of Cabinet and Chair Work*, settees had upholstered seats and wooden backs made as multiples of chair-backs (**4:89**).[91]

87. Houghton Hall, Mss RB 1 57.
88. Montagu House (1746); Murdoch (1992), p. 135, n. 23.
89. *DEFM*. The Sherborne benches are now at Temple Newsam House.
90. Gilbert (1967); information on the Hallet settees kindly supplied by Anthony Wells-Cole.
91. Kirtley (2005).

Seat Furniture

Above left:
Plate 4:90. Dressing chair (?) (1725-40). Walnut and beechwood, with later upholstery. This distinctive type of chair survives in both fully- and part-upholstered forms. The low back and rounded seat with recurved arms are surely designed with a specific function in mind.
TENNANTS AUCTIONEERS

Above right:
Plate 4:91. Dressing chair (?) 1720-40. Walnut with later upholstery.
MALLETT

---
92. Cannons (1747).
93. Gilbert (1967).
94. Ibid.

Dressing chairs

Domestic inventories frequently include 'dressing chairs' among the furniture of bedchambers and dressing rooms. These usually occur singly or in pairs, but occasionally sets of dressing chairs are recorded. In 1725 the Duchess of Chandos had 'six japanned dressing chairs with matted seats and yellow damask cushions' in her dressing room at Cannons.[92] Dressing chairs are also recorded in furniture-makers' bills, such as the 'Two fine wallnutwood veneered dressing chair frames very handsomely made wth stuft Backs & seat coverd with your gold silk made all Compleat & Fashonable', supplied by Remey George to Lord Irwin in February 1718/19.[93] At five guineas the pair these were expensive chairs. Something more modest was supplied by Thomas Green in 1723 – 'a large wallnuttree Dressing Chair with Carved feet and Carved Scrowl elbows stufft with fine Curled hair and Covered over wth linnen Silk thread cord and makeing the chair being covered with needlework compleat… 6s.6d.'.[94]

Despite the wealth of contemporary references a securely documented 'dressing chair' has yet to be identified, so we can only speculate as to what these chairs looked like and how they were distinguished from other types of chair. However, one can glean a few clues from the documents. First, they could be either wholly upholstered or with wooden backs. Second, most appear to have had arms or 'elbows'. Third, they usually occur singly or in pairs, and only rarely in sets. Fourth, they were sufficiently different from other chairs to be readily identifiable, not only to their makers, but to the compilers of domestic inventories. One relatively common type of chair that fits all these criteria is shown in **4:90** and **4:91**. The form is always distinctive, with a round or oval seat, open arms and a low, cartouche-shaped back. The low back is probably significant, because it bucks the general trend towards backs at shoulder height or higher, exposing and leaving unsupported the back of the head, neck and shoulders. It could conceivably be intended to allow access to the head and shoulders of a person having his or her wig powdered and dressed. Many of these chairs have a distinctive form of arm with recurved and hooked terminals which are now called 'shepherd's crook' arms. The design was not exclusive to dressing chairs, however, and was popular between about 1720 and 1740.

Some authorities suggest that these chairs might have been 'writing' or 'smoking' chairs, which is plausible.[95] But whereas 'writing' and 'smoking' chairs do not commonly occur in contemporary terminology, dressing chairs certainly do.

'Kentian' seat furniture

With the exception of the India back itself, the stylistic developments described thus far were essentially evolutionary rather than revolutionary. Although their cumulative effect was dramatic, most of the changes in chair design between 1715 and 1740 were incremental, and it is not difficult to see how chair-makers adapted existing models to accommodate new ideas as they arose. The adoption of 'Roman' motifs such as claw feet or masks on the knees did not alter the basic design of seat furniture, nor could it disguise its essentially baroque inspiration. But from the mid-1720s new forms of seat furniture emerged which owed very little to conventional English antecedents. Almost invariably these were linked to commissions in which William Kent or members of his circle were involved. Chairs, settees and benches were conceived *ab initio* as adjuncts to their architectural setting, at the same time introducing a strong vein of theatricality or set-dressing. The criticism often levelled at this 'Kentian' furniture is that it puts dogma before comfort, practicality and even sound construction. But this is perhaps to miss the point, since such furniture was often made not for comfort but for visual effect.

The first seats in this new architectural style were the monumental benches made for entrance halls at houses like Ditchley and Houghton (**4:92**). John Cornforth has suggested that the prototype for these, in form if not in style, can be found in the late seventeenth century benches at Ham House, which were intended to stand in loggias, colonnades and perhaps gardens (**4:93**).[96]

Below left:
Plate 4:92. Hall bench, c.1726. Painted deal. This is one of six benches made for the entrance hall in Ditchley. The design is almost certainly by William Kent, who was paid £250 in 1726 for painting the ceiling, and provided two paintings for the north wall in 1731. It is possible, however, that the benches were designed by Henry Flitcroft, who completed some interiors at Ditchley from 1736. The backs of these benches, with their splayed sides and scrolled top rails, are the progenitors of the fan back chair of the 1740s. DITCHLEY FOUNDATION

Below right:
Plate 4:93. Bench (1675-1700). Oak. It is possible that benches for loggias and colonnades, such as this one at Ham House, were the prototypes for the hall benches installed in neo-Palladian houses from the mid-1720s onwards, but see 4:94.
HAM HOUSE, THE NATIONAL TRUST

---

95. Symonds (1929), figs. 89-94, 99-100. *DEF*, I, fig. 142.
96. Cornforth (2004), p. 37.

Seat Furniture

Above:
Plate 4:94. *Cassapanca* (Italian, 1718). Painted wood. This type of large, heavily carved and decorated hall bench was presumably familiar to English designers who studied in Italy, such as William Kent and James Gibbs, and may have been the inspiration for benches made for Ditchley, Houghton, Wilton and elsewhere. This example is signed by an otherwise unrecorded artist, Jacopo Togni, and dated 1718.   PELHAM GALLERIES, PARIS & LONDON

Below left:
Plate 4:95. Bench (c.1728). Mahogany. One of four. These benches have been attributed to George Nix on the strength of an entry in the 2nd Duke of Montagu's accounts. However, the account refers to four 'mahogany couches as per bill… £14.0.0'. Is this a couch?   BOUGHTON HOUSE, THE DUKE OF BUCCLEUCH

Below right:
Plate 4:96. Bench (1730-40). Mahogany and deal. One of a pair, together with six monumental elbow chairs, made for the hall at Badminton and possibly designed by James Gibbs, who designed the hall.   BADMINTON HOUSE, THE DUKE OF BEAUFORT

Ultimately they derive from the Italian *cassapanca*, combining monumental size with a full repertoire of neo-Palladian symbolism (**4:94**).

Hall benches were ideal test-beds for neo-Palladian design, since they were static, closely linked to the architectural fabric, and comfort was not a consideration. The form was rapidly adopted by architects and craftsmen working within the extended Burlington/Kent circle such as Henry Flitcroft. Flitcroft designed a Thames-side villa at Whitehall for the 2nd Duke of Montagu, and the mahogany benches supplied by George Nix for the Banqueting Hall in 1728 are the earliest fully documented examples of their kind (**4:95**).[97] The design was later engraved in a slightly modified form and published as plate 42 in Vardy's *Some Designs of Inigo Jones & Mr. William Kent* (1744). Interestingly, similar benches are also associated with James Gibbs, an architect more often thought of in connection with baroque than neo-Palladian architecture. At Badminton is a set of benches and elbow chairs of monumental form with baroque detailing, a combination which points strongly to the authorship of James Gibbs, who also designed the hall in which they stand (**4:96**). Like many of his contemporaries, Gibbs was prepared to adopt many aspects of the new orthodoxy without surrendering to it entirely.

At Wilton formal benches were brought from the entrance hall into the heart of the house. Henry Herbert, the 9th Earl of Pembroke, inherited Wilton in 1733, and embarked on an ambitious programme of refurbishment in which Kent was almost certainly involved. A friend of Sir Robert Walpole, Herbert probably met Kent at Houghton, and he is known to have been an admirer of Kent's work.[98] Six settees were made for the Double Cube Room created by John Webb eighty years previously. They employ the full range of neo-Palladian motifs, skilfully assembled to create the impression of weight and mass while being only 5ft. (1.5m) long (**4:97**). The maker of these *tours de force* is unknown, but James Pascall, John Boson, Elka Haddock and Samuel Jones are all possible candidates.[99]

Plate 4:97. Upholstered bench (1730-40). Carved and gilded wood. These settees, attributed to William Kent, are among the best known and purest expressions of Kent's style. Neither the upholstery nor the gilding are original, and the original finish and colour scheme are a matter of conjecture.

WILTON, THE EARL OF PEMBROKE

97. John Hardy in Murdoch (1992), pp. 135-5.
98. Jackson-Stops (1985), pp. 240-41.
99. For more on these makers, see the relevant entries in *DEFM*.

Seat Furniture

Left:
Plate 4:98. Hall chair (1730). Oak. This is one of eighteen chairs supplied by George Nix to Ham House in August 1730, at a cost of £1 each. The arms on the back are those of the Tollemaches, owners of Ham House. The form is a common one, and derives from the Italian renaissance *sgabello*. The contrast in style between this and Kent's hall chair in 4:99 is marked.

HAM HOUSE, THE NATIONAL TRUST

Below:
Plate 4:99. Hall chair (1730-40). Mahogany. Probably designed by William Kent for the Tribune at Chiswick Villa.

CHATSWORTH, THE DUKE OF DEVONSHIRE

Like the *cassapanca*, the *sgabello* was also an Italian design, which in this case had first appeared in England in the early seventeenth century. Their sudden return to popularity in the 1720s was almost certainly a consequence of the neo-Palladian revival (**4:98**). However, for Chiswick Villa Lord Burlington chose a different design of hall chair for which no precedents are known (**4:99**).[100] The formality of these chairs epitomises the academic, even pedantic approach to classical design which characterises the most doctrinaire neo-Palladian interiors. The Dome Saloon in which they were placed was the central room of the villa, serving both as an entrance hall and a connecting axis for the adjacent suites. Unlike a conventional saloon it was without fireplaces or any upholstered furniture; 'In winter it must have been bitterly cold, almost uninhabitable'.[101] Fortunately Kent, unlike his patron Lord Burlington, was no pedagogue, for even the most committed neo-Palladian needed a modicum of comfort. Other seat furniture designed by Kent either for Chiswick or Devonshire House evinces a less academic approach which combines conventional chair-making with architectural forms and elements of the Italian baroque.[102] One might call this the 'Kentian compromise'. In **4:100** the rounded cabriole leg with baroque mask and headdress has been

100. Rosoman (1987).
101. Harris (1994), p. 120.
102. The 1770 inventory of Chiswick records several sets of gilt backstools and elbow chairs in the villa to which these probably belonged (Rosoman, 1986).

Plate 4:100. Chair (1730-40). Carved and gilded wood with later upholstery. This is one of a set almost certainly made for Chiswick Villa to designs by William Kent.　　　　　　　　　　　　　　Chatsworth, The Duke of Devonshire

Plate 4:101. Chair (c.1730). Mahogany, beech and oak with gilt enrichments and original crimson caffoy covers. Probably designed by William Kent, the carving attributed to James Richards. The splayed back and scrolled top rail were immensely influential in English chair design, giving rise to the fan back style of the 1740s and determining the shape of most English chair backs right through the rococo period.　　　　　　　Houghton Hall, The Marquess of Cholmondeley

transformed into a square section truss with 'money-moulding' decoration and fish-scale sides, both of which became standard neo-Palladian decorative devices. The rear leg and back posts are likewise square in section, while the crest-rail is conceived as a pair of opposed scrolls centred on a scallop shell. The splayed back and scrolled crest rail occur on many of Kent's designs, and probably derive from Italian chairs of state illustrated by Giovanni Giardini and others.

At Houghton the seat furniture made for the Saloon stands out from the other suites at Houghton because it is designed and made in a completely different idiom (**4:101**). The forelegs are modified cabrioles headed by Venus masks adorned with a shell headdress; the Venusian theme is further endorsed by the large shell-centred apron. Scrolled brackets to the forelegs offer some structural support, but not enough, for iron brackets have been added behind. The odd construction lends support to the conjecture that these chairs are probably carver's rather than chair-maker's work, and have plausibly been attributed to James Richards, who executed a number of Kent's designs. The rich caffoy upholstery, which matches that on the walls, was supplied by Thomas Roberts in 1729, which gives an approximate date for the chairs themselves.[103]

103. Houghton Hall, Mss RB 1 57.

Seat Furniture

Plate 4:102. Chair (1735-45). Mahogany with gilt enrichments and modern upholstery. This is one of a set of ten made for Francis North, 1st Earl of Guildford, about 1740. North was a friend of the Prince of Wales and would have been well acquainted with the 'Kentian' furniture at Kew and elsewhere. The shape of the back, particularly the top rail, echoes that of 4:97. A settee en suite is at Temple Newsam House, Leeds.
CARLTON HOBBS

Plate 4:103. Chair (1725-40). Carved and gilded wood with later upholstery. One of a set made for either Chiswick Villa or Devonshire House. This is a traditional X-frame design modified to conform to neo-Palladian precepts. The designer was perhaps William Kent.
CHATSWORTH, THE DUKE OF DEVONSHIRE

The chair in **4:102** is another illustration of how adroitly English chair-makers translated established forms into a neo-Palladian idiom. It comes from a set of ten made for Francis North, 1st Earl of Guildford, probably for his country house at Wroxton Abbey, Oxfordshire. The maker is unknown, but payments to both John Boson (1740) and Benjamin Goodison (1756) are recorded in the North papers.[104] It is essentially a cabriole-leg chair whose legs have been squared into architectural trusses and carved with fashionable fish scales. Similar legs occur on seat furniture made for Stourhead, Wiltshire,[105] and on tables supplied by Benjamin Goodison to Hampton Court Palace in 1733. The back has a crest rail which appears to be a derivation of the Italianate form seen in **4:100** and **4:101**, and the multiple splat is conceived almost as a type of coffering, the links between the interlaced ovals being decorated carved gilt flowerheads.

X-framed chairs acquired a new lease of life in Palladian houses. Plate **4:103** is an X-framed chair of state re-cast in a neo-Palladian mould, and was almost certainly made for Chiswick or Devonshire House. Similar chairs, with stools en suite, were supplied by Henry Williams for the Queen's Withdrawing Room at Hampton Court Palace in 1737.[106] Plate **4:104** is probably the richest and best documented example of this type, supplied by the carver James Richards for Frederick, Prince of Wales in 1733/4, and intended for the Royal Gallery at Kew. According to William Chambers, 'The Gallery, with all its furniture, is entirely executed from the designs of the same gentleman [William Kent]'.[107]

---

104. *DEFM*; Carlton Hobbs Ltd, Cat. III, No. 17. A settee from this suite is at Temple Newsam House, Leeds, and is illustrated in Gilbert (1978), Cat. No. 325, p. 269.
105. *DEF*, I, p. 269, fig. 134; III, p. 89, fig. 41.
106. Edwards and Jourdain (1955), p. 96, figs. 217 and 219; *DEFM*.
107. Geoffrey Beard in Christie's, London, *Important English Furniture*, 9 July 1998, lot 40.

Seat Furniture

4:104. Chair of State (1733/4). Carved and gilded wood with modern upholstery. Probably designed by William Kent and carved by James Richards. This chair was supplied by James Richards for the Prince of Wales' palace at Kew. Richards' bill describes '2 Very rich Chairs of state wth Sev[ll] Ornaments to fronts and sides Back and Elbows.... At Ea[ch] £12.0.0'. Six stools and two long stools were en suite.
HARRIS LINDSAY

Seat Furniture

Right:
4:105. Sofa (1735-45). Gilded beechwood with modern upholstery. This is a less 'architectural' interpretation of the X-frame form, and arguably a more appealing design as a result.
HAM HOUSE, THE NATIONAL TRUST

Below:
Plate 4:106. Chair (1725-50), Mahogany with modern upholstery. The dating of these chairs from Langley Park is debatable. The suite has been attributed to Thomas Chippendale, but the form of the chairs is early, with a waisted back and scrolled arms terminals typical of the 1730s and 1740s. CHRISTIE'S

A suite at Ham House grafts the X-frame design on to a conventional back and arms, at the same time softening the frame into a less architectural form (**4:105**). The date is probably c.1740, when many additions and alterations were made to the furniture at Ham. At least two London furniture makers, Peter Hasert and John Hele, were involved in this phase of furnishing, but this suite is not recorded in their surviving bills. Another X-frame variant is shown in **4:106**. This is one of a set from Langley Park, Norfolk; it is assumed to relate to work carried out there for Sir William Beauchamp-Proctor soon after his inheritance in 1744. Its authorship is uncertain, but William Hallet is known to have supplied furniture there in the 1740s.[108]

The origins of the fan back chair

It is often thought that the 'Kentian' style remained a relatively exclusive one, not generally taken up by furniture-makers at large. In fact, some elements of Kent's designs achieved widespread popularity, albeit in diluted form. The most obvious of these is the 'fan back' chair, which seems to have appeared about 1740 and continued in vogue for several decades (**4:107**). The splayed back with its scrolled shoulders clearly did not derive from the same lineage as the banister back, with its rounded, in-curved top. Nor did the double-scrolled variant in **4:108**. In both cases the obvious starting point seems to be Kent's splayed back chairs and benches of the late 1720s and early 1730s. There is a large set of fan back chairs (with some of a later date) at Badminton, where they seem always to have been used as dining room chairs (4:107). Another set is at

196

Seat Furniture

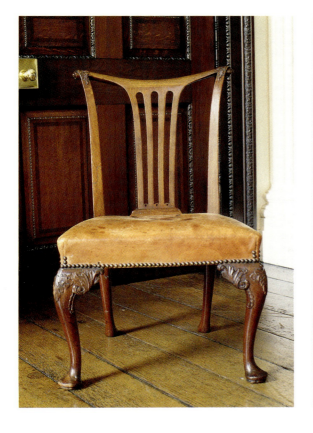

Far left:
Plate 4:107. Chair (1740-50). Mahogany and beech, with modern upholstery. The splayed back and scrolled top rail derives from Italian models adapted by Kent for Houghton Hall and elsewhere.
BADMINTON HOUSE
THE DUKE OF BEAUFORT

Left:
Plate 4:108. Chair (1745). Walnut and beech with modern upholstery. One of twenty-four supplied by John Willis of St Paul's Churchyard to Emmanuel College, Cambridge. This set of chairs is the earliest documented example of the fan back design.
ROBERT WILLIAMS/EMMANUEL COLLEGE

Plate 4:109. Design for a Garden (detail). This is from plate 16 of *Nouveaux Livre de Parterres contenant 24 pensées differants*, published by Daniel Marot about 1712. The radiating plume or fan shown at the bottom of the picture is a constantly recurring baroque device which also occurs on early rococo designs (cf. 4:111). It might also be the source of the splat design for fan back chairs.

Rousham and another at Ditchley, both also in the dining rooms.[109] Interestingly all three houses are associated with Kent. The three sets probably date from the late 1730s or early 1740s. The first documented examples dated from 1745, when the London chair-maker John Willis supplied twenty-four chairs and two settees to Emmanuel College, Cambridge (4:108). The bill describes them as 'Virginia wall't fann back Double scrole top chairs... 22s each'.[110] Willis' chairs have carved flowerheads linking the radiating bars of the splat, echoing the gilt flowerheads on the Wroxton Abbey chairs (4:102). The origins of the fan splat itself are less obvious, but the piercing on 4:108 resembles an etiolated rendering of the plume device which occurs so commonly in baroque decoration of all kinds (**4:109**). If this was the case, then there is a clear stylistic link

---
108. *DEFM*.
109. Cornforth (2004), p. 295, fig. 392
110. For more on Willis see *DEFM*.

Seat Furniture

Left:
Plate 4:110. Chair (1740-60). Mahogany, with original leather seat. The fan back model formed the basis of many subsequent designs even where, as here, rococo elements were introduced.   RIEVAULX TERRACES, THE NATIONAL TRUST

Below:
4:111. Designs for chairs (1741). These designs from William De La Cour's *First Book of Ornament* reveal how baroque forms elided seamlessly into the rococo. The first indications of the change can be seen in Bradshaw's French-style chairs at Chevening (4:112).

Opposite page:
4:112. Chair (1736). Mahogany and beech, with original tapestry covers. This set of chairs made for the 2nd Earl of Stanhope is the first in the new unequivocally French style which swept the nation in the 1740s. The stubby, leaf-carved arm terminals became known as 'French elbows', and the scroll toes feature on almost every design for 'French' chairs illustrated in English mid-18th century design books.
REPRODUCED BY KIND PERMISSION OF THE TRUSTEES OF THE CHEVENING ESTATES

111. Kent County Record Office, MS., U 1590, A 20a; '12 Large mahogany Elbow Chairs on Castors, finish'd with gilt Nails and fringe & holland Check Cases… a £5.8.4. p. Chair… £65.0 0. 2 Large Saffoys Do & Cases & Mohair to the cheeks…£29.13.10'.
112. Cornforth (2004), p. 295, fig. 393.

between the plain fan back and more complex designs such as that in **4:110**. Here there is a combination of a fan back with interlaced strapwork and paired scrolls or trusses, mixing baroque and classical or neo-Palladian motifs. At the same time the overall outline of the splat is clearly a derivation of the banister back design, as is its construction. It might be suggested, therefore, that chairs such as this demonstrate an integration of Chinese, baroque and neo-Palladian ideas which emerged in the late 1730s or early 1740s. They were soon to be joined by a new wave of rococo designs from Continental Europe. The first published signs of this new wave can be seen in the designs of Gaetano Brunetti (1736) and William De La Cour (1741) (**4:111**), but it is clear that change was already stirring among some furniture-makers in the mid-1730s. Chairs supplied by William Bradshaw for Chevening in 1736 embody some salient features of the new style, including French-style arms and legs (**4:112**). Of two sofas and twelve armchairs delivered, one sofa and eleven chairs are still in the house.[111] A similar set of walnut-framed chairs with carved frames in the French taste were supplied, probably by Bradshaw about 1740, for the drawing-room at Ditchley. John Cornforth has described these as 'one of the earliest examples of English furniture in the French taste', but the Chevening chairs are earlier and fully documented.[112] It could be argued that, despite the enthusiasm for the 'Italian gusto' which swept the country in the late 1720s and 1730s, the French taste had always been present (in the cabriole leg itself, for instance) quietly transforming itself from the baroque to the rococo. Most historians see these as distinct artistic phenomena, but to contemporaries the progression must have seemed entirely natural.

Seat Furniture

Chapter Five
TABLES AND STANDS

Plate 5:30 (Detail). Table (1735-50). See page 215

1. *DEFM*; Murdoch (2003).
2. These have long been associated with the refurbishment of Hampton Court Palace in 1715-16. See Rutherford (1927); Jourdain and Edwards (1955); Roberts (2002), pp. 153-55; Murdoch (2003). I have recently argued that they were made for the State Apartments at Kensington Palace 1722-26 (Bowett (2005)).
3. Illustrated in Edwards and Jourdain (1955); Murdoch (2003).
4. Friedman (1984), fig. 141.
5. Murdoch (2003); these were offered for sale at Sotheby's, London, 6 June 2005, lot 17.

The end of the 'triad'

The early career of James Moore, who succeeded Gerrit Jensen as cabinet-maker to the Royal Household in 1714, is obscure.[1] He must have been a furniture-maker of some substance to have been awarded the position, and he worked at a number of importance houses before 1714, including Dalkeith Palace, Boughton House and Marlborough House. However, his reputation as a maker of the first rank rests on the gilded tables and stands supplied by him and his partner John Gumley to George I between 1722 and 1726.[2] As a group they embody the final flowering of the suite or 'triad' of table, stands and mirror, which had been a key element of baroque interiors since the 1660s.

Moore's royal tables evince two distinct design influences. The first and most important was French; the pillar-leg design of **5:1** and **5:3** is a direct development of the tables supplied by Gerrit Jensen and the Pelletiers to William III and Queen Anne, and these in turn were derived from tables made in the 1690s for Louis XIV (**5:2**).[3] The decision to use these stately but perhaps rather old-fashioned designs to furnish the new state apartments of Kensington Palace may have been governed by a desire to demonstrate continuity with the palace style of the late Stuarts. Elsewhere fashion had moved on, for tables with 'claw' or cabriole legs were already current. Among James Gibbs' designs for Sudbrook House, Surrey (1715-19), is one for the saloon showing a cabriole-leg table in the French Régence style placed centrally below a niche (this is in fact the earliest English depiction of a cabriole leg table).[4] Nevertheless, the Royal Wardrobe was not alone in favouring the older model. Tables similar to **5:1** were supplied to Thomas Parker, 1st Lord Macclesfield before 1721, and to the Duke of Marlborough before 1722.[5] Neither pair matches the richness and mature sophistication of the royal examples, which represent the apotheosis of Moore's work in this vein. Plate **5:3** was also an established Moore design, first employed for a pair of tables made for Richard Temple, Baron Cobham, which can be dated between 1714 and 1718.

Tables and Stands

Plate 5:1. Table (1724). Carved and gilt wood. One of a pair. This table and its accompanying stands (5:6) were probably made for the Privy Chamber in the King's apartments at Kensington Palace. The form of the table is similar to examples made for the Duke of Marlborough and Lord Macclesfield, but the execution is richer and the design more sophisticated. This is arguably the finest example of Moore's work in the late baroque style. THE ROYAL COLLECTION © 2008 HER MAJESTY QUEEN ELIZABETH II

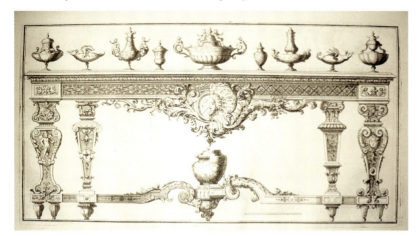

Plate 5:2. Designs for tables (c.1700). Engraving by Pierre Le Pautre. This is plate 4 from Le Pautre's *Livre de tables qui sont dans les apartements du Roy*. Copies of these engravings occur in English collections (at Boughton House, for example) and probably influenced the design of tables produced in England by Gerrit Jensen, the Pelletiers, and eventually James Moore.

Plate 5:3. Table (1724). Carved and gilded wood, inscribed MOORE on the top. Only one example of this model survives in the Royal Collection, but it was conceivably one of a pair supplied for the King's Drawing Room at Kensington. A pair of similar but less rich tables was made for Richard Temple, Baron Cobham, between 1714 and 1718.

THE ROYAL COLLECTION © 2008 HER MAJESTY QUEEN ELIZABETH II

201

Tables and Stands

Plate 5:4. Table (1715-16). Lacquer top with frame and legs of gilded wood. This is an old photograph of the table supplied by Gumley and Moore for the Prince of Wales' bedchamber at Hampton Court Palace. It is the first known example of the square-leg design derived from classical Chinese high tables. It was the only piece of furniture destroyed in the fire of 1986.

Plate 5:5. Table (c.1722). Carved and gilded wood, the top inscribed MOORE. The strikingly simple and original design derives from Chinese Ming period tables. The pair to this, if there was one, does not survive, but several similar examples are known in private collections.

THE ROYAL COLLECTION
© 2008 HER MAJESTY QUEEN ELIZABETH II

Tables and Stands

Plate 5:6. Candlestand (1724). Carved and gilded wood. This is one of a pair, both inscribed MOORE on the tops, made en suite with the table in 5:1. Similar stands made for Blenheim Palace are now lost.   THE ROYAL COLLECTION © 2008 HER MAJESTY QUEEN ELIZABETH II

The second influence on Moore's table designs was radically new and of exotic origin. A table with a lacquer or japanned top made for the Prince of Wales' bedchamber at Hampton Court Palace in 1715-16 was of a form without precedent in English furniture (**5:4**).⁶ It had a moulded rectangular frame and straight, square-section legs ending in claw feet and, as we have seen in Chapter One, the design almost certainly came from China (1:36). Another table by Moore, probably made for the Kensington apartments in 1722, is of a similar form (**5:5**). The key-pattern decoration of the frame could derive from either classical European or Chinese art, but the small reserves of shallow relief carving in the centre and corners of the frame rails are decidedly Oriental, and the double-radiussed or 're-entrant' corners to the tops are taken directly from contemporary Chinese tables and lacquer trays. Their original purpose was probably to make the corners less vulnerable to damage, but they soon became a standard feature of English table-tops in gesso, wood and marble. A number of similar key-pattern stands and tables with both lacquered and gilded tops are known; all are currently attributed to Moore, although the validity of such a blanket attribution is questionable. All Moore and Gumley's gilt tables for the royal palaces were supplied with pairs of stands en suite (**5:6**). There were also pier glasses to complete the 'triad', but none of the ensembles has survived in its entirety (cf. 6:49).

Moore's furniture for Blenheim Palace was probably supplied between 1716 and the death of the 1st Duke of Marlborough in 1722. The 'nothing done' plan prepared by Tilleman Bobart for Sarah Churchill in 1716 showed the principal floor at Blenheim still unfinished. Many rooms were without floors, some were without chimney pieces and ceilings.⁷ It was at this point that Sarah called in James Moore, her 'Oracle', who had already done much work for the Duchess at Marlborough House in London, and on whom the responsibility for finishing both the fabric and the interiors at Blenheim now devolved.⁸ A letter from William Jefferson, clerk to Henry Joynes, the comptroller at Blenheim, to his master, and dated 15 October 1716, describes the Duchess, together with the architects Sir John Vanbrugh and Nicholas Hawksmoor, showing Moore through the uncompleted rooms; 'wher it was Ready for furniture, and as soon as Mr Hawksmoor had Set Downe Everything wanting, then order'd Moor to have a Coppy and he had one, the very next Day she alter'd her mind Entirely and Said Come Mr Moor I will leave all to you and you shall Doe everything as you think fit, and tho' Sir John has Contracted with Several Workmen, if you Can Get any Body to Doe it cheaper they shall be turn'd out, notwithstanding the progress they have made in the Works...'.⁹

---

6. Royal Archives, GEO/81174-5; 'for A Table and Stands with Indian Tops and the fframes finely carved and gilt... £50.0.0'.
7. Green (1951), p. 146.
8. Ibid., p. 142.
9. Ibid.

Tables and Stands

Plate 5:7. Table (1716-22). One of a pair, attributed to James Moore. Oak with black marble top. This is probably one of the 'Two Black Marble Tables with Walnut tree [*sic*] Frames' recorded in the entrance hall at Blenheim in the inventory of 1740.
BLENHEIM PALACE

Plate 5:8. Table (1716-22). One of a pair, attributed to James Moore. Carved and gilded wood with marble top. There are five tables of this model at Blenheim. The stretchers are a later addition. BLENHEIM PALACE

Extensive refurbishments and disposals, particularly in the nineteenth century, have left very little of the arrangements orchestrated by Moore, and the inventory of 1740 is too brief in its descriptions to be of much help in identifying individual pieces. Nevertheless, a series of tables of distinctive form survives in the State Apartments which can reasonably be attributed to Moore. In the Great Hall are two plain and massive oak tables with black marble tops (**5:7**). Their 'broken' cabriole legs with square shafts and scrolled toes are repeated on five similar tables in carved and gilded wood (**5:8**). All bear either the cipher of John Churchill, 1st Duke of Marlborough, or his

Tables and Stands

Plate 5:9. Candlestand (1716-22). Carved and gilded wood, made en suite with one of the pairs of tables at Blenheim.
TREASURER'S HOUSE, YORK, THE NATIONAL TRUST

Plate 5:10. Table (1715-25). One of a pair, attributed to James Moore. Japanese lacquer top on a carved and gilded frame. Made for the Duke of Newcastle. The similarity between the frame of this table and the Blenheim tables is compelling. Moore is known to have worked for the Duke at Nottingham Castle, and possibly at Claremont, Surrey, at the same time as he was involved at Blenheim. This table also serves to reinforce the notion that the cross-stretchers on the Blenheim tables are later additions.
RONALD PHILLIPS LTD

crest and garter. A pair of stands made en suite with one of the pairs of Blenheim tables is at the Treasurer's House, York (**5:9**). As with the royal tables, the Blenheim tables had mirrors en suite, of which five pairs survive (6:48). Other tables of this idiosyncratic design survive in private collections. Some, like the examples in **5:10**, can confidently be attributed to Moore on the basis of both stylistic analogy and supporting evidence, but the design occurs so commonly, on both chairs and tables, in giltwood, walnut and japan, that it is unlikely that Moore was the sole source.

Kensington and Blenheim Palaces were among the last great English houses to have their parade

Tables and Stands

Plate 5:11. Table (1726-7). Carved and gilded wood. This is the survivor of a pair of tables supplied for the King's Gallery at Kensington by Gumley and Turing after Moore's death in 1726. It originally had a decorated apron with crown and cipher similar to the other tables. The four stands en suite also survive.

THE ROYAL COLLECTION © 2008 HER MAJESTY QUEEN ELIZABETH II

Plate 5:12. Table and stands (c.1675 and 1741). Japanned beechwood with Bantam-work lacquer tops. This 17th century triad was repaired and updated in 1741 for the 4th Earl of Dysart by the London cabinet-maker John Hele. The table frame and legs, and the shafts and bases of the stands, are Hele's work.

HAM HOUSE, THE NATIONAL TRUST

floors furnished with suites of tables, stands and looking glasses in the baroque manner. At Kensington Moore's work was unfinished when he died in 1726, and it was left to his partners John Gumley and William Turing to complete it by supplying a further pair of tables, four stands and two mirrors for the King's Gallery in 1727 (**5:11**).[10] These are the last documented examples of the baroque 'triad' of state furniture to be made in England.

At a more domestic level, Gumley and Moore's successor Benjamin Goodison supplied sets of walnut tables and stands (both with and without mirrors) for secondary apartments in the royal palaces well into the 1730s.[11] Elsewhere the evidence for the continuing viability of the 'triad' is more ambiguous. Although matching suites of tables, stands and mirrors occur in many inventories at this time, this evidence is potentially misleading, since many were old suites remaining in use after they had ceased to be fashionable. At Boughton, Drayton, Dyrham, Ham and Knole, suites of tables, stands and mirrors have been listed in every inventory since the late seventeenth century and many of them survive to this day. In some cases they were still performing their original function in the early Georgian period, and there are instances of such suites being repaired or updated at this time. At Ham House in 1741 the cabinet-maker John Hele made a new frame for a seventeenth century Bantamwork table and turned bases for its matching stands (**5:12**).[12] Three years later Hele made new bases for two scagliola tops, part of a suite which had stood in the Gallery since at least 1677 (**5:13**).[13] In both cases the style of the new bases with their columnar shafts reflects a move away from baroque forms towards more up-to-date models.

One of the drawbacks of the formal 'triad' was its inflexibility, and there is some evidence to suggest experimentation with the conventional arrangement. At Chandos House in 1725 there were several pairs of stands associated with tables of different types. In his 'visiting room' the Duke of Chandos had 'A Large Tea Table cover'd wth Silver' and a pair of stands en suite, valued at the enormous sum of £750. In his bedchamber there was a bureau flanked by a pair of stands, and in his son's dressing room there was a tea table flanked by stands. At Cannons the Duke's bedchamber contained a japanned card table and a pair of matching stands, and in other rooms the stands were again associated with bureaux of various types.[14] At Kiveton there was a similar arrangement in the South East Bedchamber, where a 'Philegrine [marquetry] Card Table Lin'd wth Green Velvet' stood with two walnut stands underneath a 'Large Looking Glass in Gold & Glass frame'.[15] However, the absence of references to sets of tables and stands on furniture-makers' trade cards or in bills after 1720 suggests that 'triads' were on the way out. Most newly furnished houses did without them. At Erddig in 1726 there were no candlestands at all. Instead, almost every room was fitted with arms or 'branches' to hold candles. These were either mounted on the walls or on mirrored sconces. Most of the chimney glasses were also fitted with candle arms of brass or glass, set into brass sockets. A similar picture emerges from the inventory of Sherborne House in 1726, where sconces had also entirely replaced candlestands as the primary source of lighting.[16] In purely practical terms these wall-mounted lights were undoubtedly an improvement, for candlestands took up floor space and presented something of a fire hazard. Even at Chandos House, where there were several sets of stands, branches attached to chimney glasses and sconces seem to have provided most of the lighting.[17]

Plate 5:13. Stand (1744). Mahogany with scagliola top. This is one of a pair of 17th century scagliola tops given new bases by John Hele in 1744. His bill describes 'Two Neat Stands made To two Stone tops The Pillars & Claws Ornamented…£6.0.0.'. Note the much higher price of the carved mahogany stands, compared with the plain turned examples in 5:12.

HAM HOUSE, THE NATIONAL TRUST

---

10. Murdoch (2003).
11. PRO LC 9/286-8.
12. Ham House, bills of John Hele, 14 February 1741:
    ' Two Neat Pillers & Claws for Two Indian Tops of Stands Black't & Varnished & Polisht… £1.2.0
    A frame for an Indian Top all packt & sent to Ham… £0.16.0'.
13. Ham House, bill of John Hele, 27 July 1744.
14. Chandos House (1725); Cannons (1725).
15. Kiveton (1727).
16. Sherborne (1726).
17. Chandos House (1725).

Tables and Stands

208

Opposite page:
Plate 5:14. Candlestands (1715-40). Carved and gilded wood. The faceted and knopped shaft derives from late 17th century stands, but the swelling trumpet-shaped top and claw (cabriole) base are early Georgian features. MALLETT

Above left:
Plate 5:15. Candlestand (1730-50). Padouk (?). The leaf-carved baluster shaft is a simplified version of those on Moore's giltwood tables and stands for Kensington Palace. The paw feet suggest a date after c.1730. CHRISTIE'S IMAGES LTD 1991

Above centre:
Plate 5:16. Candlestand (1740-60). Indian rosewood. The similarities between this and the previous stand are obvious, but the cabochon-and-leaf carved tripod suggests rococo influences and therefore a slightly later date. FAIRFAX HOUSE, YORK

Above right:
Plate 5:17. Candlestand (1741). Mahogany. This is one of a pair supplied by Peter Hasert to the 4th Earl of Dysart in 1741: 'A pair of high Mahogany Stands with cut rims the Heads 17 inches over the Pilars & Claws richly carved… £6.10.0.'. The stop-fluted pillar suggests the influence of neo-Palladian design, contrasting with the essentially baroque forms of figures 5:14-6.
HAM HOUSE, THE NATIONAL TRUST

One possible contributing factor in the disappearance of the 'triad' is suggested by the pair of candlestands from Blenheim shown in 5:9. The asymmetric, uni-directional design suggests that the cabriole form which now dominated table design proved difficult to adapt harmoniously to a stand. Indeed, Moore may have been the only man who bothered to try, for no other stands of this form are known. Instead, candlestands tended to be based on baluster or pillar forms, with pillar and claw bases, unrelated to accompanying furniture (**5:14-5:17**). The arrival of rococo designs in the 1740s gave a new lease of life to candlestands, offering opportunities for imaginative designers and virtuoso carvers which conventional designs had hitherto lacked.

Right:
Plate 5:18. Table (1720-26). Carved and gilded wood. This is the 'Large Carved & Guilt Table' recorded in the Lady's Drawing Room at Chicheley in 1755. The top bears the arms of Sir John Chester, who died in 1726. This is of much higher quality than the other tables at Chicheley (cf. 5:40-42), and was accompanied by seat furniture of similar richness (4:60). There are interesting parallels between this table and one at Chevening, Kent, attributed to William Bradshaw.
MONTACUTE, THE NATIONAL TRUST

Below:
Plate 5:19. Table (1720-26). Carved and gilded wood. This was made for the Second Best Bedchamber at Erddig, where it was recorded in the inventory of 1726.
ERDDIG, THE NATIONAL TRUST

18. Chicheley (1755).
19. Erddig (1726).
20. Hawarden Record Office, D/E/1542/107, 6 June 1726:
'To a silver table with a glass top and a coat of Arms cut and Gilt on it... £14:00:00'.

Tables with gilt tops

The absence of paired candlestands in no way diminished the importance of the table and its associated looking glass, both of which continued to occupy a prime position in rooms of state or parade. As the example of James Moore's tables shows, the same frame could be supplied with marble, lacquer, japanned or gilded tops, and it is worth considering whether there was any logic behind the choice. One might reasonably assume that gilt tops, which were both expensive and relatively vulnerable, were reserved for high status rooms, or rooms which saw little regular or informal use. Some support for this hypothesis comes from contemporary inventories. At Chicheley, built for Sir John Chester between c.1718 and c.1722, the only room to have a table with a gilt top was the Lady's Drawing Room (**5:18**), whereas the Gentleman's Drawing Room, hall and dining room and parlours had marble ones.[18] Even so, the gilt top was protected by a leather case, and this was common practice. At Blenheim the State Bedchamber was the only room to have a gilt-topped table, the rest being marble. At Erddig pairs of marble tables were placed in the Hall and Salone while the only gilt table was in the Second Best Bedchamber (**5:19**).[19] This too had a leather cover. Also at Erddig is a silvered table with an engraved glass top supplied by John Belchier in 1726, the only firmly documented one of its kind (**5:20**).[20] The cost of £14 seems modest when compared with the £21 charged for the sconce hanging above it. It is interesting that the sconce and table were supplied three years apart (the sconce in 1723), perhaps indicating that another arrangement was first envisaged.

The design of the Erddig tables is typical of the 'claw' or cabriole-leg style which superseded pillar legs from c.1715 onwards. One has an ogee-section frame, the other coved.

Plate 5:20. Table (1726) **and Sconce** (1723). Silvered wood and glass. This table was supplied by John Belchier to John Meller at Erddig in 1726, at a cost of £14. The top is glass, engraved and reverse-painted with the arms of Meller, and was originally protected by a walnut cover. It was made for the Withdrawing Room adjacent to the Best Bedchamber. The mirror hung above it was made earlier, in 1723, for £21. The silvered finish matched the silver-framed chairs (4:42) in the same room. ERDDIG, THE NATIONAL TRUST

Belchier supplied Erddig with another table with a 'cove frame', this time in walnut, and his contemporary John Phillips referred to several 'cove tables' in walnut and japan in his bill to the Duke of Beaufort – the type was obviously well known.[21]

Both the Erddig tables are embellished with shallow relief decoration on a punched ground. Many of the details of the carving are similar, but there are also sufficient differences to raise doubts about a common authorship (**5:21** and **5:22**). The decorative vocabulary and the techniques used to execute them must have been common to virtually every workshop engaged in this kind of work, and we simply do not know enough about how London furniture-makers organised their workmen and subcontractors to make definitive statements of authorship without supporting information. In this case Belchier's bill for the silver table survives, but the one for the gilt table does not, perhaps reinforcing the case for a different supplier.

---

21. Badminton archives, bill of John Phillips, 3 December 1733.

Plates 5:21 and 5:22. Details of 5:19 and 5:20. The two tables are basically similar in form, but differ in detail. The probability of two different makers is strengthened by the lack of any mention of the gilt table in Belchier's bill. Meller also bought furniture from John Gumley and John Pardoe. Note the white bole used for the silvered table, compared with the dark red for the gilt one.

Tables and Stands

Right:
Plate 5:23. Table (1720-28). Carved and gilt wood. This was made for the 4th Earl of Arundell and his wife Eleanor, who died in 1728. It is an unusually powerful design, and the lion's mask in the frieze is an early manifestation of a device which became common in the 1730s.
PORTSMOUTH MUSEUMS

Below left:
Plate 5:24. Table (1720-40). Gilt wood. One of a pair. Small gilt tables such as this are quite numerous and were clearly a popular type.
PRIVATE COLLECTION

Below right:
Plate 5:25. Table (1718-30). Gilt wood. This bears the cipher WKH, for William, Marquess of Hartington and his wife Katherine, who married in 1718. The plainness of the slim frieze contrasts with the fine detail of the top.
CHATSWORTH

Tables and Stands

Plate 5:26. Table (1720-30). Gilt wood. A typically neat and nicely detailed example of the type.
NORMAN ADAMS LTD

Plate 5:27. Detail of 5:42, showing the method of securing the detachable top. NORMAN ADAMS LTD

One of the most powerfully modelled gilt-top tables to survive from the 1720s is shown in **5:23**. The top bears the combined arms of Henry, 4th Lord of Arundell (1694-1756?) and Eleanor Everard. They were married in 1716 and Eleanor died in 1728, which provides a firm date *ante quem* for the table. The frame is unusually deep, and the modelling much bolder than customary. The masks at the top of the legs are one of the most characteristic devices of the period. Modern texts sometimes call these 'Indian' masks, because of their plumed headdresses, but they actually have a Renaissance origin, occurring commonly in sixteenth century Italian grotesques, and were later taken up by French baroque artists such as Jean Berain, Jean Le Pautre and André-Charles Boulle. It is probably from published works of these designers that the motif entered the repertoire of English furniture-makers. The lion's mask and accompanying paw feet on the Arundell table are unusually early, predating the Houghton tables and seat furniture by several years.[22]

Plates **5:24-6** show a selection of smaller gilt-topped tables probably made for bedchambers and dressing rooms of the 1720s and early 1730s. A peculiarity shared by many of them is that they were made with detachable tops, located by battens at either side and secured with dowels (**5:27**). It is not clear why they were made in this fashion, but the most obvious explanation is that it was done to eliminate the potential problem of differential movement between the frame and the top, which would caused the gesso to crack and fail. Support for this hypothesis arises from the fact that most of these table tops were not cleated at the ends as they would be in solid or veneered wood. Elimination of differential shrinkage between cleats and longitudinal boards is the obvious rationale.

---

22. Other early lion's mask tables are illustrated in Macquoid (1906), fig. 22; and Lennox-Boyd (1998), fig 53.

213

Tables and Stands

Plate 5:28. Table (1730-40), carved and gilt wood. This is one of a pair probably made for the Saloon or Drawing Room at Stowe, Buckinghamshire. Their owner, Richard Temple, 1st Viscount Cobham, patronised James Moore (d.1726) and possibly his eventual successor, Benjamin Goodison, to whom these have been attributed. The heroic scale and rich decoration make these some of the most exceptional products of their age, but in design terms little has changed since the 1720s.

CHRISTIE'S IMAGES LTD 1998

A pair of gilt tables almost certainly made for Stowe House in Buckinghamshire represents the ultimate development of the type (**5:28**). They were supplied together with a famous suite of seat furniture (cf. 4:75), probably for the Saloon or Drawing Room at Stowe.[23] The design is conventional but extremely ambitious in its sculptural quality and rich detail. The sheer splendour of the Stowe tables disguises the fact that in design terms such tables had arrived at a point of stasis. Similar designs published in William Jones' *The Gentleman or Builder's Companion* (1739) and Batty Langley's *The City and Country Builder's and Workman's Treasury of Designs* (1740) show that there had been no real change since 1730; the same basic forms adorned with the same repertoire of late baroque and neo-Palladian motifs occur repeatedly. In Langley's case, he even went back to Pierre Le Pautre in the search for ideas; plate CXLVII of his *Treasury* is a line-for-line re-drawing of a Le Pautre engraving first published about 1700 (**5:29**). Some of Jones' designs exhibit more obvious neo-Palladian influence, but the essential form is the same (**5:30**). All the indications are that by 1740 these tables, like many other furniture forms, were ready for a radical change of stylistic direction.

23. Christie's, London, sale catalogue, 9 July 1998, lot 100.

Above:
Plate 5:29. Batty Langley, designs for tables (1740). This is plate CXLVII from *The City and Country Builder's and Workman's Treasury of Designs*. The upper design is taken directly from Pierre Le Pautre's engravings, first published c.1700. These old-fashioned ideas were soon to be swept away by the dynamism of the rococo.

Left:
Plate 5:30. Table (1735-50). Gilded wood with later marble top. This table bears comparison with some of William Jones' designs published in *The Gentleman or Builder's Companion* of 1739. It combines stock neo-Palladian motifs such as the mask of Apollo, the shell and the Vitruvian scroll frieze with indications of an early rococo or 'French' treatment of the legs and feet.
COURTESY OF SOTHEBY'S

Tables and Stands

Plate 5:31. Sideboard table (c.1715-17). Marble top on a walnut frame. This table was recorded in the Canons Ashby inventory of November 1717, and dates from the refurbishment of the house by Edward Dryden between 1710 and 1717. One of the twelve walnut chairs en suite is shown in 4:24. Present location unknown.
COUNTRY LIFE

24. Erddig (1726).
25. Canons Ashby (1717) For a discussion on the use of parlours as dining and/or drawing rooms see Cornforth (2004), pp. 38-42.
26. Cannons (1747).
27. For example, Ditchley (1743).

Sideboard tables

The term 'sideboard' or 'sideboard table' had two meanings in the early eighteenth century, one specific, the other general. Its specific meaning related to dining or other rooms where meals were taken. Thus in 1717 the Left Hand Parlour at Canons Ashby contained (among other things) an oval cedar table, twelve cane chairs and an 'Inlaid Stone Sideboard'. There is an implicit link here between the oval dining table and the sideboard, which was used for serving food and drink. In the same vein, there was a 'Marble Side-Board' in the Eating Parlour at Erddig in 1726.[24] In a more general sense a sideboard could be any table which stood at the side of a room. The Right Hand Parlour at Canons Ashby was more richly furnished than the Left, with four looking glasses of various kinds, a settee and twelve walnut chairs, and a 'Marble sideboard' (**5:31**). There is no reason why this sideboard could not have been used to serve food and drink, but the comfortable furnishings and the absence of a dining table suggests this was not its primary function.[25] In the Duke of Chandos' study at Cannons was 'a walnut tree side board table' which it is difficult to imagine had anything to do with eating or drinking.[26] Thus the inventory evidence suggests that 'sideboard' might be applied to any table standing against the wall, and it is not clear how such a table differed from any other kind. It is perhaps best defined by what it was not. A sideboard table was not a pier table, nor a dressing table, card, tea, dining or breakfast table. It was essentially static and stood against the wall but probably not on a pier. It had no drawers in the frame, and often had a stone or marble top. Some bills and inventories use the term 'slab table' or 'slab frame' to describe such tables, but without specifying how the table was used.[27]

The difference between specific and general use of sideboards, as well as their bewildering variety, is amply demonstrated by the Cannons inventories. The dining rooms all had sideboards.

Plate 5:32. Sideboard (1731). Carved and gilt wood and iron. One of a pair, supplied by John Phillips to the Duke of Beaufort at a cost of £70. These remain in the 'Great Parlour' for which they were probably made.
BADMINTON HOUSE
THE DUKE OF BEAUFORT

Plate 5:33. **Table frame** (c.1710). Wrought iron. One of three probably made by John Gardam for Castle Howard. This is a rare survival of a once numerous class of metal-framed sideboards and tables.
COURTESY OF SOTHEBY'S

In the Steward's Dining Room was one with a cracked marble top, and the Marble Dining Room (which was the second-best dining room) had two marble sideboard tables over 6ft. (1.8m) long, each supported on brass pillars and with marble wine cisterns underneath. For great occasions there was the Great Dining Room on the first floor, which had a 'sideboard Room' en suite, containing 'A magnificent large black and gold marble side board table, 7 feet by 3 feet 11, on a carved walnut tree frame', and another of similar size.[28]

There were also 'sideboard tables' of a general kind throughout the principal rooms, many associated with looking glasses. In the 'Smoking Room' was 'a large marble side-board table, 6ft.8in. by 2ft.9in. on an iron frame with carved and gilt ornaments'. The Great Drawing Room had three, of which the largest had an Italian marble top 'curiously inlaid, representing a lute, a dead bird, cards, &c', on a japanned frame. A similar table stood in the upstairs Drawing Room; 'A most magnificent large sideboard table, 5ft. by 3, inlaid with a variety of curious Italian stones, so beautifully disposed, as to exhibit birds, fruit, flowers, and insects; and supported by a frame elegantly enriched with figures, festoons, masks, shells, and other ornaments richly carved and gilt'.

Several of the Cannons sideboard tables had iron or brass frames. Most such tables have long since disappeared, but there are some rare survivals. A pair of tables similar to the one described in the 'Smoking Room' at Cannons is still *in situ* at Badminton, the marble slab being supported on iron brackets disguised by carved and gilt dolphins (**5:32**). These may be the 'pair of peers wh Dolphin's heads' supplied by John Phillips in 1731, at a cost of £70.[29] The 1758 inventory of Dunham Massey, Cheshire, records a number of marble slabs with brackets on landings, staircases and in several rooms, none of which survives.[30] Some metal table frames have survived in an altered or vestigial state, such as those sold from Castle Howard in 1990 (**5:33**). These were probably made about 1710 by the blacksmith John Gardam, who also worked at Chatsworth, where in October 1711 he was paid for making 'table frames'.[31]

---

28. Cannons 1747.
29. Badminton archives, bill of John Phillips, 3 December 1731.
30. Dunham Massey (1758).
31. Sotheby's, Castle Howard, 11-13 November 1991, lots 22 and 23.

Tables and Stands

Plate 5:34. Buffet (c.1732). This is one of the double niches designed by William Kent for the buffet in the Marble Parlour at Houghton. Unlike at Drayton, the solid marble sideboards have survived intact. HOUGHTON HALL

Furniture for 'sideboard rooms' adjoining the dining room was sometimes freestanding and sometimes built in. At Boughton there were two such rooms, one for great occasions adjoining the Great Hall and one for more intimate gatherings next to the 'little painted Hall'. Both had marble or stone tables for serving food and cisterns for washing glasses and cutlery.[32] The 'buffett room' at Drayton contained '3 marble tables wth wallnut tree frames, 2 marble neeches with 2 marble cisterns in them'. The ceiling, niches and buffet were painted by 'Mr Lanscroone'.[33] When separate sideboard rooms went out of use in the later eighteenth century, the rooms together with their fittings were often broken up, so that few survive in their original form. The best known example with its marble furniture *in situ* is at Houghton, where it adjoins the Marble Dining Room (**5:34**).

The placing of large stone or marble tables in entrance halls probably derived, as John Cornforth has suggested, from the traditional function of the hall as a place of communal dining.[34] At Dunham Massey there were two marble tables in the Hall, and it is interesting that there were '2 large Folding Mahogany Tables' at the foot of the stairs adjacent to it, perhaps indicating that the Hall was still used for dining on occasion. There were a number of marble tables elsewhere in the house, including '3 Egyptian Marble Tables on Mahogany Frames' located in the first floor Great Gallery.[35] Plate **5:35** show one of the latter; its plain mahogany frame and angular legs are matched by a number of other tables in the house, all presumably bought at the same time and probably from the same source. The tables in the Great Hall at Ham House are manifestly more expensive articles (**5:36**). The frames are emphatically moulded and the strongly formed legs are carved to a considerable depth. The carving of the masks and their attendant oak leaf swags is as good as any of this date. Although no bills survive for these tables, they probably date from the refurbishment of Ham undertaken by the fourth Earl of Dysart during the 1730s.[36] The more powerfully conceived form is typical of the generally more weighty, Palladian influenced furniture of the 1730s. Plate **5:37** shows one of a pair of sideboard tables supplied by John Hodson to the Duke of Atholl in 1738. The invoice describes them as 'two neat carv'd and painted sideboard frames for marble tables…£8. 8. 0'.[37] They were originally painted stone colour, and are now white. The tops were supplied by the Duke, and repaired, cleaned and polished by Hodson at a cost of £1. 6s.

---

32. Boughton (1709).
33. Drayton (1710 and 1724).
34. Cornforth (2004), pp. 37-38.
35. Dunham Massey (1755).
36. Thornton and Tomlin (1980), p. 181.
37. Coleridge (1963).

Tables and Stands

Plate 5:35. Sideboard table (1720-40). Marble top on a solid mahogany frame. This is one of numerous large marble slabs on mahogany frames which were placed in the parlours, halls and galleries at Dunham Massey.
DUNHAM MASSEY, THE NATIONAL TRUST

Plate 5:36. Sideboard table (1730-40). Marble top on a mahogany, deal and oak frame. One of three now standing in the Great Hall at Ham House. Marble-topped tables in halls served as sideboards when the halls were required to fulfil their ancient function as dining halls. HAM HOUSE, THE NATIONAL TRUST

Plate 5:37. Sideboard table (1738). Marble top on a painted deal frame. This is one of a pair supplied by John Hodson to the Duke of Atholl in 1738. It was originally painted stone colour. The table has been reduced in height by cutting off the upper egg–and-dart moulding and re-fixing it about 2in. (5cm) lower, thereby obscuring the tops of the flutes in the frieze.
BLAIR CHARITABLE TRUST

Tables and Stands

Plate 5:38. Sideboard table (1720-30). Veined yellow marble top on a gilded wood frame. This table bears the coronet and double C cipher of James Brydges, 1st Duke of Chandos. It cannot be identified in the Cannons inventory of 1725, but may have been one of a pair recorded in his London house at the same date.

TREASURER'S HOUSE, YORK, THE NATIONAL TRUST

Plate 5:39. Sideboard tables (c.1724). Italian scagliola tops on gilded wood frames. A pair, probably supplied to George Treby (1684-1742), MP for Plympton House, Devon, and perhaps made at the time of his marriage in 1724. The central scene on one of the tops depicts David giving thanks after slaying Goliath, and is signed by the noted Italian artist in scagliola, Petrus Antonius de Paulinus. The gilded frame has a number of features typical of tables made in the 1720s. The ogee section frieze is a variant of the more common coved section, and the apron has a dropped centre, which is found with equal frequency on both tables and chairs of this date. The angular section of the legs, also commonly found on chairs, became less fashionable after c.1730.   CHRISTIE'S IMAGES LTD 2002

While dining room sideboard tables were often rather plain (and were perhaps covered with a cloth when in use), those for saloons, drawing rooms and principal bedchambers often had richly decorated frames. The table in **5:38** bears the coronet and double C cipher of the Duke of Chandos, owner of Cannons, and has plausibly been identified with the pair of 'marble Tables in guilt frames' in the 'Salone' at Chandos' London house in St James's Square.[38] It is tempting to attribute

---

38. Murdoch (2003), n. 52.

Plate 5:40. Sideboard table (c.1720-30). Inlaid marble top on a gilded wood frame. This table is recorded in the 1755 inventory of Chicheley Hall as 'A Curious Inlaid marble Table with magpyes & Snakes on a Gilt Frame'. The flying brackets could be a fashionable accessory or merely an indication of some doubt in the maker's mind as to the ability of the frame to support the top.
PRIVATE COLLECTION

these to James Moore, on the strength of payments to Moore made in 1721,[39] but there is nothing in their design which significantly distinguishes them from gilt tables supplied by other prominent London makers. Stylistically they are typical of the 1720s, with a coved frame and convex apron decorated with strapwork, scrolls and leaves on a punched ground, the legs headed by plumed Renaissance masks.

Bills reveal that the marble tops were usually the most expensive part of such tables, even when the frames were gilt. A common expedient, used in the case of the Chandos table, was to use figured marble veneers on a plain substrate, often of slate. The veneers were usually about ¼in. (6mm) thick, which must have required considerable skill in sawing, but the saving in precious stone was worth it. Of course, it is a moot point whether the buyers of veneered tops were aware of the subterfuge.

Tables with inlaid pietra dura or scagliola tops were very much more expensive even than solid marble, and these were located in the rooms of state or parade where they could be seen and admired. The tables made for George Treby, MP (1684-1742), are of this type (**5:39**). Treby spent his money carefully; the frames are decorated with shallow-relief carving cut into the gesso, which was naturally much cheaper than carving in wood. Most of the expense is in the imported scagliola tops, one of which is signed by Petrus Antonius de Paulinus, a noted Italian artist in scagliola working between c.1720 and c.1740.[40]

A group of sideboard tables from Chicheley Hall, Buckinghamshire, is more typical of those found in wealthy but non-noble houses. Chicheley was built for Sir John Chester by Francis Smith of Warwick between 1719 and 1723.[41] The furnishing may not have been completed by the time of Chester's death in 1726, but those pieces that survive are stylistically consistent with a date in the 1720s. One of the most interesting features of Chicheley's interior layout was the vertical division between the parade rooms on one side and private or family rooms on the other. The two halves were divided by the central hall and staircase. The division is reflected in the furnishings, with those on the parade side being very much richer than those on the family side.[42] Thus all the gilt tables, together with the best mirrors and seat furniture, were on the parade side. The largest and most imposing table, with an inlaid stone top, was in the Great Parlour (**5:40**) on the ground floor. In the first-floor Dining Room was a pair of smaller tables with gilt pier glasses over them

---

39. Murdoch (2003), n. 51.
40. Christie's, London, Important English Furniture, 28 November 2002, lot 150.
41. Gomme (2000), pp. 348-364.
42. Chicheley (1755).

Tables and Stands

Above left:
Plate 5:41. Sideboard table (1720-30). Marble top on a gilded wood frame. One of a pair, probably that recorded in the Dining Room at Chicheley in 1755. The shaped sides are relatively uncommon, but occur on contemporary French tables.   PRIVATE COLLECTION

Above right:
Plate 5:42. Sideboard table (1720-30). Marble top on a gilded wood frame. This is one of a pair, the smallest and simplest of the Chicheley gilded tables.   PRIVATE COLLECTION

Left:
Plate 5:43. Sideboard table (1720-40). Scagliola top on a walnut and deal frame. This is one of numerous survivors at Dunham Massey, Cheshire, which was rebuilt by George Booth, 2nd Earl of Warrington, from the 1720s onwards. Tables of this simple form were common in English houses during the early Georgian period. In this case the table top is inlaid with scagliola playing cards.   DUNHAM MASSEY, THE NATIONAL TRUST

(**5:41**). Either side of the Dining Room was a Bedchamber each with 'A marble Table on a Gilt frame' with a gilt sconce over (**5:42**). The frames of these have pulvinated friezes, a variation on the more usual coved frame. The frames of the whole group are much less richly treated than, for instance, the Chandos and Treby tables, with a palpable diminution in quality, as one might expect from the more modest proportions of Sir John's purse.

On the family side of Chicheley all the tables had either walnut or japanned frames, not gilt. Here there was a subdivision between tables in the first-floor bedchambers, which were variously described as japanned or inlaid, and those on the ground floor, several of which had marble tops. At Dunham Massey numerous marble tables with plain wood frames survive; **5:43** has a scagliola top inlaid with cards for a game of piquet and is the 'Marble Table with Cards Letters &c' located in the Yellow Feather Bedchamber in 1758.[43]

---

43. Dunham Massey (1758).

Plate 5:44. Slab table, c.1719. Carved and gilded wood with Italian marble top. One of a pair. The variable quality of the carving and the curious construction of these tables suggest they may not be English. It is conceivable they were bought in Italy by Burlington and thus became the prototypes for English tables of this form.
CHISWICK VILLA, ENGLISH HERITAGE

Neo-Palladian tables

The rise of neo-Palladian taste in the 1720s introduced a new form of table into English houses which, perhaps for the first time, placed carvers to the fore among fashionable furniture-makers. These tables tended to be closely associated in form and style with the internal architecture of the house, and the frames supporting their marble tops were conceived as sculptural works in their own right. Almost invariably they are associated with or attributed to William Kent, often with little justification, for they are simply too numerous to have all been designed by a single presiding genius. Nevertheless, Kent's responsibility for promoting and developing the form is generally accepted.[44] In contrast to the previous generation of designers and craftsmen who took their cue from France, Kent drew on models studied during his ten-year stay in Italy. His was a bolder, more vigorous and three-dimensional style, inspired by the rich baroque culture of Rome and Venice. The marrying of a rather academic architectural shell with these dramatic tables is one of the most revolutionary aspects of the neo-Palladian style.

If there is a prototype for the new Palladian style of table, it is probably the pair made for the Gallery at Chiswick Villa (**5:44**). The tops are Italian, executed in specimen marble in the form of a mosaic pavement. It is probable that they were among five slabs brought back from Genoa by Lord Burlington in 1719. The authorship of the frames is problematic. It has been suggested that they were the result of a collaboration between John Boson and Giovanni Battista Guelfi (fl.1714-34), an Italian sculptor whom Burlington met in Italy, and who was employed by Burlington at Burlington House, Piccadilly, and at Chiswick.[45] The objection to this is that the quality of the carving and the construction of the frame are very much inferior to most English work, let alone that of a man of Boson's abilities. The modelling of some elements, such as the central mask, is well executed, but the detail of the frame is poor and, in places, perfunctory. A London carver would not have remained long in employment producing work of this quality. The inconsistent quality suggests a workshop production, with only the most important elements executed by a master carver, and the rather theatrical lack of detail is reminiscent of some contemporary Italian work. The design is certainly Italian. It is worth considering whether Burlington did not buy the frames as well as the slabs in Italy. If so, it is possible they were first installed in the old house at Chiswick, since the gallery was not ready for furniture until at least 1728.

Other tables made for Chiswick display a much higher quality of carving and demonstrate how

44. Wilson (1984); Cornforth (2004).
45. Christie's, London, sale catalogue, 3 July 1996, lot 35.

Tables and Stands

Right:
Plate 5:45. Slab table (c.1730). Marble top with gilt brass edge on a carved and gilded wooden frame. One of four. Maker unknown, the design attributed to William Kent. Originally made for the Dome Saloon at Chiswick, these are now in the Great Dining Room at Chatsworth in Derbyshire. CHATSWORTH

Above:
Plate 5:47. Slab table (c.1730). Marble top on a carved mahogany frame. Maker unknown, the design attributed to William Kent. One of a pair in the Marble Hall at Houghton. HOUGHTON HALL

Left:
Plate 5:46. Slab table (c.1730). Sienna marble top with gilt pine frame. One of a pair made for Chiswick Villa, designed by William Kent and probably carved by John Boson. The pair to this table is in the Victoria and Albert Museum.
CHATSWORTH

Plate 5:48. Slab table (c.1731). Marble top on carved and gilded wooden frame. This is the largest of three tables designed by Kent for the Saloon at Houghton.
HOUGHTON HALL

Plate 5:49. Slab table (c.1732). Marble top on a carved and gilded wooden frame. Designed by William Kent for the Marble Parlour at Houghton Hall. The cornucopiae overflowing with grapes allude to the original purpose of the room as a Dining Parlour.
HOUGHTON HALL

completely Kent and the carvers in Burlington's employ mastered the new style. The four tables made for the Dome Saloon, probably made about 1730, are wonderfully accomplished, both in design and execution (**5:45**).[46] Another pair, made either for Lady Burlington's bedroom or for the Gallery, demonstrates the facility with which Kent could adapt his designs to a more intimate scale, evincing a feeling of concentrated mass and power (**5:46**).[47] A characteristic feature of almost all English tables in this style is the bold architectural moulding beneath the top, which not only gives a strong visual finish to the frame but endows it with a structural integrity lacking in many Continental examples.

The tables designed by Kent for Houghton Hall are contemporary with those made for Chiswick and remain for the most part *in situ*. The pair of tables in the Stone Hall is the least well known, possibly because they are the least typically 'Kentian' in style (**5:47**). Nevertheless, their form and decoration is perfectly in accord with Kent's debt to the Roman baroque. Three tables in the Saloon combine several primary motifs of the neo-Palladian style – scrolled square section trusses, putti, sphinxes, scallop shells and fish scale ornament (**5:48**). The black and gold *porte venere* marble tops contrast with and enrich the appearance of the frames. Two tables in the Carlo Marratti Room and the Marble Parlour respectively are very similar in design. That in the Marble Parlour is hung with festoons of grapes spilling from opposing cornucopiae to illustrate the theme of the room (**5:49**).

While Kent's responsibility for the design of these tables is not seriously in doubt,[48] the identity of their maker is less certain. James Richards, who succeeded Grinling Gibbons as Carver in Wood in the Office of Works in 1721, seems the most likely candidate.[49] He was certainly responsible for the fine mahogany staircase, doors and doorcases at Houghton. But the large number of undocumented tables in Kent's style make it certain that several workshops (at the very least) were able to produce carved frames of this quality. Among the names known to be producing furniture to Kent's designs are James Moore (both senior and junior), Benjamin Goodison and John Boson.

46. Rosoman (1985).
47. Rosoman (1985); Wilk (1996), pp.88-9.
48. Moore (1996).
49. Beard, p. 27, in Moore (1996).

Tables and Stands

Plate 5:50. Slab table (c.1730-40). Marble top on carved, painted and part-gilt softwood frame. This is one of a pair of tables in the Double Cube Room at Wilton. The principal details of the design are 'Kentian', but it lacks Kent's usual compact and powerful form. The deep apron and top-heavy trusses owe something to more conventional cabriole-leg tables.
WILTON HOUSE

Plate 5:51. Slab table (c.1726). Carved, painted and gilt deal. This table, made for the 'tabernacle' niche in the hall at Ditchley, is associated with a payment made to the carver James Richards in 1726. If the association is valid this is a precocious early example of a pure neo-Palladian form.
DITCHLEY

Kent's name is connected with the furnishing of numerous grand houses in the late 1720s and 1730s. Some, like Raynham, are reasonably well documented, and others, like Wilton, are not. At Wilton there are tables which are pure 'Kent' and others which mix Kentian features with a more conventional form (**5:50**). At Ditchley, Oxfordshire, Kent worked partly in conjunction with Henry Flitcroft, a neo-Palladian zealot known to his friends as 'Burlington Harry'.[50] The table in the hall, probably carved by James Richards, is likely to have been designed by Kent (**5:51**),[51] whereas the superb scagliola-topped table in **5:52** and **5:53** is usually attributed to Flitcroft. With its scrolled eagle-headed trusses, it bears more than a passing resemblance to a pair formerly in the Blue Velvet Room at Chiswick (now at Chatsworth). The scagliola top was made either in Florence or in Livorno, where Litchfield's brother, Admiral Fitzroy Lee, saw it in July 1726: 'I have seen this morning your table which is entirely finish't only the arms and supporters wich I writ to you of ten months ago, and you have not sent them yet which is a great pity, for I'm sure it will be the finest of the sort in Europe.'[52]

Henry Flitcroft might also have designed another pair of tables made for Ditchley (**5:54**). It is known that Flitcroft supplied five designs for table frames for Ditchley in 1740-41, but on the other hand a drawing for these tables, or one very similar, is attributed to Matthias Lock, c.1740.[53]

50. Wilson (1984), p. 167.
51. Cornforth (2004), p. 294.
52. *DEF*, III, p. 288.
53. V&A 2848.98.

Tables and Stands

Left:
Plate 5:52. Slab table (1726). Made for George Henry Lee, 2nd Earl of Litchfield, in 1726.
VICTORIA AND ALBERT MUSEUM

Below:
Plate 5:53. Detail of 5:52, showing the Italian scagliola top. The arms of the Earl of Litchfield impaling those of Frances Hales, his wife.
VICTORIA AND ALBERT MUSEUM

Whether this indicates a collaboration between the two men, or whether Flitcroft's designs, now vanished, were for some completely different tables may never be known. The link to Flitcroft is strengthened by the existence of near-identical examples at Wentworth Woodhouse, where Flitcroft also worked, and Shugborough Hall, Staffordshire, a house also owned by the Earl of Litchfield.[54] The style is strongly architectural, and epitomises the close link between neo-Palladian furnishings and the architectural shell in which they stood. Indeed, the design would work equally well in stone, which is perhaps how it was meant to be perceived.

Although the names of Kent, Flitcroft and others are regularly put forward in connection with these neo-Palladian tables, in many cases it was probably craftsmen, not architects, who designed them, for draughtsmanship was one of the essential skills of a top-class carver. The mechanics of the relationship are made clear in the case of George Mercer, a London carver who produced work for Dumfries House in the 1750s. The architect William Adam noted: 'Between the windows there should be fine Marble tables with handsome frames. From the floor to the surbase moulding that goes round the room is 2 feet 8 ins and to the top of it is 3 feet which dimensions will regulate the height of these frames and tables, and their length must not exceed 4 feet 2 ins'.[55]

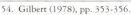
54. Gilbert (1978), pp. 353-356.
55. *DEFM*.

Plate 5:54. Slab table (c.1740). Yellow Sienna marble top on carved, white-painted and part gilt deal frame. One of a pair made for Ditchley House, Oxfordshire. The design corresponds to a drawing attributed to Matthias Lock in the Victoria and Albert Museum. Near identical tables were made for Wentworth Woodhouse, Yorkshire and Shugborough Hall, Staffordshire. Other similar tables are also known.
TEMPLE NEWSAM HOUSE, LEEDS CITY ART GALLERIES

Tables and Stands

Plate 5:55. Eagle console table (1731). Carved and gilt wood. One of a pair supplied by John Phillips to the Duke of Beaufort at a cost of £40. The black plinths are later. These are the earliest documented examples of their type.
BADMINTON HOUSE
THE DUKE OF BEAUFORT

56. Badminton archives, bill of John Phillips, 3 December 1733.
57. The architects principally concerned at Badminton in the 1720s and 1730s were Francis Smith of Warwick and James Gibbs (Jackson-Stops (1987)).

Eagle, sphinx and dolphin tables

Tables with bases carved as eagles, sphinxes and dolphins were one of the most popular manifestations of neo-Palladian taste, perhaps because of their compact form. Each was deeply imbued with classical symbolism appropriate to the new Augustan age – the eagle emblematic of Jupiter, also symbolising power and victory, the dolphin an attribute of Neptune and of Venus, and the sphinx a creature of power, vigilance and wisdom. All three designs are popularly associated with William Kent, but it is difficult to document his responsibility. Pairs of all three were supplied to Badminton in Gloucestershire in 1731.[56] This is a house with which Kent became involved only later, and the supplier of the furniture, John Phillips, is not known to have worked on any of Kent's commissions.[57]

Of the three types, eagle tables are the most common (**5:55-5:56**). The design was almost

Plate 5:56. Eagle console table, (1730-40). Marble top on a base of carved and gilded wood. This is one of a pair, originally with iron brackets helping to support the top.

RIEVAULX TERRACE,
THE NATIONAL TRUST

certainly taken from Italian sources. Examples are shown, for instance, in Giovanni Giardini's *Disegni Diversi*, published in Rome in 1714 (**5:57**). This book was probably known to Kent and was probably available to his contemporaries in England. The earliest known reference occurs in John Phillips' bill for the tables at Badminton: 'A pair of peers w[it]h Eagles att £40.00'. These are the only English documented eagle tables still in their original home. A single table is recorded in an account of furniture supplied by Thomas Moore to Dudley Ryder in May 1734: 'To an Eagle frame & Top carved and Guilded in burnished gold… £12. 0. 0.'. Like the Badminton tables, this had a gilt top rather than marble, and was supplied with a pedimented pier glass en suite.[58] Eagle tables were also among furniture supplied by William Bradshaw to the Rt. Hon. Earl of Stanhope in 1737: '2 Rich Carv'd and gilt Eagle Tables with Frames and Bracketts… £27. 4. 0'. The 23ft.9in. (7.2m) of marble used for the tops came to a further £10.13.9.[59] The 'brackets' referred to are the iron brackets supporting the tops and fixing them to the wall.

58. Strange (1928).
59. Kent Record Office, Stanhope of Chevening MSS.

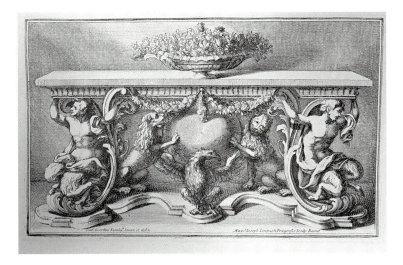

Plate 5:57. Giovanni Giardini, design for a sideboard table (1714). From *Disegni Diversi*, published in Rome but almost certainly known to English architects/designers. This engraving may be one source for the design of Georgian eagle console tables.

Tables and Stands

Left:
Plate 5:58. Giovanni Giardini, design for a sideboard table (1714). From *Disegni Diversi.* Dolphin tables were an established form in Italy before Giardini produced this engraving.

Below:
Plate 5:59. Console table (1730-40). Marble top on a base of carved and gilded deal. One of a pair. Dolphin consoles are much less common than eagles, although there is sufficient variety in their execution to suggest more than one maker.

APTER-FREDERICKS

Plate 5:60. Sphinx table (1731). Carved and gilded wood. One of a pair supplied by John Phillips to the Duke of Beaufort at the high cost of £150. These are the only documented Sphinx tables to survive. BADMINTON HOUSE THE DUKE OF BEAUFORT

Eagle tables also appear on trade cards of the 1730s and 1740s, including that of William Tomkins in London (c.1743) and Francis Brodie in Edinburgh (1739).[60] Brodie is known to have supplied eagle tables to at least three noble patrons. One may be identified with a table now in the Palace of Holyrood House, and another survives at Dumfries House, supplied in 1753. Two more at Innes House are attributed to Brodie on the strength of similarities with the design on his billhead.[61]

Giovanni Giardini was also a possible source of ideas for dolphin tables (**5:58** and **5:59**), although these were already known in Italy before 1700.[62] As far their occurrence in England is concerned, John Cornforth recently commented that these 'can be definitely associated with Kent'.[63] Dolphins certainly occur in several Kent designs; a tailpiece for Alexander Pope's translation of the *Odyssey* (1725-6) depicts a pair of dolphins ridden by Venus' swans, supporting a scallop shell and winged putto, and an illustration for John Gay's *Fables* (1726) shows a fountain whose base is composed of three dolphins entwined. Most famously, the barge designed by Kent for Frederick, Prince of Wales in 1732 is carved with shells, sea-lions and dolphins along its length. However, of the score or so of genuine eighteenth century dolphin tables recorded, none is linked to Kent by documentary evidence. Instead, they are usually attributed to Benjamin Goodison, on the strength of a bill for furniture supplied to the 4th Earl of Cardigan at Deene Park, Northamptonshire. In 1741 Goodison invoiced a 'carved and gilt dolphin table frame to match another'.[64] A pair of dolphin tables at Boughton has been attributed to Goodison because of his known association with Henry Flitcroft, who was employed by the 2nd Duke of Montagu to build a house in Whitehall in the early 1730s.[65] There must, however, have been other makers, for the dolphin tables that survive are sufficiently different in their details to suggest a number of different hands.

Sphinx tables are known to have been supplied to houses where Kent was involved, including Houghton, Badminton (**5:60**) and Ditchley, and others where he was not, such as Moore Park, Hertfordshire. The Houghton and Badminton tables are *in situ*, but the Ditchley table has gone.[66] Most famously, six were supplied by Gumley and Moore for the King's apartments at Kensington in 1724-5, although Kent's responsibility for these is conjectural.[67] A proposal by Kent's rival Sir James Thornhill for the hall at Moore Park (1725) shows a sideboard table supported on a pair of sphinxes.[68] Either Thornhill conceived the idea independently or he was very quick to emulate the Kensington scheme.

60. A set of three eagle consoles attributed to Francis Brodie is at Innes House, Morayshire (Bamford (1983), pl. 24B). See also the trade card of William Tomkins at *The Royal Bed*, active from c.1743 to c.1760 (Heal (1953), pp. 182 and 184; *DEFM*). Designs for Adderbury House, Oxfordshire include eagle tables with tabernacle glasses above (Cornforth (2004), fig. 252). See also a design by John Vardy (Royal Institute of British Architects, K9/19).
61. Bamford (1983); Pryke (1990).
62. A dolphin table is illustrated in Cornelis Meyer's *Nuovi ritrovamenti*, published in 1689, and reproduced in Jervis (1985).
63. Cornforth (2004), p. 186.
64. Edwards and Jourdain (1955), p. 45.
65. Hardy, in Murdoch (1992), pp. 134-5, fig. 136.
66. Illustrated in *DEF*, III, p. 284, fig. 31.
67. Bowett (2005).
68. Cornforth (2004), p. 32, fig. 32.

Plate 5:61. Term stand (1733). Carved and gilt deal and oak. This is one of six supplied by Benjamin Goodison for Frederick, Prince of Wales at Hampton Court Palace in 1733. The architectural form, the classical bust and the fish-scale decoration are all typical of the neo-Palladian style. HAMPTON COURT PALACE, THE ROYAL COLLECTION
© 2008 HER MAJESTY QUEEN ELIZABETH II

Term stands

Terms were an essential accessory for any formal apartment conceived in the neo-Palladian style. A term was originally an architectural device; '… Termini are sometimes employed… to support the entablatures of monuments, chimney pieces and such-like compositions. These figures owe their origin to the stones used by the ancients to mark the limits of particular possessions… In a short time, what was formerly large upright stones, were represented in human shape; and afterwards introduced as ornaments to temples and other buildings'.[69] The chief difference between terms and conventional candlestands, apart from their architectural form, is that they were intended to be static rather than movable. Hitherto, even the largest stands could, in theory, be moved to wherever they were needed, and their design was such that they could be viewed from any angle. Term stands, on the other hand, were conceived as part of the fixtures of an interior scheme, with their backs to the wall. They were not suited to occasional use, and tended to be confined to formal areas such as halls, staircases and galleries, with sconces or smaller, conventional stands providing lighting in other rooms. In these areas they served equally well as stands for candelabra or for

---

69. *Encyclopaedia Britannica* (1771), I, p. 353.
70. Houghton Hall, Inventory, 25 May 1745.
71. PRO LC9/288.
72. *DEFM*.
73. Rosoman (1985).

classical sculpture. In the hall at Houghton stood 'Four Terms at [the] Corners with Busts on Each Two Terms with Busts on D⁰ in Nitches'.[70]

The terms supplied by Benjamin Goodison for the Prince of Wales' apartments in Hampton Court Palace in 1733 are the earliest documented examples known (**5:61**). They were described in his bill as carved 'term fashion', and the wording suggests this might have been a form unfamiliar to some.[71] The stands originally supported four-branched candelabra (described as 'girandoles' in the warrant) which are now lost. Other terms attributed to Goodison are at Longford Castle, Wiltshire, where Goodison's name occurs in bills for furniture supplied between 1737 and 1745.[72]

A pair of terms supplied by John Boson to Chiswick Villa in 1735 survive at Chatsworth (**5:62**). These were invoiced by Boson as 'Stands with Boys heads' at a cost of £5 each, of which £1.16s. was to be paid to 'Mr Davis the Joiner' for constructing each one.[73] The relative costs of basic joinery and skilled carving are here clearly expressed.

A considerable number of undocumented terms survives in various collections, all broadly similar in form (**5:63**). Most were of painted or gilt deal, but mahogany examples were also made (**5:64**).

Above:
Plate 5:62. Term stand (1735). Carved and gilt wood. Joinery by 'Mr Davis', carving by John Boson. These were supplied in 1735 for Chiswick House, at a cost of £5 each.
©DEVONSHIRE COLLECTION, CHATSWORTH
REPRODUCED BY PERMISSION OF CHATSWORTH SETTLEMENT TRUSTEES
PHOTOGRAPH BY JUNE BUCK

Far left:
Plate 5:63. Term stand (1740-60). Carved, gilt and painted wood. The architectural key-pattern top is modified by a leafy collar with pierced cartouches, suggesting a rococo influence. The paint and gilding are modern.
RIEVAULX TERRACE, THE NATIONAL TRUST

Left:
Plate 5:64. Term stand (1735-60). Mahogany and part gilt. The asymmetric carved decoration on the side of the stand suggests some slight rococo influence on this otherwise typically neo-Palladian furniture form.
TEMPLE NEWSAM HOUSE, LEEDS CITY ART GALLERIES

Tables and Stands

Dressing and other small tables
Large sideboard and pier tables almost always merited a specific mention in bills and inventories if only because of the value of the marble, but the great majority of smaller tables in walnut, mahogany and wainscot received only the briefest of descriptions. At Dunham Massey there were tables of walnut and mahogany in most rooms whose size, shape and function were unspecified.

Tables and Stands

Opposite:
Plate 5:65. Table with drawer (1715-35). Walnut, oak and deal. This is typical of the small, single-drawer tables which performed a multiplicity of domestic roles in Georgian houses. The coved frame is typical of the 1720s, while the narrow, angular cabriole legs and folded feet suggest a similarly early date.
NORMAN ADAMS LTD

Plate 5:66. Table with drawer (c.1725-40). Mahogany, oak and deal. The only substantive difference between walnut and mahogany tables was that the latter were usually made in solid timber. This was a reflection of the relative cheapness of mahogany in the 1720s and 1730s. In this respect they were closer to contemporary wainscot furniture than walnut.
HOUGHTON HALL

Although these nondescript tables were predominantly associated with bedchambers and dressing rooms, they might also be found in parlours, passages, ante-rooms, studies and libraries. Only occasionally are their functions or appearances described. The furniture supplied by John Phillips to Badminton House between 1728 and 1730 included several tables of walnut and japan which were simply described as 'cove tables' because of the shape of their frames, with no further elaboration.[74] Some inventories, however, are more helpful than others, and it is clear that the most common type of small table found in bedchambers and dressing rooms was a dressing table.

The term 'dressing table' occurs rarely in seventeenth century inventories, but it is nevertheless clear that the 'triad' table functioned as a dressing table when placed in bedchambers and dressing rooms. In the Tapestry Bedchamber at Dyrham in 1710 there was a looking glass, a pair of stands and a table, on which was 'a Dressing Glass & sett of red & gold dressing boxes containing a large Comb Box a pincushion 2: Salvers 2: powder Boxes 4 patch Boxes 2: Comb Brushes 2 other sort of Brushes & a Comb Trey'.[75]

As the 'triad' fell from favour, the dressing table emerged as a piece of furniture in its own right. One of the earliest references to a dressing table occurs in the 1709 inventory of Boughton House, where there were 'two wainscot dressing tables' in Lord Monthermon's apartment,[76] but not until the 1720s are they cited with frequency. At Erddig in 1726 almost every bedchamber had a dressing table, and some other rooms besides.[77] About 1730 dressing tables entered the repertoire of the royal cabinet-maker Benjamin Goodison; in that year he supplied the Royal Wardrobe with 'a Walnuttree Dressing Table wth Drawers' for £2.10s.[78] Significantly, no stands or mirror were supplied with it.

Whereas seventeenth century 'triad' tables were consistently similar, having a single, wide drawer beneath the top, eighteenth century dressing tables took a variety of forms. When Francis Croxford advertised his stock-in-trade in 1733, it included '… dressing glasses and dressing tables of several sorts…'.[79] Most inventories do not specify whether dressing tables had drawers or not, but it is fair to assume that many single-drawer tables were used as dressing tables (**5:65-5:66**).

74. Badminton archives, bill of John Phillips, 3 December 1733.
75. Dyrham (1710).
76. Boughton (1709).
77. Erddig (1726).
78. PRO, LC9/288, f. 53.
79. *DEFM*.

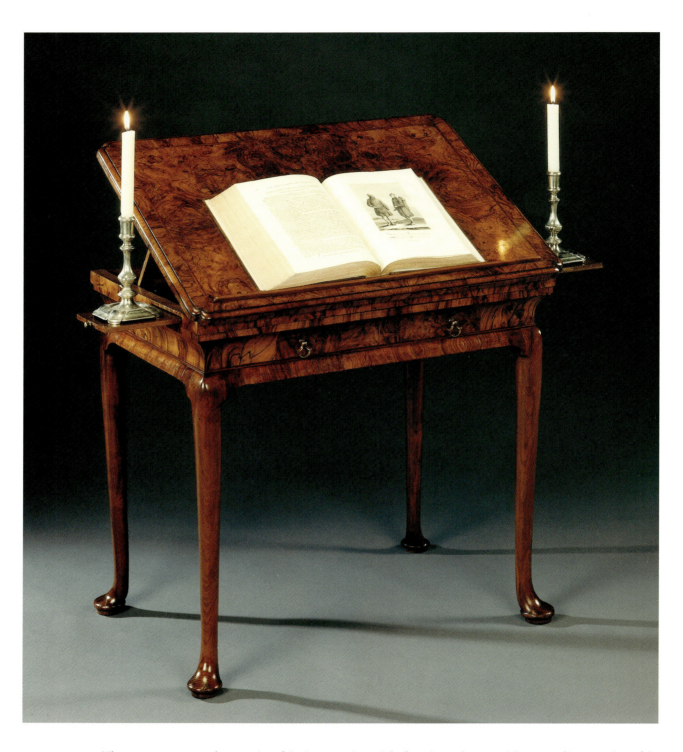

Plate 5:67. Reading/writing table (1720-40). Walnut, oak and deal. This adaptation of the single-drawer form incorporates an adjustable book-rest or desk and candle slides to each side.
MALLETT

80. Thornton (1978), p. 302 *et passim*.

They were commonly associated in inventories with dressing-glasses, either standing on the table or on the wall above it, and some had a cloth or 'toilet' to cover them. Peter Thornton has explained how the *toilette* developed in seventeenth century France from a linen cloth to protect valuable table carpets from spilt powders and cosmetics.[80] By the beginning of the eighteenth century the 'toilet' was decorative as well as practical. The 1709 inventory of Montagu House, London, records several 'twilights', including one of green silk, one of spotted calico and another of satin. At Dyrham in 1710 there was 'a Twilight upon y^e Table' in the Tapestry Bedchamber, and at

Tables and Stands

Plate 5:68. 'Architect's' or writing table (1725-45). Rosewood, brass, oak and deal. This is an extremely sophisticated variant of the common side table. The adjustable top rises to reveal a fitted interior with writing slope, brass candle arms and drawers to each side. From Ince Blundell Hall, Liverpool.

NATIONAL MUSEUMS AND GALLERIES ON MERSEYSIDE

Plate 5:69. Dressing table (1710-30). Walnut, elm, oak and deal. As with other forms of furniture, the pillar leg continued in use until about 1730. The ogee moulded top suggests a date after 1710, and the shaping of the apron reflects similar shapes on contemporary mirrors.

REPRODUCED FROM SYMONDS, ENGLISH FURNITURE FROM CHARLES II TO GEORGE II

Ditchley in 1743 the Lady's Dressing Room contained 'a wainscot Dressing Table, with a blue quilted peeling toilate'.[81] The Green and Straw Damask Bedchamber at Cannons had not only the *toilette* but all the accompanying accoutrements as well: 'A black dressing table, with a green and straw damask toylet, 2 round boxes, 2 brushes, a large dressing glass, a small ditto, and 3 covers for books laced with silver'.[82] Most inventories described the *toilette* in more prosaic language; at Erddig in 1726 the Best Dressing Room had '1 Walnut Tree dressing Table wth a Cover'.[83]

The simplicity and versatility of single drawer tables allowed them to be adapted to almost any purpose. Many are fitted for writing and reading (**5:67**) and some house ingenious mechanisms which belie their simple exterior (**5:68**). As with bureaux tables, single-drawer tables were distinguished by function, not form.

I have suggested elsewhere that three-drawer dressing tables may have developed from the French bureau rather than the English single-drawer 'triad' table.[84] Certainly it was a rare configuration in England before 1700, but the stylistic evidence suggests they were commonplace by 1730. It is difficult, however, to support this with documentary proof since inventories are rarely specific about the configuration of dressing table drawers. Early three-drawer tables with pillar legs and cross-stretchers are not common; almost all have either first or second-phase drawer construction and brassware (where original) which suggests dates between c.1700 and c.1730 (**5:69**). On veneered examples the legs are invariably dowelled up into the carcase in the

81. Montagu House (1709); Dyrham (1710); Ditchley (1743).
82. Cannons (1747).
83. Erddig (1726).
84. Bowett (2002), p.287.

Tables and Stands

seventeenth century manner. Some early cabriole-leg tables are made in a similar way; the example in **5:70** could have been made with either pillar or cabriole legs. Others have the top of the leg extended up into the carcase, which was undoubtedly a stronger arrangement (**5:71-5:72**). The strongest construction of all was to make the leg a principal structural member, with the carcase sides tenoned into it (**5:73**).

Opposite page:
Plate 5:70. Dressing table (1715-30). Walnut, oak and deal. The cabriole leg superseded the pillar leg from c.1715 onwards. The carcase of this example is made in the same way as with pillar legs, the legs being dowelled up into the carcase. Note that that the cap or abacus at the top of the leg has been retained, as with pillar leg tables.   APTER-FREDERICKS

Right:
Plate 5:71. Dressing table (1735-55). This is typical of many walnut-veneered dressing tables, having a dovetailed box carcase with the legs glued up into the corners. Brasses not original.   TENNANTS AUCTIONEERS

Below:
Plate 5:72. Detail of 5:71, showing blocks supporting the top of the leg glued and nailed in place. Note how the backs of the blocks and the shoulder pieces have been pared away with a chisel to reduce their visibility from the front.

Plate 5:73. Dressing table (1730-40). Walnut on deal and oak. On this example the carcase sides are tenoned into the tops of the legs, creating a very strong frame. This was essentially a return to joiner's construction, rather than the cabinet-style construction of the previous examples. The cockbeaded drawers suggest a date of c.1730 or later.
DUNHAM MASSEY, THE NATIONAL TRUST

Tables and Stands

Above left:
Plate 5:74. Dressing table (c.1730-40). Walnut, oak and deal. This is a nice quality example with good original brasses. Ovolo-moulded drawers suggest a date after 1730.
PRIVATE COLLECTION

Above right:
Plate 5:75. Dressing table (1730-50). Mahogany, oak and deal. Early dressing tables in plain, solid mahogany are quite numerous. This example has a relatively early pattern of handle but the insertion of a rail between the drawers and the top argues for a later date, perhaps after 1740.
MELVIN HAUGHEY

Right:
Plate 5:76. Dressing table (1735-60). Walnut, oak and deal. This table has a rail above the top drawer, a feature associated with third-phase carcase work from about 1735 onwards (see Chapter 2). The re-entrant corners to the carcase are unusual.
CHRISTIE'S IMAGES LTD 1995

From about 1730 most multi-drawer tables conformed to a more or less standard design, with either three or five drawers, on cabriole legs. Variations in timber, brassware and decorative detail gave interest to what was an otherwise mundane object (**5:74-5:76**). These were probably typical of the dressing tables recorded in most well-to-do bedchambers or dressing rooms. A more expensive variant was the 'bureau dressing table' whose origins and development have been discussed in Chapter Three.

Plate 5:77. The Norris Family (c.1736). Gawen Hamilton, oil on canvas. Henry Norris was a prosperous merchant in the Russia trade. This painting shows him and his family grouped around a rectangular mahogany tea table with raised rim. It testifies to the social importance of tea drinking and the equipage and furniture associated with it.
PRIVATE COLLECTION, UK

Tea tables

Early Georgian portrait and genre paintings often show individuals or families sitting at a small table taking tea. In many cases, the table has a central pillar and tripod base, generally called a 'pillar and claw' table, but in others the table is of rectangular form with a raised tray-like rim (**5:77**). In Chapter One it was suggested that this type of table was developed from the lacquer trays or 'tables' imported by the East India Company in the late seventeenth and early eighteenth centuries. The Customs returns reveal that tea tables were the most numerous class of lacquered ware imported by the East India Company and, according to a Parliamentary petition produced by the Joiners' Company in 1701, some 6,582 tea tables had been imported in the past four years.[85] They were usually imported in sets or nests of six to a set.[86] 'India' or 'Japan' tea tables commonly occur in domestic inventories, and seventeenth century examples survive at Ham House and Dyrham. In both cases the tables were placed on japanned frames or stands. Something similar was created by Gerrit Jensen in 1690 when he charged £2 for supplying 'a frame wth 4 Carved feet for an Indian Tea Table' to Kensington Palace.[87]

The numbers of tea tables imported fell significantly after the end of the War of Austrian Succession (1702-13), so that from c.1715 onwards importations were measured in dozens rather than thousands.[88] It is possible that this merely reflects a change in the way such importations were recorded, for the frequently used term 'lacquered ware' might cover many types of artefact, including tea tables. On the other hand, it might signify a decline in the profitability of such imports, as English japanned tea tables undercut the market.

It is often difficult to determine whether the 'tea tables' mentioned in bills and inventories were tables in the modern sense or merely trays. In some cases it was clearly a tray that was being described, as at Drayton in 1710: 'a Tea Table upon ye Chest of Drawers, 4 Cups & 4 Sawcers, 4 Chocolate cups a Bason sugar Dish & Tea pot a Dish for it to Stand in'.[89] In the 1724 inventory the same tray and its equipage was described as follows: '1 fine indian Tea-table with 8 coloured china cups & 4 saucers, a sugar dish, a plate & cover, a small china Bason and a red Tea-pott'.[90] Anyone reading the latter without the benefit of the former might reasonably assume that the tea table was a

---

85. B.L., 'THE CASE OF THE JOYNER'S COMPANY AGAINST the Importation of manufactured CABINET-WORK from the EAST INDIES'.
86. Clunas (1987), p. 260.
87. PRO, LC 9/280, f. 43.
88. PRO Cust 3.
89. Drayton (1710).
90. Drayton (1724).

Tables and Stands

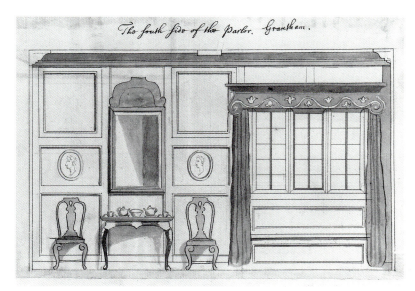 

Above left:
Plate 5:78. The South Side of the Parlour, Grantham (1728). William Stukeley, watercolour. This charming sketch shows a tea table *in situ* with its equipage. The top appears to be a tray, on a japanned frame. BODLEIAN LIBRARY

Above right:
Plate 5:79. Tea table, (1730). Chinese lacquer top on a japanned beechwood frame. This was probably supplied by George Nix to Ham House in 1730. In form and style it is probably typical of many thousands made in the late 1720s and 1730s.
HAM HOUSE, THE NATIONAL TRUST

fully formed table in the modern sense. In the same vein, the 'Black Japan Indian Tea Table' in the Drawing Room of Sherborne House in 1726 might have been either a tray or a table.[91] Occasionally the term 'hand tea table' occurs, an unmistakable reference to a tray, also known as a 'hand board'. The stock-in-trade of the cabinet-maker Thomas Halfhide, advertised for disposal in March 1723, included 'a Parcel of fine lacquer'd Tea-Tables'; the term 'parcel' suggests these too were just trays.[92]

In some cases the table is described as being on a frame or stand. In the South East Drawing Room at Kiveton there was a 'Large Japan'd Tea Table and Stand', and at Chicheley in 1755 there was 'An India tea table on a Black frame' in an upstairs passage.[93] At Cannons in 1747 the Duchess of Chandos' Drawing Room contained 'A large *India* scollopt tea table on a carved and gilt frame'.[94] In these instances we can be sure that a table in the modern sense is implied, although the tray top might well have been detachable. In 1724 the cabinet-maker Lazarus Stiles had a number of tea tables in his house and workshops; some were probably trays, as in '13 Tea Tables 15 hand boards', of which some were to be fitted with frames, since he had at least '2 Tea Table Frames' to hand.

The typical tea table of the 1720s had a tray-top on a rectangular frame with slender cabriole legs. One example, complete with its equipage, is shown in William Stukeley's watercolour sketch of his parlour (**5:78**). A table of this form survives at Ham House; it was probably supplied by George Nix in 1730 (**5:79**). Nix's bill describes 'a Black Japann'd frame for an Indian Tea Table & gilding & mending the table where it was broke… £1.5.0'.[95] The top is now fixed, but was originally detachable.

A characteristic feature of almost all tea tables is the double-radiussed or re-entrant corners to the top. This is commonly found on Chinese furniture, and in the case of lacquered trays its purpose was to make the corners less vulnerable to damage. The feature was retained by English furniture-makers even when the top was of a robust material such as walnut or mahogany. It was also adopted, as we have seen earlier in this chapter, for gilt table-tops from about 1715 onwards.

Japanned tea tables are now uncommon, probably because of their poor survival rate, but mahogany examples with fixed tops are relatively abundant (**5:80**). As early as June 1724 Robert Hodson supplied Lord Irwin with 'a Neat Mohogoney Tea Table… £1. 15. 0.'.[96] The price, though modest, probably indicates more than a mere tray. An inventive alternative to the standard tea table is shown on the trade card of Thomas Potter, probably the man recorded as a cabinet-maker in High Holborn in 1737 (**3:85**).[97] A table corresponding to this design was acquired by Leeds City Art Galleries in 1992 (**5:81**). It has a rectangular top divided in the middle which can be slid aside to reveal a well fitted with a tray which can be raised and fixed with brass catches. When not in use the tray can be lowered complete with its equipage and the top closed to keep dirty china and leftover food out of sight.

---

91. Sherborne (1726).
92. *The Daily Post*, 18 March 1723.
93. Kiveton (1727); Chicheley (1755).
94. Cannons (1747).
95. Ham House, bill of George Nix, 12 September 1730.
96. Gilbert (1967).
97. Gilbert (1998), p. 661.

Plate 5:80. Tea table (1730-50). Mahogany. This is typical of the genre, albeit with a rather idiosyncratic treatment of the legs. The simplicity of these tables often belies the quality of workmanship involved.

MELVIN HAUGHEY

Plate 5:81. Tea table, (1730-45). Mahogany and deal. This table is of the same metamorphic design as one illustrated on Thomas Potter's trade card (3:85). The tray is raised and lowered by the brass pulls which engage with ratchets inside the well. The leaves slide and close the top when the tray is not in use.

TEMPLE NEWSAM HOUSE, LEEDS CITY ART GALLERIES

Tables and Stands

Plate 5:82. Billhead of Francis Brodie, c.1740. This shows a wonderful range of furniture including an eagle table and, on the left, a dressing table with a drawer and tray top.

Plate 5:83. Tea or dressing table (1730-50). Mahogany with brass inlay. This stylish table has had its top shaved to remove the rim. The presence of a drawer which was originally divided into compartments suggests this may have been a dressing table rather than a tea table (see 5:82). An almost identical table with its rim, and probably from the same workshop, is at Haddo House, Aberdeen.
PRIVATE COLLECTION

Although the raised rim was a standard attribute of tea tables, not all tables with rims were intended for taking tea. The bill-head of the Edinburgh furniture-maker Francis Brodie shows a table with raised rim which is clearly used as a dressing table (**5:82**). It may be that where such tables are fitted with a drawer they are dressing tables rather than tea-tables. One such is shown in **5:83**. This originally had a raised rim which has subsequently been planed off, perhaps having become damaged.[98]

---

98. This is illustrated in Gilbert and Murdoch (1993), fig. 73, where it is described as walnut.

'Dutch' tables

From 1697 onwards (the year when the first complete Customs returns survive) Dutch 'tea tables', either plain or 'lackered', were the second most numerous class of furniture imported from Holland, after the ubiquitous matted chairs. The fashion for 'Dutch' tables became something of a phenomenon in early Georgian England, and few well-to do houses were without one or more examples. Among the earliest domestic references are Dutch tables at Montagu House, London (1709) and Boughton House, Northamptonshire (1709).[99] There were also Dutch tables at Drayton in 1710. They occur not only in noble houses but in the houses of successful tradesmen and merchants. In 1715 two Dutch tables stood in the house of the recently deceased upholsterer Francis Lapiere,[100] and in the same year a Dutch table was recorded in the house of Henry Woolball, a grocer and general merchant.[101] These were not expensive things - the Customs returns cite values of between 5s. and 10s. apiece – but they were fashionable.

The problem of nomenclature regarding tea tables has already been discussed, and applies equally to these Dutch tables. Their modest price raises the possibility that these were trays rather than complete tables, and this possibility is strengthened by occasional references to Dutch 'tea table frames' in the Customs returns. Similarly, some inventories distinguish between the top or 'table' and its base; the 1743 inventory of Ditchley House, near Oxford records ' a round Dutch table on a pillar and claw' in one of the secondary bedrooms.[102] In all probability the phrase 'Dutch table' could refer either to a tray or a complete table. However, it seems that the distinguishing feature of a Dutch table was that it stood on a pillar-and-claw base. The following description was written by J.T. Smith in 1828:

Plate 5:84. 'Dutch' table (1700-1730). Painted deal. Few English houses of any status were without one or more tables such as these in the early 18th century. Although obscured by a later dark varnish, the paintwork appears to be largely original.
DRAYTON HOUSE

> This description of table, the pride of our great-grand-mothers, in which the brightest colours were most gorgeously displayed, was first imported from Holland into England in the reign of William and Mary. The top was nothing more than a large oval tea-tray, with a raised scalloped border round it, fixed upon a pillar, having a claw of three legs. They are now and then to be met with in our old-fashioned family mansions, and brokers' shops. They were formerly considered by our Aunt Deborah to be such an ornament to a room, that in order to exhibit them to advantage, they were put in the corner of a waiting-parlour for the admiration of the country tenants, when they brought their rents, or sat waiting their turn for an order for coals in a severe winter.[103]

The notion that the Dutch tables were imported as tops only is one possible interpretation of the fact that English furniture-makers advertised them among their stock in trade. One of Coxed and Woster's trade labels dating from the early 1730s includes 'Wisk, Ombre, *Dutch* and *India* Tea Tables' among their stock. Perhaps they were fitting the imported tops to English bases? Or were they making tables in the Dutch style? Both possibilities are suggested by the presence of '12 kitches [catches] for dutch Tables some brass some iron' in the workshop of the Bastard brothers of Blandford, Dorset, in 1731. Their stock also included several 'Dutch fashion' tables,[104] and they may even have supplied some to nearby Sherborne House, where in 1726 there were tables 'after the Dutch fashon', one of which was described as oval.[105]

As the Coxed and Woster trade card reveals, Dutch tables were used primarily as tea tables. Painted oval and circular tea tables remained popular in Holland well into the nineteenth century but, as Smith's account implies, they were little more than old-fashioned curiosities in England by the beginning of the nineteenth century. This may partly be a question of survival, for the tables were relatively cheap, and, being made of non-durable woods such as deal or beech, were prone to damage, worm, damp and rot. Additionally, the survival rate of painted furniture has always been poor, because once the decorated surface became damaged it quickly lost its appeal. One rare survivor at Drayton is shown in **5:84**. It is made of softwood, painted and grained. The top has a border simulating a burr wood, perhaps walnut, and the raised rim suggests veined marble. The

99. Montagu House (1709); Boughton (1709).
100. CLRO, Orphans' Court Inventory, Roll No. 3097; Westman (1994).
101. CLRO, Orphans' Court Inventory, Roll No. 3097.
102. Ditchley (1743).
103. Smith (1828), II, p. 228. For more on these tables in Dutch interiors, see Thornton (1984), fig. 95.
104. Legg (1994), pp. 27, 30 and 31.
105. Sherborne (1726).

Tables and Stands

Plate 5:85. 'Dutch' table (1700-1800). Japanned deal (?). This is probably more typical of the tables described in the Customs Returns as 'Tea tables, lackered'. Although popular in Holland for all of the 18th century, 'Dutch tables' tend to disappear from English domestic inventories after about 1740. COURTESY OF SOTHEBY'S

narrow, profile-cut legs are typical of the genre. A similar table survives at Boughton. Plate **5:85** shows another version which might correspond to the 'lackered' tea tables recorded in the Customs returns.

Inventory references to Dutch tables become less common after 1740, perhaps because of the prevalence of mahogany pillar-and-claw tables which fulfilled the same purposes in a more robust fashion.

Pillar and claw tables

The term 'pillar-and-claw' occurs in bills submitted by Gerrit Jensen in the 1690s for candlestands with three scrolled feet,[106] but it does not appear to have been applied to larger tables until the 1720s. It was probably the popularity of the ubiquitous Dutch table which induced English furniture makers to create their own version of it.[107] However, it is surely significant that the first documentary references to pillar-and-claw tables, which occur in the Lord Chamberlain's accounts for 1729, describe them as being made of mahogany, the only wood which provided boards wide enough and stable enough to make one-piece tops:

a Mohogony table on a pillar… £1.15. 0
a large round Mohogony Table on a pillar and claw… £2.10. 0.[108]

---

106. E.g., PRO, LC/9, f.44 (1691).
107. For a North American view on the development of the pillar and claw table, see Fayen, 2003.
108. PRO, LC 9/287, f. 180; 288, f. 19.

Tables and Stands

Plate 5:86. Pillar-and-claw table (1725-40). Mahogany. This is a rare and probably early form, with profile-cut legs in the Dutch manner. The top is made in two pieces and the bearers are fixed to the top by tapered sliding dovetails, rather than the usual screws. Curiously, it has a 'birdcage', but the top is located by a square tenon and cannot revolve. PRIVATE COLLECTION

Plate 5:87. Pillar and claw table, c 1730-50. Mahogany. The plain tapered pillar seems to have been the most common design for early pillar and claw tables. This is a typically plain and robust example. GEFFRYE MUSEUM, LONDON

Some mahogany pillar-and-claw tables were made in a similar fashion to the Dutch ones, with profile-cut legs tenoned into the base of the pillar (**5:86**). The main problem with this construction was that the tenon provided no mechanical resistance to the force exerted by the top; it was secured solely by glue or pegs. The English solution was to dovetail the legs into the base of the pillar to prevent them spreading, while the rounded section of the leg gave it broad shoulders to support the joint. This much stronger method of construction allowed the table to support a bigger top (**5:87**). The base of the pillar was often reinforced, either at the time of making or retrospectively, by a three-spoked metal brace which tied pillar and claws together (**5:88**); later in the century this was known as a 'triangle'.[109] So long as the claw, pillar and top were kept in proportion, there was no theoretical limit to the size of table that could be made. However, a practical limit was imposed by the width of timber available for the top, for although it was possible to make tops of several boards glued together, this was less satisfactory, both aesthetically and structurally, than a one-piece top.

With the introduction of mahogany the pillar-and-claw table became the most versatile of all English furniture forms, large enough to serve variously as a tea, supper, or even a dining table, and small enough with the top raised to stand discreetly in the corner of a room. With a variety of differently configured tops, it also formed the basis for firescreens, reading tables, desks and worktables. In 1731 Benjamin Goodison supplied St James's Palace with '2 round mohogony Tables on claw feet the tops to move for different

Plate 5:88. Reinforcing plate or 'triangle'. These reinforcements were commonly fitted, either at the time or making or subsequently. Their purpose was to prevent the legs from spreading and hence splitting the base of the pillar.

---
109. *The Cabinet-Maker's London Book of Prices* (1793), p. 266.

Tables and Stands

Plate 5:89. Family portrait (1736) by Thomas Bardwell (1704-67). Oil on canvas. The detailed painting shows a prosperous English family, thought to be the Brewster family of Beccles, Suffolk, seated around a pillar and claw table. The table has a dished top and fluted pillar. The wife and eldest daughter sit on India-backed chairs, while the husband sits on a low backed corner chair. Two brass candle branches are fixed to the panelling above the fireplace. The boarded floor with a carpet placed under the table for a special occasion is typical.
GEFFRYE MUSEUM, LONDON

heights… £5. 0. 0' and 'a Mohogony Table on a Claw Foot to rise & fall, with a Desk for Books & 2 foulding wro^t Arms for Candles… £4.15. 0.'.[110] Several tables with adjustable tops survive at Hampton Court Palace.

The rapidity with which pillar-and-claw tables were adopted by Georgian furniture-makers is reflected in their inventories. The probate inventory of Thomas Roberts (1733) records several mahogany pillar-and-claw tables in his workshop, both complete and in the process of manufacture. There were in addition 'three pillars and Claws for fire Screens'.[111]

Because wide mahogany boards suitable for table tops fetched a premium, the price of pillar-and-claw tables was mainly determined by the diameter of their tops, as in the following bill of 1739 from the London furniture maker Peter Hasert:

For a Fine mahogany Table on a Pillar & Claw 30 inches £1.10. 0.[112]

The social significance of the pillar-and-claw table is amply reflected in the numerous early Georgian conversation pieces in which such tables play an important role. As with their precursors, the Dutch tables, pillar and claw tables were not necessarily expensive but they were fashionable; painters gave the tables a central role, their mahogany tops uncovered and boasting their brash red timber. They are variously represented as being used for writing, reading, gaming and, most commonly, for taking tea, coffee or chocolate (**5:89**). A japanned table supplied to Ham House about 1730 was almost certainly primarily a tea table, the link with tea being emphasised by the Chinese style decoration (**5:90**). Tables with multi-dished tops were also clearly intended for taking tea, chocolate or something similar (**5:91**). The tops were lathe-turned, using a counter-balance clamped to the top to offset the eccentric positioning of the separate dishes.

110. PRO LC 9/288, ff. 153 & 159.
111. Beard & Cross (1998).
112. Ham House, bill of Peter Hasert, 1739.

Far left:
Plate 5:90. Pillar-and-claw table
(1730-50). Japanned oak, deal and beech. The japanned finish of this table emphasises the link between the table and tea drinking.
HAM HOUSE, THE NATIONAL TRUST

Left:
Plate 5:91. Pillar and claw table
(1730-60). Mahogany, brass and mother-of-pearl. The function of these showy, multi-dished tables remains obscure.

Below:
Plate 5:92. Pillar and claw table
(c.1741). The top of this table is designed to hold the silver tea table made by the silversmith David Williaume II (1693-1761) in 1741. The fashion for 'pie-crust' mahogany tops was inspired by silver tables such as this.
DUNHAM MASSEY, THE NATIONAL TRUST

The tables of the kind shown in **5:92** are now rare. This is one of two made to support silver salvers intended for tea and coffee services. The maker of the pillar-and-claw is unknown, but the salvers are marked for David Williaume II, 1741. In the 1758 inventory the tables were described as '2 Mahogany Stands to Set the Silver Tea & Coffee Tables on'.[113] It was from silver trays such as this that the fashion for shaped mahogany tops (generally called 'pie-crust' tops by modern pundits) was developed. One wonders whether the tops were covered with a cloth, in which case it would be impossible for visitors to tell whether the top was silver or wood.

Pillar and claw tables were also made specifically for gaming. Versions with circular, triangular, square and pentagonal tops are known, sometimes covered with baize or needlework.[114] A bill for a table with a 'five square' top, supplied by Gumley and Turing to Hampton Court Palace in 1728, corresponds to a table with a pentagonal top which is still at the Palace.[115] This was described as a card table, presumably for the five-handed variant of Quadrille known as 'Quintille'. There is another bill of 1730 from Benjamin Goodison for a 'Mohogany Cinquil Table' also for Hampton Court, which might equally apply to this piece.[116]

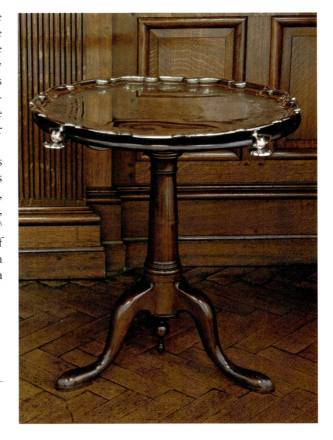

---
113. Dunham Massey (1758).
114. See, for instance, *DEF*, II, pp. 198-99.
115. PRO, LC 9/287, f. 151.
116. PRO, LC 9/288, f. 82.

Tables and Stands

Plate 5:93. Pillar and claw table (1730-50). Mahogany. Baluster stems were a common alternative to the plain tapered pillar. The restrained carving on the knees and feet is typical of many early tables, but most seem to have been plain.
CHRISTIE'S IMAGES LTD 1995

As the illustrated examples show, the most common form of stem on these early pillar-and-claw tables was either a plain tapered pillar or a baluster (**5:93**). Plain shafts might be stop-fluted, but elaborately carved pillars seem to have been a product of the rococo. Similarly, the decoration of the feet seems to have been fairly restrained until the advent of rococo designs in the 1740s and '50s.

The catches for pillar and claw tables were usually of iron and steel with a brass cover. Plates **5:94-5:95** show the most common forms. Blacksmith's iron catches were also used, although these tend to be characteristic of provincial and 'country' tables, often made of oak or other native woods (**5:96**).

Above left:
Plate 5:94. Table catch (after 1730). Brass, iron and steel. This form of catch was very solidly made and tended to last well.

Above centre:
Plate 5:95. Table catch (after 1730). Brass iron and steel. The circular catch was more common, and probably cheaper. This view shows the inside of the catch, with its iron shoot and steel spring. The brass case was first cast and then finished on a lathe. Note the founder's mark - W.

Right:
Plate 5:96. Table catch (after 1720). Iron. These blacksmith-made catches tend to be found on provincial rather than metropolitan furniture.

Dining tables

The oval dining table introduced during the 1660s had a long span of fashionable life, even occurring in Gillows' sketch books of the 1790s.[117] In the first forty years of the eighteenth century oval tables predominated in fashionable English houses almost to the exclusion of other types. Few inventories of the period are without at least one oval table and in many houses there were several. In smaller houses they might be found in any room but particularly in parlours, which usually served as family eating rooms in middle-class houses. At Catherine Morgan's house in Teddington in 1722 the common parlour contained 'two oval wainscot tables' while the adjacent 'best parlour and drawing room' had none. The relative status and functions of the two rooms is clearly expressed by their titles and contents.[118] A similar division between 'common' and 'best' parlours is found at Sherborne House in 1726, where the Common Parlour contained, among other things, 'One Walnut Oval Table' and '8 Walnut Chaires coverd with black leather'. It also had scarlet camlet curtains (a relatively inexpensive cloth) and a half-length portrait of the late owner, the Honourable Henry Portman. This was the family's eating room, whereas the nearby Best Parlour used for formal dining was more luxuriously equipped with a large oval walnut table, twelve walnut chairs 'ye bottumes and backs silver stuff', together with curtains of purple mantua silk and full-length family portraits. Across the hall there was also a Drawing Room, without dining furniture but replete with damask seat furniture and glass sconces.

In contrast to the multi-functional parlour, larger houses often had designated 'eating' or 'dining' rooms which performed no other role. In the early part of the period these rooms did not

117. Westminster City Archive, Gillows 97/1284, sketch dated 22 October 1796.
118. For more on parlours and their functions see Cornforth (2004), pp. 38-42.

necessarily contain dining tables. At Drayton in 1710 the 'Eating Parlour' or family dining room contained a dozen chairs but no table.[119] In such cases the table was usually to be found in the passage outside, or in an adjacent room, as at Ditchley in 1743, where the Dining Parlour contained twelve leather-seated chairs and two marble slabs on walnut frames, but the tables – 'A large Mohogoney table with a leaf to add, 3 Mohogoney oval Dineing Tables one wainscot breakfast Table on a claw' – were stored in the adjacent lobby.[120] By 1724 the Eating Parlour at Drayton accommodated '1 large oval wainscot table and 1 of a smaller size' as permanent furnishings, and there was in addition a dining table and an additional leaf stored in the passage outside.[121] At Erddig in 1726 the permanent furniture of the Eating Parlour included eight black leather chairs, a mahogany table and a marble sideboard, as well as a tea table with China tea-cups, a Dutch table and a corner cupboard containing crockery.[122] One suspects, however, that on important occasions dining took place either in the Hall or the Saloon, since there was no dining room as such and the Eating Parlour was too small and perhaps too homely for a large or distinguished company.

Houses planned on a truly grand scale might have several dining rooms, ranging in status from the servants' hall to the great dining room. Cannons was typical of such houses, having a Steward's Dining Room, a Marble Dining Room and a Great Dining Room. The first had a nondescript 'wainscot table', the second 'a large oval wainscot table', and the last 'a large mahogany dining table, 5ft 7 inches over' and another of 5ft. (1.5m).[123] Similarly, at Kiveton there was a first-floor Great Dining Room and a smaller ground floor Dining Room, neither of which was furnished with tables.[124] It is interesting to note what was considered a 'large' table at Cannons – this table was unlikely to seat more than ten people in comfort, but it was customary for a large company to dine at several tables. Thomas Burnet recorded such an occasion at the court of George I in 1717: '… at three a Clock all the world went to Dinner, as they were invited: some at the King's own table, which consisted of fifteen, some to Baron Berensdorf's, which seldom consisted of more than five or six, some to the Earl of Sunderland's, or Count Bothmar's each a table for a dozen, some to the dukes of Kent or Newcastle, which was about as large as the others…'.[125] If contemporary illustrations are reliable, diners generally sat closer together than would be thought comfortable nowadays.[126]

Given the frequency with which they are recorded in domestic inventories, it is not surprising to find oval wainscot dining tables from this period surviving in large numbers. Many are built on the gate-leg principle and differ little from their seventeenth century forebears. The example in **5:97** is typical, strongly made and with few stylistic clues as to its date. The edge of the top is lightly radiussed, and there is a tongue and groove joint between the leaves and the fixed top. Both these features are found on seventeenth century tables. On the other hand, the tapered pillar legs suggest an early eighteenth century date, as does the opposed baluster stretcher. The handle of the drawer, which is original, probably places the table somewhere between c.1715 and c.1740.

One obvious indicator of an eighteenth rather than seventeenth century date is the scrolled foot, which was introduced around 1710 and remained popular until about 1740 (the term 'Spanish' or 'Braganza' foot, often applied to this style of foot, is a nineteenth century misnomer).[127] Very often the foot was reduced to a slight outward 'kick' at the base of the leg, thus avoiding the expense of a carver while still paying lip-service to fashion (**5:98**). Increasingly, the hinges used for these tables were of a recognisably modern rectangular shape, distinct from the forged 'dovetail' or 'fishtail' hinges used in the seventeenth century. They were also usually secured by screws rather than nails (see Appendix I).

During the 1720s mahogany became the favoured wood for dining tables in fashionable houses. Indeed, the earliest known bill for mahogany furniture was for the '2 Mohogeny Tables' supplied by 'Mr. Hodson' (probably Robert Hodson) to Jacob de Bouverie (later 1st Viscount Folkstone) in December 1723.[128] Mahogany was roughly comparable in price to wainscot and was available in wide boards which were dimensionally stable. This allowed joiners to make the tables with the leaves made from single boards, rather than from narrower boards butt-jointed together as with oak and walnut. It is probably no coincidence, therefore, that tables are cited more commonly than

---

119. Drayton (1710)
120. Ditchley (1743).
121. Drayton (1724).
122. Erddig (1726).
123. Cannons (1747).
124. Kiveton (1727).
125. Quoted in Thurley, (1993), p. 255.
126. See for instance, Marcellus Laroon's painting *Desert* [sic] *being served at a Dinner Party,* 1725. This is reproduced in Day (2000), fig 42.
127. The terms 'Braganza' and 'Spanish' foot are 19th century inventions, based on the erroneous supposition that this style of foot was introduced with the arrival of Charles II's Portuguese queen, Catherine of Braganza. In fact there are no documented examples known before c.1708-10.
128. I am indebted to Lucy Wood for this reference.

Tables and Stands

Plate 5:97. Dining table (1715-40). Oak. This was probably the most common form of dining table made in the 18th century. It is constructed in an identical manner to late 17th century examples, but the shaped drawer rail, the double-baluster front stretcher and the plain pillar legs all suggest an 18th century date. The drawer handle, which is original, was a popular model between c.1715 and 1740.
BENINGBOROUGH HALL,
THE NATIONAL TRUST

Plate 5:98. Dining table (1710-30). Oak. This small gateleg table is typical of its kind. The tapered pillar legs and scroll feet both indicate a date after c.1710 and possibly as late as 1740. This may be a London piece, since it is constructed of high quality wainscot oak.
PRIVATE COLLECTION

Tables and Stands

Plate 5:99. Dining table (1715-30). Mahogany. The scroll feet and relatively complex turnings suggest a relatively early date for this table. Note the width of the boards used in the top. Single boards of this width were simply not available in any European wood. ALASTAIR SAMPSON

Plate 5:100. Dining table (1715-30). Mahogany. A more sophisticated mahogany gateleg, with fluted pillars and nicely modelled scroll feet.
HAMPTONS

Plate 5:101. Knuckle or finger joint. This type of hinge was devised to compensate for the loss of strength resulting from the omission of stretchers on 18th century dining tables. It was also commonly used for the hinged legs of contemporary fold-over tea and card tables.

Plate 5:102. *The south and east sides of the Dining Room, Grantham* (1727). Watercolour by William Stukeley. This is the earliest known depiction of a Georgian pad-foot table. It was customary to place the table against the wall when not in use, with the dining chairs also ranged around the walls. BODLEIAN LIBRARY

any other form of mahogany furniture in bills and inventories of the 1720s. The scrolled foot is a common feature of early mahogany dining tables (**5:99** and **5:100**), and indeed their design and construction is identical to contemporary wainscot tables except for the one-piece leaves.

With the growing popularity of the 'claw' or cabriole leg, makers of dining tables had to alter the design of their tables frames, for cabriole legs were not easily combined with stretchers. The solution was to abandon the stretchers and make the frame deeper to compensate for the loss of rigidity. One or two legs on each side were hinged on a knuckle joint to support the open leaves (**5:101**). The same construction was adopted for tables with plain turned legs and pad feet. Contemporary bills and inventories are not detailed enough to determine when the new type of frame was introduced, but they were certainly in use by the mid-1720s, when Dr. William Stukeley furnished his new house at Grantham. His watercolour of the Dining Room (1727) shows an oval dining table with turned legs and pad feet folded against the wall (**5:102**). Whether this was made of oak or mahogany we cannot tell.

Many bills for dining tables cite the measurements of the top, which suggests that, other things

Tables and Stands

Plate 5:103. Dining table (1730-60). Mahogany and oak. This bears the traces of three of Giles Grendey's trade labels. It is typical of the sort of plain mahogany tables made in huge numbers from about 1720 onwards.   GEFFRYE MUSEUM, LONDON

Plate 5:104. Pad foot (detail), showing the two lathe centre-marks used to turn the leg and the pad independently.

129. Ham House, bill of Peter Hasert, 1739.

being equal, they were priced according to size. The following bill from Peter Hasert in 1739 is typical: 'For a Mahogany Dineing Table 3ft 6 by 3ft 1… £2. 0. 0'.[129] The only other variables were the style of leg and the amount of carved embellishment applied to the knee and foot. The basic model had straight tapered legs with pad feet (**5:103**). The legs were turned on two centres, one to form the shaft of the leg and the second to make the foot (**5:104**). The junction between the two was finished by hand. The cabriole leg version was probably more expensive because of the greater work and more extravagant use of timber (**5:105**), while carved work was more expensive still. In most cases the carving was restricted to the knee and foot, matching in style that found on contemporary chairs. The same standard repertoire of shells, bellflowers, masks and acanthus leaves occurs with formulaic predictability, but occasionally one comes across tables whose masterful execution and sheer physical presence set them apart (**5:106**).

The chief limitation of oval tables was one of size, for few seated more than ten people comfortably. Plate **5:107** shows an exceptional table capable of seating at least twelve people, which at the same time reveals in its long oval shape the shortcomings of the gateleg design. The width of the top was limited by the table's height, for the leaves could be no wider than the table was high. A further limitation was the sheer weight of large leaves, which placed a strain on the frame and hinges. They also needed to be kept relatively narrow because otherwise diners sat too far away from their companions opposite and too far from dishes placed in the centre of the table.

Plate 5:105. Dining table (1730-60). Mahogany, oak and deal. The most common alternative to the pad foot table had plain cabriole legs. This table has an unusually well-figured top, and demonstrates the remarkable stability of mahogany compared with most other woods. MALLETT

Plate 5:106. Dining table (1730-50). Mahogany and oak. There is little to choose between the majority of oval tables, but occasionally one finds examples such as this which stand out in terms of workmanship and sheer presence. PRIVATE COLLECTION

Plate 5:107. Dining table (1730-1760). Mahogany and oak. The physical and aesthetic limitations of oval tables become apparent when attempting to accommodate more than about ten diners. This one from Kedleston Hall, Derbyshire, is nearly 8ft. (2.4m) across when open. The flattened oval is a consequence of the boards for the leaves not being wide enough to create a true oval. CHRISTIE'S IMAGES LTD 2002

Tables and Stands

Plate 5:108. Set of dining tables (c.1730). Mahogany and oak. This is perhaps the earliest extant example of a set of dining tables made to seat a variable number of people. There is no evidence, however, that it was made for the Marble Parlour where it now stands. It may have been made for the Hunting Hall or family dining room on the lower floor. HOUGHTON HALL

Formal dining in the early eighteenth century was *à la Française*. The table was covered with a selection of dishes from which the diners helped themselves, so dishes placed more than an arm's length away were awkward to get at.[130] For all these reasons tables above a certain size, typically eight to ten seats, tended to be long in relation to their width, and this was probably the genesis of the long, narrow tables popularly called 'wake' tables. The name arises because of the fanciful notion that they were used to support the coffin at a funeral gathering but the shape was actually determined by more practical considerations.

So long as it was fashionable to dine at several small tables the gateleg design presented no difficulty, but if a larger table were needed, then another solution was called for. This was perhaps the rationale behind the square 'flapp' tables supplied by Richard Roberts to the Royal Palaces in the 1720s:

1722:	for a large Oval Table…	£3.10.0
	for two large Wainscot flapp Tables…	£4. 0.0.[131]

The bills do not make explicit whether these 'flapp' tables were intended for dining, but the context, being often listed together with oval tables, suggests they were. Occasionally one finds bills couched in more descriptive language which tells us explicitly of their purpose. In 1733 John Hodson supplied Sir Herbert Pakington of Westwood Park, Worcestershire, with 'a Large Oblong mohogeny dining Table with 2 flapps to hold 12 people', at a cost of £3.10s.[132] In the *Daily Advertiser* of 13 October 1742 the stock of Thomas King, a cabinet-maker based in Long Acre, was advertised for auction, including 'Mahogany, Oblong, Oval and Claw Tables'. The advantage of rectangular over oval tables was twofold: they could accommodate more people for the same breadth of top, and if the size of the company required it they could be placed one against the other to make a larger table.

At Houghton Hall is a set of tables which represents a logical extension of this principle, comprising four tables, each with folding leaves and supporting gates, of which two have one square and one half-round leaf to form the ends (**5:108**). This arrangement seats any number of guests from four to twenty-four.

The history of this table is less certain than at first appears. It is now in the Marble Parlour, which was originally conceived as a dining room with a sideboard room adjoining, but it was not there

---

130. Day (2000), pp. 49 et seq. Day shows a plan (fig. 23) of the Duke of Newcastle's feast of 1710 in which the dishes are arranged on an oval table with the dessert in the centre.
131. PRO LC 9/287, f. 22.
132. *DEFM*.

Plate 5:109. Dining table (1740-60). Mahogany and other woods. This appears to be a rare early example of an extending dining table, formerly at Hamilton Palace. It is not clear how the table was constructed, but the frame appears to be hinged concertina-fashion. COUNTRY LIFE

when the inventory of Houghton was taken in 1745. During his visit to Houghton in 1731, Sir Thomas Robinson noted that the Marble Parlour had still to be completed, so that he dined elsewhere in the house, where 'we were generally between twenty and thirty at two tables'.[133] It appears that by 1745 the idea of using the Marble Parlour as a dining room was already abandoned, and it is conceivable that it was never used for its original purpose. There was, in any event, a 'Common Parlour or dining room' on the opposite side of the Marble Hall, and this was certainly furnished for dining, with six tables of various sizes and twenty-four chairs.[134] The most likely location for the present table was on the ground floor, perhaps in the Hunting Hall where in 1745 there were 'four tables'.[135] The terse language of the inventory tells us no more than this, but this would have been the conventional way of describing a dining table of four sections. The Hunting Hall served as the principal eating room on the ground floor, where both breakfast and dinner were served for family and guests.[136] The plain, robust design of the table is certainly compatible with such use, and it appears to have been constructed with strength rather than elegance in mind. Each section is double-gated on each side, so that, when fully open, the top is supported on a forest of thirty-two legs. The crowded effect is compounded by the relatively narrow boards used for the top, suggesting some economy in their selection. In the 1792 inventory it is possible to identify the table split into two parts, with 'a Pair of mahogany two flap Dining Tables to join' in the Marble Hall and 'Two mahogany dining Tables with circular ends to join those in the Hall 8 ft. long' on the Grand Staircase.[137] This suggests that at this date the table was used for large gatherings in the Marble Hall.

No other tables of the Houghton model are known, suggesting it may have been an isolated example rather than a generic type. Indeed, extending tables of any kind are rare at this date. One early looking example was formerly at Hamilton Palace, which appeared to extend by means of a concertina-action frame, but its present whereabouts are unknown (**5:109**).[138] Thomas Potter's trade card of c.1735-40 shows a rectangular dining table with a top of five hinged leaves supported on square legs, but it not clear how the frame was constructed (3:85). A bill from William Hallet for furniture supplied to Langley Park, Norfolk, in 1748, includes one of the earliest references to what became known as a 'set' of dining tables: '3 large Mahog. Dining Tables to join'.[139] This is unusual, however, and the overwhelming evidence of inventories from houses of all sizes suggests that ordinary oval dining tables remained the usual form throughout the period. Bills for sets of dining tables with half-round ends and drop-leaf centres do not become common until the 1760s.

133. Robinson (1731).
134. Houghton Hall (1745). The 1792 inventory records five tables, two oval and three square.
135. Ibid.
136. Moore (1996), p. 90.
137. Houghton Hall (1792).
138. *DEF*, III, p. 221, fig. 28.
139. *DEFM*.

Tables and Stands

Plate 5:110. Card table (1710-20). Walnut, deal and oak. Pillar-leg card tables of this half-round form were introduced about 1700 and were probably made as late as 1730. The decorative finials on the stretcher act as pins on which the rear gates pivot.
COURTESY OF SOTHEBY'S

Folding card and tea tables

Purpose-made card tables, forming part of the permanent furnishings of a room or apartment, were uncommon before 1700. By 1720 the frequency of their mention in bills and inventories suggests they were commonplace. For the first twenty years of the eighteenth century half-round tables were the most popular. The inventory of Kiveton, a house probably furnished between its completion in 1704 and the death of its owner, the 1st Duke of Leeds, in 1712, includes numerous card tables of which most were described as 'Ovall'.[140] It is probable that pillar-leg examples, popularly attributed to the 'William and Mary' and 'Queen Anne' periods, were made well into the reign of George I (**5:110**).[141]

'Claw' or cabriole-leg card tables probably began to supersede pillar leg tables about 1715. Securely dated examples from this early period are scarce but one, dated April 1724, is shown in

Tables and Stands

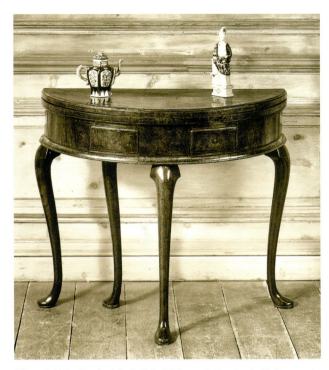

Plate 5:111. Card table (1724). Walnut, deal and oak. This example has the date April 1724 inscribed on one of the candle slides. The maker has yet to resolve the problem of joining the frame to the legs in a graceful manner. This is typical of a number of early cabriole-leg card tables.
PHILLIPS OF HITCHIN

Plate 5:112. Card table (1725-40). Mahogany, oak and deal. This table has a dual function as a tea/occasional table (first and second top) and card table (third top). The third and lowest top is also hinged to allow access to the locked well beneath. This form of table tended to go out of use after c.1740, probably because of the inconvenience of having to remove everything on top of the table to get into the well. A frieze drawer was more convenient, albeit less capacious.
CHRISTIE'S IMAGES LTD 1997

5:111. With its half-round top and deep frieze with small drawers, the design owes much to earlier tables. There is an awkwardness about the joining of the leg to the upper part which suggests that this maker had yet to satisfactorily resolve the aesthetic and structural challenges of adapting the cabriole leg to a half-round top. Nevertheless, it was possible to combine a half-round frame with cabriole legs in a satisfactory manner. The mahogany example in **5:112** has three hinged tops: the first plain, for taking tea and other purposes; the second lined with baize and with counter-wells for playing cards; the third and lowest top opens to reveal a well for cards, gaming counters, etc.. This design is a common one for early tables; in the 1760s Gillows called them 'universal' tables.[142]

Half-round tables were ideally shaped to play the most popular card game of the time, which

140. Kiveton (1727).
141. The Lord Chamberlain's accounts describe various types of furniture 'on pillars' as late as 1729. For example, PRO, LC 9/287, f. 169; 'for a neat Walnutree writing Desk on pillars... £6.10. 0.'
142. Gillows archive, 89/77.

261

Tables and Stands

Above left:
Plate 5:113. Card table (1720-40). Walnut, deal and oak. This triangular table 'made to open square' has three hinged leaves, one lined with baize for playing cards, another veneered for taking tea and other purposes, and the third rising to give access to the well.
APTER-FREDERICKS

Above right:
Plate 5:114. Triangular table (1730-60) Mahogany, deal and oak. Unlike the card table in 5:113, this design allows the table to be opened without moving it from its corner. A convenient and long-lived general purpose design, although not particularly popular in the antiques trade. CHRISTIE'S IMAGES LTD 1999

was ombre, a three-handed game. Triangular tables did equally well. An entry in the Erddig inventory of 1726 describes a '3 coner'd Omber Table', although it is not clear whether this had a folding top.[143] A bill in the Lord Chamberlain's accounts describes 'a fine 3 Corner'd Wallnuttree Table made to open square cover'd wth green velvet & trimm'd wth gold Lace... £5. 0. 0.'.[144] The table in **5:113** fits this general description. An alternative design of triangular table had the leaf hinged to fold down (**5:114**). Such tables may have been used for cards, but were equally serviceable for more general use. It seems logical that triangular tables were intended to stand in corners; this is the inference to be drawn from the Erddig inventory, where in one of the dressing rooms was listed '1 walnutree connered cubbard' and '1 walnutree connered Table', one presumably placed above the other.[145] The Gillow archives confirm that this sort of table was known as a corner table, and that they were made in Lancaster as late as 1768.[146] Three-cornered pillar-and-claw card tables are also recorded, presumably also made for ombre.[147]

Some ombre tables were square or rectangular, such as the four supplied to the Royal Wardrobe by Gumley and Moore in 1718.[148] In Lord Carnarvon's drawing room at Cannons in 1725 there was a 'four Corner Umber Table, wallnutt:Tree covered wth Cloth'.[149] It may be that since ombre was the most popular game, 'Umber Table' was simply a generic name for a card table. The greater abundance of square tables from the 1720s onwards could simply reflect stylistic change, but it might also be a consequence of the craze for quadrille, a new four-handed game recently introduced from France:

It will not be necessary to aquaint the Reader that the following game of QUADRILLE has been about two years, and is at present, the favourite game at the French Court... QUADRILLE is more amusing and entertaining than OMBRE, or any other Game on the Cards; either because evr'y Deal is play'd out, or that it better suits the Genius of the Ladies, to whom Complaisance and good Manners must Prejudice the Gentlemen in its favour

Anon, *The Game of Quadrille or Ombre by Four* (London, 1726)

143. Flintshire Record Office, D/E/280.
144. PRO LC9/287, f. 47.
145. Flintshire Record Office, D/E/280.
146. Westminster City Archive, Gillows 90/111.
147. *DEF*, III, p. 198, fig.20.
148. PRO LC/286, f. 56.
149. Cannons (1725).

One of the ladies smitten by the new game was Queen Caroline, and quadrille tables were made for the Royal Palaces from 1727 onwards.[150] There is no reason why quadrille tables should not be half-round, but square tables afforded more playing area for the same width of table.

The chief structural difference between the early Georgian card tables and their pillar-legged forebears is the method of supporting the open leaf. Most pillar-leg tables had an additional pair of legs at the rear, opening on gates hinged at the outside (5:110). The design was not particularly robust, nor were six legs convenient on such small tables. The Georgian version was simpler, with either one or both of the rear legs hinged on the same deep knuckle joint used on dining tables. A less common alternative was to hinge the frame concertina-fashion, allowing it to extend backwards to support the open leaf. An early example of this type of frame is shown in **5:115** and **5:116**. This is possibly the 'Walnuttree foulding Table' recorded in the Dressing Room to the Worked Room in the Erddig inventory of 1726.[151] The inside top is plain oak, rather than being lined with baize, and it does not have counter wells and candle dishes. Perhaps it was intended for general use.

Counter wells and candle dishes were de rigueur for tables of quality. The most common shape for the latter was round, giving card tables the lobed top which characterises many tables of this period. The simplest (and possibly earliest) versions have a rectangular frame without shaping (**5:117**). A pair of tables supplied to Hampton Court Palace either by Gumley and Moore or by Benjamin Goodison are of this type. A more sophisticated and presumably more expensive design

Left above:
Plate 5:115. Folding table (1720-26). The inside top of this table is plain oak, without veneer or cloth lining, suggesting multi-purpose use.
ERDDIG, THE NATIONAL TRUST

Left below:
Plate 5:116. Detail of 5:115, showing the method of locking the hinged 'concertina' joint with a hook and eye, and the original iron hinges fixing the rails to the top of the rear leg.

Above:
Plate 5:117. Card table (1720-40). Cocus wood veneers on beech and deal. Note that the rectangular frame does not conform to the shaping of the top. Compare with 5:118.   TEMPLE NEWSAM HOUSE, LEEDS CITY ART GALLERIES

---

150. PRO, LC 287, f. 151; 'For 3 very large Walnuttree Quadrille Tables covered wth green velvet.... £15.0.0.'.
151. Erddig (1726).

Tables and Stands

Plate 5:118. Card table (1730-48). Walnut on deal and oak. This bears the trade label of Benjamin Crook, who worked at *The George & White Lyon* in St Paul's Churchyard between c.1732 and c.1748. The shell knee and claw foot were two of the most common decorative motifs of the 1730s. The frame of this table is shaped to conform to the shape of the top.
FROM R.W. SYMONDS, *ENGLISH FURNITURE FROM CHARLES II TO GEORGE II*

Plate 5:119. Card table underside. The rounded corners are formed by simply adding wood to the corners of the frame. The drawer has been removed to show the underside of the top.

is shown in **5:118**, which bears the trade label of Benjamin Crook, who worked in St Paul's Churchyard between c.1732 and 1748.[152] Here the frame conforms to the shape of the top, and this was done by adding shaped sections to the rectangular frame (**5:119**). It bears the stylistic hallmarks of a table of the 1730s, with shell-carved and pendant-flower knees on claw feet.

Tables with square corners are conceivably slightly later in date, their shape possibly reflecting the outset corners found on tabernacle mirrors and picture frames (**5:120**). Decoration was generally confined to adding carved details similar to those found on contemporary chairs and side-tables – shells or masks on the knees, scrolled brackets and claw or paw feet.

Left:
Plate 5:120. Card table (1735-60). Mahogany, oak and beech. Tables of this form were made in large numbers, mostly in mahogany rather than walnut. The square outset corners appear to reflect the styling of contemporary 'tabernacle' mirror frames.
TEMPLE NEWSAM HOUSE, LEEDS CITY ART GALLERIES

Opposite:
Plate 5:121. Folding writing table (1730-60). Mahogany, oak and deal. This versatile table has a plain top for tea or occasional use and a baize-lined top for writing with a rising stationery compartment. Unlike a card table, the hinged leg is at the front so the table does not have to be moved to be opened. A similar table is shown on the trade card of Thomas Potter (3:85).
PHILLIPS

Tables and Stands

The space saving hinged top could of course be adapted to almost any purpose. The table in **5:121** has its hinged leg to the front, so that the top of the table folds towards the user. The first top is plain and the second has a leather-covered writing surface in front of a spring-loaded rising till fitted with pigeon-holes and drawers. The top of the till has a hinged slope supported on a ratchet. When not in use, the whole assembly sinks into the body of the table. Metamorphic tables like this were very common, popular no doubt because of their small size and practicality. The success of the folding table, whether for cards or any other purpose, is testified by its continuing popularity into the nineteenth century.

152. Crook's details in the *DEFM* are incorrect. He was apprenticed in 1718 and made free of the Joiners' Company in 1725, not 1734. On 13 September 1734 he was called to the Livery of the Company.(GL).

265

Chapter Six
MIRRORS

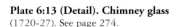

Plate 6:13 (Detail). Chimney glass (1720-27). See page 274.

1. The Customs returns record looking-glasses as one of the most valuable English furniture exports (PRO Cust 3).
2. Quoted in Wills (1965), p. 45.
3. Ibid.
4. Child (1990), pp. 23-25.

Looking glass production

From 1700 onwards the manufacture of looking glass plates in England was a considerable industry, supplying glasses to both the domestic and export markets.[1] The growth in manufacturing might have been due to the repeal in 1699 of the 20 per cent excise duty imposed in 1695. One suspects that the noticeable increase in the size of mirror plates after 1700 was encouraged by this measure, as well as by improvements in manufacturing proficiency. In February 1700 the Vauxhall manufactory advertised in *The Post-man*: 'Large Looking-glass Plates, the like never made in England before, both for size and goodness, are now made at the old Glass House at Foxhall… Where all persons may be furnished with rough plates from the smallest sizes to those of six foot in length and proportionable breadth, at reasonable rates'.[2] Note the mention of 'rough plates'; grinding, polishing and foiling was done elsewhere. A rival operation at the Bear Garden Glass House on Bankside responded two years later with a notice in the same newspaper: 'At the Bear Garden Glass-House in Southwark are Looking-Glass Plates, Blown from the smallest size upwards, to 90 inches, with proportionable breadth, of lively Colours, free from Veins and foulness, incident to the large Plates that have been hitherto sold'.[3] This was not mere hyperbole. *The Daily Journal* of 11 April 1728 advertised the sale of the 'Entire Furniture of a Person of Quality', which included 'two of the finest large Pier-Glasses in London, whole Plates, one 7 Foot by 3 Foot 6 Inches, the other 5 Foot 9 Inches by 3 Foot 6 Inches…'. It is possible, of course, that these were imported plates, for the French led the way in the manufacture of cast or plate-glass, which could be made in larger sheets than blown glass.[4]

One of the most successful glass manufacturers, and a rival to both Vauxhall and the Bear Garden, was the cabinet-maker and glazier John Gumley, whose Lambeth manufactory was established about 1705. In 1714 Gumley went into partnership with James Moore to supply cabinet-work and looking glasses to the Royal Wardrobe. In *The Lover* of 24 April 1714 Gumley announced the opening of new premises in the Strand:

These are to give Notice. That John Gumley hath taken for a Ware-house, and furnished all the upper Part of the New Exchange in the Strand… with the largest and finest Looking Glasses in

Frames, and out of Frames… Likewise all sorts of Coach-Glasses, Chimney-Glasses, Sconces, Dressing Glasses, Union-Suits, Dressing Boxes, Swinging Glasses, Glass Schandeleres, Lanthorns, Gilt Brockets, Desks and Bookcases, Indian Chests and Cabinets, Screens, Tea Tables, Card-Tables of all kinds, Strong Boxes, and the like… Also John Gumley's House and Shop the Corner of Norfolk-street, is to be Lett…[5]

That same year Richard Steele, owner/publisher of *The Lover*, described the new warehouse and commented: 'We are arrived at such perfection in this ware of which I am speaking that it is not in the power of any Potentate in Europe to have so beautiful a mirror as he may purchase here for a trifle. It is by modest computation that England gains £50,000 a year by exporting this commodity, for the service of foreign nations'.[6]

Something of the variety of types, sizes and combinations of mirrors available can be gauged from a bill submitted by Gerrit Jensen to the Marquess of Salisbury in 1714. Among other things Jensen supplied:

> A large glass sconce 38x30, 4 blue sconces, 8 square oval sconces, sconces engraved with figures, narrow chimney sconces, large looking glass, frame glass drawn with scarlet & silver the mouldings gilt & the top carved and gilt. Table to suit the glass. Large glass, the frame Right Japan, & folding Japan table, white japan glass. Walnut tree Writing desk, the top for books & paper, and glasses in the door, arched. Union Suite of Japan & one of walnut. Various dressing glasses, Break Corner cupboard, glass in the door 31 x 15 … Dressing glass in a walnut Swing frame. Glass in a carved gilt frame, the bottom glass 50 x 24, the top 24 x 21. Chimney glass in a carved gilt frame, the middle glass 41 x 18, the two ends 18 x 10.[7]

Dressing glasses and 'union suites'

Dressing glasses of various sorts occur with reasonable frequency in early Georgian domestic inventories, and are noticeably more common than they were even in 1700. In many inventories the glasses are clearly associated with dressing tables, as in the 'one Walnut dressing table one dressing glass' in the Purple Chamber at Sherborne House in 1726.[8] We are only rarely given details of form or appearance, such as the 'arched dressing Glass walnut frame' also at Sherborne. At Chandos House in 1725 there was 'A Wallnutt: Wood dressing glass wth Drawers' in the marquess's bedchamber, and at Erddig a year later there was '1 blew Japan dressing glass upon a frame' in 'the closet within the blew mohair Room'.[9] At Kiveton in 1727 there were numerous dressing glasses in 'swing' frames, some plain, others japanned.[10]

A bill for furniture supplied by John Phillips to Badminton House, Gloucestershire, between 1728 and 1730, includes dressing mirrors of several kinds. There were small 'swing glasses' at 8s. each, 'neat Dressing Glasses' at £1.5s., two Wal[nu]t 3 draw dress[in]g Glasses' also at £1.5s., 'A Dressing Glass with a Desk' at £1.5s., and two 'Union setts', one walnut and one japanned red and gold, costing four guineas each.[11]

Some of these items are self-descriptive. An early 'swing glass' is depicted in the engraving of *The Ladies' Library* (3:73). It has a rectangular plate suspended between baluster-turned supports. Later versions tended to have square-section supports like those in **6:1**, and this simple style of mirror continued in production for most of the eighteenth century. The ordinary 'dressing glass' is more obscure; it

5. *DEFM*.
6. *DEF*, II, p. 323. It must be said that this figure is not borne out by the surviving export figures, which value England's total furniture exports at around £20-30,000 per annum at this period (PRO Cust 3).
7. Coleridge (1967).
8. Sherborne (1726).
9. Chandos House (1725); Erddig (1726).
10. Kiveton (1727).
11. Badminton Archives, bill of John Phillips, 3 December 1731.

Plate 6:1. Swing dressing glass (1730-80). Walnut, deal and glass. The 'swing glass' was much the simplest and cheapest form of dressing mirror. The earliest examples, which are rare, have baluster-turned uprights (cf. 3:73). Square section uprights like those shown here were in use by the 1720s. The basic form of the simplest glasses scarcely changed over the 18th century. PRIVATE COLLECTION

Mirrors

Above:
Plate 6:2. Dressing glass (1720-40). Gilded gesso, deal and glass. Easel dressing glasses such as this are now scarce, but must once have been common (cf. 5:82). The evidence of previous fixings on the back of the mirror suggests it could also be hung if desired.   NORMAN ADAMS LTD

Right:
Plate 6:3. Dressing glass (1730-60). Mahogany, oak and deal. With either one or three drawers in the base, this is the most common type of dressing glass to survive. Cove-fronted bases such as these continued to be made into the 1760s.   TENNANTS

may have been a free-standing mirror with a leg or stay at the back, of the sort shown in **6:2**. One is also shown standing on a dressing table on the billhead of the Edinburgh cabinet-maker Francis Brodie (5:82). These are no longer common, and one wonders how many have lost their stays and become hanging mirrors instead. Glasses 'with drawers' were another standard type. The most common configuration was either one or three drawers (**6:3**), but more complex arrangements also survive (**6:4**). 'A Dressing Glass with a Desk' presumably describes one like that shown in **6:5**, with a slope enclosing drawers.

Mirrors

Plate 6:4. Dressing glass (1720-40). Japanned deal and glass. This has a more complex arrangement of drawers than the previous example. The plate has the double-arched head typical of the 1720s, and the new style flat-section frame in place of the earlier ovolo. CHRISTIE'S IMAGES LTD 2006

Plate 6:5. Dressing glass (1715-30). Japanned deal and glass. Dressing glasses with desk bases were a common type. This example has turned uprights and an ovolo-moulded frame, both early features. CHRISTIE'S IMAGES LTD 2001

The term 'Union Suite' needs explanation. The earliest known citation occurs in a bill for furniture supplied by Gerrit Jensen to the Royal Wardrobe in 1711: 'For a Dressing Glass made in a Union Suite £3.10.0'.[12] References occur more commonly from about 1714, and at Sherborne House there were several union suites recorded in the 1726 inventory. The term persisted into the second half of the eighteenth century, but seems to have gone out of use by 1800. Some authorities have suggested that 'union suite' described a dressing mirror with a base conceived as a miniature desk, of the sort shown in **6:5**. However, John Phillips' bill cited above mentions both a 'Dressing

12. PRO, LC 9/284.

Mirrors

Plate 6:6. Union Suite (1715-30). Chinese lacquer on softwood, glass; japanned pearwood stand (1738). This is one of a pair imported from Canton and repaired in 1738 by John Hodson, who also supplied the stand. The style of the mirror and frame suggests they were made about 1720. Most of the interior boxes which made up the full 'suite' have been lost.

BLAIR CHARITABLE TRUST

Glass with a Desk' and two 'Union Setts', and the difference in price between them was considerable. Similarly, the cost of the one cited in Jensen's bill of 1711 suggests something more than just a mirror with drawers. Clarification is offered by a bill submitted by John Hodson for repairing a pair of lacquered union suites at Blair Castle in 1739 (**6:6**):

To mending and repairing in the japan 2 Union suits compleat with boxes brushes and etc., taking off the brass work new lacquering do, and putting on a again and new looking glasses to do...
To 2 neat black stain'd peartree frames with a drawers in each with good locks and brass work for ye Union suits to stand on... £5.5.[13]

Thus the 'union suite' was much more than a dressing mirror with a desk – it also contained boxes, brushes and all the paraphernalia associated with dressing (**6:7**). When Richard Roberts died in 1733 he had in his bedchamber a 'Dressing Glass with Union Set Japanned', which confirms that the 'union set' was distinct from or in addition to the glass.[14] By inference, it seems likely that dressing glasses could be bought with or without the union set, and this makes sense of Phillips' bill quoted above. It is a moot point at what stage such an article ceased to be a union suite and became a full sized dressing desk with all its fittings (**6:8**).

13. Quoted in Coleridge (1963). The original bill can no longer be found in the Blair Castle archives.
14. Roberts (1733).

Left above and below:
Plate 6:7. Union Suite (1720-40). Red japanning on deal, glass. The detail below left reveals the fitted drawer with compartments and removable boxes which comprised a full 'union suite'. The square-section uprights, ogee section moulding and triple-arched plate all suggest a date in the 1720s or 1730s.
VICTORIA AND ALBERT MUSEUM

Below:
Plate 6:8. Dressing glass and desk (1730-45). Walnut, oak and deal, glass. Combined desks and dressing glasses were not uncommon. Cockbeaded drawers suggest a date not before 1730, which is consistent with the shell knee and ogee-section mirror frame.
CHRISTIE'S IMAGES LTD 2006

Mirrors

Plate 6:9. Chimney glass (1710-20). Painted and gilded wood, glass. This probably dates from the first period of furnishing at Castle Howard, c.1710-20, although it is not in its original position. *Verre églomisé* borders remained fashionable until the 1720s.
CASTLE HOWARD

Plate 6:10. Chimney glass (1715-30). Black japanned wood and glass. This is one of the many overmantel mirrors recorded in the Erddig inventory of 1726. Black frames for both mirrors and pictures occur commonly in early 18th century inventories.
ERDDIG, THE NATIONAL TRUST

---

15. For the early development of overmantel mirrors see Bowett (2002), pp. 297-8.

Chimney glasses

Overmantel mirrors or 'chimney glasses' were very much a new thing at the beginning of the eighteenth century, but their popularity spread so rapidly that they were a commonplace in middle- and upper-class interiors by 1720.[15] They were originally conceived as part of the fixed furniture of the room, either built into the panelling over the fireplace or, more commonly, in

Mirrors

Plate 6:11. Chimney glass (1700-1720). Arched and shaped glasses such as this were highly fashionable until the 1720s, as were *églomisé* borders. SWORDERS

Plate 6:12. Chimney glass (1718-26). Glass with gilt wood slip. This mirror is set into the marble fire surround in the Great Parlour at Chicheley. Note how the foxing on the plate reveals the position of the deal battens behind. CHICHELEY

plain frames which more or less matched the panelling. Glasses of this kind survive in considerable numbers, and tend to follow a three-plate, rectangular format, with different treatments of the surrounding frame (**6:9** and **6:10**). Arched glasses were highly fashionable but more expensive and consequently less common (**6:11**). In some houses the mirrors were built into the stone or marble of the chimney breast itself. Plate **6:12** shows a rectangular overmantel in the Great Parlour at

273

Mirrors

Plate 6:13. Chimney glass (1720-27). Glass with gilt and painted wood slip. This shaped overmantel in the Saloon at Ditchley may have been designed by James Gibbs. It originally had multiple plates.
DITCHLEY FOUNDATION

Plate 6:14. Chimney glass (1720-50). Gilded gesso and deal, original glass plates. This is a more common style of frame, with scrolled brackets and conventional late baroque detail. Candle branches are replaced.
GEFFRYE MUSEUM, LONDON

Plate 6:15. **Chimney glass** (1730-50). Gilded gesso, deal and glass. This bears the trade label of John Belchier. The form is conventional, although the plate may originally have been in three parts. Outset square corners suggest neo-Palladian influence. The candle branches and backplates are later additions, perhaps replacing lost originals. CHRISTIE'S IMAGES LTD 1999

Chicheley, probably installed in the early 1720s, and **6:13** shows a shaped one from the saloon at Ditchley of about the same date.

Compilers of inventories had various ways of describing chimney glasses, and it is often difficult to determine whether they were part of the fixed fabric or not. At Drayton a number of rooms contained 'a marble chimney piece and slab, wth a glass over it' which could have been built in.[16] At Kiveton almost all the chimney glasses were described as 'fix'd', which is self-explanatory, but the Dining Room had simply a 'Chimney Glass in a gilt frame', which was probably not a fixture.[17]

Chimney glasses were often associated with some form of lighting. Since mantelshelves were not usual at this date, arms or 'branches' were attached to the panelling above the fireplace or to the glass itself. In the *Salone* at Erddig there was '1 large Glass over the Chimly wth a gold fram' together with '1 pair of Branches with nosles to each'.[18] Here it seems that the branches were not attached to the mirror but close to it. In other rooms there were candle branches at the chimney even where there was no mirror; the same arrangement can be seen in 5:89. At Marlborough House in 1740 several of the smaller rooms had 'A Glass over the Chimney and two arms for Candles'; here the wording is too vague to determine whether these were attached to the mirror or to the panelling.[19]

In many Georgian parlours pictures were hung over the fireplace in lieu of a chimney glass, and sometimes a picture was hung over the glass, often mounted within a common frame (see Frontispiece). At Erddig there was a 'very large Glass over the Chimley wth a Picture' which was lit by '1 pair of silver'd Sconches at ye Chimley'.[20] In a closet at Kiveton there was a 'Chimney Glass fix'd in a Black & Gold jap^d frame' together with a 'Landskip in Carvd frame fix'd over ye Chimney'.[21]

An obvious problem with built-in chimney glasses was that they were difficult to alter or remove. The last was particularly a consideration for tenants in urban houses or lodgings who wanted to take their furniture with them when they moved. This may be one reason for the great number of chimney glasses in frames of walnut, mahogany or gilt wood which were not fixed into panelling. They usually conformed to the three-plate format, with or without candle branches, and in frames more or less elaborate, according to the purse of the owner. Plate **6:14** is a common model, with scrolled brackets to the sides and a slim, carved and punched gesso frame. Note that the section of the frame has changed from the ovolo or bolection section of the earlier examples. Plate **6:15** bears the trade label of John Belchier; its outset square corners reveal neo-Palladian influence, suggesting a date in the 1730s or later.

Horizontal chimney glasses remained popular for the whole of the eighteenth century and designs for chimney pieces with built-in glasses occur in William Jones' *The Gentleman or Builder's Companion* (1739), Abraham Swan's *The British Architect* (1745) and others. With the rise of neo-Palladian taste in the late 1720s and 1730s chimney glasses became larger as the chimney and fireplace assumed greater significance in the room's internal architecture. The most important source for the new style was Inigo Jones' drawings for chimney pieces of the 1630s, which Lord

16. Drayton (1724).
17. Kiveton (1727).
18. Erddig (1726).
19. Marlborough House (1740).
20. Erddig (1726).
21. Kiveton (1727).

Mirrors

Above left:
Plate 6:16. Fireplace and overmantel, c.1725. Carved and gilt wood, glass. The design for this fireplace in the Gallery at Chiswick was taken from two designs of the 1630s by Inigo Jones. The fireplace derives from the Queen's House, Greenwich, and the overmantel from Somerset House. CHISWICK VILLA, ENGLISH HERITAGE

Left:
Plate 6:17. Design for a fireplace and overmantel (1731), by Isaac Ware. Plate 33 from *Designs of Inigo Jones and Others*. The pediment design was used for the Channon bookcase shown in 3:80.

Above right:
Plate 6:18. Chimney glass (c.1740). Gilded wood and glass, attributed to William Kent. This overmantel was made for Worcester Lodge, designed by William Kent for the Duke of Beaufort. BADMINTON HOUSE, THE DUKE OF BEAUFORT

Burlington purchased as part of a larger collection in 1720 and 1721. Versions of Jones' designs were created at Chiswick Villa in the 1720s (**6:16**). The publication of these and other designs by Isaac Ware in *Designs of Inigo Jones and Others* in 1731 spawned a generation of neo-Palladian chimney pieces and glasses in houses all over Britain. Every one of the designs included a large panel above the mantel slab suitable for either a mirror or a painting set into an architectural frame (**6:17**). It would be otiose to illustrate many of these, which in a sense belong more to architecture than furniture, but the example from Worcester Lodge, almost certainly designed by William Kent, is worth showing because of its sheer panache (**6:18**).

Far left:
Plate 6:19. Lantern (1725-40). Gilded wood, glass and metal. This is one of four hanging in the hall at Ditchley, and perhaps designed by William Kent. This might technically qualify as a sconce, but lights with glass shields were more usually called lanterns. DITCHLEY FOUNDATION

Left:
Plate 6:20. Sconce (1730-31). Silver. This is one of a set of sconces made by Peter Archambo for the 2nd Earl of Warrington. It was among twenty-four silver sconces recorded at Dunham Massey in 1758. The central image depicts Prometheus bound.
DUNHAM MASSEY, THE NATIONAL TRUST

Sconces

A sconce or 'sconch' was a wall-mounted device to hold candles; its purpose was to provide light but it was not necessarily mirrored. The derivation is probably from medieval Latin *sconsa*, a hiding place, via the medieval French *esconse* and old German *schanze*, a screen or defence. Thus a sconce was perhaps originally a fitment intended to screen a candle from the wind, and the light in **6:19** might conceivably be called a sconce. At Kiveton in 1727 there were 'glass lamp sconces' in passageways and staircases which might have been of this type.[22] However, lights in glass enclosures were more commonly known as lanterns. The example shown here was recorded in the Ditchley inventory of 1743 as one of four 'Carved and gilt compass side lantrons'.[23]

The inventories of many early eighteenth century houses cite both candle branches and sconces, so there was a clear distinction between the two in the mind of the compilers, and the distinguishing feature of a sconce seems to have been its decorative backpiece. This might originally have protected the flame from draughts, but now served primarily as a reflector. The inventory of plate in the royal palaces drawn up in 1721 listed 195 silver sconces of different sorts ranging between 16 and 147 ounces (454 and 4167g) in weight.[24] Similar sconces were found in private houses At Dunham Massey there were twenty-four recorded in the 1758 inventory, of which fourteen were in the Great Gallery (**6:20**).[25] Lord Warrington's expenditure on silver was perhaps exceptional. Sconces of silvered brass were more common, such as the 'pair of silvered

22. Kiveton (1727).
23. Ditchley (1743).
24. Temple Newsam (1992), p. 35.
25. Dunham Massey (1758).

Mirrors

Left:
Plate 6:21. Sconce (1730-50). Gilded wood and brass. This is a powerfully conceived expression of neo-Palladian ideas and an impressive sculptural work in its own right, regardless of the mere four candle power it produces.
KNOLE, THE NATIONAL TRUST

Below:
Plate 6:22. Designs for mirrors (1703). This is Plate 4 from Daniel Marot, *Nouveaux Livre d'Orfeuverie*. Of the three small sconces shown, only the right-hand one is mirrored. This is perhaps the earliest known published design for a mirrored sconce.

sconches at ye Chimley' in the Withdrawing Room at Erddig.[26] At Marlborough House there were 'four Silver'd Sconces' in the Hall and a pair of gilt sconces at the chimney in the Drawing Room.[27] At Kiveton there were sconces of lacquered brass, silvered brass, and carved and gilded wood.[28] Indeed, wooden sconces were quite common and occur in numerous contemporary high status inventories. The exceptional example in **6:21** is one of a pair made for Lionel Sackville, 1st Duke of Dorset. The Duke's friendship with Lord Burlington makes it possible that the designer was William Kent. Providing a mere four candle-power, the sconce is nevertheless a powerful expression of wealth and status, combing high baroque and neo-Palladian motifs in a typically Kentian manner. The central mask represents the sun-god Apollo with his laurel garlands below. The snake candle branches suggest Apollo's mythical victory over the python, and the plumed female masks are borrowed from Jean Berain's engravings. The lion mask suspending the whole ensemble was a favourite neo-Palladian device (cf. 6:19).

Glass sconces were uncommon before 1700. Probably the earliest illustration of a mirrored sconce occurs in Daniel Marot's *Nouveaux Livre d'Orfeuverie*, published in 1703. Plate 4 shows three sconces, two of metal and one annotated 'Placque en Miroire Glacé' (**6:22**). Others, apparently mirrored, are shown on the walls in *Second Livre D'Apartements* (1703). At Boughton in 1709 there were glass sconces in the Drawing Room and Music Room, and at Drayton in 1710 there were 'looking-glass sconces' in a Drawing Room and 'Two pair of Scollopt looking glass

26. Erddig (1726).
27. Marlborough House (1740).
28. Kiveton (1727).

Mirrors

Plate 6:23. Sconce (1700-1730). Glass and brass. Small, narrow glass sconces such as this are now rare, but were probably once common and relatively cheap. Perhaps they were intended for chimney breasts. The brass sockets and glass arms are replacements. One of a pair.
CHRISTIE'S IMAGES LTD 2000

Plate 6:24. Pair of sconces (1710-30). Walnut, glass, brass and embroidery. The arched and shaped tops correspond to the tops of contemporary pier glasses and the doors of desks-and-bookcases. The needlework is protected by clear glass.
HOTSPUR LTD

Sconces' in the Long Gallery.[29] This was not just a country house phenomenon, for in the parlour of Thomas Diaper, a London salter, was a glass sconce as early as 1705.[30]

Inventories give us no idea what size these were, but sconces which appear stylistically appropriate for this date tend to be rather small, similar in scale to the metal ones. A sconce like the one shown in **6:23** might correspond to the 'narrow chimney sconces' described in Gerrit Jensen's bill for Hatfield House (quoted above, page 267). At Kiveton there were chimney sconces in several rooms, although their size was not specified.[31] Sconces with needlework or other cloth backing, such as the pair shown in **6:24**, seem at first improbable, because the non-reflective backs offer no benefit in terms of light, and would be vulnerable to candle grease, soot or even fire, unless protected by glass. However, the 1725 inventory of John Evendon, a London joiner and

29. Boughton (1709), Drayton (1710).
30. CLRO, Orphans' Court Records, Roll 2686.
31. Kiveton (1727).

279

Mirrors

Left:
Plate 6:25. *Sconce* (1720-40). Walnut, glass and brass. The ogee-section frame and shouldered tops to the plates are typical of the 1720s, while the shaped base and cresting is a simplified version of those found on larger gilded mirrors. The brass arms and one plate are replacements. One of a pair. COURTESY OF SOTHEBY'S

Above centre:
Plate 6:26. *Sconce* (1720-40). Gilded wood, glass and brass. This rare triple branch sconce has a narrow, delicately moulded frame. The double arched top is typical of the 1720s. For a contemporary illustration see Stukeley's watercolour, 3:40. The candle arms are replaced. CHRISTIE'S IMAGES LTD 1991

Above right:
Plate 6:27. *Sconce* (1720-40). Gilded wood, glass and brass. Another simple double-arched example, this time with a cut gesso and gilt frame. Candle arms are replaced. BENINGBOROUGH HALL, THE NATIONAL TRUST

picture dealer, records 'a pair of workt [embroidered] Sconces' in his 'fore chamber' or parlour.[32] It could be that embroidered sconces were modestly priced versions of the 'picture sconces' owned by Lord Warrington (6:20). Plate **6:25** shows a sconce in a later style, incorporating the ogee-section frame and shouldered plate typical of the 1720s. Other examples are shown in **6:26** and **6:27**. The narrow frames have an understated appeal to modern eyes, but this was originally surely more a question of price rather than stylistic preference. By way of contrast, **6:28** shows a small sconce which mimics the more ambitious large sconces and pier glasses of the 1720s. It bears the trade card of Thomas Cleare, who worked at the *Indian Chair* in St Paul's Churchyard from about 1725.[33] It is a moot question whether Thomas Cleare actually made the sconce; the inventory of Lazarus Stiles, a cabinet-maker who died in 1724, records a 'Mr Odell, Sconcemaker' among his creditors.[34]

The rise in popularity of mirrored sconces may in part have been due to the absence of candle stands, which had hitherto provided the lighting component in the suite of mirror, table and stands. At Erddig and Sherborne House, both fashionably furnished in the 1720s, sconces and candle branches appear to have completely replaced candle stands.[35] In the latter house, the sconces were all in pairs, with either glass or brass arms. At the same time there was a noticeable increase in average size. Among the many sconces supplied by Gerrit Jensen to the Marquess of Salisbury in 1714, a

32. CLRO, Orphans' Court Records, Roll 3208.
33. Thomas Cleare was apprenticed in the Joiners' Company in 1706. For further details see *DEFM*, p. 177; Gilbert (1996), p. 145.
34. Stiles (1724).
35. Erddig (1726); Sherborne (1726).

Above:
Plate 6:28. Sconce (1725-40). Gilded wood, brass and glass. This bears the trade card of Thomas Cleare (cf. 4:35). Though of modest size it is stylistically ambitious, with a cresting similar to those found on large sconces and pier glasses of the period.
BEARNE'S

Right:
Plate 6:29. Sconce (1724). Gilt wood, glass and brass. This is one of a pair supplied by John Belchier for Erddig at a cost of £14 each. They were installed in the *Salone*, where they were recorded in the 1726 inventory as '2 large Sconches with gold lackered frames & 2 pair of glass Arms to Each'. See also the silvered sconce in 5:20, also supplied by Belchier.
ERDDIG, THE NATIONAL TRUST

single 'large glass sconce' measured 38 x 30in. (96.5 x 76.22cm) – see above, page 267. This was a good-sized plate, but small compared with a pier glass. A few years later the sconces provided for Erddig by John Belchier were as big as some pier glasses and in a sense performed the same role, with the added benefit of lighting (**6:29**). Thus from their origins as small light fittings ancillary to the main furniture, sconces had become by the 1720s one of the primary furnishing elements of many middle and upper class interiors.

Aside from the presence of candle branches, Belchier's sconces differed from pier glasses in having shaped bases, whereas the pier glasses generally had a flat base to sit on top of the dado rail (cf. 6:39). The scroll-cornered style was derived from the French Régence model, also used for pier glasses such as those at Blenheim Palace (6:48), but the treatment of the cresting is typically English. As we shall see, the shape of these crestings influenced the design of cheaper wooden-framed mirrors with what are now called 'fret-cut' frames.

Mirrors

Left:
Plate 6:30. Sconce (c.1725). Gilded wood, glass and brass. After a design by James Gibbs. This is one of the few sconces for which an original design on paper survives.
TEMPLE NEWSAM HOUSE, LEEDS CITY ART GALLERIES

Opposite page:
Left:
Plate 6:31. Sconce (1733). Gilded wood, glass and brass. One of three supplied by Benjamin Goodison for the Prince of Wales' apartments at Hampton Court Palace. Although the frame is modelled in the architectural or neo-Palladian style, this sconce nevertheless has the double-arched top found on baroque mirrors of the 1720s.
HAMPTON COURT PALACE, ROYAL COLLECTION

Right:
Plate 6:32. Sconce (1730-50). Glass and gilded deal. The rectangular plate and 'tabernacle' frame are both indications of a stylistic change associated with the neo-Palladian style. SOTHEBY'S

Below:
Plate 6:33. Candle branch socket (1720-50). Brass. This engraved socket is marked on the back J*G, possibly for the brass-founder John Giles.

The diversity of size and quality is reflected in the great range of prices charged for sconces. The 'pair of large Looking Glass Sconces in a carv'd and gold frame with double glass branches' supplied by John Pardoe to Erddig in 1720 (which do not survive) were not as impressive as they sound, for the cost of the pair was only £12.[36] By contrast the two 'fine large' sconces supplied by John Belchier in 1724 cost £14 each (6:29).[37] The difference in price is reflected in their position in the house; Belchier's sconces hung in the *Salone*, Pardoe's in the family's Eating Parlour.[38] Belchier's detailed bill, when correlated with the surviving mirrors at Erddig, reveals that the price of mirrors increased disproportionately with size. The largest cost 5d. per square inch of glass, the smallest 1d. This was because of the greater difficulty in making, grinding and foiling larger plates. Also, because glass was taxed by weight, the thicker larger plates paid proportionately more.

While shaped square plates predominated, other forms occur, including ovals and octagons. The octagon mirror in **6:30** follows a design by James Gibbs, whose original drawing survives in the Ashmolean Museum.[39] Oval sconces occur quite frequently in inventories throughout the period, such as the 'Two Glass Oval Sconces with three Branches Each' in the Cabinett at Houghton.[40] Neo-Palladian influence is apparent in the three sconces supplied by Benjamin Goodison for the Prince of Wales' apartments at Hampton Court Palace (**6:31**) They were supplied in 1733 as 'three

36. Clwyd Record Office, D/E/1542/533.
37. Clwyd Record Office, D/E/1542/107.
38. Belchier's sconces have hitherto been attributed to John Pardoe (Drury 1978) but, for the reasons given in the text, I have reassigned them to Belchier. There is also a strong stylistic similarity between the sconce and Belchier's silvered sconce made for the Withdrawing Room.
39. Friedman (1972); Gilbert (1998), pp. 645-6.
40. Houghton (1745).
41. PRO LC9/288.
42. *DEFM*, p. 409.

Mirrors

glass sconces in carved and gilt frames, with two wrought arms each…'.⁴¹ These are the first documented examples in this quasi-architectural style, and they have attributes which soon became standard for mirrors of the 1730s and 1740s – outset corners, a sanded fascia, egg-and-dart and Vitruvian scroll mouldings. The most common manifestation of neo-Palladian taste was the pedimented 'tabernacle' frame. The example in **6:32** is perhaps similar to the 'Sconce in a tabernacle frame carv'd and guilt… with a pair of brass branches' supplied by Peter Hasert to Lady Mary Fortescue of Sawston Hall, Cambridgeshire, in May 1736.⁴² The development of tabernacle frames will be discussed in more detail below.

The candle branches fitted to sconces were generally of glass or brass. Because the branches were removable from their sockets they frequently became detached and lost, and so original branches, especially glass ones, are rare. It is probable that many sconces now fitted with brass branches were originally furnished with glass ones. The sockets for the branches seem always to have been made of brass and, being screwed to the mirror, their survival rate has been higher. As the trade card of John Giles reveals, candle branches and sockets were part of the stock in trade of cabinet brass-founders. Plate **6:33** shows a socket stamped on the back with the initials J*G, possibly his founder's mark.

283

Mirrors

Left:
Plate 6:34. Looking glass (1720-26). Gilded gesso, deal and glass. This is one of a pair from Chicheley Hall, Buckinghamshire, and probably formed part of the original furnishings of the house before the death of Sir John Chester in 1726. It was clearly designed with the possibility of candle branches in mind, but none appears to have been fitted. Carved rosettes cover the place where they would have been fixed. Perhaps supplied by the sconcemaker William Odell.
PRIVATE COLLECTION

Below left:
Plate 6:35. Looking glass (1720-40). Gilded wood and glass. The shaping of the lower edge of the plate allows for the fitting of candle branches if desired.
BENINGBOROUGH HALL, THE NATIONAL TRUST

Hanging glasses

Mirrors without candle branches and with no specific role in the interior architecture of the house were usually referred to just as 'looking-glasses' or sometimes 'hanging glasses'. The Lord Chamberlain's accounts record dozens of 'looking glasses' supplied to the royal palaces by Gumley and Moore and their successors. Some were supplied together with tables and stands, and many with tables alone, as in these bills for St James's Palace in 1722:

for 3 Hanging glasses in Wallnuttree frames…	£25.10. 0.
for 3 Wallnuttree Tables wth Drawers…	£ 7.10. 0.[43]

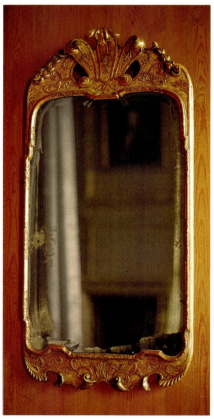

Other than the lack of candle branches, there was no real difference between a plain hanging glass and a sconce. Indeed, it seems likely that many hanging glasses were designed with the option of candle branches in mind. The mirror in **6:34**, which looks like a sconce, has a pair of gilt rosettes at the point where branches would normally be fixed, but they do not appear to be later additions. These may have been supplied by Mr Odell, a sconcemaker who supplied a number of looking glasses to Chicheley, including two sconces in burnished gilt frames in April 1722.[44] Similarly, the smaller example in **6:35** is designed in such a way as to allow space for candle branches to be fixed to the base if desired. Both mirrors have the double-arched top and shaped base to the plate which was the most common style of the 1720s and '30s.

It seems probable that the ubiquitous mid-Georgian fret-cut mirror frame emerged at this period, the shaping of the bases and crestings being based on those of gilt mirrors. Plate **6:36** shows a simple early version, whereas **6:37** is a little more complex and perhaps later. The profile of the frame closely follows that of the gilt sconce in 6:28. These veneered frames executed in walnut or mahogany were undoubtedly cheaper than gilt ones, and remained popular for most of the eighteenth century, with minor modifications to take account of prevailing stylistic trends. The Gillow sketch books contain drawings of mirrors with fret-cut frames made in the 1790s almost unchanged from those of fifty years earlier.

While plain walnut or mahogany frames predominated, by about 1730 part-gilt or 'parcel' gilt frames had become highly fashionable. Benjamin Goodison's bills for the royal palaces describe these as 'ornamented with gold'.[45] Most examples have either fret-cut frames or are 'tabernacle' mirrors in the neo-Palladian manner (**6:38** and **6:63**).

---

43. PRO LC 9/287, f. 24.
44. *DEFM*. William Odell, son of George, was apprenticed in the Joiners' Company in October 1708 (GL, MSS 8052). A 'Mr Odell' is listed among the creditors of Lazarus Stiles as a 'Sconcemaker' (Stiles 1724).
45. PRO, LC 9/288, f. 143 et seq.

Mirrors

Left:
Plate 6:36. Looking glass (1720-40) Walnut and deal, glass. The ubiquitous Georgian fret-cut mirror frame had its origins in the simple veneered frames of the early Georgian period. Brass candle sockets were once screwed to the base, in which case this would have been described as a sconce.

CHRISTIE'S IMAGES LTD 2001

Below:
Plate 6:37. Looking glass (1725-45). Walnut and deal, part gilt, and glass. One can see how the more elaborate profiles of some fret-cut frames derived from gilt gesso mirrors such as that in 6:27. These shapes were easily adapted to rococo profiles from the 1740s onwards.

SOTHEBY'S

Plate 6:38. Looking glass (1740-80). Mahogany (part gilt), deal and glass. This is typical of many thousands of similar looking glasses made over a very long period. As a rule, it seems that the more complex profiles, such as this one, are later than the simpler ones. The gilt slip is a vestige of the part-gilt style popular in the 1730s.

PRIVATE COLLECTION

285

Mirrors

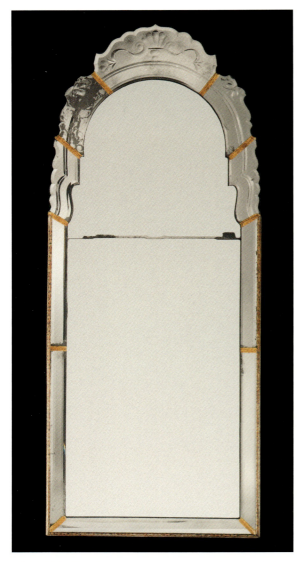

Plate 6:39. Pier glass (1710-20). Glass and gilded wood. The arched head is the most common form of pier glass to survive from this early period. The glass border was known as the 'frame', and in this case the shaped cresting is cut and 'scolloped'. The flat base is a defining characteristic of most pier glasses, allowing them to be positioned on the dado rail. One of a pair. RONALD PHILLIPS LTD., LONDON

Plate 6:40. Pier glass (1710-20). Glass, gilded wood and composition. *Verre églomisé* frames, sometimes termed 'mosaic work', were popular from about 1700 until the 1720s. The frame retains the decorative gilt 'corners' and 'middles' typical of picture frames of about 1690-1710, but 'arched heads' are not commonly cited in bills until c.1710. The main plate is replaced. CHRISTIE'S IMAGES LTD 2002

Plate 6:41. Pier glass (1710-20). Glass and gilded wood. One of a pair made for Castle Howard, probably for the initial phase of furnishing after completion in 1708. This is a fine quality glass, with glass borders, 'scolloped' upper plate and finely wrought cresting.

CASTLE HOWARD

Pier glasses

Pier glasses were distinguished from other types of looking glass in several ways. They were intended to be hung on the 'pier' or wall between two windows. They were generally larger than other mirrors, usually narrower in proportion and often (but not always) had straight bases to allow them to sit on the dado rail. It seems likely that they were initially fixed into the panelling, as were Gerrit Jensen's glasses at Hampton Court Palace (1699), and were thus conceived as part of the interior fixtures rather than as movable furniture. Inventories of some older houses include pier glasses of this type, such as at Montagu House, where in Room 53 there was a 'Peer covered with Glass'.[46] However, it soon became usual to construct the mirrors with frames independent of the panelling, and these were either hung from hooks or screwed to the wall.

At the beginning of the period the most common design had a rectangular main plate with an arched 'head' or upper plate. Among Gerrit Jensen's last bills for mirrors supplied to the royal household are numerous references to 'arched' glasses. The following description is for a pair of mirrors and tables supplied to St James's Palace in 1714:

> for two very large arched Peer Glasses in Glass frames for the dressing Room, two oval Indian folding tables to stand under the Said Glasses…[47]

Mirrors conforming to this general description survive in numbers, most with either plain glass or *églomisé* borders (**6:39** and **6:40**), some with carved and gilt crestings (**6:41**). The chief difference between these and mirrors of a few years earlier was the omission of a horizontal frame dividing the main plate from the head, although in most cases the division was clearly demarcated by an engraved border or an applied gilt strip. However, the terminology of the time, which describes pier glasses in terms of a main plate and a 'head', indicates that the glasses were still conceived as being of two parts, and it wasn't until the 1720s that this began to change. The continuing popularity of the two-part glass was assisted by the fact that it was easier and cheaper to make glasses of two plates rather than one large one.

Glasses with cut or engraved edges to the plates were often described as 'scolloped'. *Verre églomisé* frames, introduced in the 1690s, were still highly fashionable in 1714. A surviving pair at Castle Howard, probably made about 1710-15, were recorded in the inventory of 1759 as having 'Mosaic' frames; the term also occurs in earlier references in the Lord Chamberlain's accounts.[48] Gerrit Jensen's bill for glasses supplied to the Marquess of Salisbury in 1714 describes a *verre églomisé* mirror with carved gilt cresting in the following terms:

> … large looking glass, frame glass drawn with scarlet & silver the mouldings gilt & top carved and gilt.[49]

---

46. Montagu House (1733).
47. PRO, LC 5/45, f. 318.
48. Castle Howard, Inventory 1759, ff. 6 and 9; PRO LC 9/282, f. 3 (1704).
49. Coleridge (1967).

Mirrors

Left:
Plate 6:42. Pier glass (1715-30). Japanned wood and glass. This glass retains the bold, ovolo-moulded frame and 'corners and middles' decoration carried over from 17th century glasses, but narrow proportions and flattened arch suggest a date towards 1720. The flower painting is uncommon, although other examples are known.   CHRISTIE'S IMAGES LTD 2006

Below:
Plate 6:43. Pier glass (1715-25). Glass and gilt wood. This bears the painted arms of Viscount Montagu in the upper plate. The flattened arch occurs on contemporary desks-and-bookcases, such as that in 2:13. One of a pair, originally from Cowdray Park.   ALTHORP

In other documents *églomisé* frames are described simply in terms of their colour. Kiveton, lavishly furnished after completion in 1704, had numerous mirrors with coloured glass frames, such as the 'Looking Glass in a purple & Gold frame of Glass' in the North East Drawing Room, and these were all still in place in 1727.[50] But by about 1720 the fashion for *verre églomisé* had passed its height, and no documented examples made later than this have come to light. A notice published by Benjamin Goodison in 1727 refers to such mirrors as 'old-fashioned':

> Stolen out of the Shop of Benjamin Goddison, Cabinet-Maker, at the Golden Spread Eagle, in Long-Acre, on or about the 5th Day of this present August, a large old-fashioned Glass Sconce, in a Glass Frame, with Gold Flowers painted on the Glass Frame, and a green Ground, the Bottom Border of the Frame is Wanting: This is to give Notice, that if any Person shall bring the said Glass, or give any Account of it to the said Benjamin Goddison, shall receive three Guineas Reward.
>
> *Daily Courant*, 24 August 1727

Towards 1720 pier glasses with arched heads, often shaped or shouldered, began to give way to glasses with squarer or flatter tops (a comparable development can be observed in the shapes of the mirrored doors of contemporary desks-and-bookcases). Plate **6:42** shows a pier glass in the newer style, with a japanned or black varnished frame, the upper plate painted with a basket of flowers. A more common form of decoration was to have the upper plate painted or engraved with arms, as in the case of a pair of glasses made for Cowdray Park, and now at Althorp, Northamptonshire (**6:43**). At the same time the ovolo-section frame, which had seventeenth century origins, began to be replaced by a flatter section, usually in the form of a shallow ogee. A walnut-framed mirror at Erddig has a new-style frame (**6:44**). This is perhaps the 'walnuttree hanging glass' recorded in the Yellow Mohair Room in 1726.[51] For a while the two styles were concurrent; also at Erddig was a 'hanging glass in a black frame' which has a broad ovolo frame in the old style. Interestingly, neither was perceived as a pier glass, despite being tall and narrow and having the necessary flat base. Perhaps they were hung on interior walls. Another example of the new style frame, this time decorated in silvered gesso cut in low relief, is shown in **6:45**. This was made for the drawing room of Streatlam Castle during the refurbishment of 1717-21.[52]

The development of the double-arched head, which became a dominant form in the 1720s, can be traced in mirrors supplied to the royal palaces by the Gumley and Moore partnership. Given Gumley's involvement with a glasshouse at Lambeth, it seems reasonable to assume that the supply of mirror plates was largely Gumley's

Above:
Plate 6:44. Pier or hanging glass (1720-26). Walnut, deal and glass. This glass now hangs in the drawing room at Erddig but it is not possible to identify it with certainty on the inventory of 1726. Although it is tall, narrow, and has a flat base, it may not necessarily have hung on a pier.
ERDDIG, THE NATIONAL TRUST

Left:
Plate 6:45. Pier glass (1717-21). Silvered wood and glass. This bears the Bowes crest, and was probably made for the newly refurbished Streatlam Castle. The squared-off top plate and flat-section frame are relatively recent stylistic developments.
THE BOWES MUSEUM

---

50. Kiveton (1727).
51. Erddig (1726).
52. Wills and Coutts (1998).

Above left:
Plate 6:46. Pier glass (1715). Gilded wood and glass. Supplied by Gumley and Moore, probably for the Prince of Wales' Privy Chamber at Hampton Court Palace. The formal, rather stilted design of this and the following mirror combines baroque scrolled crestings or 'heads' with Berainesque detail and architectural pilasters. Many of these elements can be seen in diluted form on mirrors of the 1720s. HAMPTON COURT PALACE, THE ROYAL COLLECTION ©2008 HER MAJESTY QUEEN ELIZABETH II

Above right:
Plate 6:47. Pier glass (1715). Gilded wood and glass. Supplied by Gumley and Moore, probably for the Prince of Wales' Drawing Room at Hampton Court Palace.   HAMPTON COURT PALACE, THE ROYAL COLLECTION ©2008 HER MAJESTY QUEEN ELIZABETH II

responsibility. Together, Gumley and Moore furnished the new apartments of George, Prince of Wales, and his wife Princess Caroline at Hampton Court Palace in 1714/15.[53] Three mirrors associated with this phase of work at Hampton Court survive, but their correct identification is not without problems.[54] While the attribution to Gumley is not in doubt (one bears the name 'Gumley' incised on a gilt slip), it is difficult to reconcile the descriptions given in the bills with the surviving mirrors. The chief difficulty is that the dimensions cited appear to differ from the mirrors now *in situ*. The usual practice, where measurements were given, was to cite the dimensions of the main

53. For an account of this phase of building and furnishing at Hampton Court, see Thurley (2003), pp. 245-253.
54. Rutherford (1927); *DEF*, II; Jourdain and Edwards (1955).

plate, but in this case the dimensions cited, in one case nearly 12ft. (3.7m) high, exceed the largest sizes of mirror plate that England was capable of producing. Hence the dimensions probably refer to the total area of the mirror, and not just the main plate. If this was the case, then the bills begin to make sense. The glass supplied for the Privy Chamber was described as follows:

> for a large Glass in a gilt frame and top containing ten foot four Inches high by three eleven inches and a half wide…

The mirror in **6:46** corresponds to this description. It is the only one with a solid rather than a glazed top, and the width of 3ft.11½in. matches exactly. The vertical dimension is more problematic, since the mirror is a good 18in. (45.7cm) higher than the bill states. If, however, one ignores the eagle and measures only the area contained within the frame, the measurements correspond.

The bill for the Drawing Room mirror is as follows:

> For a large Glass in a Glass frame and festoon finely done with carved and gilt work containing eleven foot ten inches and a halfe by four foot nine inches…

As with the previous mirror, the general description fits the one shown in **6:47** and the width corresponds exactly. When the plume and mask are ignored and the dimension within the frame is measured, the height also corresponds.

Following the same method of measurement, the third mirror corresponds with the description of that made for the Dining Room:

> For a large Glass in a Glass frame and festoon finely done with carved and gilt work containing eight foot eight inches by four foot six Inches and three Quarters.

The formal, rather stilted design of Gumley's Hampton Court mirrors is due largely to the treatment of the main plate and cresting as distinct elements, in the seventeenth century manner. They are the direct linear descendants of the mirrors supplied by Gumley to the Duke of Devonshire in 1703 and 1705, not only in form, but also in their Berainesque decorative repertoire.[55] The design of the crestings evokes comparisons with the headboards of state beds produced around 1700; there are clear parallels in contemporary engravings, such as the *Dossiers de Lits* published by Daniel Marot in 1703.[56] The style was, however, common to mirrors produced in much of western Europe at this time, and particularly in France, where glass-framed mirrors with scroll-topped crestings were popular between c.1700 and 1730.[57]

It is not difficult to see how the paired scrolls at the head of the Hampton Court mirrors evolved into the double-arched form popular in the 1720s. Indeed, the next stages can be seen in mirrors supplied by James Moore for the State Apartments at Blenheim and Kensington Palace in c.1720 and 1724 respectively. The Blenheim mirrors, of which there are four pairs surviving, are very French in character, both in their overall form and broad proportions, and in their decoration (**6:48**). Though still a two-plate design, the clear distinction between cresting and main plate has gone, and the double-scrolled top has become integrated into the frame. Glasses of a similar type

Plate 6:48. Pier glass (c.1720). Gilded wood and glass. Attributed to James Moore, and supplied for the State Apartments at Blenheim Palace. This more unified design represents a clear stylistic advance on the Hampton Court mirrors. One of a pair.
BLENHEIM PALACE,
THE DUKE OF MARLBOROUGH

---

55. Bowett (2002), pp.301-302.
56. Daniel Marot, *Nouveau Livre Da Partements*, The Hague (1703), plate 6.
57. Child (1990), pp. 183-5.

Mirrors

Plate 6:49. Pier glass (1724). Gilded wood and glass. Probably made for George I's state apartments at Kensington Palace, and showing yet another progression from the Blenheim mirrors.
HAMPTON COURT PALACE, THE ROYAL COLLECTION
©2008 HER MAJESTY QUEEN ELIZABETH II

Plate 6:50. Pier glass (1723). Gilded wood and glass. Supplied by John Belchier for the Second Best Bedroom at Erddig, at a cost of £36. The flat frame decorated in low relief is typical of the 1720s, as is the shouldered, flattened arch top. Compare with 6:37.
ERDDIG, THE NATIONAL TRUST

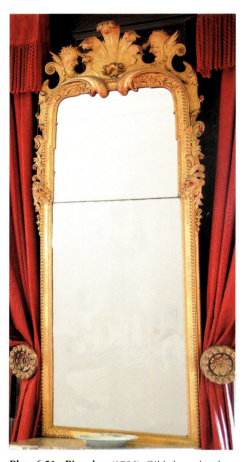

Plate 6:51. Pier glass (1726). Gilded wood and glass. At £50 this was the most expensive of the glasses supplied by Belchier to Erddig, and was installed in the Best Bedchamber. The frame is palpably richer than 6:50, with deeper relief. This double-scrolled top is probably the most common form for pier glasses of the 1720s.
ERDDIG, THE NATIONAL TRUST

were supplied for the State Apartments at Kensington Palace in 1724 (**6:49**).[58] These are later in style, less obviously French and the scrolled top has evolved into a true double-arch.

John Belchier's pier glasses for Erddig show how by the 1720s the French model had evolved into recognisably English style. That made for the Second Best Bedchamber is characteristically narrow, in order to fit the pier, with a shouldered head centred by a small quirk (**6:50**). This was supplied in 1723 at a cost of £36[59] with a gilt table which also survives (5.19). In the Best Bedchamber hung the most expensive glass, supplied by Belchier in 1726 at a cost of £50, and below it was a French brass and turtleshell marquetry bureau (**6:51**).[60] The plates are bigger, and the frame palpably richer in treatment. The flattened arch to the top incorporates a bold double-scroll flourish surmounted by a plume. Judging by the number of extant examples, this style of mirror was a popular one; on the strength of the Erddig examples they are often attributed to Belchier, but the style is unlikely to have been a Belchier monopoly.

The construction of the frames, even of the best mirrors, was surprisingly crude, requiring only the most basic joinery and confirming Campbell's opinion that the frame maker was often no more than 'a cobbling Carpenter or Joiner' (**6:52**).[61] To the basic frame were glued, nailed or screwed the carved elements, which, of course, were produced by the carver. Pier glasses with glass borders or frames

---

58. Bowett (2005).
59. Hawarden Record Office, D/E/1542/107.
60. Ibid; Erddig (1726).
61. Campbell (1747), p. 174.

Plate 6:52. Pier glass frame (1720-40). Gilded wood. This back view shows the crude joinery typical of Georgian mirror frames. The main frame was made by a frame maker, and the carved elements added by the carver. According to Robert Campbell (1747), most carvers were also gilders. Note that the angled joints between the sides and top act as a crude dovetail, preventing the weight of the glass pulling the frame apart.
PRIVATE COLLECTION

Plate 6:53. Pier glass (1720-26). Glass and gilded wood. This was originally installed in the Lady's Drawing Room at Chicheley Hall, where the panelling was shaped to accommodate it. It demonstrates the continuing popularity of glass borders in the 1720s, with the double-arched top bringing it up to date.
PRIVATE COLLECTION

dispensed with the services of a carver altogether. The example in **6:53** is from Chicheley, where it was installed in the Lady's Drawing Room, the panelling being shaped to accommodate it. It can thus be dated with reasonable certainty to 1722-25, when Chicheley's interiors were being fitted out.

The arrangement of mirrors on the parade floor at Erddig was typical of many new-built grand houses of the 1720s. Along the east side of the ground floor from the Best Bedchamber, Withdrawing Room, Saloon, and Second Best Bedchamber was a sequence of looking glasses, either pier glasses or large sconces, and beneath each was placed a table. Each pairing was placed against a pier on the outside wall, presenting an enfilade of splendid tables and mirrors running the length of the house. Despite the abandonment of the traditional 'triad' with candlestands, the association of pier glasses and tables was still very strong, and was to remain so for the whole of the eighteenth century. At Erddig and many other houses there were, in addition, large overmantel mirrors over each fireplace. Lesser houses replicated the arrangement on a more modest scale. While the pairing of mirrors and tables was quite usual, small sconces might well be placed independently. Several different styles of mirror are shown in William Stukeley's sketches of 1726-8. That in the parlour has a rectangular bevelled plate and separate cresting in the seventeenth century manner (5:78), while the dining room has a shouldered, truncated ogee plate and shaped cresting in the style of about 1720-25 (5:102). The two sconces in the best bedchamber are roughly rectangular, with rounded and indented corners, while the overmantels are plain, three-plate rectangles (3:40). The presence of so many different styles of mirror in one modest house is a good indication of the plurality of tastes of the Georgian middle classes. There was no such thing as a single 'Georgian style'.

Mirrors

Plate 6:54. Design for a looking glass (1746). Plate 4 from *Six Sconces*, by Matthias Lock. Lock's designs evince the continuing influence of the baroque double-scrolled head, adapted and embellished with rococo detail.

Plate 6:55. Tabernacle (1722). This tabernacle in the hall at Chicheley was designed by William Kent and carved by James Richards. It was originally painted by Kent with a *trompe l'oeil* figure of Mercury in the niche. CHICHELEY

The 'tabernacle' frame

The double-arched glasses of the 1720s evinced a direct design lineage from the end of the seventeenth century and were essentially baroque in form and inspiration. It is difficult to determine when they finally went out of fashion; documented or otherwise firmly datable mirrors of this type are not known after 1730, but they probably continued to be made and to evolve. The influence of the double-scroll top can be seen, for instance in Matthias Lock's designs of the 1740s, suggesting a seamless transition from late baroque to rococo styles (**6:54**). The introduction of a new architecturally-based style in the 1720s and 1730s did not, therefore, replace the baroque mirror but offered an alternative to it. One sees hints of the new style in Gumley's mirrors of 1715, whose frames have sides conceived as classical pilasters (6:46-6:47). But frames directly taken from architectural templates did not apparently appear until the 1720s, when the 'tabernacle' frame came into vogue.

In early eighteenth century nomenclature the term 'tabernacle' originally referred to a niche in a wall housing a statue or bust. Thus in 1722 James Richards was paid 'for carving ye Tabernacle & ye Frontispiece for ye Hall' at Chicheley, Buckinghamshire, in which was painted a figure *en grisaille* of Mercury by William Kent (**6:55**).[62] The idea came ultimately from classical temples such as the Pantheon in Rome, where the statues of deities were placed in niches around the walls

---

62. *DEFM*, p. 742.

Plate 6:56. Designs for tabernacle mirrors (c.1720-25), by James Gibbs. Gibbs' use of a 'tabernacle' frame for mirrors and paintings predates similar designs by Kent and his circle.
ASHMOLEAN MUSEUM

Plate 6:57. Tabernacle glass (1717-1721). This mirror bears the Bowes crest, and was made for Streatlam Castle, Co. Durham. If it was made for the refurbishment of 1717-21, then this is the earliest known example of a tabernacle mirror. If the candle branches are original, then this was technically a sconce. One of a pair.
BOWES MUSEUM

of the building. In the case of a tabernacle mirror the figure of the deity was replaced by that of the viewer, seemingly without any sense of irony. There was also a stylistic link between tabernacle mirrors and the rectangular architectural style of wall panelling introduced around 1720. Many interior elevations of the 1720s show the walls above the surbase divided into panels with bold egg-and-dart frames, outset corners and scrolled pediments.[63] The space within the frame served equally well for plain stucco, a painting, or a mirror.

The first known designs for tabernacle mirror frames occur in some of James Gibbs' drawings of 1721-22, predating by several years similar designs by Kent (**6:56**).[64] Indeed, such frames are characteristic features of Gibbs' interiors thereafter, and the tabernacle frame cannot therefore be seen as a purely neo-Palladian innovation, but as part of a more general development in interior design and planning. However, in doctrinaire neo-Palladian houses such as Chiswick the tabernacle frame remained rooted in Jonesian precedents, whereas in other hands, such as Gibbs', it was interpreted with greater freedom.

Although no documented tabernacle mirrors from this early date are known, an example from Streatlam Castle, County Durham, might well have been made at this time (**6:57**). It has been assumed that the mirror relates to the second phase of refurbishment at Streatlam (c.1743),[65] but could be part of an earlier scheme executed in 1717-22. Some elements of the design, particularly

63. See numerous examples in Friedman (1984).
64. Friedman (1972).
65. Wills and Coutts (1998).

Mirrors

Right:
Plate 6:58. Tabernacle glass (1720-26). Another early tabernacle frame, this time bearing the arms of Sir John Chester (d.1726). It combines an architectural form with baroque details such as the plumed head and lambrequin. The volute scrolls in the corners also have parallels in contemporary baroque style mirrors (cf. 6:59). The rosettes in the lower corners presumably allowed for the option of candle branches which, if fitted, would have made this a sconce rather than a pier glass. CHICHELEY

Far right:
Plate 6:59. Hanging glass (1720-26). Gilded wood and glass. This is one of a set of four at Chicheley, contemporary with the tabernacle glass in 6:58. Like James Moore's mirrors for Blenheim, this shows a strong French influence. Clearly, Sir John Chester did not recognise the rigid division created by polemicists like Isaac Ware (and endorsed by modern scholars) between the neo-Palladian and baroque styles. CHICHELEY

the flanking pilasters with their shallow-relief strapwork and composite capitals, suggest affinities with Gumley's mirrors of 1715-16, and the retention of baroque-style 'corners and middles' decorating the inner frame also suggests an early date. The eagles' heads at the base of the mirror echo those found, for instance, on the headboard of John Meller's bed at Erddig, supplied in 1720, and on numerous baroque mirrors of the 1720s.

A tabernacle mirror at Chicheley Hall bears the cipher of Sir John Chester, who died in 1726 (**6:58**). In this case the scrolled corners of the French-style mirrors like those at Blenheim have been adapted to the tabernacle form with the addition of an egg-and-dart border and scrolled pediment. In the centre of the pediment the plumed mask and lambrequin bib also derive from baroque rather than neo-Palladian imagery. Like other mirrors at Chicheley, this was conceivably supplied by 'Mr Odell', who in between August 1722 and January 1724 provided gilt tables, frames and glasses to the value of £156.12s.[66] This mirror makes an interesting comparison with a set of four other mirrors at Chicheley which are contemporary, but conceived in the baroque style with double-arched tops (**6:59**). Most owners were happy to mix 'old' and 'new', and we should regard the arguments of neo-Palladian propagandists like Isaac Ware with caution.

By about 1730 the tabernacle frame had achieved widespread popularity, partly due to the publication of design books such as James Gibbs' *Book of Architecture* (1728). Overtly polemical neo-Palladian design books such as Ware's *Designs of Inigo Jones and Others* (1733) undoubtedly gave impetus to the movement, and it was aided by powerful sponsors, such as the Earl of Burlington and Frederick, Prince of Wales. The latter was an early convert, and for his apartments at St James's Palace Benjamin Goodison supplied 'A Large Pier Glass in a Tabernacle Frame gilt… £88.0.0.' in 1732.[67]

66. See note 44.
67. PRO. LC9/288, f. 168.

Mirrors

Left:
Plate 6:60. Tabernacle glass (after 1732). Gilded wood and glass. This is one of a pair bearing the crest of Anthony Ashley-Cooper, 4th Earl of Shaftesbury, and made for St Giles House, Dorset.
CHRISTIE'S IMAGES LTD 2000

Below:
Plate 6:61. Tabernacle glass (1730-60). Gilded wood and glass. This is typical of the very numerous tabernacle mirrors made over a long period. The design was somewhat formulaic, but had the advantage of being able to fit into almost any scheme of interior architectural joinery. One of a pair.
APTER-FREDERICKS

During the 1730s the tabernacle frame achieved near universal acceptance, an emblem of what came to be conceived as the national or 'British' style. It was promoted by a host of design books issued by Isaac Ware, William Jones, Batty Langley, Edward Hoppus, and Abraham Swan, to name but a few. Their widespread availability helped the tabernacle frame remain popular into the 1760s. The majority are predictably formulaic (**6:60-6:61**), but one which offers a humorous and

Mirrors

Plate 6:62. Hanging glass (1735). Carved and gilded wood and glass. One of a pair carved by John Boson for Lady Burlington in 1735 and probably designed by William Kent. Boson charged £15 for carving the two frames. The owl is a punning reference to Lady Burlington's maiden name of Saville.

© DEVONSHIRE COLLECTION, CHATSWORTH
REPRODUCED BY PERMISSION OF CHATSWORTH SETTLEMENT TRUSTEES

Plate 6:63. Tabernacle glass (1730-60). Walnut, deal and glass. The part-gilt walnut veneered tabernacle frame was produced in huge numbers from about 1730 onwards.   APTER-FREDERICKS

original slant within the conventions of the type is shown in **6:62**. This is one of a pair made for Dorothy, Lady Burlington, in 1735, en suite with the bureaux-tables shown in 3:59. The carving is by John Boson and the design, with its punning allusion to Lady Burlington's maiden name of Saville, almost certainly by William Kent.

It is probable that many tabernacle frames which are now gilded were originally painted, sometimes with part-gilt details. This was entirely consistent with their perceived function as part of the internal architecture of the house. It was also cheaper, but as paint chipped or became discoloured, it was often easier to gild completely rather than renew the paint.

Tabernacle frames were principally carvers' work, but cabinet-makers' versions, veneered either in walnut or mahogany, were very common (**6:63**). These tended to be smaller and less obviously linked to the formal planning of the house. In many cases they combine the stylistic attributes of both tabernacle and fret-cut frames.

The prevalence of rectangular forms tends to obscure more imaginative interpretations of the neo-Palladian style. Oval glasses had long been popular, occurring in inventories from 1700 onwards; it was merely the style of the frames which changed. The design of the glass shown in **6:64** has been attributed to William Kent; there is a strong resemblance between some elements of the frame and Kent's designs for the state barge of Frederick, Prince of Wales. The making of the mirror has been attributed to Benjamin Goodison, although the actual execution would have required the hand of an expert carver, not a cabinet-maker. C-scrolls and a pierced fronded leaf at the base of the mirror hint at rococo influence, probably placing this mirror in the 1740s. The mirror shown in **6:65** is one of quite a number with bold egg-and-dart frames wrapped with leaves at the mid-point, possibly from a common source but more probably based on an engraved design. In this case the frame is surrounded by naturalistically carved fruit and a putto's head, recalling the work of Grinling Gibbons. Overpainting has been removed to reveal the original stone and white colour scheme.

Above left:
Plate 6:64 Hanging glass (1735-50). Carved and gilded wood and glass. The design of this bold, sculptural mirror frame has been attributed to William Kent. Ostensibly a full-blown neo-Palladian design, the base has rococo details which suggest a date perhaps after 1740.
VICTORIA AND ALBERT MUSEUM

Above right:
Plate 6:65. Hanging glass (1730-50). Oval mirrors were a popular alternative to the rectangular tabernacle. In this case the fruit and foliage is reminiscent of Grinling Gibbons – such anachronisms were not uncommon. The stone-coloured finish is thought to be original. CARLTON HOBBS

Appendix I
CABINET METALWARE

Locks

The standard iron drawer lock used on the great majority of early Georgian furniture had given good service since the late seventeenth century. It had an iron case fixed with six iron nails (four in the back and two in the top) and a narrow single bolt or shoot (**1** and **2**). Many had no wards or tumblers, relying for security on variations in the size and shape of the key and the length and diameter of its hollow shank or 'pipe'. Better locks were 'warded'; that is, the bolt was protected by thin semi-circular strips of iron known as 'wards' which impeded the turning of the key unless it was cut to correspond with the wards. Some also had shaped pins to which the pipe had to correspond, thus affording additional security. The two nails in the top of the lock case were necessary to prevent the lock working loose through repeated use, or from being forced off deliberately by pressure applied through the keyhole.

Door locks for cabinets were often also of iron, usually with three or four bolts and often screwed rather than nailed. However, in such a conspicuous place it was usual to fit a more expensive lock with a brass case, even if the drawer locks were iron (**3**). The same applied to the locks for desk slopes. The locks were available in all sizes. The Bastard inventory of 1731 records dozens of locks, from 'small iron lox' at 3s. the dozen to 'drawer lox' at 5s., and 'Cubbord lox & desk locks' in both brass and iron at 18s. the dozen.[1] **4** shows a tiny iron lock from a cabinet door of about 1730.

1. Legg (1994).

1 2 3 4

High quality furniture was fitted with brass locks all round. Those on the drawers were usually nailed with brass-headed pins (**5**), but screwed locks also occur in exceptional cases (**6**). Only four screws were used, since the screws afforded much better grip than nails. The cases were usually finished with a bevelled edge, with steel or iron showing through where the lock mechanism was riveted to the case. The desk and door locks on exceptional pieces were often engraved (**7**).

5

6

7

Bolts

Door bolts were of either iron or brass, with brass becoming almost universal on good quality furniture by the 1720s. Even where the casing was brass, the bolt was usually iron, because of its superior strength and resistance to wear. Whereas seventeenth century door bolts generally had pierced casings and decorative knobs, early Georgian bolts tended to be plainer (**8-10**). They varied in size and quality, the upper bolt on cabinet doors tending to be longer than the lower to remain within arm's reach (**10**). At this date most bolts were still applied to the face of the door, rather than being set into the door's edge as was the case later in the century. Almost invariably they were nailed rather than screwed, although many have subsequently had nails replaced by modern screws.

8   9   10

Hinges

The Bastard inventory of 1731 records a vast number of hinges of every conceivable type, including: 'table hinges' at 7s. the dozen, 'common butts' at 3s., 'setts [of hinges] for desks and bookcases at 12s.', 'setts for whisk tables' at 6s., 'side hinges' at 8s. the dozen, dovetail hinges in brass and iron of various sizes, 'brass hinges for cuppords' at 9s. the dozen, and 'HL' hinges at 30s. the dozen.[2] Many of these, such as the HL hinges, were joiners' stock for house doors, and the range used for furniture was somewhat narrower. Common dovetail hinges for table leaves and

2. Legg (1994).

Appendix I

doors were still used (**11**), but these were increasingly replaced by stronger, screwed hinges of a recognisable modern form (**12**). Fancy brass variations on the dovetail hinge occur, and were especially popular for japanned corner cupboards, presumably because of their pseudo-exotic appearance (**13**). Similarly, external cabinet hinges of a type copied from lacquer cabinets were still popular, either plain or engraved (**14**). Tiny hinges for interior cabinet doors survive quite well because they get little use, although the original pins have frequently been replaced by screws (**15**).

Cabinet door hinges were sometimes of the butted type, but were more usually pintles. These ranged in quality from the simplest iron (**16**) to cast brass of increasing size and ornateness, often with a cranked axis (**17** and **18**). The advantage of the latter, apart from their greater strength and longer 'throw' (the distance by which the hinged edge of the door opens clear of the cabinet) is that they can be disassembled, so that the doors can be removed without disturbing the hinge. Almost invariably these good quality brass hinges were fixed with screws.

Appendix 1

Handles and escutcheons

There was probably a greater variety of handles and escutcheons than any other type of cabinet brassware. This reflects not only the size and variety of the manufacturing base, but also the fact that handles and escutcheons had an important visual and decorative role. As the doors and windows on a house present its visage to the world, so escutcheons and handles do the same for case furniture. The variety of patterns was truly astonishing, and it is possible here only to illustrate a few of the more common ones.

Among the cheapest handles were the plain rings with circular backplates which were made in huge numbers (**19-21**). They were by far the most numerous type of handle recorded in the Bastard workshop inventory of 1731: '18 doz: of brass drawer rings of different sorts 15d per doz…'.[3] Most were fixed in the time-honoured fashion, with a strip of brass or iron hammered back against the inside of the drawer front (**22**). Occasionally, however, one finds ring handles fixed with a threaded bolt and nut (**23** and **24**), but this is confined to high quality pieces. Small interior drawers were often fitted with a small brass knob fixed by a threaded shank (**25**). Plain ring handles were generally matched with equally plain oval lock escutcheons (**23**), although more decorative versions are found (**26** and **27**).

3. Legg (1994).

19 20 21 22

23 24 25 26 27

Appendix I

The florid, pierced style of escutcheon in figure **28** is generally found in conjunction with brass 'drops'. These were first introduced in the late seventeenth century and continued to be used as late as 1730 (**29**), but loop or bail handles with shaped backplates superseded them from 1710-15 onwards. It seems likely that this style of handle was copied from imported lacquer cabinets. In Japan, loop handles with or without backplates were in use long before they appeared in England (**30**), and many of the early English patterns bear a strong resemblance to Japanese versions. It is possible that these were originally designed for use on japanned furniture, before being applied more generally. Figures **31-35** show a variety of patterns introduced about 1715; these are probably the commonest early type and variations are legion. In a significant departure from seventeenth century practice, sets of brasses now began to be made with escutcheons and handle backplates matching.

28

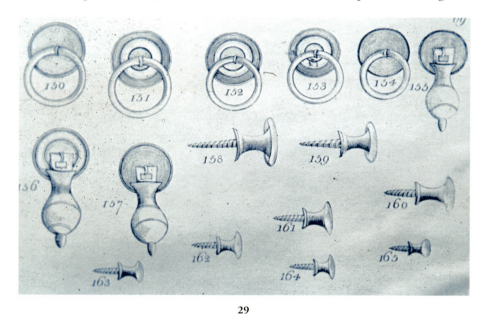

29

30

31

32

33

34

35

Appendix I

In the 1720s new designs came thick and fast. The so-called 'bat's wing' style (a modern epithet) was also probably derived from Oriental prototypes (**36-39**), while others are less obviously Oriental in style (**40-43**). Some designs were modified to a more European shape; **44-46** show examples in which the 'bat's wing' has been transformed into a double-baluster.

Until at least 1730 loop handles were usually fixed with brass or iron strips rather than threaded bolts. This was primarily a factor of cost, since bolts and nuts were hand made and consequently expensive, but by 1720 better quality furniture was almost always fitted with handles with pillar bolt and nut fixings (**47**). In many cases the bolts are retrospective fittings, the original strip fixings having worked loose and been replaced.

36 37 38
39 40 41
42 43 44
45 46 47

Appendix I

48

A significant change in the design of cabinet brassware occurred about 1730, with the introduction of cartouche shapes derived from patterns for armorials and inscriptions. These were published in design books like those issued by Thomas Bowles, a print-seller who issued numerous sets of engravings of this type in the late 1720s and 1730s.[4] Examples of brasses taken from Bowles' plates have been found on surviving furniture. It is surely no coincidence that Bowles was situated in St Paul's Churchyard, squarely in the midst of a furniture-making area and adjacent to the engravers and brass founders of Cheapside and Aldermanbury. Bowles' designs were high baroque in style, but for the more architecturally inclined there were sources such as James Gibbs' *Book of Architecture*, in which modified escutcheons suitable for stone memorials were published (**48**). In tracing the development of the new style the Antrobus desk-and-bookcase is of key importance (cf. 2:41), since it is the first dated example (**49**). The Antrobus brasses are of remarkable quality, and were probably specially commissioned, but mass-produced examples soon followed. Figures **50-52** show some of the simplest and cheapest variants, all subtly different.

A multitude of other designs were available, many of them conflating Oriental and European forms (**53-60**). Larger versions of the same patterns were used for carrying handles (**61-63**).

4. Snodin (1994).

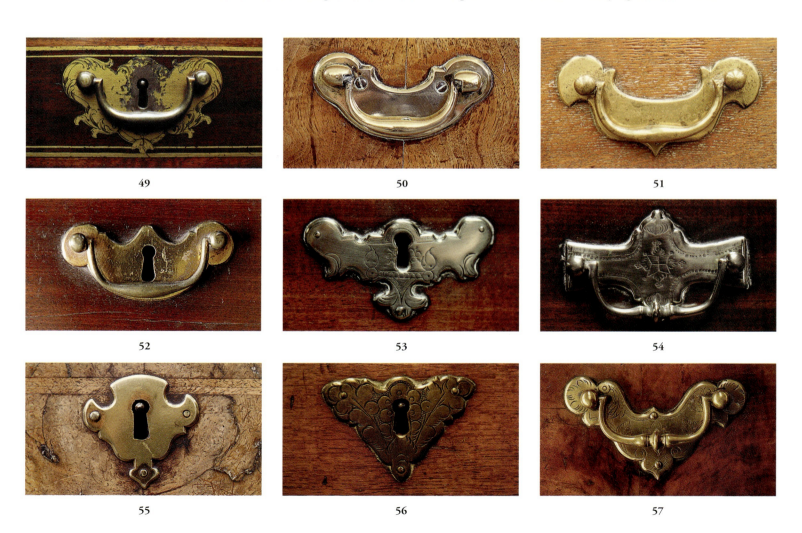

49 50 51

52 53 54

55 56 57

Appendix 1

Most of the patterns produced in the 1730s were solid rather than pierced, but around 1740 open or pierced designs became common. The example in **64** is from the mahogany commode in 3:33. The source of the design has not been discovered, but it was almost certainly taken from an engraving. This example could date from c.1735, but in general pierced designs are indicative of the period after 1740 (**65-66**). Almost invariably they are associated with third-phase carcase construction. The example in **66** is a relatively common design, taken from the desk and bookcase shown in 1:28. The brasses are marked IC; this unknown brassfounder exported his wares to North America, where they have been found on a high chest of drawers made in Massachusetts.[5] Pierced designs may have been less robust and more difficult to cast, but on the other hand they used less brass. These paved the way for the complex rococo designs of the following decades.

5. Fennimore (1996), p. 433.

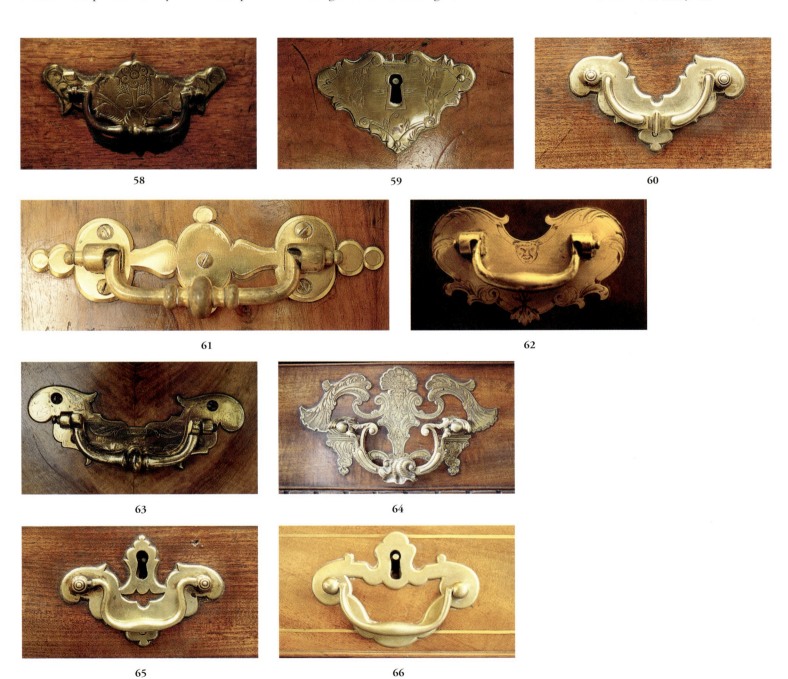

58

59

60

61

62

63

64

65

66

307

Appendix II
GLOSSARY OF WOODS MENTIONED IN THE TEXT

Beech (*Fagus sylvatica*)
Beech was the most important home-grown timber used by London furniture makers. It was a common tree in most of England and Wales, growing particularly well on the chalky soils of the Chilterns and the Thames valley. According to Defoe, it was from here that London received a 'vast Quantity' of beech for the use of turners and chair-makers, as well as for firewood.[1]

The wood is fine and even-textured, pale brown in colour, with little or no figure. Quartered surfaces show prominent rays, and these make it easy to distinguish beech from other secondary woods. Although easy to work, it is moderately heavy, and hard and tough; surprisingly, seasoned beech is superior to oak in these last respects, but its durability is poor, being prone to both furniture beetle and rot.

Beech is sometimes recorded in cabinet-makers' inventories, but its bland appearance and low lustre gave it little appeal as a show-wood. It was occasionally used for drawer linings and other secondary purposes, but rarely on London-made furniture. For chair-makers, however, beech was of primary importance. Cane chair-makers employed it as a cheap alternative to walnut. The inventory of chair-maker Thomas Warden, who died in 1702, records 'Ordinary Beach Chaires' at 3s.6d. each, compared with walnut chairs from 4s.8d. upwards.[2] Such chairs were often stained to resemble walnut or japanned in colours. In the latter case the wood's fine texture provided a good base on which to lay the coloured varnish. Chair-makers' inventories usually include quantities of beech timber, generally in the form of plank (boards 2in. (5cm) or more thick) and 'quarters' (generally 4in. x 2in. – 10cm x 5cm). Robert Loveland, a cane chair-maker who died in 1706, had 657ft. of beech plank in his workshop, together with large quantities of walnut.[3] Thomas Perkins, who died in 1723, had beech plank, quarters and clapboards (thin boards – for splats?) on hand.[4] In 1733 Thomas Roberts had beech in 4in., 3in. and 2in. (10cm, 7.5cm and 5cm) thick planks, as well as quarters and some clapboards.[5]

On upholstered chairs beech was used for the hidden parts of the frames – mainly seat rails and backs. Its tough, close texture made it an ideal material to grip tacks and webbing, and it could stand repeated nailing. In the longer term, however, its vulnerability to rot and worm were serious drawbacks, and this accounts for the relatively low survival rate of upholstered seat furniture. On

1. Defoe (1724-5), II, p.72.
2. CLRO, Orphans' Court Record 2439.
3. CLRO, Orphans' Court Record 2760.
4. CLRO, Orphans' Court Record 3214.
5. PRO, Prob 3/32/127.

gilded chairs the whole frame was often of beech, since it carved well and offered a good surface for the gesso foundation. The rear legs on cheaper walnut chairs were sometimes of beech stained to resemble walnut, and the walnut splats on India-back chairs were frequently veneered on to beech.

The other artisans for whom beech was of primary importance were turners. Not only was beechwood used for all sorts of kitchen ware, but their cheap rush-seated chairs were usually made with beechwood frames. The trade card of Francis Thompson, a turner in St John's Lane, advertised 'all Sorts of dy'd Beach Chairs' (1:5). These were produced in tens, possibly hundreds, of thousands, but almost all have perished due to worm.

Cedar (various spp.)
The name cedar was given by furniture-makers to any wood with an aromatic scent, but true cedars (*Cedrus* spp.) were rarely (if ever) used. The most common variety employed in the late seventeenth and early eighteenth centuries was red cedar imported from North America, Bermuda and the West Indies. These are all varieties of juniper (*J. virginiana, J. bermudiana,* etc.,) which, although botanically distinct, are similar in all respects and microscopically indistinguishable. The best red cedar is deep red-brown in colour with a fine, smooth texture and a fragrant scent. It was used both as a primary wood, for tables, chests, etc., and as a secondary wood, for drawer linings and internal divisions. It appears to have been less common in the early eighteenth century than it was in the late seventeenth. The customs returns show occasional shipments from 1700 onwards, primarily from Virginia and Maryland, the Carolinas and the West Indies, valued at between 5d. and 12d. per foot.[6] This was expensive, on a par with good quality walnut, and may account for its relative scarcity. The only known record of cedar in furniture-maker's stock-in-trade before 1740 occurs in the inventory of Lazarus Stiles, who had '58 foot of 2 Inch Cedar' in stock.[7]

Other North American 'cedars' include Atlantic white cedar (*Chamaecyparis thyoides*) and northern white cedar (*Thuya occidentalis*) both of which occur in seventeenth century English furniture, but their incidence in eighteenth century furniture is as yet unresearched.

The most abundant West Indian cedar was a hardwood, *Cedrela odorata*. This is similar to mahogany, but lighter and softer, with a more open texture and a pronounced scent. Although popular later in the eighteenth century, there is little or no evidence for its importation and use in the earlier period.

Deal
Together with wainscot oak, deal was one of the twin foundations of the London furniture industry. Deal was the term used in the timber and woodworking trades for softwoods imported from Scandinavia and the Baltic. The word derives from the Germanic verb *deelen*, to divide, and the noun *deel*, meaning a part or portion. Strictly speaking, a *deal* was therefore a sawn board of pine, spruce or fir, but the term was also used in a generic sense for objects made from such boards, as in 'a deal table' or 'a deal chest of drawers'.

Timber merchants and furniture-makers classified deal by its appearance. Scots pine (*Pinus sylvestris*) and, possibly, larch (*Larix decidua*) were marketed as *red deal*. *White deal* was the produce of Norway spruce (*Picea excelsa*) and (probably) silver fir (*Abies alba*). The identity of *yellow deal* is less clear; some authorities cite Scots pine, others larch or Norway spruce. It is possible that all three were marketed as yellow deal, where conditions of growth produced timber neither obviously red nor white. As a general rule, red deal was used for general joinery, exterior work and lesser quality furniture, while white deal, easier to work and with a lower resin content, was preferred for cabinet-work.

Deals were further classified by place of growth or shipment. In the period covered by this book, Norway was the principal source of deals for furniture making, and references to Norway deals abound in the documentary sources. Red and white *Christiana* deals were exported from the vicinity of Christiana, the capital of Norway (now Oslo), and were generally regarded as the best quality. *Dram* deals from nearby Drammen were also highly regarded. Other significant sources

6. PRO, Cust 3.
7. Stiles (1724).

were Gothenberg (Sweden), Danzig (Prussia), Narva and St Petersburg (Russia). The price of deals varied according to size and quality, but the average was about 1d.-1½d. per superficial foot, compared with 3-5d. for wainscot oak.

Deals were imported sawn into standard sizes which were largely determined by the specifications of the London Rebuilding Act of 1667. 3in. (7.5cm) deals were used for house joists, general construction, framing, etc. 1in. or 1¼in. (2.5 or 3cm) deals were used for flooring and panelling. All sizes were used in furniture-making, but standard 1in. deals occur most commonly in furniture-makers' inventories. They varied in width and in length; the most common widths were 9in. and 11in. (23cm and 28cm), and lengths commonly between 8ft. and 14ft. (2.4 and 4.3m). Deal 'ends' were under 8ft. in length. Deals could be further reduced in thickness for panelling, dustboards etc., by 'slitting' or sawing lengthways by hand.

During the period covered by this book some North American softwood timber was imported, but this was primarily for naval use and made little, if any, impact on furniture-making. Cultivation of home-grown British softwoods for commercial use was at this time in its infancy and there is no record of their use in fashionable English furniture.

Holly (*Ilex aquifolium*)

Holly is the whitest wood of native British growth. It is moderately hard, fine and even in texture, and easy to work. It was the first choice for stringing or other white detailing, although prone to yellowing over time (and hence usually misidentified as 'boxwood' by modern pundits). It was extensively used in arabesque marquetry and, when dyed in colours, for floral marquetry.

References to holly are rare in early Georgian furniture-makers' records. In 1731 Samuel Jakeman had 'a parcel of Holly Peartree & Wallnuttree Finiers' on his premises, but this is the only reference so far discovered in a London workshop. 'Holly venears' also occur in the inventory of the Bastards' workshops in Blandford. The most likely use of these veneers was for inlaid work, either on case furniture or on the splats, legs and frames of chairs.

Because of its close similarity to sycamore, it is usually not possible positively to identify holly on historic furniture except by microscopic analysis.

Mahogany (*Swietenia* spp.)

There were two varieties of mahogany employed by English furniture-makers in the eighteenth century. The first was West Indian mahogany (*Swietenia mahagoni*), variously called Jamaica, Spanish, St Domingo, Hispaniola and Cuba, depending on its source. The second was Honduras mahogany or 'baywood' (*S. macrophylla*). *S. mahogani* is native to the islands of the West Indies, Bahamas and the southern tip of Florida. *S. macrophylla* grows on the mainland of Central and South America, from Mexico southwards to Bolivia, Brazil and Peru. However, during the period covered by this book there is no record of mahogany from the mainland being imported into England, so it is probable that all early mahogany furniture was made from West Indian mahogany, *S. mahagoni*. Between 1722 and 1763 more than 90% of the mahogany imported into England came from Jamaica, with the remainder coming principally from the Bahamas.[8] Wood from Cuba, Hispaniola and other foreign islands was not imported until the 1760s.

S. mahagoni came in many grades of quality. The best was moderately hard and dense, fine textured, deep reddish brown in colour, strong, durable and highly stable in use. Contemporary observers are consistent in saying that the best wood came from trees growing on poor, rocky soils. Faster-grown timber from fertile lowland sites tended to be lighter in colour and weight, with plainer figure and a less lustrous surface. Raw mahogany often has white mineral deposits in its pores, as if the surface had been rubbed with chalk, and it was probably these which gave the wood a reputation for blunting tools. The deposits vanish when oil, wax or varnish is applied and hence remain only on untreated surfaces, such as drawer linings and carcase interiors.

The customs returns show small, sporadic shipments of mahogany entering London and other ports from 1700, but large scale importations did not commence until after the Naval Stores Act of 1721, which removed the import duty on all timber imported from British possessions in North

---

8. PRO, Cust 3.

America and the West Indies.[9] From a total value of just over £695 in 1723 (equivalent to 86 tons), mahogany importations rose rapidly to £5,744 (718 tons) in 1731 and £14,736 (1,842 tons) in 1738.

The wood was initially fairly cheap, with typical values ranging from 3d.-5d. per foot in the 1720s. This placed it on a par with wainscot, and considerably cheaper than walnut. In the 1720s mahogany was initially regarded as a joinery wood, recommended by Batty Langley for wainscotting,[10] and also employed for staircases and flooring. The halcyon age of cheap mahogany lasted until the outbreak of war with Spain in 1739. Between 1738 and 1740 the average price of mahogany doubled from 4d. to 8d. per foot.[11] Long before this, however, mahogany had become well established as a furniture wood, and records of mahogany furniture in bills, inventories and advertisements occur from the early 1720s onwards.

Because of its relatively low market value, and because freight was charged by volume, not weight, loggers tended to 'top and tail' their trees to remove buttresses, forks and other irregular timber, and hew the logs square. This meant that much of the best figured timber, such as curl or crotch wood which came from the butt and from the fork of the tree, was left behind as unprofitable. This accounts for the bland, straight-grained character of much of the mahogany used in early Georgian furniture, and it is generally this wood which the antiques trade misidentifies as 'red walnut'. Mahogany was shipped mainly in squared logs or sawn into planks of 2in. to 10in. (5cm to 25cm) thickness – thinner boards were prone to damage in transit. The broadest planks were destined for 'table wood' and usually cut 'through and through', whereas small logs from slow-grown trees producing hard, heavy and dark timber were employed for chair-making, table pillars and framing. There was initially very little commercial incentive to cut the wood into veneers, but as prices rose, particularly after 1740, veneering became increasingly common.

While wood sawn 'through and through' maximised the width of mahogany boards, furniture-makers soon found that quarter-cutting, although more wasteful, exposed a decorative striped or 'roey' figure, frequently mixed with a mottled or rippled cross-grain. One finds this wood used on chair splats, drawer fronts and desk slopes, either in the solid or as a veneer. It is not uncommon to find drawer fronts of figured wood veneered on to a plain mahogany substrate, suggesting a marked differential in cost between plain and figured wood.

Several modern authorities state that early mahogany was sometimes called 'Jamaica wood'. In fact this term was not used until it became necessary to distinguish Jamaican mahogany from wood from other sources. The first of these was 'Rattan' mahogany, grown on the Mosquito coast of Central America and named after the island of Ruatan off the coast of Nicaragua. This was poor quality stuff, fast-grown, light and porous, but suitable for secondary purposes. Shipments of Rattan mahogany began to arrive in England in the 1740s, followed by Honduras mahogany in the 1760s.[12]

Maple (*Acer* spp.)
The field maple (*Acer campestris*) is Britain's only indigenous maple. It is typically a hedgerow tree, much less common now than formerly. In many areas of the country it has been overtaken by introduced species such as the Norway maple (*A. platanoides*) and the sycamore (*A. pseudoplatanus*).

Maple wood is pale creamy or light brown, moderately hard, with a uniform, fine and even texture. It works easily and is stable in use, though not particularly durable. Usually straight-grained, it occasionally shows a rippled 'fiddle-back' figure, and the scarce burr wood is exceptionally decorative.

Both maple and sycamore were very widely used by turners, particularly for kitchen ware. Among cabinet-makers the wood was less common; Lazarus Stiles was one of the few known London makers to include 'Mapell' in his workshop (see page 33).

On fashionable furniture maple is most frequently found as a burr veneer, often stained in colours. The most popular treatment was to create a mottled yellow and black tortoiseshell or marbled effect which the antiques trade used to call 'mulberry'. This was done using *aqua fortis*

9. Bowett (2004).
10. Langley (1728), p. 136.
11. Bowett (1997).
12. For a detailed analysis of the 18th century mahogany trade see Bowett (1997).

(nitric acid) and heat to turn the wood yellow, then washing it over with lampblack. The firm of Coxed and Woster are the best known practitioners of this technique, but it was undoubtedly used by others.

It is possible that maple and sycamore were also used for stringing and other decorative details. In such cases it is usually indistinguishable from holly without microscopic analysis.

Oak *(Quercus* spp.*)*

London furniture-makers made a clear distinction between native oak and imported oak, which they called *wainscot* (q.v.). As a general rule, where references to *oak* occur in contemporary documents, particularly in tradesmen's bills or inventories, the home-grown variety is implied. Because of the London trade's preference for wainscot it is quite rare to find oak listed in furniture-makers' stock-in-trade, although it does occur in the records of carpenters and house joiners. For instance, when the joiner John Gilham was fitting out the New Church in Greenwich, he charged oak quarters at 3d. per foot and 1in. wainscot boards at 5d. The former was home-grown, the latter imported.[13]

Provincial furniture makers were much more likely to use home-grown timber, particularly if their business involved building and joinery as well as furniture-making. In 1731 the Bastard family workshops in Blandford, Dorset, contained both wainscot and 'dry English oak' in board and plank.[14] In inland areas beyond easy reach of a navigable river, particularly in the north and west of Britain, native oak was probably the only variety readily available. Thus vernacular or 'country' furniture is often characterised by the use of fast-grown native oak, whereas wainscot typically indicates the product of an urban workshop.

Although the North American oaks were known in Britain, there is no evidence that they were imported for furniture-making until the second half of the eighteenth century. *See wainscot.*

Pear (*Pyrus* spp.)

Domestic pear trees, cultivated for fruit, rarely produce timber of sufficient size to be of use to furniture makers. The wild pear, however, is a much larger tree and was once relatively common, particularly in central and southern England. Its timber is hard, moderately dense and very fine textured. The colour is generally pale fleshy brown, with little figure. It is easy to work and reasonably stable in use.

Pear wood is the only fruitwood which occurs with frequency in the inventories of early Georgian furniture-makers. It was commonly used by picture-frame makers for japanned frames, because its smooth, hard surface provided an ideal ground for gilding or japanning. Similarly, it was favoured by makers of japanned furniture to veneer the carcase before japanning, allowing the japan to be applied directly on the veneer without the need for gesso. This explains the presence of pear tree veneers in the inventories of cabinet-makers like Samuel Jakeman, who died in 1731.[15] Most of the japanned case furniture examined for this book has carcases veneered with pear wood.

Rosewood

The identity of the 'rosewood' used in early Georgian furniture has been the subject of debate for some decades. R.W. Symonds believed that the wood was Indian rosewood (*Dalbergia latifolia*), and described as 'a popular fallacy' the notion that the wood was padouk (*Pterocarpus* spp.).[16] The problem is partly one of identification, since it is often difficult to tell the two woods apart, even at a microscopic level.[17] It is also one of terminology, since the name rosewood has been applied to different woods at different times. After combining research into documented pieces with microscopic analysis and etymological data, it now seems clear that the early eighteenth century 'rosewood' was padouk, and was so called because of its rosy red or pink colour, and not, as most authorities state, because it was rose-scented. Thus the 'rosewood' furniture imported from China by the East India Company was made from padouk, as was that made in England by English furniture-makers using imported padouk timber.

There are many species of padouk distributed throughout Asia and Africa. The most likely

---

13. Lambeth Palace Library, *Records of the Commissioners for the Fifty Churches*, MSS 2697, Book of Works, fol. 199.
14. Legg (1994).
15. Jakeman (1731).
16. Symonds (December 1934).
17. In theory the two woods are separated at a microscopic level by several features, but in practice the differences are not always definitive. A reliable chemical test has been developed by Ian Fraser, furniture conservator for Leeds City Art Galleries. Samples of padouk placed in acetone will stain the solvent orange, whereas Indian rosewood will stain it purple.

sources for the wood used by eighteenth century furniture-makers are southern India, the Andaman islands and parts of Indonesia. The wood varies in colour from straw yellow to pink, blood-red and purple, often with darker streaks. The grain is strongly interlocked, producing a striped figure on quartered surfaces. It is hard, heavy and durable, with a coarse texture. Despite this, it is capable of a high finish, and is a first-class cabinet wood. It fades badly in sunlight, however, and old padouk furniture is often pale brown or grey.

The use of padouk tends to be associated with élite London-made furniture of the 1730s and 1740s, when importations of rosewood via the East India Company were at their height.[18] It is probable that the wood was relatively expensive compared with mahogany and walnut, but it also occurs on furniture by non-metropolitan makers such as John Brodie of Edinburgh.

Because of its darker colour Indian rosewood (*Dalbergia latifolia*) was known as black rosewood, or blackwood. However, importations of black rosewood were uncommon before 1750, becoming more abundant in the 1760s and 1770s.[19] In the absence of evidence to the contrary, it is therefore reasonable to assume that most references to 'rosewood' furniture in the early Georgian period imply padouk. The name padouk did not become current until the second half of the nineteenth century.

Wainscot

Wainscot, or quarter-sawn oak from continental Europe, was the wood of choice for English joiners and furniture-makers from medieval times onwards. It was straight-grained, free of knots and low in tannin. Although it was more expensive than home-grown oak, it was better quality, less wasteful, easier to work and more stable. Medieval supplies came from the Baltic, but by the early eighteenth century most came from Holland, where timber floated down the Rhine from central Germany was milled in multi-bladed water and wind-powered sawmills for export to England.

Dutch wainscot formed the mainstay of the London furniture trade for most of the eighteenth century. It was used for carcase work and drawer linings on veneered furniture and in the solid for plain wainscot case furniture. Contemporary documents almost always distinguish between oak – the home-grown variety – and wainscot – the imported variety. The latter are always in the form of boards or 'leaves', and graded according to thickness (usually between ½ and 1½in. (1.25 and 3.8cm)).

The use of high quality wainscot is one of the most characteristic features of London cabinet-work, and distinguishes it from vernacular or 'country' furniture. However, wainscot was available not only in London, but in most ports on the south and east coasts. Consequently, provincial furniture-makers in seaports and major inland towns on navigable rivers also had ready access to wainscot, and it is often impossible to distinguish between London work and good provincial furniture. Thus the use of wainscot is always an indication of quality, but not necessarily of metropolitan manufacture.

Walnut (*Juglans* spp.)

There were two species of walnut used in early Georgian furniture making. The first was European walnut (*Juglans regia*) and the second was North American black walnut (*Juglans nigra*). European walnut is moderately hard and heavy, medium textured, strong and tough (hence the preferred wood for gunstocks). The colour is mid-brown with a greyish tinge, with smoky grey, brown and black figuring. Well-figured root and burr timber is exceptionally decorative. It is easy to work and, if well seasoned, it is stable in use but not durable, being prone to rot and worm.

Black walnut is similar to European walnut but tends to have a uniformly darker, chocolate or even purple-brown colour (hence the epithet 'black'). It is also often rather heavier, and has a much better resistance to furniture beetle.

J. regia is typically a tree of warm, Mediterranean and Middle-Eastern climates, but it has been semi-naturalised in England since Roman times. Some of the walnut used by English furniture-makers was home grown. In the workshop of the Bastard family of joiners in Blandford, Dorset, which was destroyed by fire in 1731, was 'a large quantity of English and foreigne walnut...'.[20] For provincial furniture makers without ready access to a sea-port home-grown wood was probably the

18. PRO Cust 3.
19. Ibid.
20. Legg (1994).

only kind of walnut they were able to obtain. London furniture-makers also used home-grown stock; the inventory of Richard Roberts, taken in 1733, includes English walnut in 4in., 3in., 2in. and 1½in. (10, 7.5, 5 and 3.8cm) planks and boards.[21]

Before 1721 most imported walnut came from France, but this trade dropped off sharply after the French export ban of 1720, with only small, sporadic shipments thereafter. The rest of Europe and the Mediterranean made up the shortfall. Campbell's *London Tradesman* tells us that London timber merchants were furnished 'with Wallnut-Tree from Spain'.[22] The customs returns reveal that walnut was also imported from Holland, Flanders, Germany, Portugal, Italy, Turkey, and the 'Streights' (North Africa). The bulk of this went into London. Between 1720 and 1740, walnut to the value of £12,922 was imported from Europe to London, and only £380 (2.9%) to other ports.[23] These figures reinforce the notion that imported European walnut was something of a rarity for provincial workshops. It was mostly imported as board and plank, occasionally as logs and veneer. The customs returns show that Holland in particular was a source of walnut veneers in the 1740s.

North American black walnut was a negligible quantity in English furniture-making until the passing of the 1721 Naval Stores Act, which removed the import duty on timber imported from British possessions in the Americas.[24] Thereafter it played an increasingly important role until the 1760s. Between 1720 and 1740, walnut to the value of £24,525 was imported from North America, primarily from Virginia and Maryland. Of this £18,914 went into London and £5,611 into provincial ports. The greater proportion of North American timber going to provincial ports (some 29% of the total) was due to greater representation of the west coast ports in Atlantic trade. The beneficiaries of the more equitable distribution of North American timber (compared with the European variety) were the furniture makers of Bristol, Liverpool and Lancaster. The archives of Gillow of Lancaster reveal them to have been considerable users of American walnut for most of the eighteenth century. In London, 'Virginia' walnut occurs commonly in advertisements and in furniture-makers' inventories and bills from the early 1720s onwards.

The customs returns give the lie to the oft-repeated story of the walnut 'famine', said to have been caused by the severe winter of 1709 and the French export ban which followed it in 1720. This appears to have been first propagated by J.C. Loudon's *Arboretum et Fruticetum Britannicum* (1838) and was given further credence by G.S. Boulger in *Wood* (1902). Not only did supplies of European walnut not cease after 1720, but due to the influx of North American timber there was far more walnut available after 1720 than before.[25]

Juglans regia and *J. nigra* can only be positively distinguished by microscopic analysis (and even then sometimes only with difficulty). It is therefore unwise to rely on colour, figure or other superficial characteristics to attempt identification on old furniture. Among North American furniture historians it is axiomatic that if a piece of walnut furniture has woodworm it is probably made from European wood. This has some basis in fact, since *J. nigra* is generally more resistant to worm than *J. regia*.

There is some indication that particular types of walnut were favoured for particular roles. 'Virginia' walnut seems to have been particularly favoured for chair construction. In 1725 the widow Jamidge advertised for sale 'All Sorts of Chairs and Couches' in both mahogany, Virginia walnut and English walnut.[26] In 1733 Richard Roberts' stock included a number of 'Virginia chairs' completed and in hand.[27] The frequency with which Virginia walnut is specified as a chair wood suggests that it had a certain cachet, perhaps because of its greater durability or deeper, more uniform colour. Some European walnut, on the other hand, had a reputation as a veneer wood. 'Grenoble' walnut is occasionally mentioned, even after the French export ban of 1720. It is likely that 'Grenoble' was by this time a term indicative of quality rather than of specific origin.

The different uses of North American and European walnut, one used primarily in the solid, the other as a veneer, may have been due to the difference in cost. European walnut paid duties of 20% by value, which tended to encourage the importation of only the better quality wood, whereas American walnut paid no duty, and was often shipped to make up freight when more lucrative cargoes were lacking. Typical prices of American walnut at source in the 1720s were between 1d.-6d. per foot, depending on quality; with the addition of freight charges this increased to a market

---

21. PRO, Prob 3/32/127.
22. Campbell (1747), p.167.
23. PRO Cust 3.
24. 8 George I, cap. 4.
25. Total value of walnut imported from all sources 1700-1719, £9,843 [PRO Cust 3].
26. *Daily Courant*, 13 March 1725.
27. PRO, Probate 31/479.

value of about 3d.-8d. per foot in London. High quality veneers, on the other hand, cost as much as 2s. per foot.

Although the quantity of walnut imported from both North America and Europe was greatly exceeded by the quantity of mahogany even before 1730, this was to some extent offset by supplies of home grown walnut and by the greater use of walnut veneers. Bills and advertisements offer ample testimony to the continuing popularity of walnut furniture though the 1730s and 1740s, but the sheer quantity of mahogany meant that in time walnut declined into a minor role. By the time the stock-in-trade of Paul Saunders was inventoried in 1760, he had only 306ft. (93m) of Virginia walnut in stock, compared with 11,986ft. (3,653m) of mahogany.[28]

Yew (*Taxus baccata*)

Yew is a softwood which belies it name, being tough, strong and relatively hard. The tree grows commonly in many parts of the British Isles but rarely produces timber of sufficient breadth to interest cabinet-makers. Trees of any size usually have a deeply fluted bole with a good deal of sapwood, in-grown bark and numerous knots which make it difficult to obtain clean boards of any width. Yew burrs are highly decorative, tightly knotted with a deep amber colour and lustrous surface, and it is in this form that yew most commonly occurs on fashionable furniture.

The only known reference to yew wood in a furniture-maker's stock-in-trade before 1740 occurs in the inventory of Lazarus Stiles (1724), who had some 'Ewe Feniers' in his workshop when he died.[29] A spectacular gilt gesso desk-and-bookcase of about 1720, sold at Christie's in 2002, has an interior fitted with drawers and cupboards veneered in burr yew.[30] A fine cabinet of similar date entirely veneered in burr yew is at the Georgian House in Bristol (3:86). These are exceptional examples, however, and the use of yew was on the whole confined to provincial and vernacular furniture making.

28. Kirkham (1969).
29. Stiles (1724).
30. Christie's London, 4 July 2002, lot 100. This was one of a pair; the other was sold at Sotheby's London, 3 June 1977, lot 93.

SELECT BIBLIOGRAPHY

Manuscript sources

Domestic inventories

Blenheim 1740	*British Library ADD MSS 61473
Boughton 1709	*Northampton County Record Office
Cannons 1725	Huntington Library, San Marino, California, ST 83 (copy in the V&A archive)
Cannons 1747	Private collection (copy in the V&A archive)
Canons Ashby 1717	Northampton County Record Office
Chandos House 1725	Huntington Library, San Marino, California, ST 83 (copy in the V&A archive)
Chicheley 1755	Buckinghamshire Record Office
Dalkeith 1739	National Archives of Scotland GD224/1040/44
Ditchley 1743	*Private collection
Drayton 1710	*Drayton archive
Drayton 1724	*Drayton archive
Dunham Massey 1758	John Rylands Library, Manchester, EGR7/17/1
Dyrham 1703	Gloucester County Record Office
Dyrham 1710	Gloucester County Record Office
Elmfield 1722	PRO, Prob 3/21271
Erddig 1726	Flintshire Record Office
Houghton (1745)	*Houghton Hall archive
Houghton (1792)	*Houghton Hall archive
Kiveton 1727	*National Art Library, NAL. 86 22 55A
Marlborough House 1740	*British Library ADD MSS 61473
Montagu House 1709	*Northampton County Record Office
Montagu House 1746	*Northampton County Record Office
Sherborne House 1726	PRO, Prob C, 107, 126.

N.B. Inventories marked * have been transcribed and published in Murdoch (2006)

Workshop inventories

Samuel Jakeman 1731	CLRO, Orphans Court Record 3332, Common Sergeant's Book 6, fol. 143.
Robert Loveland 1706	CLRO, Orphans Court Record 2760, Common Sergeant's Book 5, fol. 164B.
Thomas Perkins 1723	CLRO Orphans Court Record 3214, Common Sergeant's Book 6, fol. 93.
Richard Roberts 1733	PRO, Prob 3/32/127: 31/119/497.
Lazarus Stiles 1724	CLRO Orphans Court Record 3197, Common Sergeant's Book 6, fol. 86.
Thomas Warden 1701	CLRO, Orphans Court Record 2439, Common Sergeant's Book 5, fol. 82B.

Published sources

ANON.	*The State of the Island of Jamaica*, London (1726).
	A General Description of all Trades, London (1747).
BAARSEN, Reinier	*Nederlandse Meubelen, 1600-1800*, Amsterdam (1993).
BAMFORD, Francis	'A Dictionary of Edinburgh Wrights and Furniture Makers, 1660-1840', *Furniture History*, XIX (1983).
BEARD, Geoffrey	'Three eighteenth-century cabinetmakers: Moore, Goodison and Vile', *The Burlington Magazine* (July 1977), pp. 478-486.
	Craftsmen and Interior Decoration in England, 1660-1820, Edinburgh (1981).
	'William Kent's furniture designs and the furniture makers', *Antiques* (June 1986), pp. 1278-89.
	Upholsterers and Interior Furnishing in England 1530-1840, New Haven and London (1997).
	'Kentian Furniture by James Richards and others', *Apollo* (January 2003), pp. 37-41.
BEARD, Geoffrey, and CROSS, John	'Thomas and Richard Roberts, Royal chair-makers', *Apollo* (September 1998), pp. 46-48.
BEARD, Geoffrey, and GILBERT, Christopher, eds.	*Dictionary of English Furniture Makers, 1660-1840*, Leeds (1986).
BOULGER, G.S.	*Wood – A Manual of the Natural History and Industrial Applications of the Timbers of Commerce*, London (1902).
BOWETT, Adam	'The Commercial Introduction of Mahogany and the Naval Stores Act of 1721' *Furniture History*, XXX (1994), pp. 43-57.
	'After the Naval Stores Act: Some Implications for English Walnut Furniture', *Furniture History*, XXXI (1995), pp. 116-123.
	'Thomas Ripley and the early use of mahogany', *The Georgian Group Journal*, VII (1997), pp. 140-145.
	'The Jamaica Trade: Gillow and the Use of Mahogany in the Eighteenth Century', *Regional Furniture*, XII (1998), pp. 14-57.
	'The mahogany pulpit, reredos and altar table at St George's Church, Bloomsbury', *The Georgian Group Journal*, IX (1999), pp. 166-175.
	'Myths of English Furniture History: Rosewood', *Antique Collecting* (February 1999), pp. 12-17.
	English Furniture from Charles II to Queen Anne, 1660-1714, Woodbridge (2002).
	'Design sources for the Powderham Bookcases', *Furniture History Society Newsletter* (November 2002), pp.1-5.
	'The India-back chair, 1715-1740', *Apollo* (January 2003), pp.3-9.
	'George I's Coronation Throne', *Apollo* (January 2005), pp. 42-47.
	'George I's Furniture at Kensington Palace', *Apollo* (November 2005), pp. 37-48.
BOWETT, Adam, and LINDEY, Laurie	'Furniture from the White Swan workshop in St. Paul's Churchyard, 1711-1735', *Furniture History*, XXXIX (2003), pp. 71-98.
BOYNTON, Lindsay	The Moravian Brotherhood and the Migration of Furniture Makers in the Eighteenth Century', *Furniture History*, XXIX (1993), pp. 45-58.
BUTLER, Roderick and Valentine	'Furniture Furniture', *The Journal of the Antique Metalware Society* (June 2000), pp. 29-32.
CAMPBELL, Colen	*Vitruvius Britannicus, or, The British Architect* (London 1717).
CAMPBELL, Robert	*The London Tradesman*, London (1747).
CESCINSKY, Herbert	*English Furniture of the Eighteenth Century*, 3 vols., London (1912).
CHARLESTON, R.J.	*English Glass and the Glass Used in England*, London (1984).
CHAUDHURI, K.N.	*The Trading World of Asia and the English East India Company, 1600-1760*, Cambridge (1978).

CLEMMENSEN, Tove	'Some Furniture Made in China in the English Style, Exported from Canton to Denmark 1735, 1737 and 1738', *Furniture History*, XXI (1985), pp. 174-180.
CLUNAS, Craig	'Design and Cultural Frontiers; English Shapes and Chinese Furniture Workshops, 1700-90', *Apollo* (October 1987), pp.256-263.
	Chinese Furniture, London (1988).
COLERIDGE, Anthony	'John Hodson and some cabinet-makers at Blair Castle', *The Connoisseur* (April 1963), pp. 223-230.
	'English Furniture and Cabinet-makers at Hatfield House – I, c.1600-1750', *The Burlington Magazine* (February 1967), pp.63-70.
COLLINS BAKER, J.	*The Life and Circumstances of James Brydges, First Duke of Chandos*, Oxford (1972).
CORNFORTH, John	'Houghton Hall, Norfolk – II', *Country Life* (7 May 1987), pp. 104-108.
	Early Georgian Interiors, New Haven and London (2004).
CRAGG, Jeremy	'A new light on a set of chairs at Erddig', *Furniture History Society Newsletter* (August 2001), pp. 1-3.
CROSS, John	'The Changing Role of the Timber Merchant in Early Eighteenth Century London', *Furniture History*, XXX (1994), pp. 57-64.
CROSSMAN, Carl L.	*The Decorative Arts of the China Trade*, Woodbridge (1991).
DAY, Ivan, ed.	*Eat, Drink & Be Merry: The British at Table, 1600-2000*, London (2000).
DEFOE, Daniel	*A Tour thro' the Whole Island of Great Britain*, 2 vols., London (1724-5).
DRURY, Martin	'Early Eighteenth-Century Furniture at Erddig' *Apollo* (July 1978), pp. 46-55.
EDWARDS, Clive	*Eighteenth-century furniture*, Manchester and New York (1996).
EDWARDS, Ralph, ed.	*The Dictionary of English Furniture*, 3 vols., London (1954).
EDWARDS, Ralph and JOURDAIN, Margaret	*Georgian Cabinet-Makers*, rev. edn., London (1955).
ELLSWORTH, R.H.	*Chinese Furniture*, New York (1971).
FARRINGTON, Anthony	*Trading Places: The East India Company and Asia*, London (2002).
FAYEN, Sarah Neale,	'Tilt-Top Tables and Eighteenth-Century Consumerism', *American Furniture* (2003), pp. 95-137.
FENNIMORE, Donald L.	*Metalwork in Early America*, Winterthur (1996).
	'Marked English Cabinet Handles and Knobs', *The Journal of the Antique Metalware Society* (June 1997), pp. 1-10.
FLANIGAN, J. Michael	*American Furniture in the Kaufman Collection*, Washington (1986).
FORMAN, Benno	*American Seating Furniture 1630-1730*, New York and London (1988).
FRIEDMAN, Terry	'James Gibbs' Designs for Domestic Furniture', *Leeds Arts Calendar*, No. 71 (1972), pp. 19-25.
	James Gibbs, Newhaven and London (1984).
FUHRING, Peter, and RATZKI-KRAATZ, Anne,	Late Seventeenth- and early Eighteenth-century French Designs for Upholstered Furniture', *Furniture History*, XXV (1989), pp. 42-60.
GARNETT, Oliver	*Erddig*, National Trust Guide Book, London (1995).
GILBERT, Christopher	'The Temple Newsam Furniture Bills', *Furniture History*, III (1967), pp. 16-28.
	'Furniture by Giles Grendey for the Spanish Trade', *Antiques*, XCIX (1971), pp. 544-50.
	'An Early Cabinet and Chair Work Price List from York', *Furniture History*, XXI (1985), pp. 227-8.
	Furniture at Temple Newsam House and Lotherton Hall, 3 vols. (Leeds 1978 and 1998).
	Marked London Furniture, 1700-1840, Leeds (1996).

GILBERT, Christopher, and MURDOCH, Tessa	*John Channon and brass-inlaid furniture, 1730-1760*, New Haven and London (1993).
GOMME, Andor	*Francis Smith of Warwick*, Stamford (2000).
GOW, Ian	'The Buffet-Niche in Eighteenth Century Scotland', *Furniture History*, XXX (1994), pp. 105-116.
GRAF, Lanie E.	'Moravians in London: A Case Study in Furniture-Making, c.1735-65', *Furniture History*, XL (2004), pp. 1-52.
GRAHAM, Clare	*Ceremonial and Commemorative Chairs in Great Britain,* London (1994).
GREEN, David	*Blenheim Palace*, London (1951).
GRINDLEY, Nicholas,	*The Bended Back Chair*, exhibition catalogue, London (1990).
GUSEVA, Natalia Iurevna	'Fedor Martynov, Russian Master Cabinet Maker', *Furniture History*, XXX (1994), pp. 92-99.
HARRIS, John	*The Palladian Revival*, London (1994).
HAYWARD, John	'English Brass-inlaid Furniture', *Victoria and Albert Museum Bulletin* (January 1965), pp. 11-23.
	'The Channon family of Exeter and London chair and cabinetmakers', *Victoria and Albert Museum Bulletin* (April 1966), pp.65-70.
HEAL, Ambrose	*London Furniture Makers, 1660-1840*, London (1953).
HEPPLEWHITE, George	*The Cabinet-Maker and Upholsterer's Guide*, 3rd edn., London (1794).
HOLMES, Geoffrey	*The Making of a Great Power, Late Stuart and Early Georgian Britain, 1660-1722*, London and New York (1993).
HUSSEY, Christopher	'Furniture at Longford Castle – I', *Country Life* (12 December 1931), pp. 679-682.
JACKSON-STOPS, Gervase (ed.)	*The Treasure Houses of Britain*, exhibition catalogue, New Haven and London (1985).
	'A Set of Furniture by Thomas Phill at Canons Ashby', *Furniture History*, XXI (1985), pp. 217-219.
	'Badminton, Gloucestershire', *Country Life* (6 April 1987), pp.128-33; (16 April 1987), pp. 136-9.
JAFFER, Amin	*Furniture from British India and Ceylon*, London (2001).
JERVIS, Simon	'A Great Dealer in the Cabinet Way', *Country Life* (6 June 1974), pp. 1419.
	'Multum in Parvo', *Furniture History*, XXI (1985), pp. 1-10.
	'Seat Furniture at Bowringsleigh', *Furniture History*, XXIX (1993), pp. 38-44.
JOURDAIN, Margaret	'Furniture at Erddig, Denbighshire', *Country Life* (22 March 1930), pp. 441-445.
	'Furniture at Erddig, Denbighshire – II', *Country Life* (26 April 1930), pp.623-26.
	The Work of William Kent, artist, painter, designer and landscape gardener, London (1948).
JOY, Edward	'Some Aspects of the London Furniture Industry in the Eighteenth Century', unpublished MA thesis, London (1955).
	'The Overseas Trade in Furniture in the Eighteenth Century', *Furniture History*, I (1965), pp. 1-11.
KIRKHAM, Pat	'Samuel Norman: a study of an eighteenth-century Craftsman', *The Burlington Magazine,* (August 1969), pp. 501-13.
	'The London furniture trade 1700-1870', *Furniture History*, XXIV (1988).
KIRTLEY, Alexandra A.	*The 1772 Philadelphia Furniture Price Book*, Philadelphia (2005).
LANGLEY, Batty	*A Sure Method of Improving Estates*, London (1728).
	The City and Country Builder's and Workman's Treasury of Designs, London (1740).
LAWSON, Philip	*The East India Company, a history*, London (1993).
LEGG, Polly	'The Bastards of Blandford: an Inventory of their losses in the fire of 1731', *Furniture History*, XXX (1994), pp. 15-42.

Bibliography

LENYGON, Francis	*Decoration in England from 1640-1760*, 2nd edn, London (1927).
LESLIE, Charles	*A New History of Jamaica*, London (1740).
LINDEY, Laurie,	'The Orphan's Court record of Thomas Warden, a cane chairmaker', *Furniture History Society Newsletter* (August 2004), pp. 2-4.
	'William Old and John Ody at The Castle in St Paul's Churchyard', *Furniture History Society Newsletter* (February 2006), pp. 1-4.
LOVEDAY, John,	*Diary of a Tour in 1732*, London (1890).
LUNSINGH SCHEELEUR, Th. H.	'A la recherche du mobilier de Louis XIV', *Antologia di Belle Arti*, nos. 27-28 (1985).
MACQUOID, Percy	*The Age of Mahogany*, London (1906).
MOORE, Andrew (ed.)	*Houghton Hall*, London (1996).
MORSE, H.B.	*The Chronicles of the East India Company trading to China, 1635-1834*, 5 vols., Taipei (1966).
MORTIMER, T.	*The Universal Directory*, London (1763).
MOXON, Joseph	*Mechanick Exercises*, London (1678).
MURDOCH, Tessa	'The king's cabinet-maker: the giltwood furniture of James Moore the Elder', *The Burlington Magazine*, (June 2003), pp. 408-420.
	Noble Households: Eighteenth-Century Inventories of Great English Houses, Cambridge (2006).
PRYKE, Sebastian	'The Extraordinary Billhead of Francis Brodie', *Regional Furniture*, IV (1990), pp. 81-99.
ROBINSON, Sir Thomas	*Historic Manuscripts Commission* (1731), Appendix pt vi, Carlisle, p.84.
ROSOMAN, Treve	'The decoration and use of the principal apartments of Chiswick House, 1727-70', *The Burlington Magazine* (October 1985), pp. 663-667.
	'The Chiswick House Inventory of 1770', *Furniture History*, XXII (1986), pp. 81-106.
RUTHERFORD, F.J.	'The Furnishing of Hampton Court Palace 1715-37', *Old Furniture*, II, No. 6 (November 1927), pp. 76-86.
SCOONES, Francesca	'Dr. William Stukeley's House at Grantham', *The Georgian Group Journal*, IX (1999), pp. 158-165.
SHERATON, Thomas	*The Cabinet Dictionary*, London (1803).
SHIXIANG, Wang	*Connoisseurship of Chinese Furniture*, Hong Kong (1990).
SMITH, J.T.	*Nollekens and His Times*, 2 vols., London (1828), republished Turnstile Press, London (1949).
SNODIN, Michael	'Thomas Bowles and Baroque Ornament: Some More Printed Sources for engraved brass Inlay', *Furniture History*, XXX (1994), pp. 86-91.
STABLER, John	'"We Always Stamped All We Made, Not being Asham'd of Our Work"', *Furniture History*, XLI (2005), pp. 13-20.
	'A Dictionary of Norfolk Furniture Makers, 1700-1840', *Regional Furniture*, XX (2006).
STRANGE, E.F.	'Some Early 18th Century Furniture Bills', *Old Furniture* (May-August 1928), pp.48-53.
SYMONDS, R.W.	'Furniture from the Indies III', *The Connoisseur* (July-December 1934), pp. 111-119.
	'Early Imports of Mahogany for Furniture – II', *The Connoisseur* (December 1934), pp. 375-381.
	'Early Mahogany Furniture', *The Connoisseur* (February 1935), pp. 68-73.
	'Giles Grendey (1693-1780) and the Export Trade of English Furniture to Spain', *Apollo* (December 1935), pp. 336-42.
	Masterpieces of English Furniture and Clocks, London (1940).

	Veneered Walnut Furniture, 1660-1760, London (1946).
	'The New Wood', *The Antique Collector* (July-August 1949), pp. 138-144.
	'Eagle Pier-Tables', *The Antique Collector* (March-April 1950), pp. 54-9.
	The Chair with the "Bended Back", *The Antique Collector* (July-August 1951), pp. 155-161.
	'A Chair from China', *Country Life* (5 November 1953), pp. 1497-1499.
	'The Chair with the Mask on the Seat Rail', *The Antique Collector* (December 1954), pp. 222-227.
TEMPLE NEWSAM	*Country House Lighting*, Country House Studies No. 4, Leeds (1992).
THORNTON, Peter	*Seventeenth-Century Interior Decoration in England, France and Holland*, New Haven and London (1978).
	Authentic Décor – The Domestic Interior 1620-1920, London (1984).
	Form and Decoration – Innovation in the Decorative Arts, 1470-1870, London (1998).
THORPE, W.A.	'Stoneleigh Abbey and its furniture', *The Connoisseur* (December 1946), pp. 71-78 and 152.
THURLEY, Simon	*Hampton Court Palace*, New Haven and London (2003).
WALTON, Karin-M.	'An Inventory of 1710 from Dyrham Park', *Furniture History*, XXII (1986), pp. 25-80.
WESTMAN, Annabel	'Francis Lapiere's Household Inventory of 1715', *Furniture History* (1994), pp. 1-14.
WILK, Christopher, ed.	*Western Furniture 1350 to the Present Day*, London (1996).
WILLIAMS, Robert	'Two pieces of dated walnut furniture', *Furniture History*, XIV (1978), pp. 65-67.
WILLS, Geoffrey	*English Looking-glasses*, London (1965).
WILLS, Margaret, and COUTTS, Howard	'The Bowes Family of Streatlam Castle and Gibside and Its Collections', *Metropolitan Museum Journal*, 33 (1998), pp. 231-243.
WITTKOWER, Rudolf	*Palladio and English Palladianism*, London (1974), reprinted in paperback (1983).
WOOD, Lucy	*The Lady Lever Art Gallery Catalogue of Commodes*, London (1994).
WOOLER, Colin	*Dictionary of Old Trades, Titles and Occupations*, London (2002).
WORSLEY, Giles	*Classical Architecture in Britain: The Heroic Age*, New Haven and London (1995).

INDEX

Page numbers in bold refer to illustrations and captions
Page numbers in italics refer to footnotes

A General Description of all Trades, 19
Acts of Parliament
   London Rebuilding, 310
   Naval Stores, 10, 32, 310, 314
Adam, William, 227
Adderbury House, *231*
Addle Street, 24
Africa, 312
   North, 37, 314
   West, 32
Aken, Joseph Van, **44-45**, 45
Alden, Anne, 127
Aldermanbury, 10, 14, 15, 78, **118**, 306
Aldgate, 10
Althorp, **288**, 289
Amelia, Princess, 72, *106*
America
   Central, 310, 311
   North, 32, 36, 36, 58, 114, *151*, 187, 309, 310-315
   South, 310
American Revolution, 36
Andaman islands, 313
Anne, Princess, 72, *106*
Anne, Queen, *151*, 200
Anne, Queen of Russia, *175*
Antrobus, 40, 74, **74**, 75, **75**, 80, 306
Antrobus, Daniel, John and Richard, 75
Antwerp, 138
apprenticeships, 12-13
Arbuthnot, Philip, 23, 131
Archambo, Peter, **277**
architectural pediments, 80-81, **80**
Arley Castle, 162
Arlington Street, 187
Arundell, Earl of, **212**, 213
Ashley-Cooper, Anthony – *see* Earl of Shaftesbury
Asia, 32, 312
Aske Hall, 183, **183**
Astell, Wm, 33
Atholl, Duke of, 218, **219**
Avery, Abraham, *11*

BA, 24, **24**
Badminton House, 138, **190**, 196, **197**, **216**, 217, 228-229, **228**, 231, **231**, 235, 267
Bahamas, 310
Baltic, 32, 36, 313
Banks, Joseph, 29
Bankside, 266
Bardwell, Thomas, **248**
Basket-makers' Company, 15
Bastard brothers, 24, 35, 245, 300, 301, 310, 312, 313

Bateman, Sir William, 95, **95**
Bath, Earl of, 32
Bear Garden Glass House, 266
Beauchamp-Proctor, Sir William, 196
Beaufort, Duke of, 19, 138, 211, **216**, **228**, **276**
beech, 33, 308-309
Belchier, John, *11*, 20, 31, 60, 77, **77**, 79, **79**, 80, 122, **123**, 128, **128**, 134, **134**, **138**, 210-211, **211**, 275, **275**, 281, **281**, 282, 292, **292**
Bell, Daniel, and Moore, Thomas, 180, **180**
Bell, Elizabeth, **82**, 83, 122, **123**
Bell, Henry, 80, **82**, 83, 122, **123**
Bell Lane, **99**
Bell, Philip, **123**
Belton House, 166
benches, 189, **189-191**
Bennet, Samuel, 31, *75*
Bent, Thomas, 18, **19**
Berain, Jean, 50, 95, **95**, 137, 161, 162, **163**, **164**, 173, 213, 278, **290**, 291
Berensdorf, Baron, 252
Bermuda, 309
Berry, William, 66-68, **68-69**, 70, 72, 92
Bicester, 172
Birmingham, 24
Black Swan Court, 15
Blackfriars Stairs, 10
Blair Castle, 270, **270**
Blandford, Dorset, 24, 35, 245, 310, 312, 313
Blathwayt, Madam, 127
Blathwayt, William, 131
Blenheim Palace, 27, 138, **154**, 155, 203-205, **203-205**, 209, 210, 281, 291, **291**, 296, **296**
Bobart, Tilleman, 203
Bolivia, 310
bolts, 301, **301**
bookcases, 131-137, **132-136**
Booth, George – *see* Earl of Warrington
Boson, John, 21, 112, 124, 125, **125**, 150, 191, 194, 223, **224**, 225, 233, **233**, **298**, 299
Boston, Mass., *151*, 171
Bothmar, Count, 252
Boughton House, 96, 130, 187, 200, **201**, 207, 231, 235, 245, 246, 278
Boulger, G.S., 314
Boulle, André-Charles, **95**, 151, 173, 213
Bouverie, Jacob de – *see* Viscount Folkstone
Bowes family, **289**, **295**
Bowes-Blakiston, Elizabeth, 155, **155**
Bowles, Thomas, 306
Bowringsleigh, 186, **186**
Bradshaw, William, 166, **167**, 175, 183, **183**, 198, **210**, 229

Bramshill Park, Surrey, **44**, 45
Brazil, 310
Brewster family, 248
Bristol, 10, 315
British Architect, The, 275
Brodie, Francis, 175, 231, 244, **244**, 268
Brodie John, 313
Brook Street, 90
Brown, John, 20, 172, **172**
Browning, George, 29, **29**, 30
Brunetti, Gaetano, 198
Brydges, James – *see* Duke of Chandos
Buck, Henry, *11*, 20
Buckinghamshire, 32
buffets, 218, **218**
Bull, James, *11*
bureau-tables, 120-125, **121-125**
bureaux, 125-126, **125-126**
Burlington House, 223
Burlington, Lady, 21, 112, 124, 184, **184**, **298**, 299
Burlington, Lord, 191, 192, 223-225, **223**, 276, 278, 296
Burnet, Thomas, 252
Burton Agnes, 44
Burton Constable, 137
Bushnell, Thomas, *11*
Butt, Samuel, 12, 13, **13**, 18-19, 118
Byrom, William, 23

Cabinet Dictionary, 137
Cabinet, The, 31, **76**
Cabinet-Makers' London Book of Prices, 89
cabinets, 137-143, **137-143**
   and stands, **43**
cabinet-makers, 12
caffoy, 166, *166*, 193
Cambridge
   Emmanuel College, 197, **197**
   Magdalene College, 125, 131
Campbell, Robert, 292, **293**, 314
Cannons, 32, 43, 54, 94, 96, 106, 121, 125, 137, 138, 161, **162**, 169, **169**, 170, 175, 188, 207, 216-217, 220, **220**, 237, 242, 252, 262
Canons Ashby, 152, **152**, 153, 157, **157**, 158, 216, **216**
Canton, 49-50, **50-51**
carcase damage, 81
Cardigan, Earl of, 231
Carnarvon, Lord, 262
Carolinas, 36, 309
Caroline, Princess, 290
Caroline, Queen, 263

322

carvers, 21, 23
cassapanca, **190**, 191
Casteels, Pieter, **Frontispiece**
Castle Baynard, 33
Castle Howard, 217, **217**, 272, 287, **287**
Castle, The, 13, 20, 160
castors, **126**
Caversfield, 172
cedar, 309
Chair and Crown, The, 17
chairs, 144-199, **145-149**, **152-186**, **188**, **192-199**
  cane, 15
  Chinese, **157**
  compass seat, 171-172, **171-172**
  coronation, 144, **146-147**
  dressing, 188-189, **188**
  'Dutch', 16, **16**
  elbow, **52**, **153**, **154**, **156**, **158**, **169**, **182**, 185, **185**
  fan back, 196-198, **197-198**
  hall, **48**
  India back, 47, **47**, 48, 156-159, **156-159**, 182
  pillar leg, 144-147, **145-146**
  walnut and ash, **38**
Chambers, William, 194
Chandos, Duchess of, 188, 242
Chandos, Duke of, 32, 94, 96, 161, 169, **169**, 207, 216, 220, **220**, 222
Chandos House, 127-128, 161, 207, 267
Channon, John, 40, **136**, 137
Charing Cross, 10
Charlecote Park, Oxfordshire, 52
Chatsworth, **184**, 186, **186**, 217, **224**, 226, 233, **233**
Cheapside, 11, 75, 306
Chelsea, 20
Chester, Sir John, 173, 210, **210**, 221-222, **284**, 296, **296**
chests
  and stand, **44**
  clothes, 94-96, **95-96**
  of drawers, **13**, **18**, 96-105, **97-105**
    double, 118-120, **118-120**
  -on-stands, 112-117, **113-117**
  with folding tops, 105-108, **106-110**
Chevening, 183, 198, **198-199**, 210
Chicheley Hall, 173, **173**, 210, **210**, 221-222, **221-222**, 242, **273**, 275, 284, **284**, **293**, 294, **294**, 296, **296**
Child, Sir Francis, 149, **149**
Chilterns, 308
chimney-glasses – *see under* mirrors
China, 312

Chippendale, Thomas, 32, 116, 124, 126, 142, 183, **183**, **196**
  Gentleman and Cabinet-Maker's Director, 116-117, 124, 126, 142
Chiswick Villa, 21, 112, 124, 184, **184**, 192, **192**, 193, 194, **194**, 223-225, **223-224**, 226, 233, **233**, 276, **276**, 295
Christian VI, King of Denmark, 50
Christiana, 309
Chupain, Elijah, 118
Church Street, 37
Churchill, John – *see* Duke of Marlborough
Churchill, Sarah – *see* Duchess of Marlborough
City and Country Builder's and Workman's Treasury of Designs, 134, **134**, **135**, 142, 215, **215**
Clandon Park, 72
Claremont, **205**
Cleare, Thomas, 122, 162, **162**, 280, **281**
Clerkenwell, 10, 11, 32
Clinch, Thomas, 23
clothes presses, 130-131, **130-131**
Cobham, Viscount, **181**, 200, **201**, **214**
cockbeading, 72-80, **76**, **78**, 101, **101**, **110**
Colchester, 112, **113**
commodes, 111-112, **112**
Cooke, Richard, 138
Cornbury Park, **172**
Cornhill, 10, 29, 30, **76**
cornices, 58-64, **59-60**
couches, **154**, 187, **187**
Cour, William De La, 198, **198**
Covent Garden, 10, 11, **28**, 29, 31, **40**, 150
Cowdray Park, **288**, 289
Cox, Joseph, 21
Coxed and Woster, 18, **19**, 68, **68**, 77, **77**, 82, 83, **85**, 121, **121**, 245, 312
Coxed, Grace, *11*, 68, **77**, 85
Coxed, John, 11, 13, 19-20, **57**, 58
Crook, Benjamin, 80, **81**, 264, **264**
Crown, The, 14, **118**
Croxford, Francis, 20, 235
Cuba, 310
cupboards
  corner, 126-129, **127-129**

Dahl, Michael, *151*, 164, **164**
Daily Advertiser, 258
Daily Courant, The, 30, 127, 131, 289
Daily Journal, The, 34, 266
Daily Post, The, 20, 23, 30, 39, 86
Dale, William, 32
Dalkeith Palace, 94, 200
Danzig, 310

Davis, Mr, 124, 233, **233**
deal, 32, **35**, 309-310
Decker, Sir Matthew, 49, **49**, 52, **53**
Deene Park, 231
Defoe, Daniel, 32, 308
Delafield, Erasmus, **182**
Denmark, 39, **50**
Designs of Inigo Jones and others, 137, 276, **276**, 296
desks, writing, **40**
desks-and-bookcases, **22**, 23, 24, **24-25**, 39, **41**, 50, **51**, 52, **53**, 54-93, **54-93**
Devonshire, Duke of, 291
Devonshire House, 192, 194, **194**
Diaper, Thomas, 279
Dieckard, Henry, 40
Disegni Diversi, 229, **229-230**
Ditchley House, 94, 189, **189**, **190**, 197, 198, 226, **226**, 231, 245, 252, **274**, 275, 277, **277**
Dorset, Duke of, 278
dovetails, 65, 108, **109**
Drammen, 309
drawers
  construction, 56-58, **57-58**, 65-68, **65-66**
  edge mouldings, 72-80, **75**, **78**
Drayton House, 94, 97, 160, 207, 218, **218**, 241, 245, **245**, 252, 275, 278
Dresden, **41**
Drury Lane, 29
Dryden, Edward, 152, **152**, 157, **216**
Dumfries House, 227, 231
Dunham Massey, **95**, 97, 160, 217, 218, **219**, 222, **222**, 234, 277, **277**
dustboards, 56, **56**
Dyrham Park, 26, 96, 127, 130, 131, 207, 235, 236, 241
Dysart, Earl of, 150, **206**, **209**, 218

East India Company, 32, 42, 49, **49**, 50, 149, 155, 241, 312
East Indies, 36, 43, 47, 52
ebony, 32
Edinburgh, 175
Eldin, Daniel, *11*
Elizabeth I, Queen, 52
Elmfield House, *97*
Erddig, **23**, 27, 54, **59**, 60, **60**, 94, 96, 127, 137, **138**, 161, **161**, 166, **166-167**, 171, 207, 210-211, **210-211**, 235, 237, 252, 262, 263, 267, **272**, 275, 278, 280-281, **281**, 282, 289, **289**, 292, **292**, 293, 296
escutcheons, 303-307, **303-307**
Evendon, John, 279
Everard, Eleanor, **212**, 213
export trade, 36-42

Falck, Joachim, 40, *116*
Far East, 148
Faucon, James, 30
Feet
   bracket, 70-71, **70-71**
   claw, 150
   French, 150
   Indian, 148-149
   pad, **256**
   'Spanish or 'Braganza', 252
Fetter Lane, 163
Fish, Peter, 84, **85**
Fitzwilliam, Viscount, *49*
Flanders, 314
Fleet Ditch, 10, 11, 18, 19, 29, 31, 33
Fleet River, 33
Fleet Street, 10, *149*, **182**
Fletcher, Jeremiah, **153**
Fletcher, Joseph, *11*
Flitcroft, Henry, **189**, 191, 226-227, 231
Florence, 226
Florida, 310
Folkstone, Viscount, 185, 252
Fordham, James, 83, **83**
Fort St George, 52
Fortescue, Lady Mary, 283
Framlingham, 37
France, 151, 314
Fredensborg Castle, 50
Frith Street, **31**

Gamage, Robert, *11*
Gardam, John, 217, **217**
Gardner, William, *11*
Gatehouse, John, 19, **57**, **59,** 64, 68
Gay, John, 231
General Advertiser, 20
Gentleman or Builder's Companion, The, 215, **215**, 275
George & White Lyon, 80
George I, King, 17, 94, 114, 200, 252
   coronation chair, 144, **146-147**
George II, King, 17, 72
George & White Lyon, The, **264**
George, Remey, 148, 188
Georgian House, Bristol, 315
Germany, 36-37, 39, 313, 314
Giardini, Giovanni, 193, 229, **229-230**, 231
Gibbons, Grinling, 225, 299, **299**
Gibbs, James, 72, 169, **169**, 170, **190**, 191, 200, *228*, **274**, 282, **282**, 295, **295**, 296, 306
   Book of Architecture, 80, 296, 306
Gibraltar, 37
Gibson, ?, *11*
Giles, John, 24-26, **26**, **282-283**, 283
Gilham, John, 312
Gillman, William, 117
Gillows, 251, 261, 262, 284, 314
Golden Cup, 30
Golden Plow, The, 15

Golden-Square, 30
Goldsmiths' Company, 75
Goodison, Benjamin, 40, *106*, 111, 125, 127, 140, 175, 185, **185**, 194, 207, **214**, 225, 231, **232**, 233, 235, 247, 249, 263, 282, **282-283**, 284, 289, 296. 299
Gosfield Hall, 126, **126**
Gothenberg, 310
Grant, Samuel, *151*, 171
Grantham, 114, **115**, 165, **242**, 255, **255**
Graveley, J., 26, 40
Great Marlborough Street, 30
Great Queen Street, 23
Green, Thomas, 188
Green, William, *11*
Greenwich
   New Church, 312
   The Queen's House, **276**
Grendey, Giles, 32, **36**, 37, 80, 104, **104**, 120, **120**, 122, 178, **178**, *186*, **256**
Grenoble, 314
Greyhound and Hat, 13
Gubbay Collection, *72*
Guelfi, Giovanni Battista, 223
Guilbaud, John, 11-12
Guildford, Earl of, 194, **194**
Gumley and Moore, 43, 72, 86, 94, 114, 121, 127, 131, 133, **202**, 203, 231, 262, 263, 266, 284, 289-291, **290**, 294, 296
Gumley and Turing, **206**, 207, 249
Gumley, Elizabeth, 114
Gumley, John, 30, 32, 200, 207, **211**, 266
Gutter Lane, 75

Haddo House, **244**
Haddock, Elka, 191
Hague, The, 37
Hales, Frances, **227**
Halfhide, Thomas, 23, 242
Hallet, William, 32, 176, **176**, 187, 196, 259
Ham House, 46, **46-47**, 166, **167**, 189, **189**, **192,** 196, **196**, **206-207**, 207, 218, **219**, 241, 242, **242**, 248, **249**
Hamilton, Duke of, 175
Hamilton, Gawen, **241**
Hamilton Palace, 259, **259**
Hampton Court Palace, 46, 111, 121, 131, 153, *157*, 160, 164, 185, 194, *200*, **202**, 203, **232**, 233, 248, 249, 263, 282, **282-283**, 287, 290-291, **290**
handles, 303-307, **303-307**
Harcourt, Viscount, 156, **156**
Harles, Thomas, 88
Harley, Edward, 170, **170**
Harlot's Progress, The, 16
Harrison, Edward, 52
Hartington, Marquess of, **211**
Hartland, Richard, *11*
Hasert, Peter, 196, **209**, 248, 256, 283
Hatfield House, 112, 279

Hatton Garden, 23
Hawksmoor, Nicholas, 203
Haymarket, 10
Heasman, Henry, 150
Heathcote, Lady, 14
Hele, John, 196, **206-207**, 207
Helme, Isaac van den, 127
Hepplewhite, George, 150
   Guide, 151
Herbert, Henry – *see* Earl of Pembroke
Herbert, Sidney, *49*
Hervey, Lord, 175
Hibbert, 32
hinges, 301-302, **302**
Hinton House, Dorset, 21
Hintz, Frederick, 39-40, **39**
Hispaniola, 310
Hodgson, John, *11*
Hodson, John, 31, **31**, *137*, 162, *173*, **173**, 218, **219**, 258, 270, **270**
Hodson, Robert, *173*, 242, 252
Hoese, Peter, 37, **41**
Hogarth, William, 16
Holborn, 10, 11, 31, 33, 90, 120
   Bridge, 11, 29, 163
   High, 141, 242
Holker Hall, **184**
Holland, 32, 36, 39, 84, 245, 313, 314
holly, 33, 310
Holyrood House, Palace of, 231
Hoppus, Edward, 297
Hopton, 84, **85**
Hornby Castle, 148
Houghton Hall, 125, 169, 183, 189, **190**, 191, 193, **193**, **197**, 213, 218, **218**, **224-225**, 225, 231, 233, 258-259, **258**, 282
   suites, 173-176, **173-176**
Houndsditch, 10
How, Thomas, **177**
Huali wood, **46-47**, **48**, **49**, **150**, **154**
Hubert, William, 137, 142
Hutt, Elizabeth, 186, **186**
Hutt, John, 27
Hyde, Robert, 40, **40**

IG, **159**
Ince and Mayhew, 124
Ince Blundell Hall, **237**
India, *49*, 313
Indian Chair, 162, 280
Indonesia, 313
Infantado, Duke of, **36**, 37
Innes House, *231*
Ioannovna, Empress Anna, 42, **42**
Ipswich Journal, 37
Ireland, *49*
Irwin, Lord, 126, 171, 176, **176**, 187, 188, 242
Isleworth, 32
Italy, 37, 314

JG, 26, **26**, **282-283**, 283
Jakeman, Samuel, 21, *26*, 31, 33, 35, 310, 312
Jamaica, 310
Jamidge, widow, 314
'Japan Cabinet and Cistern, The', 23
Jefferson, William, 203
Jensen, Gerrit, 93, 112, 126-127, 200, **201**, 241, 246, 267, 269, 270, 279, 280, 287
Johnson, Thomas, 21
Joiners' Company, 12-14, 90-93
    Petition, 50, 241
Jones, ?, *11*
Jones, Inigo, 275-276, **276**, 295
Jones, Richard, 127
Jones, Samuel, 191
Jones, Thomas, *11*
Jones, William, 215, **215**, 275, 297
journeymen, 13
Joynes, Henry, 203

Kedleston Hall, **257**
Kendall, John, 112-114, **113**, 116
Kensington Palace, 126-127, 144, 151, *157*, 200, **201**, 203, 205, **206**, 207, **209**, 231, 241, 291-292, **292**
Kent, Duke of, 252
Kent, William, 72, 125, **125**, 142, 175, 189-196, **189-195**, 218, 223-231, **224-226**, 276, **276**, **277**, 278, 294, **294**, 295, **295**, **298-299**, 299
Kenward, Robert, **48**
Kew Palace, 194, **194-195**
Kilmansegge, Madame, 121
King & Queen, Bicester, 172
King, Mr, 172
King, Richard, *11*
King, Thomas, 258
Kiveton Hall, 137, 148-149, **148**, 161, 242, 252, 260, 267, 275, 277, 278, 279, 289
Kneller, Sir Godfrey, 165
Knole, 207
Knowles, John, *137*
Kremlin, *175*

lacquer, 42-48, **43-44**, 50, **50**, **51**, **61**, **62**, **70**, 70
Ladies' Library, The, **132**, 133, 267
Lambeth, 30, 266, 289
Lancaster, 262
Landall, Thomas, 40
Langley, Batty, 58, 72, 134, 142, 215, **215**, 297, 311
Langley Park, 196, **196**, 259
Langley, Stephen, 184, **184**
Lanscroone, Mr, 218
lanterns, 277, **277**
Lapiere, Francis, 97, 245
Lee, Admiral Fitzroy, 226
Lee, George Henry – *see* Earl of Litchfield
Leeds, Dukes of, 148, 260

legs
    cabriole, 150-156, **151-156**
    horsebone, 151
    Marlboro(ugh), 47, 149
Leicester, Earl of, 52, **65**
Lincoln Street, 30
Lincoln's Inn Fields, 30
Lion & Lamb, The, 29
Litchfield, Earl of, 226, 227, **227**
Little Wild Street, 30
Livorno, 226
Lock, Matthias, 21, 226-227, **227**, **294**, **294**
locks, 300-301, **300-301**
Lomax, Francis, 37
London, *passim*
    Bridge, 10
    furniture trade, 10-53
    map of, **11**
    Record Office, 11
    West End, 12
London Evening Post, 90
Long Acre, 10, 11, 258
Longford Castle, 185, **185**, 233
Lord Chamberlain, 126-127
Lothbury, 31
Loudon, J.C., 314
Louis XIV, King, 200
Loveland, Robert, 308
Lover, The, 30, 266-267
Lucas, William, 138-140
Ludgate Hill, 10
Luvarick, Samuel, 12
Lyttleton family, **163**

MA, **159**
McClellan, James, 37
Macclesfield, Lord, 200, **201**
mahogany, 32, 86-90, **86-89**, 310-311
    'Grenoble', 314
    Honduras, 90, 310
    oil polished, 88-89
    'Rattan', 311
    West Indian, 310
Maiden Lane, 40, **40**
Mainz, 37
maple, 33, 311
Mardol, 37
Marlborough, Duchess of, 27, 95, **95**, 138, 203
Marlborough, Duke of, 138, **154**, 200, **201**, 203-205
Marlborough House, 200, 203, 275, 278
Marot, Daniel, **197**, 278, **278**, 291
Marshall, John, 37
Martynov, Fedor, 42, **42**
Mary, Queen, 126-127
Maryland, 36, 309, 314
Marylebone St, 17
Mash, Mr, 20
Mason, Edward, 150

Massachusetts, 307
Massey, Abraham, 23
Massey, Mr. Joseph, 37
Matthews, Timothy, **182**
Maxwell, Charles, 29, 30
Mayo, John, 13
Meaux, Bishop of, 151
Mediterranean, 32, 313, 314
Meller, John, 27, 31, 58, **59**, 92, 166, **211**, 296
Mercer, George, 227
Mercier, Philip, 160
metalware, 24-26, **26**, 300-307, **300-307**
Mewburn, James, 88
Mexico, 310
Middle East, 313
Middlesex, 32
Miller, Peter, 14, **14**, 65, 66, **67**, 71, 72, 93, 142, 1**42-143**
Mills, Daniel, 23
mirrors, 266-299, **267-299**
    chimney glasses, 272-276, **272-276**
    dressing, 267-272, **267-271**
    hanging glasses, 284, **284-285**, 296, **298-299**
    looking glasses, 284, **284-285**
    overmantel, **Frontispiece**
    pier glasses, 287-293, **286-293**
    tabernacle glasses, 294-299, **294-298**
Montacute House, 158, **159**
Montagu, Duke of, 94, 96, 130, **190**, 191, 231
Montagu House, 94, 96, 126, 130, 187, 236, 245, 287
Montagu, Viscount, **288**
Monthermon, Lord, 235
Moore, James, 27, 46, 93, **95**, **154**, 155-156, **156**, 169, **169**, 180, 200, **201-206**, 203-205, 207, 209, **209**, 210, **214**, 221, 225, **291**, 296
Moore, James, the Younger, 187, 225
Moore Park, 231
Moore, Thomas, 229 – *see also under* Daniel Bell
Moorfields, 23
Moorgate, **83**
Moravians, 39, 40
Morgan, Catherine, 84, 97, 111, 130, 251
Mortimer's *Universal Director*, 31
Moscow, 42
Mosquito coast, 311
mouldings, 58-64, **63-64**, 99-101, **100**, **117**

Narva, 35, 310
Nash, Elkington and Whitehorn, 163
Nash, Hall and Whitehorne, 27-29, **28**, 120
Nash, Thomas, **28**, 29
New England, 36
New Exchange, 32
New York, 36
Newcastle, Duke of, **205**, 252
Newhailes, 160

Index

Newman, Edward, *11*, 17-18, **18**
Newport church, *186*
Newton, Sir Isaac, 165
Nicaragua, 311
Nix, George, 46-47, **46-47**, 187, **190**, 191, **192**, 242, **242**
Norman, Samuel, 32
Norris family, **241**
Norris, Henry, **241**
North, Francis – *see* Earl of Guildford
Norway, 32, 309
Norwich, 10, 39, 117
Nottingham Castle, **205**

oak, 312
Odell, William, 280, 284, **284**, 296
Ody, John, 13, 20, **20**
Old and Ody, **20**, 70, **71**, 76, 108, **108**, 140, **140**, 160, **160**
Old Bailey, The, 23, 142
Old, Henry, **20**
Old, Mary, 13, 20
Old, William, *11*, 13, 20, **20**
Orders of Architecture, 58, 72
Oriental influence, 42-53
Orphans' Court Records, 138
Oslo, 309
Oxford, Earl of, 170, **170**

Packer, Thomas, 172
padouk, 32, **76**
Page, Sir Gregory, **48**, 49, **154,** 155
Pakington, Sir Herbert, 258
Palladio, 137
Palleday, John, 14
Palleday, William, 14, **14**, 78, **78**, 118, **118**, 119
Palleday, William senior, 14
Pardoe, John, 56, 58, **59**, 92, 111, **111**, 120, **120**, 122, *137*, **211**, 282
Parham House, West Sussex, **149**
Parish Clerks, Company of, 144, 144-145, 146
Parker, Thomas – *see* Lord Macclesfield
Pascall, James, 191
Paul I, Czar, *175*
Paulinus, Petrus Antonius de, **220**, 221
Pautre, Jean Le, 213
Pautre, Pierre Le, 151, **151**, **201**, 215, **215**
Peabody Essex Museum, 52, **53**
pearwood, 33, 312
Pelletier family, 200, **201**
Pembroke, Earl of, *49*, 191
Pepys, Samuel, 131
Perkins, Thomas, 24, 34, 308
Peru, 310
Peter I, Tsar, 40
Philadelphia, 116
  Furniture Price Book, 116, 187
Philippines, *49*

Phill, Thomas, 152-153, **152-153**, 157
Phillips, John, 19, 20, **76**, 77, 89-90, 211, **216**, 217, 228-229, **228**, 231, 235, 267, 269, 270
Plympton House, **220**
Pope, Alexander, 231
Portman, Honourable Henry, 251
Portugal, 37, 314
Post-man, The, 127, 266
Potter, Thomas, 140-141, **140-141**, 242, **243**, 259, **264-265**
Povey, Thomas, 131
Powderham Castle, 74, **136**, 137
Price, John, *137*
Price, William, 60, **60**
Prices of Cabinet and Chair Work, 116
Prussia, 37, 310
Puller, Isaac, 15
Puller, Jonathan, *11*, 15
Puller, Sarah, 15
Pulteney, William, 32
Purefoy, Elizabeth, 172

RF, 23, **23**, 60, **60-61**, **138**
Rannie & Haig, 32
Raquet Court, *149*
Raynham, 226
Renshaw, John, 90
Reynolds, Mrs Mary, 99, **99**
Reynolds, Thomas, 99, **99**, 101
Rhine, River, 313
Richards, I., 129, **129**
Richards, James, 193, **193**, 194, **195**, 225, 226, **226**, 294, **294**
Richardson, Samuel, 33
Rider, Honourable Counsellor, 180
Rigaud, Hyacinthe, 151
Roberts, Richard, 17, 32, 33, 111, 131, **146-147**, 153, *157*, 158, 160, 163-165, **164**, 172, 258, 270, 308, 314
Roberts, Thomas, 150, 151, 171, 173, 174, 183, 187, 193, 248
Robinson, Sir Thomas, 259
Rochester Bridge, Wardens of, 182
Rochester Cathedral, 149
Rodwell, James, 20
Rodwell, William, *172*
Roentgen, Abraham, 39
Rokeby Park, 125
rosewood, 47, 49, 312
Rousham, 197
Rowland, John, *11*
Royal Bed, the, **28**, 29, 120, *231*
Royal Bed and Rising Sun, **182**
Royal Chair, 17
Royal Collection, 125, **201**
Royal Exchange, 30
Royal Household, 40, 86, 111, 140, 200, 235, 262, 266, 269

Royal Palaces, 121, 140, 153, 158, 164, 182, 258, 263
Ruatan, 311
Russell, William, 163
Russia, 36, 40, 310
Ruyvan, Samuel Van, *11*
Ryder, Dudley, 229

Sackville, Lionel – *see* Duke of Dorset
St Alfege, Greenwich, *151*
St Catherine Coleman, 21
St Domingo, 310
St George's, Bloomsbury, 89-90, 150
St Giles House, Dorset, 297
St Giles, Cripplegate, 34
St. James's, 10
St James's Palace, 72, *106*, 127, 131, 151, 163, 247, 284, 287, 296
St James's Square, 220
St John's Lane, 16, 309
St Martin's Lane, 11, 26, 31, *137*
St Mary Aldermanbury, 33
St Paul's Churchyard, 10, 11, 12, 13, 15, 17, 19, 20, 27, 31, 33, **76**, 80, **82**, 83, **128**, 160, 162, 172, 186, **197**, 264, **264**, 280, 306
St Paul's School, 11
St Petersburg, 40, 42, *175*, 310
Salisbury, Marquess of, 267, 280, 287
Sandon Hall, Stafford, 180
Sarnesfield Court, 172
Saunders, Paul, 315
Saville, Dorothy – *see* Lady Burlington
Savoy, 13, **67**
Sawston Hall, 283
sawyers, 34-35
Saxony, 37
Say, Richard, *149*
Scandinavia, 36
Scarsdale, Earl of, 177, **177**
sconces, 277-283, **277-283**
scriptors, 54, **55**, 58
seat construction, 178, **179**
Seaton Delaval Hall, 88
Second Book of Architecture, 137
second-phase construction, **99**
  summaries of, 64, 81
Seddon, 32
Seddon, George, 33
settees, 187, **187**
sgabello, 192, **192**
Shaftesbury, Earl of, 297
Sharp, Samuel, **38**, 39
Shaw (sawyer), 34
Shepheard, Samuel, **137**
Sheraton, Thomas, 88, 101, 137
Sherborne House, 84, 105-106, 138, 187, 207, 242, 245, 251, 267, 269, 280
Shrewsbury, 37
Shugborough Hall, 227, **227**

326

Sidney, Elizabeth, **65**
Simms and Metcalf, 32
Simpson (joiner), 131
Sloane, Sir Hans, 165
Smith, Francis, 221, *228*
Smith, J.T., 245
Smith, Joseph, **11**
Sir John Soane's Museum, 49, 125
sofas, **153**, **167**, 187, **196**
Soho, 20, 31
Soho Square, 30
Some Designs of Inigo Jones & Mr. William Kent, 191
Somerset House, **276**
South Carolina Gazette, 37
Southwark, 10, 19, *116*, 266
   map of, **11**
Spain, 37, 90, 310
Spencer, Lady Anne, 95, **95**
Spindler, Nathaniel, 40
Spitalfields, 99
Stamford Baron, 150
Stamford Mercury, 150
stands, 203-265, **206-207**
   candle, **203**, **205**, **208-209**
   term, 232-233, **232-233**
Stanhope, Earl of, **183**, **198-199**, 229
Stanwix, Mr, **31**
Steele, Richard, 267
Steinfeldt, Heinrich, 40
Stiles, Lazarus, 14-15, 24, 31, 33, 280, 309, 311, 315
Stoneleigh Abbey, 182, **182**
stools, **146**, 185, **185**
Stourhead, 194
Stowe House, 180, **181**, **214**, 215
'Straits/Streights', 37, 314
Strand, 10, 23, 30
Streatlam Castle, 155, **155**, 289, **289**, 295, **295**
Stukeley, Dr. William, 114, **115**, 165, **165**, 242, **242**, 255, **255**, 293
Suckling family, 177
Sudbrook House, 200
Suffolk, 177
Sunderland, Earl of, 252
Sutton Scarsdale, 177
Swan, Abraham, 275, 297
Sweden, 37, 310

tables, 200-265, **201-202**, **204-206**, **210-231**, **234-250**, **253-265**
   bureau- – *see* bureau-tables
   'architect's', **237**
   card, 260-264, **260-264**
   Chinese, **46-47**
   dining, 251-259, **253-259**
   dressing, **106**, 234-240, **237-240**
   'Dutch', 245-246, **245-246**
   eagle, sphinx and dolphin, 228-231, **228-231**
   folding, 260-265, **260-265**
   k'ang, **150**, 151
   pillar and claw, **17,** 246-250, **247-250**
      catches, 250, **251**
   sideboard, 216-222, **216-222**, 230
   slab, 223-227, **223-227**
   tea, 44-46, **44-45**, 241-244, **241-244**
   writing/reading, **236**, **237**, **264-265**
Teddington, 84, 97, 111, 130, 251
Temple Newsam House, 126, **194**
Temple, Richard – *see* Viscount Cobham
Tennet (Tennant), Paschal, 75
Thames, River, 32, 33, 308
Thames Street, 33
third-phase construction, 81-84
   summary of, 84
Thompson, Francis, 16, **16**, 309
Thornhill, Sir James, 231
Three Chairs, the, 16
Three Cover'd Chairs and Walnut Tree, 172, **172**
Three Pillows, The, 27
timber, 32-35, **35**
   sale of, 33-34
Togni, Jacopo, **190**
Tollemaches, **192**
Tomkins, William, 231
Tonkin, 50
Townsend, John, *137*
Treasurer's House, York, 205
Treasury Offices, Whitehall, 186, **186**
Treby, George, **220**, 221, 222
Troester, John George, 40
Trotter, Thomas, 171
Turin, 37
Turing, William, **206**
Turkey, 37, 314
turners, 16-17
Turners' Company, 20
Two Candlesticks and Bell, The, 24

union suites, 267-271, **270-271**
Universal System, 124
upholsterers, 12, 27-29
Upholsterers' Company, 12, **28**, 31

Vanbrugh, Sir John, 32, 88, 203
Vansittart, Arthur, **164**
Vardy, John, 191, *231*
Vaux, Mr., 172
Vauxhall glass manufactory, 266
Verlander, Mrs, **85**
Versailles, 151, **151**
Virginia, 36, 309, 314, 315
Vizagapatam, 52, **52-53**

wainscot, 32, **35**, 313
   furniture, 84-86, **85**
Wales, Frederick, Prince of, 46, 153, **194**, **195**, **202**, 203, 231, **232**, 233, 282, **282-283**, 290, **290**, 296, 299
walnut, 32, 313-315
Walpole, Horace, 142
Walpole, Sir Robert, 125, 150, 171, 173, 174, 187, 191
Walton, Henry, 26
Wapping, 10, 127
Warden, Thomas, 15, 308
Warden, William, 15
Wardour Street, 20
Ware, Isaac, 137, 276, **276**, 296, **296**, 297
Warrington, Earl of, **96**, 97, **222**, 277, **277**, 280
wars
   Austrian Succession, 241
   Spanish Succession, 43, 90, 148
Warwickshire, 182, **182**
Watling Street, 11
Webb, Hon. General, 30
Webb, John, 191
Webb, Robert, **28**, 29
Wellwood, Dr, 86
Wentworth Woodhouse, 227, **227**
West Indies, 10, 32, 36, 309, 310-311
Westminster, 10, 17
   Abbey, **146**
   map of, **11**
Westwood Park, 258
White, John, *11*
White Swan workshop, *11*, 13, **82**, 83, 122
Whitehall186, **186**, 191, 231
Wierne, John, 14
Wild, Daniel, 80
William III, King, 200
Williams, Henry, 160, 194
Williams, Samuel, *11*
Williaume, David II, 249, **249**
Willis, John, 197, **197**
Wills, John, 29
Wilton House, **49**, **190**, 191, 226, **226**
Wimpole Hall, 170, **170**
Windsor Castle, 131
Wood, Stephen, 19, *137*
Woolball, Henry, 245
Worcester Lodge, 276, **276**
'working masters', 13-15
Wormell, Joseph, *11*
Woster, Thomas, **68** – *see also* Coxed and Woster
Wrexham, **23**
Wroxton Abbey, 194, 197

yew, 315
York, 205
York, John, 182, **182**